The History of Canada

The History of Canada

Second Edition

Scott W. See

Grey House
Publishing

4919 Route 22
PO Box 56
Amenia, NY 12501-0056

PUBLISHER:	Leslie Mackenzie
EDITOR:	Richard Gottlieb
EDITORIAL DIRECTOR:	Laura Mars
EDITORIAL ASSISTANT:	Diana Delgado
PRODUCTION MANAGER:	Kristen Thatcher
MARKETING DIRECTOR:	Jessica Moody

Grey House Publishing, Inc.
4919 Route 22
Amenia, NY 12501
518.789.8700
FAX 845.373.6390
www.greyhouse.com
e-mail: books@greyhouse.com

Publisher's Cataloging-In-Publication Data
(Prepared by The Donohue Group, Inc.)

See, Scott W., 1950–
    The History of Canada / Scott W. See. — 2nd ed.

        p. : ill., maps ; cm.

    First ed. published: Westport, Conn. : Greenwood Press, 2001.
    Includes bibliographical references and index.
    ISBN: 978-1-59237-610-0

    1. Canada—History. I. Title.

F1026 .S44 2010
971

For Mylese

Contents

Foreword

This retelling of my story, the story of my country and of my ancestors and relatives, is vividly accomplished. Scott See's narrative encompasses many Canadian stories: French and English fur-traders taking "country wives" *à la façon du pays;* the impact of France's decision to cede New France to England after "The Conquest"; insurgents fighting the Family Compact in Ontario in the 1830's; refugees arriving in Grosse Île, dying or fanning out across the country; soldiers returning from the killing fields in France only to march in the Winnipeg General Strike (1919) for justice; soldiers serving with the UN peace-keeping forces in Cyprus; and Canadians anxiously watching Québécois voters deciding the fate of Canada in two referendums on separation. Stories similar in broad strokes to American stories, yet different in details.

Why study the history of Canada? Professor See believes that studying another country's history helps those with inquiring minds to better understand themselves. *The History of Canada,* a sweeping overview written by an American, certainly helped this Canadian understand the forces that have shaped Canada, her history and her culture.

See captures the essence of what it is to be a Canadian, our pride in our country and our preoccupation with self-identity. He discloses the historical reasons behind Canadians' patriotism: social programs that leave no citizen behind; the Canadian role on the world stage as a middle power contributing to a more just and peaceful world; contributions to science, medicine, the arts. The Canadian Broadcasting Corporation was created with a mandate to encourage the development of a national identity and culture. It succeeded. Today, I can instantly bond with Canadians anywhere by name-dropping: *As It Happens; Man Alive; Friendly Giant; Hockey Night in Canada;* and *The McKenzie Brothers.*

Other than by rebels and Fenians, no shot has been fired across the border since the horrific battle at Lundy's Lane in July 1814, but that doesn't mean Canadians and Americans see the world the same. Canadian historians would disagree with the reasons given by Professor See to explain why Quebec was so dramatically against conscription during both world wars. See argues that it came from an underlying anger in Quebec against France for ceding New France to England under the Treaty of Paris, 1763. Canadian historians see it as anger against citizens being drafted to serve in wars on a foreign soil. In another example, Professor See presents the American point of view when explaining the cessation of the Avro Arrow program, but not the prevalent Canadian viewpoint.

Canadians and Americans may never agree on many historical questions. In *The History of Canada*, Scott See has produced a thoughtful commentary on Canadian history for Americans. It provides the groundwork for understanding and debate on themes and questions about Canada's history. The essence of Canada's history and our quest for self-identity is captured. I am glad to have read this retelling of my heritage.

Marianne E. Reid, MLS, Librarian
Brandon University
Brandon, Manitoba, Canada

Preface to the Second Edition

This Second Edition includes a new chapter that covers the first decade of the twenty-first century as well as revisions to the material from the 2001 edition that was published by Greenwood Press as part of its *Histories of the Modern Nations* series. The section on the Notable People in the History of Canada has been expanded, a number of maps and photographs have been added, and the Timeline of Historical Events has been brought up to date. This edition also includes a new section of Primary Documents. These were selected to enhance the text and give the reader insight to the kinds of evidentiary material that historians use to construct the complex portrait of a nation. I sought to provide a representative assortment that addresses the country's political, economic, diplomatic, social, and cultural experiences. It is my hope that they will supplement and thereby enrich the basic narrative of Canada's history from the contact period between Native peoples and European explorers to the close of the twenty-first century's inaugural decade.

As I stated in Chapter 1:

> *Why study the history of Canada? For seven consecutive years in the 1990s, the United Nations Human Development Program proclaimed the vast nation that sits atop the North American continent to be the best country on earth, according to an index that includes quality of life, income, and education. By 2005, the UN ranked Canada fourth in the world. Yet in spite of this powerful and compelling evidence of the country's global stature, misconceptions continue to skew our sense of the Canadian past.... A persistent and misleading assumption implies that Canada's history, while occasionally distinctive, is essentially a pale reflection of the more intriguing and lively saga of the nation to its immediate south: the United States. The Americans, the*

*idea has it, [believe that] their essentially passive neighbors,
while occasionally worthy of some note, have essentially trod
a national trail that was clearly blazed by others. Neither
point holds merit.*

Acknowledgments

For a number of years I considered the possibility of updating and
enhancing *The History of Canada*, so I was pleased when Grey House
Publishing invited me to do so.

I am thankful for the support and creative guidance I received from
Laura Mars, Kristen Thatcher, and Diana Delgado at Grey House. The
planning and initial work for this edition was made possible by a
generous Senior Fellowship from the Canadian Embassy in Washington, DC. In addition, I am grateful for the support of Stephen Hornsby
and the Canadian-American Center at the University of Maine. Thanks
to Tanya Buckingham for producing the maps, and to the staff at
Library and Archives Canada for their help in selecting and ordering
many of the visuals that were used in this edition. The staff at the
University of Maine's Fogler Library, especially Betsy Beattie, cheerfully
offered their assistance in finding sources. I greatly appreciate Stefano
Tijerina's efforts to identify some of the paintings and photographs that
were added to this edition. I also owe a debt of gratitude to my
colleague Richard Judd for reading sections of the new material and for
his helpful suggestions. I value the constant encouragement that I
receive from my daughters, Hadley and Hilary. As has been the case in
every one of my major writing projects, Mylese See read the entire
manuscript and offered her insightful editorial advice. Any mistakes
and shortcomings in this revised edition, of course, remain my own.

Scott W. See

Introduction

This second edition of *The History of Canada* is the first published by Grey House Publishing. The first edition was published by Greenwood Press in 2001. This ten-year update not only reflects Canada's trials and triumphs in the past decade, but also includes a significant amount of new material and features.

Arrangement & Content

- **Front Matter** is an illustrated history lesson. It includes full color maps and national and provincial flags and emblems, as well as lyrics of the national anthem, and photos of prime ministers and governors general. With a Foreword written by librarian Marianne Reid of Brandon University in Manitoba, and the author's Preface, readers have a firm grasp of the world's second largest country before even turning to the first chapter.

- The main body of text in this new edition consists of **eleven chapters**, one more than in 2001. They are arranged chronologically, taking the reader from the first wave of migration 12,000 years ago to today's film and sports industries that cross international borders. Each chapter is amply subtitled, providing logical steps from one period in Canadian history to another. From *Early Exploration* to the *Quebec Experiment* to the *Canadian Nationalism Triumph* to the *Nuances of Modern Politics*, this edition offers tremendous value for novices of Canadian history as well as those whose generational family lived through every stage of the country's progression.

    In addition, this new edition is supported by photographs and maps, placed thoughtfully throughout the text, helping researchers visualize changes to the country as they happened.

- **Notable People in the History of Canada** follows the final chapter, with biographies of men and women who helped define this vast country. The list of 41 comprises politicians, journalists, explorers,

religious figures, writers, educators, activists and artists and
includes 10 more individuals than the last edition.

- The **Timeline** puts the history of Canada in order, from border
  wars to the Olympics to the passing of the French Language
  Charter. It includes hundreds of significant events, right up to the
  2010 Vancouver Winter Olympics.

- **Primary Documents** is a NEW section of *The History of Canada*. It
  includes carefully selected articles, legislation, letters and excerpts.
  Designed to support chapter themes, each document is referenced
  in the main text. A separate Table of Contents identifies the 38
  diverse documents, with "Prime Minister Harper Announces
  Measures to Strengthen Canada's Arctic Sovereignty" and the
  "Joe Canadian Rant" on the list.

- *The History of Canada* includes a **Bibliographic Essay** that not only
  lists books that would be helpful in further research on Canada, but
  is annotated with helpful descriptions and comparisons. These
  resources are categorized by topics relevant to Canada's history,
  such as international relations, Canadian women, provinces and
  regions, native peoples, Canadian workers and International
  relations, Provinces and Regions, Native Peoples, and workers in
  Canada. This essay ends with a list of recommended web sites on
  Canadian history.

Ending with a detailed **Index**, *The History of Canada* is a compellingly
written narrative that weaves the country's immense geography,
political struggles, and regional, cultural and ethnic diversity into the
complex reality of Canada.

THE ROYAL ARMS OF CANADA BY PROCLAMATION OF KING GEORGE V IN 1921

The Royal Arms of Canada were established by proclamation of King George V on 21 November, 1921. On the advice of the Prime Minister of Canada, Her Majesty the Queen approved, on 12 July, 1994, that the arms be augmented with a ribbon bearing the motto of the Order of Canada, DESIDERANTES MELIOREM PATRIAM - "They desire a better country".

This coat of arms was developed by a special committee appointed by Order in Council and is substantially based on a version of the Royal Arms of the United Kingdom, featuring the historic arms of England and Scotland. To this were added the old arms of Royal France and the historic emblem of Ireland, the harp of Tara, thus honouring many of the founding European peoples of modern Canada. To mark these arms as Canadian, the three red maple leaves on a field of white were added.

The supporters, and the crest, above the helmet, are also versions of elements of the Royal Arms of the United Kingdom, including the lion of England and unicorn of Scotland. The lion holds the Union Jack and the unicorn, the banner of Royal France. The crowned lion holding the maple leaf, which is the The Royal Crest of Canada, has, since 1981, also been the official symbol of the Governor General of Canada, the Sovereign's representative.

At the base of the Royal Arms are the floral emblems of the founding nations of Canada, the English Rose, the Scottish Thistle, the French Lily and the Irish Shamrock.

The motto - A MARI USQUE AD MARE - "From sea to sea" - is an extract from the Latin version of verse 8 of the 72nd Psalm - "He shall have dominion also from sea to sea, and from the river unto the ends of the earth."

THE NATIONAL FLAG

The National Flag of Canada, otherwise known as the Canadian Flag, was approved by Parliament and proclaimed by Her Majesty Queen Elizabeth II to be in force as of February 15, 1965. It is described as a red flag of the proportions two by length and one by width, containing in its centre a white square the width of the flag, bearing a single red maple leaf. Red and white are the official colours of Canada, as approved by the proclamation of King George V appointing Arms for Canada in 1921. The Flag is flown on land at all federal government buildings, airports, and military bases within and outside Canada, and may appropriately be flown or displayed by individuals and organizations. The Flag is the proper national colours for all Canadian ships and boats; and it is the flag flown on Canadian Naval vessels.

The Flag is flown daily from sunrise to sunset. However, it is not contrary to etiquette to have the Flag flying at night. No flag, banner or pennant should be flown or displayed above the Canadian Flag. Flags flown together should be approximately the same size and flown from separate staffs at the same height. When flown on a speaker" platform, it should be to the right of the speaker. When used in the body of an auditorium; it should be to the right of the audience. When two or more than three flags are flown together, the Flag should be on the left as seen by spectators in front of the flags. When three flags are flown together, the Canadian Flag should occupy the central position.

A complete set of rules for flying the Canadian Flag can be obtained from the Department of Canadian Heritage.

THE ROYAL UNION FLAG

The Royal Union Flag, generally known as the Union Jack, was approved by Parliament on December 18, 1964 for continued use in Canada as a symbol of Canada's membership in the Commonwealth of Nations and of her allegiance to the Crown. It will, where physical arrangements make it possible, be flown along with the National Flag at federal buildings, airports, and military bases and establishments within Canada on the date of the official observance of the Queen's birthday, the Anniversary of the Statute of Westminster (December 11th), Commonwealth Day (second Monday in March), and on the occasions of Royal Visits and certain Commonwealth gatherings in Canada.

QUEEN'S PERSONAL CANADIAN FLAG

In 1962, Her Majesty The Queen adopted a personal flag specifically for use in Canada. The design comprises the Arms of Canada with The Queen's own device in the centre. The device - the initial "E" surmounted by the St. Edward's Crown within a chaplet of roses - is gold on a blue background.

When the Queen is in Canada, this flag is flown, day and night, at any building in which She is in residence. Generally, the flag is also flown behind the saluting base when She conducts troop inspections, on all vehicles in which She travels, and on Her Majesty's Canadian ships (HMCS) when the Queen is aboard.

FLAG OF THE GOVERNOR GENERAL

The Governor General's standard is a blue flag with the crest of the Arms of Canada in its centre. A symbol of the Sovereignty of Canada, the crest is made of a gold lion passant imperially crowned, on a wreath of the official colours of Canada, holding in its right paw a red maple leaf. The standard was approved by Her Majesty The Queen on February 23, 1981. The Governor General's personal standard flies whenever the incumbent is in residence, and takes precedence over all other flags in Canada, except The Queen's.

CANADIAN ARMED FORCES BADGE

The Canadian Armed Forces Badge was sanctioned by Her Majesty Queen Elizabeth II in May 1967. The description is as follows:

Within a wreath of ten stylized maple leaves Red, a cartouche medium Blue edge Gold, charged with a foul anchor Gold, surmounted by Crusader's Swords in Saltire Silver and blue, pommelled and hilted Gold; and in front an eagle volant affront head to the sinister Gold, the whole ensigned with a Royal Crown proper.

The Canadian Forces Badge replaces the badges of the Royal Canadian Navy, the Canadian Army, and the Royal Canadian Air Force.

ALBERTA

The Arms of the Province of Alberta were granted by Royal Warrant on May 30, 1907. On July 30th, 1980, the Arms were augmented as follows: Crest: Upon a Helm with a Wreath Argent and Gules a Beaver couchant upholding on its back the Royal Crown both proper; Supporters: On the dexter side a Lion Or armed and langued Gules and on the sinister side a Pronghorn Antelope (Antilocapra americana) proper; the Compartment comprising a grassy mount with the Floral Emblem of the said Province of Alberta the Wild Rose (Rosa acicularis) growing therefrom proper; Motto: FORTIS ET LIBER (Strong and Free) to be borne and used together with the Arms upon Seals, Shields, Banners, Flags or otherwise according to the Laws of Arms.

In 1958, the Government of Alberta authorized the design and use of an official flag. A flag bearing the Armorial Ensign on a royal ultramarine blue background was adopted and the Flag Act proclaimed June 1st 1968. Proportions of the flag are two by length and one by width with the Armorial Ensign seven-elevenths of the width of the flag carried in the centre. The flag may be used by citizens of the Province and others in a manner befitting its dignity and importance but no other banner or flag that includes the Armorial Ensign may be assumed or used.

Floral Emblem: Wild Rose (Rosa Acicularis). Chosen in the Floral Emblem Act of 1930.

Provincial Bird: Great horned owl (budo virginianus). Adopted May 3, 1977.

BRITISH COLUMBIA

The shield of British Columbia was granted by Royal Warrant on March 31, 1906. On October 15th, 1987, the shield was augmented by Her Majesty Queen Elizabeth II. The crest and supporters have become part of the provincial Arms through usage. The heraldic description is as follows: Crest: Upon a Helm with a Wreath Argent and Gules the Royal Crest of general purpose of Our Royal Predecessor Queen Victoria differenced for Us and Our Successors in right of British Columbia with the Lion thereof garlanded about the neck with the Provincial Flower that is to say the Pacific Dogwood (Cornus nuttallii) with leaves all proper Mantled Gules doubled Argent; Supporters: On the dexter side a Wapiti Stag (Cervus canadensis) proper and on the sinister side a Bighorn Sheep Ram (Oviscanadensis) Argent armed and unguled Or; Compartment: Beneath the Shield a Scroll entwined with Pacific Dogwood flowers slipped and leaved proper inscribed with the Motto assigned by the said Warrant of Our Royal Predecessor King Edward VII that is to say SPLENDOR SINE OCCASU, (splendour without diminishment).

The flag of British Columbia was authorized by an Order-in-Council of June 27, 1960. The Union Jack symbolizes the province's origins as a British colony, and the crown at its centre represents the sovereign power linking the nations of the Commonwealth. The sun sets over the Pacific Ocean. The original design of the flag was located in 1960 by Hon. W.A.C. Bennett at the College of Arms in London.

Floral emblem: Pacific Dogwood (Cornus Nuttallii, Audubon). Adopted under the Floral Emblem Act, 1956.

Provincial Bird: Steller's jay. Adopted November 19, 1987.

MANITOBA

The Arms of the Province of Manitoba were granted by Royal Warrant on May 10, 1905, augmented by warrant of the Governor General on October 23, 1992. The description is as follows: above the familiar shield of 1905 is a helmet and mantling; above the helmet is the Crest, including the beaver holding a prairie crocus, the province's floral emblem. On the beaver's back is the royal crown. The left supporter is a unicorn wearing a collar bearing a decorative frieze of maple leaves, the collar representing Manitoba's position as Canada's "keystone" province. Hanging from the collar is a wheel of a Red River cart. The right supporter is a white horse, and its collar of bead and bone honours First Peoples. The supporters and the shield rest on a compartment representing the province's rivers and lakes, grain fields and forests, composed of the provincial tree, the white spruce, and seven prairie crocuses. At the base is a Latin translation of the phrase "Glorious and Free."

The flag of the Province of Manitoba was adopted under The Provincial Flag Act, assented to May 11, 1965, and proclaimed into force on May 12, 1966. It incorporates parts of the Royal Armorial Ensigns, namely the Union and Red Ensign; the badge in the fly of the flag is the shield of the arms of the province.

Description: A flag of the proportions two by length and one by width with the Union Jack occupying the upper quarter next the staff and with the shield of the armorial bearings of the province centered in the half farthest from the staff.

Floral Emblem: Pasque Flower, known locally as Prairie Crocus (Anemone Patens). Adopted 1906.

Provincial Bird: Great gray owl. Adopted July 16, 1987.

NEW BRUNSWICK

The Arms of New Brunswick were granted by Royal Warrant on May 26, 1868. The motto SPEM REDUXIT (hope restored) was added by Order-in-Council in 1966. The description is as follows: The upper third of the shield is red and features a gold lion, symbolizing New Brunswick's ties to Britain. The lion is also found in the arms of the Duchy of Brunswick in Germany, the ancestral home of King George III. The lower part of the shield displays an ancient galley with oars in action. It could be interpreted as a reference to the importance of both shipbuilding and seafaring in New Brunswick in those days. It is also based on the design of the province's original great seal which featured a sailing ship on water. The shield is supported by two white-tailed deer wearing collars of Indian wampum. From one is suspended the Royal Union Flag (the Union Jack), from the other the fleur-de-lis to indicate the province's British and French background. The crest consists of an Atlantic Salmon leaping from a coronet of gold maple leaves and bearing St. Edward's Crown on its back. The base, or compartment, is a grassy mound with fiddleheads as well as purple violets, the provincial floral emblem. The motto "Spem Reduxit" is taken from the first great seal of the province.

The flag of New Brunswick, adopted by Proclamation on February 24, 1965, is based on the Arms of the province. The chief and charge occupy the upper one-third of the flag, and the remainder of the armorial bearings occupy the lower two-thirds. The proportion is four by length and two and one half by width.

Floral Emblem: Purple Violet (Viola Cuculata). Adopted by Order-in-Council, December 1, 1936, at the request of the New Brunswick Women's Institute.

Provincial Bird: Black-capped chickadee. Adopted August 1983.

NEWFOUNDLAND & LABRADOR

The Arms of Newfoundland were granted by Royal Letters Patent dated January 1, 1637 by King Charles I. The heraldic description is as follows: Gules, a Cross Argent, in the first and fourth quarters a Lion passant guardant crowned Or, in the second and third quarters an Unicorn passant Argent armed and crined Or, gorged with a Coronet and a Chain affixed thereto reflexed of the last. Crest: on a wreath Or and Gules a Moose passant proper. Supporters: two Savages of the clime armed and apparelled according to their guise when they go to war. The motto reads QUAERITE PRIMEREGNUM DEI (seek ye first the kingdom of God).

The official flag of Newfoundland, adopted in 1980, has primary colours of Red, Gold and Blue, against a White background. The Blue section on the left represents Newfoundland's Commonwealth heritage and the Red and Gold section on the right represents the hopes for the future with the arrow pointing the way. The two triangles represent the mainland and island parts of the province.

Floral Emblem: Pitcher Plant (Sarracenia Purpurea). Adopted June 1954.

Provincial Bird: Atlantic puffin.

NORTHWEST TERRITORIES

The Arms of the Northwest Territories were approved by Her Majesty Queen Elizabeth II on February 24, 1956. The crest consists of two gold narwhals guarding a compass rose, symbolic of the magnetic north pole. The white upper third of the shield represents the polar ice pack and is crossed by a wavy blue line portraying the Northwest Passage. The tree line is reflected by a diagonal line separating the red and green segments of the lower portion of the shield: the green symbolizing the forested areas south of the tree line, and the red standing for the barren lands north of it. The important bases of northern wealth, minerals and fur, are represented by gold billets in the green portion and the mask of a white fox in the red.

The official flag of the Northwest Territories was adopted by the Territorial Council on January 1, 1969. Blue panels at either side of the flag represent the lakes and waters of the Territories. The white centre panel, equal in width to the two blue panels combined, symbolizes the ice and snow of the North. In the centre of the white portion is the shield from the Arms of the Territories.

Floral Emblem: Mountain Avens (Dryas Integrifolia). Adopted by the Council on June 7, 1957.

Provincial Bird: Gyrfalcon. Adopted June 1990.

NOVA SCOTIA

The Arms of the Province of Nova Scotia were granted to the Royal Province in 1625 by King Charles I. The complete Armorial Achievement includes the Arms, surmounted by a royal helm with a blue and silver scroll or mantling representing the Royal cloak. Above is the crest of heraldic symbols: two joined hands, one armoured and the other bare, supporting a spray of laurel for peace and thistle for Scotland. On the left is the mythical royal unicorn and on the right a 17th century representation of the North American Indian. The motto reads MUNIT HAEC ET ALTERA VINCIT (one defends and the other conquers). Entwined with the thistle of Scotland at the base is the mayflower, added in 1929, as the floral emblem of Nova Scotia.

The flag of the Province of Nova Scotia is a blue St. Andrew's Cross on a white field, with the Royal Arms of Scotland mounted thereon. The width of the flag is three-quarters of the length.

The flag was originally authorized by Charles I in 1625. In 1929, on petition of Nova Scotia, a Royal Warrant of King George V was issued, revoking the modern Arms and ordering that the original Arms granted by Charles I be borne upon (seals) shields, banners, and otherwise according to the laws of Arms.

Floral Emblem: Trailing Arbutus, also known as Mayflower (Epigaea Repens). Adopted April 1901.

Provincial Bird: Osprey. Adopted Spring, 1994.

NUNAVUT

The dominant colours blue and gold are the ones preferred by the Nunavut Implementation Commissioners to symbolize the riches of the land, sea and sky.

Red is a reference to Canada. In the base of the shield, the inuksuk symbolizes the stone monuments which guide the people on the land and mark sacred and other special places. The qulliq, or Inuit stone lamp, represents light and the warmth of family and the community. Above, the concave arc of five gold circles refers to the life-giving properties of the sun arching above and below the horizon, the unique part of the Nunavut year. The star is the Niqirtsuituq, the North Star and the traditional guide for navigation and more broadly, forever remains unchanged as the leadership of the elders in the community.

In the crest, the iglu represents the traditional life of the people and the means of survival. It also symbolizes the assembled members of the Legislature meeting together for the good of Nunavut; with the Royal Crown symbolizing public government for all the people of Nunavut and the equivalent status of Nunavut with other territories and provinces in Canadian Confederation. The tuktu (caribou) and qilalugaq tugaalik (narwhal) refer to land and sea animals which are part of the rich natural heritage of Nunavut and provide sustenance for people. The compartment at the base is composed of land and sea and features three important species of Arctic wild flowers.

Floral Emblem: Purple Saxifrage (Saxifraga oppositifolia). Adopted May 1, 2000.

ONTARIO

The Arms of the Province of Ontario were granted by Royal Warrants on May 26, 1868 (shield), and February 27, 1909 (crest and supporters). The heraldic description is as follows: Vert, a Sprig of three leaves of Maple slipped Or on a Chief Argent the Cross of St. George. Crest: upon a wreath Vert and Or a Bear passant Sable. The supporters are on the dexter side, a Moose, and on the sinister side a Canadian Deer, both proper. The motto reads: UT INCEPIT FIDELIS SIC PERMANET (loyal in the beginning, so it remained).

The flag of the Province of Ontario was adopted under the Flag Act of May 21, 1965. It incorporates parts of the Royal Armorial Ensigns, namely the Union and Red Ensign; the badge in the fly of the flag is the shield of the Arms of the province. The flag is of the proportions two by length and one by width, with the Union Jack occupying the upper quarter next the staff and the shield of the armorial hearings of the province centered in the half farthest from the staff.

Floral Emblem: White Trillium (Trillium Grandiflorum). Adopted March 25, 1937.

Provincial Bird: Common loon. Proposed, but not officially adopted.

PRINCE EDWARD ISLAND

The Arms of the Province of Prince Edward Island were granted by Royal Warrant, May 30, 1905. The heraldic description is as follows: Argent on an Island Vert, to the sinister an Oak Tree fructed, to the dexter thereof three Oak saplings sprouting all proper, on a Chief Gules a Lion passant guardant Or. The motto reads: PARVA SUB INGENTI (the small under the protection of the great).

The flag of the Province of Prince Edward Island was authorized by an Act of the Legislative Assembly, March 24, 1964. The design of the flag is that part of the Arms contained within the shield, but is of rectangular shape, with a fringe of alternating red and white. The chief and charge of the Arms occupies the upper one-third of the flag, and the remainder of the Arms occupies the lower two-thirds. The proportions of the flag are six, four, and one-quarter in relation to the fly, the hoist, and the depth of the fringe.

Floral Emblem: Lady's Slipper (Cypripedium Acaule). Designated as the province's floral emblem by the Legislative Assembly in 1947. A more precise botanical name was included in an amendment to the Floral Emblem Act in 1965.

Provincial Bird: Blue Jay (cyanocitta cristata) was designated as avian emblem by the Provincial Emblems Acts, May 13, 1977.

QUÉBEC

The Arms of the Province of Québec were granted by Queen Victoria, May 26, 1868, and revised by a Provincial Order-in-Council on December 9, 1939. The heraldic description is as follows: Tierced in fess: Azure, three Fleurs-de-lis Or; Gules, a Lion passant guardant Or armed and langued Azure; Or, a Sugar Maple sprig with three leaves Vert veined Or. Surmounted with the Royal Crown. Below the shield a scroll Argent, surrounded by a bordure Azure, inscribed with the motto JE ME SOUVIENS Azure.

The official flag of the Province of Québec was adopted by a Provincial Order-in-Council of January 21, 1948. It is a white cross on a sky blue ground, with the fleur-de-lis in an upright position on the blue ground in each of the four quarters. The proportion is six units wide by four units deep.

Floral Emblem: Iris Versicolor. Adopted November 5, 1999.

Provincial Bird: Snowy owl. Adopted December 17, 1987.

SASKATCHEWAN

The complete armorial bearings of the Province of Saskatchewan were granted by Royal Warrant on September 16, 1986, through augmentation of the original shield of arms granted by King Edward VII on August 25, 1906. The heraldic description is as follows: Shield: Vert three Garbs in fesse Or, on a Chief of the last a Lion passant guardant Gules. Crest: Upon a Helm with a Wreath Argent and Gules a Beaver upholding with its back Our Royal Crown and holding in the dexter fore-claws a Western Red Lily (Lilium philadelphicumandinum) slipped all proper Mantled Gules doubled Argent. Supporters: On the dexter side a Lion Or gorged with a Collar of Prairie Indian beadwork proper and dependent therefrom a six-pointed Mullet faceted Argent fimbriated and garnished Or charged with a Maple Leaf Gules and on the sinister side a White tailed deer (Odocoileus virginianus) proper gorged with a like Collar and dependent therefrom a like Mullet charged with a Western Red Lily slipped and leaved proper. Motto: Beneath the Shield a Scroll entwined with Western Red Lilies slipped and leaved proper inscribed with the motto MULTIS E GENTIBUS VIRES.

The official flag was dedicated on September 22, 1969, and features the Arms of the province in the upper quarter nearest the staff, with the Western Red Lily, in the half farthest from the staff. The upper green portion represents forests, while the gold symbolizes prairie wheat fields. The basic design was adopted from the prize-winning entry of Anthony Drake of Hodgeville from a province-wide flag design competition.

Floral Emblem: Western Red Lily (Lilium philadelphicum var. andinum). Adopted April 8, 1941.

Provincial Bird: Prairie sharp-tailed grouse. Adopted March 30, 1945.

YUKON

The Arms of the Yukon, granted by Queen Elizabeth II on February 24, 1956, have the following explanation: The wavy white and blue vertical stripe represents the Yukon River and refers also to the rivers and creeks where gold was discovered. The red spire-like forms represent the mountainous country, and the gold discs the mineral resources. The St. George's Cross is in reference to the early explorers and fur traders from Great Britain, and the roundel in vair in the centre of the cross is a symbol for the fur trade. The crest displays a Malamute dog, an animal which has played an important part in the early history of the Yukon.

The Yukon flag, designed by Lynn Lambert, a Haines Junction student, was adopted by Council in 1967. It is divided into thirds: green for forests, white for snow, and blue for water.

The flag consists of three vertical panels, the centre panel being one and one-half times the width of each of the other two panels. The panel adjacent to the mast is coloured green, the centre panel is coloured white and has the Yukon Crest disposed above a symbolic representation of the floral emblem of the territory, epilobium angustifolium, (fireweed), and the panel on the fly is coloured blue. The stem and leaves of the floral emblem are coloured green, and the flowers thereof are coloured red. The Yukon Crest is coloured red and blue, with the Malamute dog coloured black.

Floral Emblem: Fireweed (Epilobium Angustifolium). Adopted November 16, 1957.

Provincial Bird: Common raven. Adopted October 28, 1985.

National Anthem: O Canada

From "Chapter 5, Statutes of Canada 1980; proclaimed July 1, 1980." Composed by Calixa Lavallée; French lyrics written by Judge Adolphe-Basile Routhier; English lyrics written by Robert Stanley Weir (with some changes incorporated in 1967).

O Canada! Our home and native land!
True patriot love in all thy sons command.
With glowing hearts we see thee rise,
The True North strong and free!
From far and wide, O Canada, We stand on guard for thee.
God keep our land glorious and free!
O Canada, we stand on guard for thee.
O Canada, we stand on guard for thee.

O Canada! Terre de nos aïeux!
Ton front est ceint de fleurons glorieux!
Car ton bras sait porter l'épée, Il sait porter la croix!
Ton histoire est une épopée Des plus brillants exploits.
Et ta valeur, de foi trempée,
Protégera nos foyers et nos droits,
Protégera nos foyers et nos droits.

Participants to the First Ministers' Constitutional Conference on Patriation of the Constitution

(Held in Ottawa from September 2 to 5, 1981)

- The Right Honourable Pierre Elliott Trudeau, P.C., Q.C., M.P., Prime Minister of Canada;
- The Honourable William G. Davis, Q.C., Premier of Ontario;
- The Honourable René Lévesque, Premier of Québec;
- The Honourable John M. Buchanan, Q.C., Premier of Nova Scotia;
- The Honourable Richard B. Hatfield, Premier of New Brunswick;
- The Honourable Sterling R. Lyon, Q.C., Premier of Manitoba;
- The Honourable W.R. Bennett, Premier of British Columbia;
- The Honourable J. Angus MacLean, P.C., D.F.C., C.D., Premier of Prince Edward Island;
- The Honourable Allan Blakeney, Q.C., Premier of Saskatchewan;
- The Honourable Peter Lougheed, Q.C., Premier of Alberta;
- The Honourable Brian Peckford, Premier of Newfoundland.

Fathers of Confederation

Three conferences helped to pave the way for Confederation - those held at Charlottetown (September, 1864), Québec City (October, 1864) and London (December, 1866). As all the delegates who were at the Charlottetown conferences were also in attendance at Québec, the following list includes the names of all those who attended one or more of the three conferences.

*Hewitt Bernard was John A. Macdonald's private secretary. He served as secretary of both the Québec and London conferences.

DELEGATES TO THE CONFEDERATION CONFERENCES, 1864–1866

LEGEND:

Charlottetown, 1 September, 1864	C
Québec, 10 October, 1864	Q
London, 4 December, 1866	L

CANADA

John A. Macdonald	C Q L
George E. Cartier	C Q L
Alexander T. Galt	C Q L
William McDougall	C Q L
Hector L. Langevin	C Q L
George Brown	C Q
Thomas D'Arcy McGee	C Q
Alexander Campbell	C Q
Sir Etienne P. Taché	Q
Oliver Mowat	Q
J.C. Chapais	Q
James Cockburn	Q
W.P. Howland	L
*Hewitt Bernard	

NOVA SCOTIA

Charles Tupper	C Q L
William A. Henry	C Q L
Jonathan McCully	C Q L
Adams G. Archibald	C Q L
Robert B. Dickey	Q
J.W. Ritchie	L

NEW BRUNSWICK

Samuel L. Tilley	C Q L
J.M. Johnson	C Q L
William H. Steeves	C Q
E.B. Chandler	C Q
John Hamilton Gray	C Q
Peter Mitchell	Q L
Charles Fisher	Q L
R.D. Wilmot	L

PRINCE EDWARD ISLAND

John Hamilton Gray	C Q
Edward Palmer	C Q
William H. Pope	C Q
A.A. Macdonald	C Q
George Coles	C Q
T.H. Haviland	Q
Edward Whelan	Q

NEWFOUNDLAND

F.B.T. Carter	Q
Ambrose Shea	Q

Prime Ministers of Canada

Sir John A. Macdonald	Conservative	1867–1873
Alexander Mackenzie	Liberal	1873–1878
Sir John A. Macdonald	Conservative	1878–1891
Sir John Abbott	Conservative	1891–1892
Sir John Thompson	Conservative	1892–1894
Sir Mackenzie Bowell	Conservative	1894–1896
Sir Charles Tupper	Conservative	1896
Sir Wilfrid Laurier	Liberal	1896–1911
Sir Robert Laird Borden	Conservative	1911–1917
Sir Robert Laird Borden	Union	1917–1920
Arthur Meighen	Conservative	1920–1921
William Lyon Mackenzie King	Liberal	1921–1926
Arthur Meighen	Conservative	1926
William Lyon Mackenzie King	Liberal	1926–1930
Richard Bedford Bennett	Conservative	1930–1935
William Lyon Mackenzie King	Liberal	1935–1948
Louis St. Laurent	Liberal	1948–1957
John George Diefenbaker	Progressive Conservative	1957–1963
Lester Pearson	Liberal	1963–1968
Pierre Elliott Trudeau	Liberal	1968–1979
Charles Joseph Clark	Progressive Conservative	1979–1980
Pierre Elliott Trudeau	Liberal	1980–1984
John N. Turner	Liberal	1984
Brian Mulroney	Progressive Conservative	1984–1993
Kim Campbell	Progressive Conservative	1993
Jean Chrétien	Liberal	1993–2003
Paul Martin, Jr.	Liberal	2003–2006
Stephen J. Harper	Conservative	2006

CANADIAN PRIME MINISTERS
(WITH PARTY AFFILIATION AND TIME IN OFFICE)

Rt. Hon. Sir John A. Macdonald
(Conservative)
July 1, 1867 to Nov. 5, 1873
Oct. 17, 1878 to June 6, 1891

Photo credit: William James Topley/National
Archives of Canada/PA-027013

Hon. Alexander MacKenzie
(Liberal)
Nov. 7, 1873 to Oct. 16, 1878

Photo credit: William James Topley/National
Archives of Canada/PA-026308

Hon. Sir John J. Abbott
(Conservative)
June 16, 1891 to Nov. 24, 1892

Photo credit: William James Topley/National
Archives of Canada/PA-033933

Rt. Hon. Sir John S. D. Thompson
(Conservative)
Dec. 5, 1892 to Dec. 12, 1894

Photo Credit: National Archives of Canada/C-000698

Hon. Sir Mackenzie Bowell
(Conservative)
Dec. 21, 1894 to April 27, 1896

Photo Credit: William James Topley/National
Archives of Canada/PA-027159

Rt. Hon. Sir Charles Tupper
(Conservative)
May 1, 1896 to July 8, 1896

Photo Credit: National Archives of
Canada/PA-027743

Rt. Hon. Sir Wilrid Laurier
(Liberal)
July 11, 1896 to Oct. 6, 1911

Photo Credit: William James Topley/National
Archives of Canada/C-001971

Rt. Hon. Sir Robert L. Borden
Oct. 10, 1911 to Oct. 12, 1917
(Conservative Administration)
Oct. 12, 1917 to July 10, 1920
(Unionist Administration)

Photo Credit: William James Topley/National
Archives of Canada/PA-028128

Rt. Hon. Arthur Meighen
July 10, 1920 to Dec. 29, 1921
(Unionist "National Liberal and
Conservative Party")
June 29, 1926 to Sept. 25, 1926
(Conservative)

Photo Credit: William James Topley/National
Archives of Canada/PA-026987

Rt. Hon. William Lyon
Mackenzie King
(Liberal)
Dec. 29, 1921 to June 28, 1926
Sept. 25, 1926 to Aug. 6, 1930
Oct. 23, 1935 to Nov. 15, 1948

Photo Credit: National Archives of
Canada/C-027645

Rt. Hon. Richard Bedford Bennett
(Conservative)
(Became Viscount Bennett, 1941)
Aug. 7, 1930 to Oct. 23, 1935

Photo Credit: National Archives of Canada/C-000687

Rt. Hon. Louis Stephen St. Laurent
(Liberal)
Nov. 15, 1948 to June 21, 1957
Photo Credit: National Archives of
Canada/C-010461

Rt. Hon. John G. Diefenbaker
(Progressive Conservative)
June 21, 1957 to April 22, 1963
Photo Credit: Paul Horsdal/National Archives
of Canada/PA-130070

Rt. Hon. Lester Bowles Pearson
(Liberal)
April 22, 1963 to April 20, 1968
Photo Credit: Ashley-Crippen Studio/National
Archives of Canada/PA-126393

Rt. Hon. Pierre Elliott Trudeau
(Liberal)
April 20, 1968 to June 4, 1979
Mar. 3, 1980 to June 30, 1984
Photo Credit: National Archives of Canada/C-046600

Rt. Hon. Charles Joseph Clark
(Progressive Conservative)
June 4, 1979 to Mar. 3, 1980
Photo Credit: Mia & Klaus

Rt. Hon. John Napier Turner
(Liberal)
June 30, 1984 to Sept. 17, 1984
Photo Credit: Courtesy of the
Liberal Party of Canada

Rt. Hon. Martin Brian Mulroney
(Progressive Conservative)
Sept 17, 1984 to June 25, 1993
Photo Credit: Robert Cooper/National
Archives of Canada/PA-152416

Rt. Hon. Kim Campbell
(Progressive Conservative)
June 25, 1993 to Nov. 4, 1993
Photo Credit: Courtesy of the
National Speakers Bureau

Rt. Hon. Jean Chrétien
(Liberal)
Nov. 4, 1993 to Dec. 11, 2003
Photo Credit: Courtesy of the
Prime Minister's Office

Rt. Hon. Paul Edgar Philippe Martin
(Liberal)
Dec. 12, 2003 to Feb. 6, 2006
Photo Credit: Courtesy of the
Liberal Party of Canada

Rt. Hon. Stephen Joseph Harper
(Conservative)
Feb. 6, 2006 to —
Photo Credit: Courtesy of the
Prime Minister's Office

GOVERNORS GENERAL OF CANADA SINCE CONFEDERATION
(WITH DATE APPOINTED)

The Viscount Monck,
G.C.M.G.
June 1, 1867

Lord Lisgar,
G.C.M.G.
Dec. 29, 1868

The Earl of Dufferin,
K.P., G.C.B., G.C.S.I., G.C.M.G.,
G.C.I.E
May 22, 1872

The Marquess of Lorne,
K.T., G.C.M.G., G.C.V.O.
Oct. 5, 1878

The Marquess of Lansdowne,
K.G., G.C.S.I., G.C.M.G., G.C.I.E.
Aug. 18, 1883

Lord Stanley of Preston,
K.G., G.C.B., G.C.V.O.
May 1, 1888

The Earl of Aberdeen,
K.T., G.C.M.G., G.C.V.O.
May 22, 1893

The Earl of Minto,
K.G., G.C.S.I., G.C.M.G., G.C.I.E.
July 30, 1898

The Earl Grey,
G.C.B., G.C.M.G., G.C.V.O.
Sept. 26, 1904

H.R.H. The Duke of Connaught,
K.G., K.T., K.P., G.M.B., G.C.S.I.,
G.C.M.G., G.C.I.E., G.C.V.O.,
G.B.E., T.D.
Mar. 21, 1911

The Duke of Devonshire,
K.G., G.C.M.G., G.C.V.O., T.D.
Aug.. 19, 1916

Lord Byng of Vimy,
G.C.B., G.C.M.G., M.V.O.
Aug. 2, 1921

The Viscount Willingdon of Ratton,
G.C.S.I., G.C.M.G., G.C.I.E., G.B.E.
Aug. 5, 1926

The Earl of Bessborough,
G.C.M.G.
Feb. 9, 1931

Baron Tweedsmuir of Elsfield,
G.C.M.G., G.C.V.O., C.H.
Aug. 10, 1935

Major-General The Earl of Athlone,
K.G., G.C.B., G.C.M.G., G.C.V.O.,
D.S.O.
Apr. 3, 1940

Field Marshal The Viscount
Alexander of Tunis,
K.G., G.C.B., O.M., G.C.M.G., C.S.I.,
D.S.O., M.C., A.D.C.
Aug. 1, 1945

The Rt. Hon. Vincent Massey,
P.C., C.C., C.H.
Jan. 24, 1952

Major General
The Rt. Hon. Georges-P. Vanier,
D.S.O., M.C., C.D.
Aug. 1, 1959

The Rt. Hon. Roland Michener,
P.C., C.C., C.M.M., C.D., Q.C.
Mar. 25, 1967

The Rt. Hon. Jules Léger
P.C., C.C., C.M.M., C.D.
Oct. 5, 1973

The Rt. Hon.
Edward Richard Schreyer,
P.C., C.C., C.M.M., C.D.
Dec. 7, 1978

The Rt. Hon. Jeanne Sauvé,
P.C., C.C., C.M.M., C.D.
Dec. 23, 1983

The Rt. Hon.
Ramon John Hnatyshyn,
P.C., C.C., C.M.M., C.D., Q.C.
Oct. 6, 1989

The Rt. Hon. Roméo LeBlanc,
P.C., C.C., C.M.M., C.D.
Nov. 22, 1994

Her Excellency the Rt. Hon.
Adrienne Clarkson,
C.C., C.M.M., C.O.M., C.D.
Oct. 7, 1999

Her Excellency the Rt. Hon.
Michaëlle Jean,
C.C., C.M.M., C.O.M., C.D.
Sept. 27, 2005

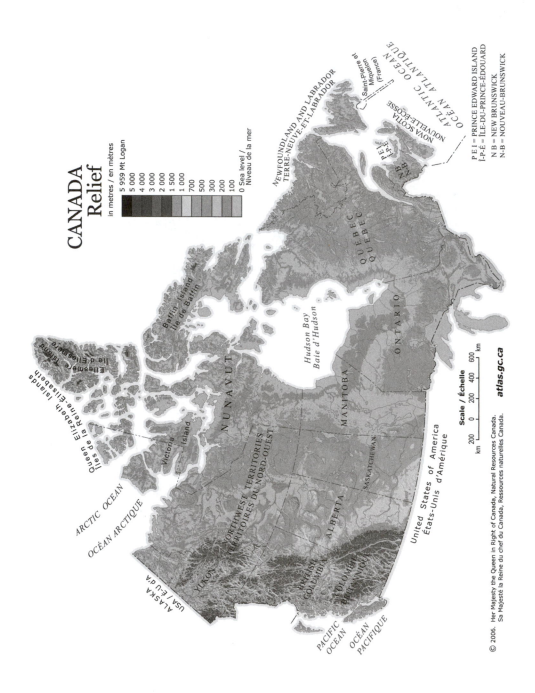

CANADA
Relief
in metres / en mètres

5 959 Mt Logan
5 000
4 000
3 000
2 000
1 500
1 000
700
500
300
200
100
0 Sea level /
  Niveau de la mer

P E I = PRINCE EDWARD ISLAND
Î.-P.-É = ÎLE-DU-PRINCE-ÉDOUARD

N B = NEW BRUNSWICK
N.-B = NOUVEAU-BRUNSWICK

Scale / Échelle
km 200 0 200 400 600 km

atlas.gc.ca

© 2006. Her Majesty the Queen in Right of Canada, Natural Resources Canada.
         Sa Majesté la Reine du chef du Canada, Ressources naturelles Canada.

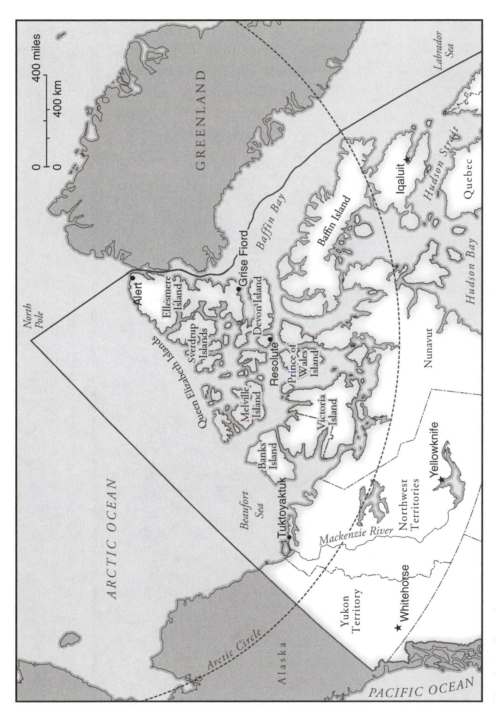

Northern Canada

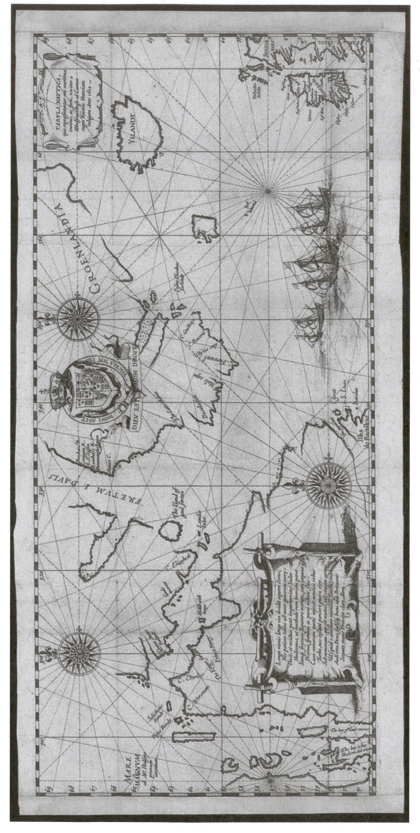

Henry Hudson arrived in Arctic waters in 1610 determined to find the Northwest Passage. He explored Hudson Bay and the mouth of the Bay. His crew mutinied and abandoned him in 1611 and returned to Europe. This map by Dutch cartographer Gerritsz is based on Hudson's discoveries.

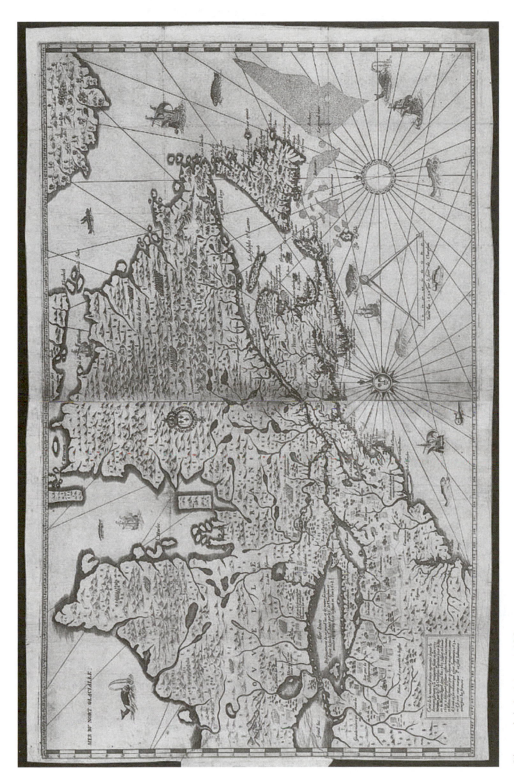

Champlain's Map 1632

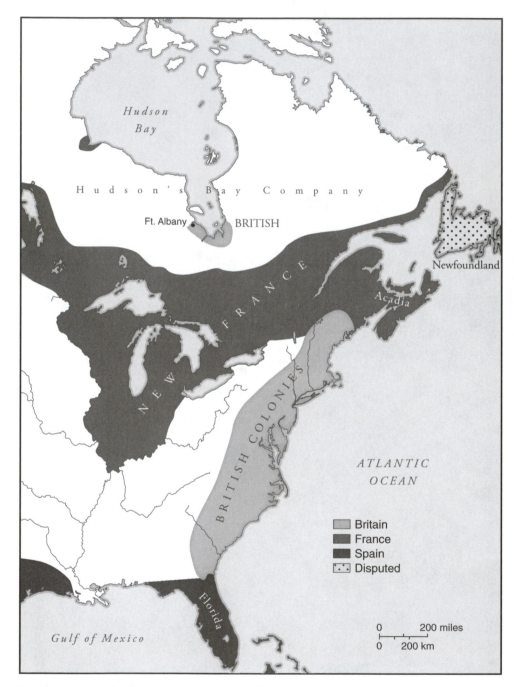

North America in the Late Seventeenth Century

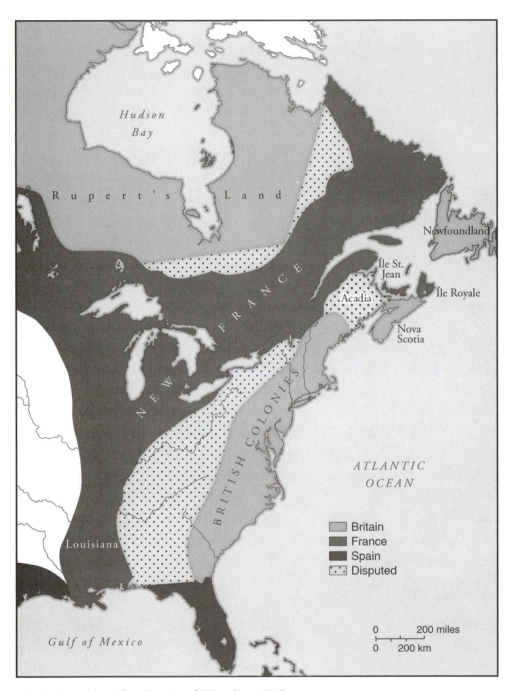

North America After Treaty of Utrecht - 1713

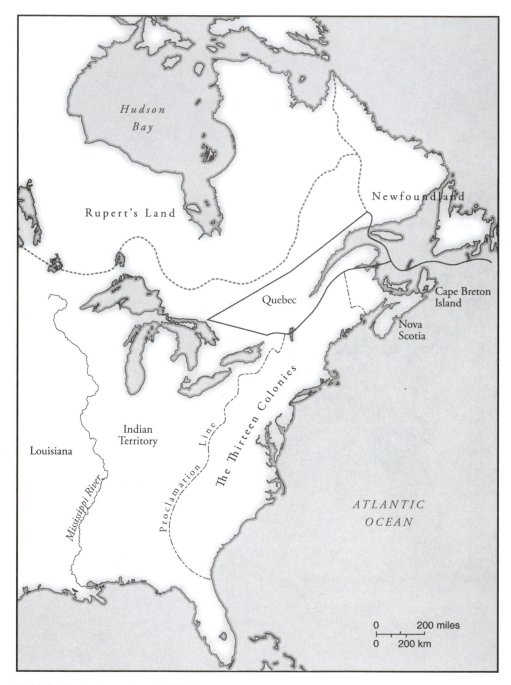

British North America in 1763

Canada in 1873

Modern Canada

Chapter 1

One of the Best Countries on Earth

Against Formidable Odds

Why study the history of Canada? For seven consecutive years in the 1990s, the United Nations Human Development Program proclaimed the vast nation that sits atop the North American continent to be the best country on earth, according to an index that includes quality of life, income, and education. By 2005, the UN ranked Canada fourth in the world. Yet in spite of this powerful and compelling evidence of the country's global stature, misconceptions continue to skew our sense of the Canadian past. These suggest that Canadian history is boring, placid, and of little import; that it is devoid of the grand or heroic elements that generally capture the attention of people both inside and outside the nation. Moreover, a persistent and misleading assumption implies that Canada's history, while occasionally distinctive, is essentially a pale reflection of the more intriguing and lively saga of the nation to its immediate south: the United States. The Americans, the idea has it, are the scriptwriters of the most powerful and captivating national story on earth.[1] Their essentially passive neighbors, while occasionally worthy of some note, have essentially trod a national trail that was clearly blazed by others.

Neither point holds merit. The history of the second largest nation on earth is neither sleep inducing nor inconsequential. Its history is

Vancouver, British Columbia, the site of the 2010 Winter Olympics.

Source: Associated Press / Bayne Stanley

unique, despite the fact that it shares patterns with other nations that have been formed by waves of immigrants that transformed a territory originally inhabited by Aboriginal peoples. Readers acquainted with the histories of countries such as Australia, Mexico, Argentina, and India, to name but a few, will certainly recognize much that is familiar. Perhaps most important, Americans will no doubt discover evocative themes as they explore Canada's story. At the same time—and this is the particular challenge of coming to grips with the history of the neighbor of a country that exercises such enormous power in the modern world—Canada's history is not an extension of the American saga.

To many non-Canadian observers, images of and references to the country are often portrayed in a stereotypical fashion. For Americans in the northern states, the country is the source of bothersome, chilly blasts of air in any season. To legions of college students, it is the exporter of decent and relatively affordable beer, a point that is underscored with advertised images of the purity of Canadian beverages, superimposed on a pristine landscape. The land of the rugged Mountie is another popular perception of Canada; strikingly, for a country that fashions itself as one of the most amicable nations on earth, the country uses the elite Royal Canadian Mounted Police as one of its most recognizable symbols. In a world rife with violence, Canada is unique in embracing a symbol of law enforcement as an image of self-portrayal. People around the globe might also think of the country as a hockey devotee's paradise, a place where the fast-paced and rough-and-tumble sport is treated simultaneously with a reverence and fanaticism that is matched only by soccer fans in Latin America and Europe.

It is entertaining to draw out the colorful stereotypes that seem to capture the essence of the country, and certainly Canadians, with genuine self-deprecating humor, are often the first to point out their idiosyncrasies. Yet below the surface of these playful and superficial images, the country is an immensely complex place where in the recent past, voters in Quebec cast ballots in two referendums to decide whether they would retain or fundamentally alter their relationship with the other provinces. The immensely successful 2010 Winter Olympics in Vancouver provided an opportunity for the country to showcase its stature as a global model of well-being and civility; at the same time, numerous critics noted a glaring regional disparity in the design of publicity and coverage for the event. The paradox of modern Canada is intriguing. Deemed a superior and thus successful model of a modern state by the United Nations, the country simultaneously struggles under a crippling—some would argue fatal—burden of regional, cultural, and ethnic diversity. The bitter irony that one of the planet's most successful nations in the first decade of the twenty-first century grapples with the persistent threat of dismantlement gives us a stark vantage point. While the factors that help to explain this striking contradiction are varied and of course open to debate, collectively they provide a suitable road map for beginning our exploration into Canada's past (see "The Vancouver Winter Olympics and the Press" in the Documents section).

Canadian history should be appreciated by non-Canadians for two essential reasons. As is the case with all other historical studies, it is an important exercise to undergo in order to make sense of the country's present. It also offers, particularly to Americans, some intriguing themes that lend themselves to comparative analysis. At the turn of the last century, Prime Minister Wilfrid Laurier shrewdly observed that "Canada is the most unlikely of regions for nation building." Even after adding another one hundred years, the observation seems particularly insightful. In many ways, the people who put their shoulder to the wheel of national development have beaten some long odds. Canada's history, even after peeling away nationalistic overtones, is fundamentally a tale of survival.

The overarching geography of the territory that Canadians inhabit accounts for one of the most dynamic survival themes. Indeed, one of the most enduring quips about the country's landmass is that it has too much geography. The immensely varied environment, with the sweeping Canadian Shield of Precambrian rock, the over one million streams, rivers, ponds, and lakes, the seemingly endless terrain of the prairies and the frozen reaches of the North, the awe-inspiring succession of mountain ranges in the West, all combined to create obstacles to exploration, settlement, transportation, and communication. In addition, the varied and dramatic climate, ranging from the temperate weather of southern Ontario and the lower Pacific coastal region of British Columbia to the ice-choked barrens of the Arctic, has given first Aboriginal peoples, and then European and Asian immigrants, particular challenges. Throughout Canadian history, day-to-day existence in an often harsh environment has consumed the energies of millions of the country's inhabitants. The geography and environment of the country shaped and continue to dictate the rhythm of life for people as varied as farmers who cope with short growing seasons, engineers who blast into the igneous rock of the Shield to extract marketable minerals, and college students who use tunnels in winter to avoid numbing temperatures and howling winds as they pass from lectures to labs. People the world around have to come to grips with the geography and environment of the region they inhabit; what makes Canada's saga particularly problematic is that its citizens have attempted to master such a large swath of the world's terrain.

Another powerful theme of persistence falls under the category of political struggles between imperial powers as the age of revolution in the late eighteenth and nineteenth centuries created modern nations. These contests shaped Canada's early history as the French and English engaged in a protracted struggle for mastery of the New World. Canada became an arena for contesting empires; it also was used periodically as a bargaining chip by agenda-driven negotiators in Europe as a means of sorting out the spoils of wars. The French imperial authority fell dramatically to the wayside in the late eighteenth century, and the British North American empire partially unraveled as the American rebellion became a successful revolution. Pursuing a political evolution in the context of the British Empire, Canadians confronted the challenge of juggling the interests of Britain and the United States. As American power surged continentally in the nineteenth century and then internationally in the following century, Canadians negotiated the tricky currents of a sometimes tempestuous relationship between their former imperial master and their neighbor. As the country sought and then achieved sovereignty in a piecemeal fashion, it attempted to ward off the encroachment of what many Canadians considered to be corrosive American economic, social, and cultural influences. Even in the early twenty-first century, magazines and Web sites regularly publish poll results that illuminate their deeply ambivalent feelings about their neighbor. Many Canadians are open to closer contact with Americans, but just as many fear that the ties between the two nations will lead inexorably to Canada's demise as an independent nation. Thus, the politically based survival game, while much altered in definition and scope over the centuries, continues to be a central national consideration.

Survival issues can also be clustered under the category of economic themes. A land that was first sought by Europeans for its seemingly inexhaustible fishing stocks and furs, it soon presented enticing possibilities for lumbering and agricultural development. The concentration on the gathering, extracting, and cultivating of staple resources is one of the most persistent economic dynamics in all of Canadian history. After the initial age of exploration and settlement, it expanded to encompass other raw materials such as minerals, petroleum, and natural gas. The staples approach to understanding Canadian history, while still of value, does not fully explain the complexity of economic themes in Canada's past. The realities of mercantilism, enforced by French and British imperial masters alike, gave way as the British embraced the capitalist model in the nineteenth century. The Western world's grinding passage through the traumatic stages of capital development, with merchants and then industrialists creating transnational economies, meant that Canadians would go through similar phases. By the twentieth century, accelerated by its participation in two global wars, Canada took its place as one of the world's leading economic powers. Even as it entered the postindustrial era late in the century, Canada would be on the cutting edge of technological innovations and changes. Yet with its dramatically skewed trading patterns, first with Britain and then with the United States, Canada would be forever positioned precariously as an extension of a foreign economic giant. Thus, from their entanglements with French mercantilists in the seventeenth century to their current economic intermeshing with the United States and Mexico under the North American Free Trade Agreement (NAFTA), Canadians have attempted to retain control over their economic fate.

Finally, the survival idea has played out in the often overlapping arenas of ethnicity, race, religion, and culture. The triangular contest involving Amerindians, French, and British was at root a struggle for survival. As the British imperial forces emerged triumphant in the late eighteenth century, the battleground with the two other groups shifted to the occupation of certain spaces and a sometimes violent resistance to assimilation. The traditional jockeying for power between francophones and anglophones, so much a catalyst for historical forces from the sixteenth to the nineteenth centuries, became over time a less satisfactory model for understanding

Canada's past.[2] As the country increasingly became an amalgam of ethnic and racial groups, the struggle of various peoples to maintain their cultural integrity often became acute. Despite the efforts of many of its architects, Canada has failed to become an assimilationist nation. Superimposed on the issues mentioned above have been an all-encompassing American culture. Significantly, as Canadians diligently sought to articulate a national identity, the fear of American absorption has provided a bonding agent for the country's disparate cultural and ethnic groups.

On another level, the study of Canadian history is tremendously useful for its comparative value. As historian Robin Winks observed, "The reason Americans should study Canadian history is to learn more about themselves, about how they differ from and how they are similar to others."[3] Winks's observation suggests that in order truly to know ourselves, it is imperative to understand other peoples. The historical record in North America points to great similarities and dissimilarities in the histories of the closely linked neighbors. Whether the focus falls on political systems, economies, foreign relationships, societies, or cultural groupings, the implicit or overt comparison of the historical paths taken by the two countries often proves of great worth.

In another vein, Canadians typically know much more about the American past and present than do Americans about their northern neighbor. With the vast majority of its population living close to the border and with thoroughly intertwined trading, defense, and communication systems, Canada is bombarded with information about the United States. The two peoples share a continent, and over centuries they have developed millions of ties that bind. Canadians have often viewed this as both a blessing and a curse. The former suggests that if Americans take an interest in Canada, then they will appreciate the country's distinctions and unique contributions to world history. The latter, conversely, might lead Americans to believe that Canadians should be absorbed into a grand continental enterprise defined according to American standards. Therefore, the consciousness raising of Americans to climb out of their ignorance of Canada is often heralded as a noble, if not problematic, effort. As a consequence, Canadianists in the United States tend to display missionary zeal in flogging their informational wares. Yet the ambiguity in Canada remains palpable. As Canadians often remark when they find out that Americans are studying some aspect of their history or culture, they feel conflicted. A sense of being pleased is offset by a nagging fear that something bad will come of it, such as closer continental integration.

Canada is not "America North." Its history must be approached on its own terms to understand how and why it is very much a distinct nation. Before we set on a course of charting the historical development of a peoples down through the centuries, it will be instructive to explore several subjects to provide a contextual platform: the country's geography, its current political systems, economic configuration, society, and culture.

An Overwhelming Landscape: The Geography of Canada

Historians have long known that although geography might not be entirely deterministic in setting the course of events in a nation's development, it profoundly shapes history. Modern geography takes into account both the study of landforms and the interaction of people with their environment. These geographical dynamics have been so thoroughly intertwined in Canada's history that it is appropriate to begin with a brief discussion of the country's basic geographical features and regions.

The Canada of the imagination—bold, rugged, varied, and vast— closely matches the country's physical geography. Covering over 3.8 million square miles, it is the second largest country on earth behind the Russian Federation. Spanning six time zones, it comprises about seven percent of the world's land mass. It is roughly the size of the European continent and occupies almost half of North America. Bordered by three oceans—the Pacific to its west, Arctic to its north, and Atlantic to its east—it has a total coastline of 146,000 miles. About eight percent of its territory is water, giving the country about nine percent of the world's freshwater supply. To its south and northwest, it shares the world's longest international boundary (5,335 miles) with its only land neighbor, the United States. The country's vastness and its position in the continent's northern reaches simultaneously present beneficial elements, such as bountiful resources and water supplies, and formidable challenges, such as rugged terrains, severe climates, and great distances.

Most of the basic landforms of Canada share continental patterns of running in a north-south direction, creating another obstacle for people as they set about carving out a distinctive nation. The country's physiographic regions vary dramatically from east to west and from south to north. The regional variety has shaped exploration, habitation, economic development, and relationships with Americans in contiguous regions. Starting from the Atlantic seaboard, the areas defined by the current Atlantic Provinces and part of Quebec, the land is an extension of the vast Appalachian region that sweeps north to south along the continent's spine. The mountain ranges and valleys that dominate this region, coupled with the extensive coastal area of the Atlantic Ocean and Gulf of St. Lawrence, lend themselves to modest agricultural pursuits, forestry, mining, and fishing. The Great Lakes–St. Lawrence lowlands, an area bordering the interior lake systems and St. Lawrence River, or the extreme southern portions of Quebec and the southern peninsular region of Ontario, is one of the most fertile and temperate areas in Canada. It is also the location of the country's two largest cities, home to most of its population, and its industrial heartland. When Canadians speak of central Canada, this is the region they have in mind.

Sweeping north of both of these regions in a dramatic U-shape is the Canadian Shield, the country's dominant landform. Also called the Precambrian Shield, it is a mass of igneous rock that blankets roughly half of Canada's geography. With Hudson Bay as the center of the cup, it encompasses Labrador, most of Quebec, Ontario, and Manitoba, and much of Nunavut and the Northwest Territories. Scoured by thousands of years of glaciation, the Shield is characterized by thin soil, a rugged terrain that includes hills and valleys, honeycombed streams and rivers, and seemingly countless lakes and ponds. Virtually uninhabitable, the Shield created a formidable obstacle to exploration, settlement, and the construction of transportation systems such as railroads and highways. At the same time, the Shield is an area of immense beauty and wilderness; it is also the vast storehouse of immense resource wealth, including minerals such as nickel, copper, iron, lead, zinc, and uranium. For centuries its fur-bearing animals were trapped by the millions to drive a lucrative fur trade. Its vast timber stands have propelled one of the country's major industries in timber, pulp, and paper; its water systems provide much of the country's hydroelectricity. A proverbial mixed blessing, the Canadian Shield looms large in Canadian history. It may be home to relatively few Amerindians and whites, but it held and continues to hold a magnetic attraction for trappers, hunters, miners, timber cutters, hikers, photographers, and artists. Perhaps no other landform kindles the imagination as much as the great Canadian Shield; it is at once a place to be admired and exploited.

Well into North America's interior, the Shield yields to another dominant landscape: the expansive interior plains. Also reaching in a north-south fashion, the plains dominate the continent's interior from the southern United States to the arctic tundra of northern Canada. The key plains landform is the prairie of southern Manitoba, Saskatchewan, and Alberta. The rolling prairies, once home to nomadic Native peoples and millions of buffalo have become over time the country's grain belt. The production of grains, including wheat, oilseed, canola, soy, and barley, is a central focus of prairie agriculture. In addition, livestock and oil and gas development became extremely important sectors of the prairie economy in the twentieth century.

The prairies abruptly run up against the Western Cordilleras, a system of magnificent mountain chains, steep valleys, and plateaus. These include the Rockies and a succession of ranges heading westward to the Pacific coast. In much of British Columbia, the mountain ranges literally drop into the sea, giving Canada's geography an abrupt and exquisite finale. This region encompasses British Columbia, the Yukon Territory, and some of the western parts of the Northwest Territories. Little of this terrain is arable, with the major exceptions being the Fraser River Valley and southern Vancouver Island. The compressed mountains, which also run in a north-south pattern, hold dense forests, mineral deposits, and water systems for hydroelectric power. Fishing stocks on the Pacific seaboard, once considered inexhaustible, are now in decline. Some of the world's most beautiful scenery is to be found in this region, so it should be no surprise to discover that some of Canada's most impressive national parks are located here.

Finally, the country's northern reaches, including the Hudson Bay Lowlands along the southwestern shores of the huge salt water bay, the Arctic Lowlands, and the Arctic archipelago of islands, encompass an area that few Canadians have ever seen. The home to Inuit and other northern Amerindians, much of the Far North is covered in ice for all or most of the year; it is characterized by permafrost, making it an area essentially devoid of agricultural pursuits. In the early twenty-first century scientists continue to amass compelling evidence that rising temperatures have had a dramatic impact on the permafrost and ecosystem of the North. Yet even with the accelerating effects of global warming, the vast region is overwhelmingly inhospitable. On the other hand, the ground holds mineral deposits and identified storehouses of oil and natural gas. The extraction of these resources, already underway in some locations, appeals to developers who want to exploit the potential of this area. At the same time, it raises questions about the territorial rights of Native peoples and environmental concerns.

Hence, the landscape of Canada is dominated by distinctive regions, most of them enormous and essentially running in a north-south direction. With the exception of the Far North and most of the Canadian Shield, these regions cut across the international border between the United States and Canada. Complicating this pattern are the country's major waterways. While there are many rivers and lakes that flow across the current international border, for the most part Canada's rivers drain into the Atlantic, Pacific, and Arctic oceans and Hudson Bay through Canadian territory. The great river systems in Canadian history, from the St. Lawrence River in the East to the Mackenzie River in the Northwest, have provided transportation and communication linkages throughout history to the modern era.

The country's regions are also typified by varied climatic patterns. Much of Canada's southern portion is temperate, with long winters and short summers. Parts of southern British Columbia experience great rainfall and mild winter temperatures, while southern Ontario's summer is often extremely hot and humid. The plains region, as in the United States, experiences great temperature fluctuations, with extremely cold winters followed by hot and dry summers. The Atlantic region has weather patterns that are quite similar to those of New England, its seasons punctuated by distinct changes. Thus, both ocean coasts moderate the temperatures, while in the interior the seasonal highs and lows tend to be more dramatic. The Far North is permanently frozen, with extremely cold temperatures through much of the year, while the tundra of the near Arctic experiences very cold and long winters and a brief summer that bring out an impressive variety of hearty vegetation. The Arctic and the central part of the prairies, especially Saskatchewan's southwestern portion, comprise the country's driest regions.

These climatic zones mean that the vast majority of people involved in agricultural pursuits are forced to cope with short growing seasons, which severely limits the kinds of crops that Canada can produce. While wine grapes and other fruits are grown in Ontario, British Columbia, and Nova Scotia, short growing seasons are the norm for the remaining productive land. Only about five percent of Canada's land is arable, and over half of the country is covered in forests and woodlands. This leads to four points that heavily influenced Canadian history. First, farmers in the country have generally been forced to use marginal soil and grapple with extremely challenging climatic patterns; thus, they have favored grains and hearty root crops that can tolerate such conditions. Second, Canadians became skilled in developing strains of crops that are adapted to the country's particular characteristics. Moreover, much of the country's landscape has been profoundly altered by damming and irrigation systems. Third, as has been the case around the globe, the transformation of Canada's ecology has triggered unintended consequences that have harmed the environment along with bringing a more bountiful production. These issues demand, but do not always receive, attention. Fourth, the northern orientation has forced Canadians to rely heavily on importing produce that either cannot be grown locally, such as citrus fruits, or can be raised in only limited quantities.

In sum, Canada's sheer size, its geographical landforms, its tremendous variety of resources, its limited but abundant vegetation, and its varied climatic patterns have combined to shape historical developments in numerous ways. While geography and weather are not entirely deterministic in any country's history, they prescribe a range of possible courses of human activity. Early settlers, for example, quickly realized that the severe and long winters along the St. Lawrence River would afford only limited possibilities for crops. Individuals have been adapting to and changing their environment for as long as they have roamed the planet, and Canadians have certainly not been an exception to that endeavor.

Canada's Political System

Canada's government springs from a fountain of Western, liberal, and democratic traditions. It integrates Britain's parliamentary behavior with aspects of federalism as designed in the United States, such as a governing constitution, a Senate, and a Supreme Court. Canada's continued attachment to the British monarchy, coupled with a democratically elected government, makes its political system unique in North America. The country's Constitution, formerly the British North America Act, was adopted in 1982. Ten provinces and three territories make up the country. The provinces, in order of joining Confederation, are: Ontario, Quebec, New Brunswick, and Nova Scotia (1867), Manitoba (1870), British Columbia (1871), Prince Edward Island (1873), Saskatchewan and Alberta (1905), and Newfoundland (1949). The three territories are the Yukon, the Northwest Territories, and Nunavut, a self-governing territory of mostly Inuit created in 1999. Citizens eighteen years of age and over in the provinces and territories elect their own governments. These governments reside in provincial capitals and have certain unique and shared powers with the federal government. Canadians also elect representatives to the federal government's House of Commons, which meets in Ottawa. The balance of powers between the federal government, the provinces, groups, and individuals sets the agenda for much of the political debate in Canada.

The Canadian head of state is the monarch of the United Kingdom, currently Queen Elizabeth II. The sole remaining connection between the country and its former imperial master, the monarchy is a mostly symbolic linkage to the past. The monarch's representative in the country is the governor general, an essentially advisory and ceremonial position that since 1952 has been held by Canadian citizens. Appointed by the monarch on the advice of the prime minister, the governor general's influence has varied widely in Canadian history according to the personality and activism of the individual, and the historical landscape of the times in which he or she has served. Although constitutionally the governor general could wield enormous powers, in practice the individual acts solely on the advice of the prime minister.

Real political power in Canada emanates from the elected House of Commons. Canada borrowed the essence of Britain's parliamentary system, which means that members of the House of Commons form the government. The party with the most members—whether a majority or a minority when the total numbers of representatives from various other parties are tallied—has the opportunity to lead the country. The head of government is the prime minister, the leader of the party with the most members. While in a parliamentary system voters in their ridings, as Canadian electoral districts are called, cast ballots for a member of Parliament to represent their interests, they also keep in mind that if they want a certain party, and a particular political leader to lead the country, then that party must have the most members. Prime ministers and their appointed cabinets are given tremendous leeway in setting the political agendas for their terms in office. If the party in power enjoys a clear majority of members of Parliament, then typically it has the potential to implement its political goals. Conversely, if a party has a minority status, it must appeal to members from other parties to gather enough votes to pass legislation.

The House of Commons currently has 308 members, elected at least every five years by law, and representing four major parties and independents. The ridings are apportioned according to a balance of tradition and population, with Ontario and Quebec having the greatest number, with 106 and 75 members, respectively; Quebec's numbers are protected by law. Members of Parliament for the rest of the country are apportioned according to population, not unlike the U.S. House of Representatives. Quebec's representative proportion, which was thirty-six percent of Parliament after Confederation in 1867, is close to twenty-five percent of the current body. This decline, for Quebecers, has been a matter of concern and has shaped political disputes in the modern era.

Canadians borrowed the name for their upper house from the United States, but with a few exceptions, the Senate barely resembles the modern U.S. version. Designed to be an elite group of appointed legislators who represent the country's regions, the Senate nominally has tremendous power to veto or amend legislation coming from the House of Commons. In practice, however, the Senate rarely exercises its prerogatives. Senators are appointed by the governor general on the advice of the prime minister, which means that the party in power has a tremendous advantage when vacancies appear. Problems with the Canadian Senate abound, including the regional apportionment that favors Ontario and Quebec and the body's nonelected status. The number of Senators allotted to each province and territory follows a model that was shaped by political wrangling and the chronological order of confederating with Canada (Quebec and Ontario have twenty-four apiece; Nova Scotia and New Brunswick have ten apiece; Newfoundland and Labrador, Manitoba, Saskatchewan, Alberta, and British Columbia have six apiece; Prince Edward Island has four; and Yukon, Northwest Territories, and Nunavut have one apiece). Originally appointed for life according to constitutional documents, Canada's 105 senators now face mandatory retirement at age seventy-five.

In judicial matters, Canada uses a federal criminal code that follows the traditions of English common law. The provinces exercise control over civil laws; thus Quebec's civil code, which still reflects traditions rooted to French civil law, is unique when compared with that of the other provinces. The final arbiter for legal cases in Canada is the Supreme Court, a body of justices created in 1875. Nine justices sit on the Supreme Court. By law, three must be from Quebec, and all are appointed by the prime minister when vacancies occur. Unlike their U.S. counterparts, the justices do not receive extensive attention in the press. The responsibilities and impact of the Supreme Court have changed dramatically since the late nineteenth century. As late as 1949 the Judicial Committee of the British Privy Council was used as the final court for Canadian cases. Since then, however, the Supreme Court has assumed more of a central role in determining not just thorny legal cases, but in ruling on Canada's laws. The creation of the Charter of Rights and Freedoms, part of the 1982 Constitution, has led to a number of cases that have placed the justices at the crossroads of politically charged cases (much like their American counterparts).

Canada's political and judicial systems have changed extensively since 1867 when the country was created. Canadians often point to the concept, as a way of distinguishing the unique nature of their country's history, that their systems evolved over time with only occasional contentious or violent outbursts. The obvious comparison is to their southern neighbor, which boisterously sought freedom in a

revolutionary struggle and then experienced bloody division in the
Civil War. The root points of the comparison are undeniable, but the
superficial contention that Canada's basically peaceful evolution is
its most important distinguishing feature is flawed on two levels.
First, Canada's past is not lacking in tumultuous themes that are
comparable to events in the United States or Western Europe. Second,
the "evolution versus revolution" differences between the two national
groups might have been an appropriate conceptual theme for an
earlier era, but events since the nineteenth century have thoroughly
complicated such a cosmetic approach to understanding the development of the country's political and judicial organizations.

Canada's Economy

Canada's economy has been intricately linked to the developing
capitalistic ideals, organizations, and trading patterns of Western
nations in the modern era. Canadians enjoy one of the highest
standards of living in the world. The country's current gross domestic
product (GDP), the value of all goods and services produced in any
given year, is close to $1.5 trillion. Fully two-thirds of that figure is
derived from service industries, and almost one-third from the
industrial sector. A small fraction of the country's GDP, about two
percent, is created by agriculture. Since the earliest years of European
settlement, Canada's economy has been rooted to the production of
raw materials that are in demand outside the country. During the
twentieth century the country became more industrial than agricultural in productive capability and outlook, and in the past few
decades it has adapted to a postindustrial climate of service and high-
tech industries.

The country's major resources are its minerals, fossil fuels, forest
products, and hydroelectric power. Its primary industries, such as
wood and paper products and oil and natural gas production, process
those resources. In addition, Canadians engage in agriculture and
fishing. The country's leading secondary industries are automobile
manufacturing, iron and steel construction, machinery and equipment production, and telecommunications. The coupling of its
abundant resources with its manufacturing output makes the

country's economy quite typical in the modern world. While some of its resources are either shrinking rapidly or endangered, such as its fishing stocks along both the Atlantic and Pacific coasts, Canada continues to rely on its abilities to market its resources to the world.

With the institution of the Free Trade Agreement with the United States in 1989 and the North American Free Trade Agreement in 1993, which included Mexico, and its participation in the G20, an organization comprising some of the world's strongest economies, Canada has intensified its international trading patterns. Almost three-quarters of Canada's exports go to the United States, while over half of its imports are from the same country. Canada also trades extensively with Japan, the United Kingdom, Germany, South Korea, the Netherlands, China, France, Taiwan, and Mexico. In 2007 its exports, which include automobiles and car parts, pulp and paper, oil and natural gas, timber products, minerals, and aluminum, were valued at $440 billion. The country imports automobiles and car parts, machinery and equipment, electronics, plastics, chemicals, consumer goods, and food. Its imports totaled $390 billion during the same year. While its trade balance is essentially favorable, the country's dependence on American markets throughout the modern era has created a series of problems that plague Canadians and elude definitive solutions.

Although the country's economy boomed in the early years of the twenty-first century, it has suffered as a result of the global recession that began in 2008. Canadians face significant problems that are typical in the modern global economy. While it copes with a mammoth debt of over $500 billion, its deficit—the gap between tax resources and expenditures—is relatively modest when compared with other industrialized countries. Unemployment in 2010 hovered around eight percent, certainly a healthy figure when considered in the light of countries whose economies are struggling, and especially when compared with Canada's decimated economy of the 1930s. Nonetheless, Canadians continue to be challenged by competition from abroad, an extraordinarily high tax base, shifting markets for their products, international corporate takeovers, and labor issues. In addition, environmental themes in modern Canada reflect problems around the globe. Dwindling resources, a reliance on petroleum products to fuel industry and transportation, pollution that fouls the country's air, water, and soil, and fierce contests between expansion-minded industries and environmentally conscious organizations are but a few of the important problems that continue to seek workable solutions. Overall, Canada's economy in the modern era is the envy of much of the rest of the world in that it helps to create a generally favorable environment so that most of its citizens enjoy a measure of well-being.

The Peoples of Canada

There are an estimated thirty-four million Canadians, most clustered in a band that hugs the U.S. border. Population experts have compared this demographic image to Chile, meaning that it is long and narrow. Most of the nation's largest cities—Toronto, Montreal, Vancouver, Ottawa, Calgary, and Winnipeg—are within one hundred miles of the U.S. border. Moreover, an estimated ninety percent of Canadians are concentrated within the same distance of the United States. The overwhelming majority of Canadians—over three-quarters—live in urban settings and larger towns, a trend that has accelerated since the early twentieth century. With a current life expectancy of eighty-one years at birth, Canada ranks as a world leader in the quality of life for its citizens. These kinds of population measures, important for achieving a benchmark for understanding any nation's history, are particularly revealing in Canada because they paint a portrait of a people who, in spite of persistent myths, are intensely urbanized and modern. Importantly, they are also affected by the economic and cultural influences of the United States.

Canada's peoples have created a nation in the modern tradition, composed of distinctive power centers that range from local communities, to provincial governments, to regional collectives, to the federal government. Although it is impossible to capture the sentiments accurately in a few words, they have also constructed various group, provincial, regional, and national identities. Sometimes these identities blend seamlessly. As often as not, however, they strike out in various directions and thus complicate and enliven societal and political debates. Canadians have certainly articulated a national identity, as evidenced in a variety of national memories, patriotic symbols such as the distinctive maple leaf flag, a national anthem ("O Canada"), and familiar characterizations such as the Mountie and the beaver (the latter endlessly and imaginatively employed by writers and cartoonists, inevitably as a foil to Uncle Sam, the standard U.S. symbol). These images directly or obliquely allude to ideals that are distinctively Canadian, such as the French "fact," the tradition of supporting Britain in war and peace, even-handed behavior in the international community of nations, and an ambivalent relationship with the United States. Often these ideals provide a powerful bonding agent for Canadians. As many observers have noted, Canadians are sometimes most unified and clear about their self-identity when they travel abroad (see "Joe Canadian Rant" in the Documents section).

Nonetheless, tensions abound in the Canadian historical landscape, so much of the following work will be given over to an introduction to some of the most important struggles that have taken place among the country's various groups. A French-English duality clearly provides one of the most enduring frameworks for understanding the context for power between governments, regions, and ethnic groups. Survival (*la survivance*) of the French language and a French-Canadian culture is a serious issue for the country's millions of francophones. For the more than one million Canadians who claim Amerindian ancestry, the issues are similar. As has been the case for centuries, issues of homeland, formal recognition, treaty rights, and ethnic intolerance infuse the current contest between Native peoples and other Canadians. Regionalism is an acute dynamic in the Canadian past and present, offering perennial challenges to maintaining a workable union and testing the skills of those Canadians who seek compromise over conflict. The citizens of Canada have long coped with what many call the "burden of unity." A vibrant and distinctive Atlantic region to the east shares little with Quebec. Neighboring Quebec and Ontario often seem like polar opposites, although in fact they are not. The prairie region has its own identity and set of priorities, and the Far West demonstrates a different orientation that looks to the Pacific Rim and the U.S. Northwest for trade and cultural linkages. Maintaining a cohesive bond between the peoples of the various regions has historically been the purview of the federal government, but in truth Canadians, acting as either individuals or in groups, have long made it their business to weigh in on the great national unity debate.

Perhaps the most difficult issue to address is the subject of culture. Constructed onto a base of Native peoples, who themselves were newcomers in the distant past, Canada is a nation of immigrant heritage and recent arrivals. Although ethnic identification is made challenging because of a high rate of marriages between groups through the generations, a basic ethnic breakdown of the Canadian population is possible. According to the 2006 census figures, about twenty-eight percent of Canadians claim the British Isles or Ireland as their ethnic orientation, and about twenty-three percent note their French heritage. Twenty-six of the respondents indicate that they are of mixed background. The remainder comprise other North Americans; Amerindians; other Europeans such as Germans, Italians, Ukrainians, Dutch, Polish, Portuguese, and Scandinavians; Asians from China, India, Southeast Asia, and Sri Lanka; and one of the most recent groups, Caribbeans. Thus, from a foundation of Native peoples, French, and British, the country has become one of the most multicultural nations on earth. This fact has been embraced by the government, which in 1988 passed an act designed to promote the country's various cultures and confront persistent discrimination and intolerance. Ethnic orientation and identification present an essential paradox in Canadian history. Considered in the past and present by many Canadians a corrosive element that undermines the formation of national identity and saps the country's strength and resources, ethnic diversity is also applauded and embraced by many as the Canadian identity. A mosaic of peoples, given the privilege of maintaining their customs, languages, religions, and ideologies under the protective umbrella of a progressive Canadian government, is the essence of modern Canada to many proud citizens. These conflicting ideas will be explored in the pages ahead, for the gap between the ideal and the reality of multiculturalism strikes at the heart of the Canadian story.

Canada in a New Century: A Product of Its Past

At the close of the twenty-first century's first decade, Canadians are quite aware of the complexity of their identities, the often conflicting interpretations of their past, and the different visions they hold for their future. Canadians are overwhelmingly affluent, educated, technologically attuned, environmentally aware, passionately protective of both group and individual rights, and relatively progressive in their political persuasions. Their country is recognized internationally as one of the leading middle powers since World War II, possessed of integrity and wisdom in navigating a course between competing empires throughout its history. And while there is certainly a clamor of viewpoints emanating from the far left and right, Canadians have become particularly adept at seeking and achieving compromise. Concerned about the economic and cultural penetration of the United States, Canadians often find their most compelling sense of identification in the disclaimer that they are *not* Americans. With a population of roughly one-tenth that of the United States, inhabiting the second largest territory on earth, and gathered overwhelmingly in locations close to the U.S. border, Canadians continue to face formidable challenges to maintain their sovereignty. They are engaged in an ongoing debate, which some would argue is tiresome and self-defeating, that is heavily colored by history. Canadians wrestle openly with questions that probe at self-identity and weigh their successes and failures in constructing a modern nation. Ultimately, they are forced to confront the essential challenge of deciding whether to continue in their existing political form or bow to the pressures of dissolution.

We look to Canada's history to understand these issues. The country's past might share similarities with its American, British, and French cousins, but it unfolds in a distinct fashion. It has navigated daunting natural and human-designed obstacles to survival. Ultimately, as is made clear by the repeated pronouncements of the United Nations in the modern era, it is a thriving nation that works despite a fracturing along political, regional, ethnic, and language lines. History has painted a canvas in northern North America that is colorful and richly textured. Clearly Canada's history is neither tedious nor a bland reflection of its more powerful neighbor.

NOTES

1. The term "Americans" can be used to describe the inhabitants of various countries in the Western Hemisphere, but for the purposes of this book it refers to the residents of the United States.

2. A francophone is a French-speaking person; an anglophone is an English speaker. An allophone is a person whose primary language is neither French nor English.
3. Robin Winks, *The Relevance of Canadian History: U.S. and Imperial Perspectives* (Toronto: Macmillan of Canada, 1979), xiv.

Chapter 2

Native Peoples, Europeans, and a Clash of Cultures (Prehistory–1663)

Canada Before the Contact Period

Canada's location in the northern reaches of the continent meant that it would be a paradoxical place. Its climate and geological landforms suggested that it would present great challenges to the people who tried to inhabit it and wrest a living from its lands and waters. On the other hand, its seemingly boundless terrain of waterways, lowlands, forests, plains, and mountains harbored a vast treasure trove of resources. For the relatively modest numbers of people, considering the larger populations of Europe, Asia, and the southern part of the America continents, the nation that we now call Canada would display essential tensions: between bounty and austerity, struggle and peace, and freedom and restraint. It is in understanding its contradictory nature that one finds the essence of Canadian history.

The contradictions lie in the initial years of fitful meetings between the peoples of two worlds: the original inhabitants of North America and Europeans. This protracted era, called the contact period, suggests themes in Canadian history that have weathered the test of time. Northern North America, rather than being a vacuum for energetic Europeans to explore and settle, was a vast landscape inhabited by a

Explorer Jacques Cartier, his crew, and Native peoples on Mount Royal, the landform that gave its name to Montreal.

Source: Library and Archives Canada / Lawrence R. Batchelor collection / C-010521

flourishing mixture of Native peoples who had fashioned a way of life over the centuries that was in tune with the environment and, as far as we can determine, was part of a complicated system of relationships between neighboring and often competing tribal groups. From a European perspective, Canada was alternately viewed as an obstacle or an objective. The obstacle idea was rooted in the energetic exploratory activity that led Europeans to find a short western ocean route to the riches of Asia. Antithetically, the objective ideal emerged in large measure as a secondary plan, at least for the place we now call Canada. If not easily and readily traversed, then perhaps the waters, soils, and rocks of northern North America would yield other substances—perhaps even riches—that would make European settlement a worthwhile endeavor. Thus for Native peoples, Canada had been an austere yet often bounteous home for countless generations. For the vanguard of European explorers and settlers, the image of Canada fluctuated between being a barrier or a magnet. Indisputably, the vast continent became the arena for a clash of peoples and cultures that would account for much of Canada's early colonial history.

In order to come to grips with precontact North America, historians must be particularly creative in seeking a variety of sources. In order to understand Native peoples before and during the early contact years, we cannot rely exclusively on the most common historical source: written documents. Instead we should make imaginative use of archaeological material, as well as the contributions of anthropologists and ethnographers. Moreover, as the written record of the contact period unfolded, it was almost exclusively the product of European males, who inevitably defined and remembered events that fit their principles and ideals. We are left with the documents, maps, and visual portraits of what they saw and how they reacted to life in the New World. Therefore, the task of determining what the lives of Native peoples were like before and during contact is a particularly challenging one. And while some conclusions about Amerindians will probably remain forever ill defined and debatable, a combination of oral testimony, Native traditions, and carefully interpreted records of European-based peoples gives us a clearer insight to life in Canada hundreds of years ago.

Until recently, Canada's Amerindians tended to be portrayed as a backdrop for the substance of Canadian history, a group to be considered during the fur trade era of the early colonial period and in the context of several nineteenth-century conflicts, or as an interesting sidebar to flesh out the complexity of the Canadian past. Thanks to a wealth of scholarly and popular literature on Native peoples in the past generation, we now know that their impact on Canadian history was and continues to be far greater than previously acknowledged. Neither background to the European invasion nor anecdotal supplement, the country's Native peoples are an essential part of the historical admixture for a rounded understanding of the Canadian past.

Migration of Native Peoples to Canada

Archaeological evidence suggests that at least two great waves of migration brought Native peoples to the Americas. The most widely recognized migration came from northern Asia over a land bridge in what is now the Bering Strait between 12,000 and 20,000 years ago. Although this is one of the oldest and most compelling theories, some recent DNA evidence has pointed to genetic connections between the peoples of Manchuria and Mongolia and some Native peoples in North America. As the mammoth glaciers retreated from the last ice age, these groups transmigrated within present-day Canada. By the era of European exploration and settlement, they occupied virtually all of the land mass that entails Canada today. The second large wave occurred from 700 to 1000 A.D., when scholars believe the Inuit of the Arctic region and various peoples of the interior of British Columbia migrated. These two surges explain the great difference between the groups and linguistic patterns of Native peoples in Canada.

Brief mention should be made of competing theories that attempt to explain the ethnically and linguistically diverse Amerindian groups of the Americas. These ideas range from oceanic connections and trade routes, made possible by favorable ocean currents and wind, with southeast Asia and Pacific islands. Similar theories explore connections with North Africans, the Phoenicians, and even one popular idea about an Irishman named St. Brendan the Navigator.

Taking the broadest of viewpoints, historians note that Native peoples in the northern reaches of the continent were complex, linguistically varied, and culturally diverse, and tribal groupings differed dramatically in size. While diversity characterized the Amerindian population, all peoples were clearly well adapted to the environment for survival. Hardship, deprivation, and war would certainly have been part of the lives of generations of Native peoples in the land that was to become Canada, yet scholars agree that these groups were resilient and highly adapted to the rigorous terrain and climate of the continent's northern part.

Native Groups, Economies, and Cultures

Although population estimates of groups before definitive census records are problematic, probably about 500,000 Native peoples lived in Canada on the eve of European contact in the late fifteenth century. Scholars place the range between a low of 300,000 and a high of 2 million, but the 500,000 figure has gained a measure of acceptance. The size of various tribal units and affiliated groups varied dramatically, with the largest populations clustered near plentiful resources and in more temperate climatic zones, such as along the present-day British Columbia coast, southern Ontario, and the lowlands along the St. Lawrence River. At least twelve major linguistic families, the two largest being the Athabaskan of the West and North and the Algonquian that dominated in the East, encompassed Canada's Native peoples. A third linguistic branch, smaller in range but of critical importance for understanding Canadian history, was the Iroquoian group located in present-day New York state. For important moments in Canadian history, they ranged into southern Ontario and along the St. Lawrence River. Within these linguistic groups, defined by similar languages and cultures, over fifty distinct languages were spoken by Canada's Amerindians.

The culture of Canada's Native peoples is as hard to characterize in a brief space as it would be to lump various ethnic groups from Africa, Asia, or Europe. Nonetheless, it is possible to make generalizations that fairly characterize the peoples whom the Europeans first encountered. These behaviors were also partially responsible for the destructive clashes, due in part to a lack of understanding of cultural differences, that largely defined European-Amerindian relations for centuries. Native peoples displayed generally egalitarian qualities, and tribal units worked according to consensus. While Amerindians had chiefs, the leader's authority rested largely on an ability to hold power to represent the common will. The belief system of Native peoples suggested a close relationship with the land and animal kingdom that provided food and clothing. Amerindian life was thoroughly intertwined with the living beings and inanimate objects of the universe. Religious behavior, characterized by a host of spirits and communal rituals, was left largely to the individual. The balance between the needs of the group and the individual was a complex one that varied from one tribe to another, but in general Amerindians highly prized personal power and skill. In addition, Native peoples played sports, such as lacrosse, and clearly demonstrated a sense of humor that transcended cultures.

The economies of tribal units varied greatly as well, from highly socialized groups such as the Iroquois and West Coast Bella Coola with their multiple family units and elaborate villages, to nomadic family units of hunters and gatherers such as the eastern Algonquian tribes. The vast majority of Native peoples were hunters and gatherers, and the interior of what would become Canada was honeycombed with well-plied trade routes. Some tribes, such as the Huron, honed their trading skills long before Europeans arrived. Other units based much of their economy on agricultural pursuits. A trademark of Iroquoian peoples was their expertise in raising corn, beans, squash, and other vegetables. Some scholars estimate that the Huron raised by farming seventy-five percent of what they consumed in bountiful years. In the prairies, tribes employed sophisticated hunting tactics to slaughter buffalo for food and clothing. West Coast Amerindians were adept at catching fish in the rich coastal waters and river systems; they were also exceptional woodworkers. The totem pole became one of the most recognizable symbols of North American Amerindians yet was the creation of West Coast Native peoples. Although tribal groups clearly had a sense of territory and familiarity with hunting, trapping, and fishing regions, they had no clear ownership tradition that a contemporary European would recognize or honor.

One of the most enduring and discernible contributions of Native peoples was their technological creations. Europeans would adapt so completely a host of Amerindian-designed tools and transportation devices that these would literally end up being considered emblematic of present-day Canada. A partial list would include the bark canoe, snowshoes, toboggans, and dogsleds. In addition, the techniques that Native peoples developed in growing edible plants, trapping animals, and curing pelts would be adopted wholesale by whites who were eager to exploit the resources of North America for their own use and European markets. Indeed, Amerindians pointed the way to the development of raw materials that would become the backbone of colonial and postcolonial economic development. The lucrative fur trade was a prime example.

Although the documentary evidence of the lives of Native peoples is more abundant after Europeans appeared, and tragically the postcontact era was rife with violent clashes between the cultures, enough evidence survives to suggest that Amerindians regularly warred on neighboring tribes in the precontact period. Native peoples typically took captives into their tribes and made hostages of women and children to facilitate intricate trading relationships over the generations. Adoption of captives and intermarriage between tribes was not uncommon, and while countless wars and skirmishes defined in part the Amerindian life cycle, scholars are in some agreement that the utter destruction of tribes in warfare, while it might have occurred, was probably not a typical objective strategy for warring groups (see "Champlain's Assessment of Native Peoples" in the Documents section).

In sum, along the northern perimeter of what one historian called the "hemispheric civilization," Canada's indigenous peoples existed above larger Amerindian populations in Central and South America.[1] Patterns of conflict and trade were already in place, and while the introduction of Europeans clearly disturbed a measure of balance between Native peoples, they often deliberately or inadvertently intensified long-standing relationships. The fragmentation and lack of cohesion among Native peoples, so clearly a hallmark of survival in the generations before contact, probably contributed to their demise after contact. Finally, while similarities between the peoples of the late Middle Ages and Amerindians were perhaps not as great as described by contemporaries and later by historians, for many of the first European traders and settlers of peasant stock adapted quite readily to Native lifestyles, a cultural gulf separated the groups.

Europeans determined that Native peoples lacked legal traditions, a sense of property rights, and a meaningful and organized religion. These were key touchstones for their lives in Europe, and all were ideals that they attempted to transplant in the New World.

Norsemen: Exploration and Settlement

Few traditional records exist to give us a clear sense of the earliest European groups that came in contact with the North American continent. Without the benefit of compasses, which were introduced in the twelfth century, Nordic peoples made their way across the Atlantic from Iceland to Greenland over several centuries. Around 1000 A.D. Leif Eriksson made a voyage that brought him in contact with Baffin Island, the Labrador Coast, and a mysterious Vinland where the group found grapes and a temperate climate for wintering over. Scholars place Vinland somewhere between Labrador and Florida. This and subsequent voyages to the coastal areas of present-day Canada brought the Norse into contact with a people called *skraelings*, or "barbarians." Scholars believe these were Inuit-related peoples. Bloody confrontations between the groups thwarted the efforts of Nordic peoples to colonize the Vinland settlement, and after repeated efforts from the eleventh to the fourteenth centuries, trade for raw materials such as wood probably accounted for the only contact between Europeans and Amerindians. According to the period's key source—the sagas, or oral accounts passed along by generations through the centuries—Norse settlements existed in northern North America for a brief time.

The only Norse site that has been confirmed is in l'Anse aux Meadows in the northwestern tip of Newfoundland. The remains of a small number of earthen huts and some artifacts indicate that Norse peoples had a temporary settlement in Canada around the year 1000 A.D. Women were known to be present because of the discovery of implements that were used to make yarn from wool. The irregular encounters probably ceased around the thirteenth century, and for about five hundred years European contact with the region that would become Canada was infrequent and poorly documented. Nordic peoples retreated even from the older Greenland settlements because of increasingly cold temperatures, so the story of Nordic contact is disconnected from the intensive European drive that erupted in the fifteenth century to explore and colonize the New World. The hearty Nordic peoples who touched on the Arctic islands and northern continental coast did, however, point to an essential truth in Canadian history. The land was rich in resources such as timber and fish. Canada had much to offer as the European continent experienced dramatic population growth and economic development.

The New World: Early Exploration

In the age of exploration, Europeans sought a sea route to Asia, primarily to facilitate a trade in spices that were crucial for the unrefrigerated European diet of meats and other foods. Northern European groups by the fifteenth century were attempting to break the trade monopolies of Italian cities. Moreover, improvements in navigational devices, such as the astrolabe, and technological developments in designing and building more seaworthy vessels helped to spur oceanic passage. Timeless human qualities explained the late fifteenth-century quest for exploring and exploiting the potential of the New World: human curiosity and a desire to earn a profit. Interwoven in this motivational mixture was the dedication on the part of some early explorers, as well as their important European-based sponsors, to spread Christianity. The growing western European sea powers—Spain, Portugal, England, the Netherlands, and France—were the prime contenders during the period under discussion. As fate would have it, France ended up focusing a great deal of energy in the region now called Canada largely because it was not on the cutting edge of the exploration quest. Rather late in joining the competition, France was habitually short of the necessary capital for the successful development of the New World.

Explorers regularly bumped into the coast of northern North America in the wake of Christopher Columbus's celebrated 1492 voyage. Virtually all of the initial explorers of Canada sought a relatively direct, and with any luck swift, northwest passage to the riches of Asia. Sailing for the English, the Italian mariner John Cabot (born Giovanni Caboto) probably landed in northern Newfoundland and Cape Breton in 1497. Although the precise locations of his landfalls continue to be contested by scholars, his contact and active attempt to claim the land for England's Henry VII almost immediately created a context for imperial rivalry. Cabot and a large contingent of mariners disappeared without trace the following year. The Portuguese Corte-Real brothers, tracking the coastline of North America, also touched on Newfoundland and Labrador in 1500 and 1501. Like Cabot, the Corte-Real brothers were lost to the sea, and the Portuguese turned their energies toward developing southern islands and territory in the New World.

Another Italian mariner who sailed for the French, Giovanni da Verrazano (1524–1528), plied a great swath of the eastern seaboard of North America, probably from North Carolina or Virginia to Gaspé at the eastern tip of present-day Quebec. The voyage, sponsored by François I, the first French monarch to be truly interested in the New World, gave the French a sense of the North Atlantic. Verrazano designated the shores of northern North America *Nova Francia*, or New France. These explorers collectively grasped the idea that a landmass blocked the northern passage to Asia, although some believed the Pacific Ocean was extremely close to the Atlantic Ocean. Also, after Cabot's voyage, explorers tapped into an old European interest: feeding a growing and increasingly urban population. Portuguese, French, and British mariners fished for cod in the rich waters off present-day Newfoundland and Nova Scotia. This endeavor became such an important Canadian practice that it was only recently altered with a cod fisheries moratorium in the waters off Newfoundland to protect dwindling fish stocks. Whalers came as well, especially from the Basque region, summering and sometimes wintering over on North America's hostile shores. By the mid-1500s, these hardy fishermen had grasped the fact that the land would yield another commodity that fetched handsome prices in Europe: furs and pelts.

Cartier's Voyages: An Attempted French Foothold

The initial series of intensive explorations for France were shaped by the desire to find a passage to Asia and to discover riches, two of the classic driving forces behind transatlantic movement in the sixteenth century. Jacques Cartier, a mariner from Saint-Malo in Brittany, made three voyages for François I in 1534, 1535–1536, and 1541–1542. Cartier and his men "discovered" little in the gulf of St. Lawrence. Instead they encountered fishing boats and visited harbors already named by Basque whalers. Cartier expressed ambiguous feelings about the land he encountered. In an obvious reference to the hostility of the landscape, he called the Labrador coast in the Strait of Belle Isle the "land God gave Cain." Cartier's voyages illustrated the French desire to gain a stake in the New World; he planted a cross on the shores of the gulf of St. Lawrence. His desire to locate a western passage to Asia brought him up the St. Lawrence River to the Amerindian communities of Stadacona (Quebec) and Hochelaga (Montreal). At Hochelaga the water passage to the west was blocked by rapids, which the French named Lachine with an expectation that China lay beyond the foaming waters of the St. Lawrence.

Cartier's voyages also yielded the first clear evidence of the clash of cultures between Native peoples and Europeans that has been such a persistent theme in Canadian history. He met both Mi'kmaq and Iroquoian groups, who eagerly sought to trade furs and other goods. On one trip, Cartier kidnaped an Iroquoian chief named Donnacona, his two sons, and other children and adults. They never returned from France; all probably fell victim to European diseases. Cartier and his men wintered over in Stadacona, a brutal time when they encountered the frozen and snow-covered landscape for many long months. One-quarter of Cartier's men perished, most because of scurvy, a vitamin C deficiency. Native peoples showed the whites how to alleviate the problem with a tea made from the bark and leaves of white cedar. The final voyage brought a more intensive group, with Cartier theoretically under the command of a nobleman named Jean-François de La Rocque de Roberval. Delayed by one year, Roberval's group, which had been prepared to attempt a settlement, endured a harsh winter where Cartier had stayed the previous year. Unable to find the mythical land of riches, called the Saguenay, Cartier made haste for home with holds filled with what he assumed were gold and diamonds. Dumped on the wharves of France, alas, was worthless iron pyrite (fool's gold) and quartz.

Cartier's and Roberval's voyages from 1534 to 1542 put the French off the scent of the New World for the remainder of the sixteenth century. Although misled by false gold and quartz, not the riches that the Spanish had encountered to the south, the French had dimly grasped the fact that furs would be a lucrative commodity. Moreover, the seas yielded fish, whales seemed plentiful, timber stands were lush, and apparently the St. Lawrence lowlands held the potential for agricultural pursuits. Yet negative factors clearly outweighed the positive prospects of the New World. Struggles and a lack of trust between the French and Amerindians led to skirmishes on several occasions. Europeans, used to the temperate climate of northwestern France, found the land austere. And the riches, promised in such abundance by Native peoples who quickly grasped the intentions of the excitable Europeans, proved elusive. Despite tantalizing information about great inland freshwater seas (the Great Lakes), the water paths, including the immensely promising St. Lawrence River, were frustratingly blocked. Finally, Cartier's voyages lent an Iroquoian word for a village to the land the French intended to master: Canada. A combination of factors led to a period of inattention: hostilities with Native peoples, the harsh terrain and dramatic climate, obstructed passages to the west, a dearth of readily accessible riches, and limited financial support. Soured on the Canadian experience, the French turned their colonizing attentions to the south in a mostly unsuccessful effort to capture territory in areas largely controlled by the Portuguese and Spanish.

Champlain and the Establishment of New France

For the remainder of the sixteenth century Spanish, English, French, and Basque fishermen exploited the abundant fisheries of the eastern seaboard of North America. The island of Newfoundland was regularly used either to dry cod or pack the fish in barrels of salt. Along the St. Lawrence, trade continued between French and Basque fishermen and Amerindians, primarily where the Saguenay River joins the St. Lawrence at the Montagnais tribal village of Tadoussac. This informal activity yields little historical evidence of European encounters with the New World, yet we know that trade and fishing continued. The next serious attempts at exploration and settlement largely resulted from the energies of a remarkable man named Samuel de Champlain.

The fur trade drove the renewed French interest in Canada. In particular the beaver was highly prized for making hats and coats for Europe's growing number of merchants and businessmen. For two and a half centuries after 1600, a struggle to create a monopoly to dominate the fur trade shaped much of Canadian history. Supported by a trading monopoly and royal permission, the French trader Sieur de Monts and Samuel de Champlain initially attempted a settlement in 1604 in the Bay of Fundy region of the current Maritime Provinces of New Brunswick and Nova Scotia. A commoner who had fought for France, Champlain first wintered near the mouth of the St. Croix River, which divides present-day New Brunswick and Maine, and then moved across the bay to Port-Royal. De Monts and Champlain started with 125 settlers, but difficulties in controlling trade and uncertainty with Amerindians led de Monts to return to France with the group in 1607. Significantly, during the brief period of abandonment of New World settlement for the French, the English located their first successful colony along Virginia's modest James River.

The following year, 1608, Champlain obtained permission from de Monts to attempt a settlement along the St. Lawrence. Champlain had determined that a colony along the majestic river would be easier to protect, there would be better prospects for development and exploration of the interior, and he hoped to improve trade with Native peoples who prized copper pots and iron goods such as axes. Champlain also found that in the years since Cartier's voyages, the Amerindians along the St. Lawrence River had changed dramatically. The Iroquoian groups that Cartier had encountered and even fought had mysteriously retreated. Algonquian Indians, primarily the Montagnais, had replaced them. Eager to trade with the French, the Algonquian tribes quickly formed a tenuous relationship with the French to offset what appears to have been a long-standing struggle with the fierce Iroquoian groups to the south and west.

Choosing the settlement where the St. Lawrence River narrows, called Quebec in the Algonquian language, Champlain's small party constructed a habitation under the looming rock that dominates the landscape. Quebec served as the administrative center of New France during the French regime and is the current capital of the province of Quebec. Nearly three-quarters of the small party died of scurvy or dysentery that first winter, a stark reminder that settlement in the

New World would continue to be a difficult endeavor. Supplies and new men came after the river thawed in the spring of 1609, thereby ensuring the survival of a permanent settlement in New France and establishing a pattern of reinforcement from the Old World that would be such a critical factor for life in early colonial Canadian history. The struggle to gain a trade monopoly and control over the St. Lawrence occupied Champlain's interests until 1612.

Champlain's mandate was to create a settlement sustained by agricultural production, yet it was in his skills as an explorer and extraordinarily perceptive cartographer that he made his mark in history. Over the next several years, after excursions to the hinterland with Amerindian guides, Champlain found a large lake that he named after himself, reached the eastern boundaries of two of the great inland seas (Lakes Ontario and Huron), and wintered with a powerful tribe of Iroquoian cousins named the Huron in present-day southern Ontario. With the help of protégés, such as Etienne Brûlé, Champlain worked to cement the relationship between Native peoples and French and gathered tantalizing news of the Mississippi system and the Pacific Ocean. The French were swiftly gaining a cursory sense of the geography of the interior of North America. As it turned out, their position on the education curve was far ahead of their English counterparts to the south, a fact that would create tensions in the decades ahead as the European powers struggled to gain control of the continent.

Champlain and his Algonquian allies clashed repeatedly with the Iroquoian confederacy. Beginning with a dramatic encounter near Lake Champlain in 1609, where Champlain and his men purportedly killed three Iroquois chiefs, the French with their guns regularly defeated smaller Iroquoian forces. The bitter encounters between the French and Iroquoian peoples would persist for generations and become one of the important themes in New France's history. Native peoples also suffered from the introduction of European diseases. Although it is hard to measure the decimation that European-borne diseases inflicted on Amerindians, the seventeenth century brought a calamity of the first order to the continent's original inhabitants. In one of the most clearly documented accounts, the Huron, once a thriving group that essentially controlled the trading routes of the Lake Huron area, lost over fifty percent of their population by 1639 through disease or warfare. Their population would never recover to predisease levels, a dramatic illustration of the fate of hundreds of thousands of Native peoples in North America.

By the 1620s, Quebec's fort was but a small outpost of the French Empire. It reflected the French trading impulse, for the early settlers hoped to make rapid fortunes in the New World. In 1627, when Quebec welcomed its first birth of a child of European extraction in New France, the settlement was home to fewer than one hundred people. Heavily dependent on regular supply ships, the settlers also survived largely thanks to their trade with the Native peoples, as well as the information they gleaned about coping with Canada's inhospitable environment.

Acadia: Early French-English Rivalry in Canada

The St. Lawrence River valley was not the only focal point for French settlement and trade in the New World. The eastern area of colonization, called Acadia, was a distinct enterprise from the more aggressively developed colony along the St. Lawrence. Settlers to Acadia were drawn from distinct regions in France, primarily centered near the port of La Rochelle. To the present day, Acadians are of a different hereditary lineage then are their French-speaking counterparts in Quebec and other regions. Their distinctive culture and linguistic patterns explain a persistent lack of cohesion between the groups.

The propertied Sieur de Poutrincourt, his family, and a handful of settlers followed the initial designs for a French settlement in the Bay of Fundy region after Champlain shifted focus to the St. Lawrence. By 1611, Port-Royal had been reestablished, only to be sacked by a raid of English settlers from the Virginia colony led by Samuel Argall in 1613. The next several decades brought a weak attempt on the part of the French to reestablish the colony and a small but bloody clash between rival groups of Acadians over trading rights. Most important, in 1621 Sir William Alexander received a grant in the same region from the English king, James I, to create a Scots settlement. Most of the original Scots settlers left the area, which they called Nova Scotia, soon after their arrival. However, the overlapping claims—Acadia for the French and Nova Scotia for the British—placed the Acadians at the crossroads of a struggle between empires in the New World well into the eighteenth century.

A European Foothold in the New World

By the 1620s, a tiny European-based population clustered in a handful of habitations along the St. Lawrence River and in some beleaguered settlements in Acadia. Far to the north, the English mariner Henry Hudson had explored a massive saltwater bay in 1610. Hudson Bay, claimed for England, would later become a strategic location for shipping furs from the interior of North America.

Few men and women in New France considered themselves permanent settlers. Compared with the relatively thriving and rapidly growing English settlements in Virginia, New France was a minuscule trading post that had modest designs on agricultural development. Trade was expanding with Native peoples of Algonquian language and culture, facilitated by energetic French trappers called *coureurs de bois* (runners of the woods). Conversely, as a result of the actions of leaders such as Cartier and Champlain, the French found themselves in perpetual conflict with the powerful Iroquoian confederacy. Spreading out of present-day New York State, Iroquoian tribes played a pivotal role in developing fur trade to the south with the Dutch and English. As French trade relations tightened with some groups, the Huron, for example, they deteriorated with the formidable Iroquois.

A hint of riches in the interior and the prospect of discovering a quick and navigable passage through the landmass of North America to get to Asia remained an enticing, if not elusive, prospect. In 1627, the Company of New France, also called the Company of Hundred Associates, was established under the guidance of Louis XIII's chief administrator for New France, Cardinal Richelieu. The company of shareholders was granted entire control over trade, land distribution, and colonial governance. In return it promised to settle hundreds of Roman Catholics annually for fifteen years. Unfortunately for the French, English raiders in 1628 led by the Kirke brothers intercepted the company's initial convoy of settlers and supplies to Quebec. The following year, with the colony near starvation, Champlain surrendered, and most of the settlers returned to France. While the territory was ceded back to the French after a peace treaty in 1632, the inauspicious beginnings of European settlement in this place called Canada pointed to a nascent conflict for a continent. Native peoples, while clearly enjoying superior numbers at the time, were rapidly becoming interwoven in the competitive trading patterns and disputes between the European interlopers. By the 1630s the seeds of the interaction among three groups—Amerindians, French, and English—were planted. Through periods of confrontation, peace, and trade, these peoples would chart Canada's colonial development.

The French Design for the New World

The persistence of the French colony along the St. Lawrence can be attributed to several factors that converged in the seventeenth century: the remarkable determination of Samuel de Champlain and a handful of colonial proponents; the growing popularity of beaver hats in Europe, which put a premium on one of the few marketable goods that the colony could produce; and the French alliance with Algonquian groups in their ongoing struggles against the powerful Iroquois. In general, life remained exceptionally strenuous for colonists in Canada. As with their English, Dutch, and Spanish counterparts in the New World, the French had to contend with a grueling and often dangerous passage across the Atlantic Ocean that could last from several weeks to months, Native peoples, a rigorous climate, and uncertainty. Moreover, the growing season was especially short, and the waterways, including the St. Lawrence River, were frozen during the winter months, thereby limiting the colony's trade and communication with France to certain seasons.

The French design for the New World encompassed three common themes of European colonial development: the prospect of discovering riches more lucrative than furs, especially gold and diamonds; finding an expeditious, easily traversable passage through the continent to the Pacific Ocean; and a relatively small number of missionaries who dedicated themselves to converting and ministering to the untold thousands of Amerindians, all of whom were considered heathens by European standards. By the eighteenth century the fledgling colony at Quebec would be used variously as an experimental model for settlement and a New World land grant system, a fur trade outlet, and a missionary base for reaching deep into the continent. As the French colony survived, and later thrived, it impinged directly on the competing and virtually identical interests of the English and Dutch empires. These were two of France's oldest rivals in Europe. An inescapable fact that governed New France's fate is that as it survived and expanded, it became more of an irritant for its historic enemies. In sum, New France's success contributed to its demise in the massive struggle for control of the continent, a victim of English imperial agendas and the growing American colonies to the south (see "The Old World Becomes the New World" in the Documents section).

New France to 1663

Champlain returned to New France in 1633 with a handful of settlers following an agreement between England and France. His energies and almost fanatical dedication to colonizing the New World explain why popular imagery grants him the title "Father of New France." When he died in 1635 before the colony had realized its full potential, he left no obvious successor, a central concern for the troubled colony until the monarch, Louis XIII, assumed full control in 1663. He directed his capable administrator, Cardinal Richelieu, to engineer the development of New France. For almost two decades, under Richelieu's tutelage, the colony struggled to survive.

Economy

A mercantile system that most expanding European powers employed at the time governed New France's economy. Countries weighed a colony's worth by its ability to enrich its economy and strengthen its position in checking the might of its rivals. Colonies were a source of raw materials, a developing market for products crafted in the mother country, and a strategic extension of empire. Although it exhibited French cultural qualities, Cardinal Richelieu's design for New France followed classic mercantile guidelines. The Company of Hundred

Associates, a group of investors, benefited from a virtual monopoly on trade and in turn received the responsibility of bringing modest numbers of settlers to New France. Mirroring the ongoing religious tensions in France, it barred Protestants from the colony. Coupled with the religious element, this ensured that New France would be exclusively Roman Catholic. Despite the backing of the crown, the company faced bankruptcy by the mid-1640s and ceded its powers to a group of settlers.

Religious Impulse

The church played a central role in New France's mission. The mandate for the religious groups was twofold: to minister to the French Roman Catholic settlers and to convert Native peoples to Christianity. The Récollets, members of the Franciscan order, were in Quebec as early as 1615. But it was the Jesuits, the Society of Jesus, who placed an indelible stamp on colonial development in New France and deeply affected Amerindians. By the time this order of dedicated, well-educated priests fixed New France in its sights for missionary work, it had already been tested by carrying the Christian message to Asia, South America, and Africa. Thanks to the Jesuits' prolific reports to France well into the eighteenth century, called the *Relations*, historians have a rich—if not biased—source for descriptions of the environment, culture, and Amerindians of New France.

The Jesuits, with the support of the Ursuline nuns, were responsible for establishing in Quebec the first college for Native American boys, a girls' school, and a hospital in the 1630s. They attempted to turn the Algonquian groups near Quebec away from their traditional lifestyle of seasonal hunting and fishing and gain an appreciation of Christianity and farming. In addition, the "Black Robes," as they were called by Native peoples, fanned into the hinterland to proselytize. Canada's most famous Jesuit missionary, Jean de Brébeuf, achieved a modest success among the Huron. Jesuits accepted in part the radically different cultures and belief systems of the Amerindians they encountered. Lamentably, they also inadvertently introduced diseases such as smallpox and measles, sicknesses for which North America's Native peoples carried no natural resistance. The diseases swept rapidly, crippling the ability of eastern tribes to survive. The Huron, for example, were decimated by the twin swords of disease and Iroquois attacks in the late 1640s. Several Jesuit priests, including Brébeuf, were tortured and killed in the raids. The tragic story of the Huron makes a dramatic, yet not unusual, example of the difficult position in which Native peoples found themselves. Even in the light of the historic conflicts that predated the arrival of Europeans, their various connections with European-based peoples put them into a vicious cycle of disease, violent clashes, and distorted trading patterns. Over time this dramatically eroded their numbers and sapped their ability to maintain control over territory that they had used for generations.

The bustling city along the St. Lawrence that represents the social and economic capital of modern Quebec was founded by a religious order in 1642. Paul de Chomedey de Maisonneuve, a soldier working for the Société de Notre-Dame, obtained a grant to set up a religious community at the location of the former Iroquois settlement of Hochelaga. Supporting the enterprise was an energetic and extra-ordinary laywoman, Jeanne Mance. Given its position as a western outpost during the early development of New France and being close to Iroquois raiding parties, the tiny settlement never truly fulfilled its original mandate to be a religious beacon to Native peoples in the hinterland. Instead, after struggling for years and all but dropping its missionary role, Montreal, as it would be called after its famous outcropping named by Jacques Cartier, would emerge as one of New France's key trading and financial centers.

New France by 1663

Manifold problems plagued the hundreds of settlers who made their way to New France in the several decades after its inception. An inadequate labor supply and low number of permanent settlers remained important issues. Clearing land from the dense forest was a backbreaking enterprise. The colony received only marginal attention from France; poor administrators oversaw its trading companies. Intense and sustained warfare with the Iroquois through the early 1660s depleted supplies and discouraged settlement. By the time that the crown took direct control over the fate of New France, there were roughly 3,000 settlers. This number paled in comparison with the nearly 90,000 English and Dutch colonists to the south. But with the reinvigorated attention of the French monarch, New France received a boost that would ensure more positive developments. Significantly, it would also make the colony a more attractive target for the English and their American colonists (see "A Portrait of Life in New France" in the Documents section).

NOTE

1. Olive Dickason, *Canada's First Nations* (Toronto: McClelland & Stewart, 1992), 82.

Chapter 3

The Age of New France (1663–1763)

The Rise and Fall of New France

Samuel de Champlain and a handful of settlers returned to Quebec in 1633 and reestablished a colony that struggled to survive into the 1660s. With royal attention and an infusion of funding, New France then flourished as an agricultural, fur trading, and commercial outpost for the French well into the eighteenth century. Although modest in numbers compared with the English and Dutch settlements to the south, the French experiment in the New World succeeded in clearing land along the St. Lawrence system using a land grant system that borrowed heavily from European feudalism. The French gained an excellent sense of the continent's interior with a fur trading network that extensively relied on Native peoples. Dedicated religious missionaries pushed into the hinterland in an attempt to convert Amerindians. Throughout this period, the French and their allies clashed periodically with the Iroquois, one of the strongest tribal networks in the Northeast. In Acadia another colonial enterprise prevailed, separated by geography from New France and distinguished by different immigration patterns and relationships with Native peoples.

Unfortunately for the peoples of New France, the relative successes of the colony helped to seal its fate as the rising tide of imperial

The pivotal battle on the Plains of Abraham in Quebec during the Seven Years' War. This illustration depicts the French forces under the Marquis de Montcalm and the British forces under James Wolfe during the clash on 13 September 1759.

Source: Library and Archives Canada / National Archives of Canada, Print Collection / C-001078

competition gained momentum. Mastery of the lucrative fur trade, strategic control of the commanding St. Lawrence water system, a persistent clash of cultures and religions, and a desire to maintain a presence in the Great Lakes region and the territory west of the Appalachian Mountains led to a large-scale rivalry for continental control. Wars, followed by unsatisfactory peace treaties, character-ized the period from the late seventeenth century into the late eighteenth century. With the final collapse of New France at the hands of the English and their American colonial allies came a crushing reality for the roughly 70,000 French in North America. They experienced bitter defeat and abandonment by an imperial regime that found the possession of Caribbean sugar islands more attractive than the scrappy Canadian settlements. The rise and fall of New France in the seventeenth and eighteenth centuries set the stage for an often contentious relationship between the French and English that underscores a great deal of Canadian history.

Royal Control and Governance

Unlike in the English colonies, where royal control irritated the relationship between colonists and imperial masters, the French experiment in the New World received new life with a monarch's attention. In 1663 New France became a royal colony, a formal province of France. The youthful Louis XIV assumed direct control of the troubled colony. He relied on an able administrator, Jean-Baptiste Colbert, to engineer the colony's economy, settlement, and defense. Crafted in a classic mercantilist framework, New France was to be a tightly knit series of settlements that would be relatively self-sufficient and defensible. It would serve as a New World trading center, a source for furs, timber, and minerals, and a market for manufactured goods from France.

The colony's power structure operated in a hierarchical fashion, with governing authority delegated from the crown through ministers such as Colbert. While the appointed Sovereign Council held the responsibility for military protection, land grants, and justice, real control lay in the hands of three individuals: the governor general, the bishop, and the intendant. No mechanisms for self-governance existed. While English settlers in some American colonies adopted the practice of town meetings, New France fashioned an elitist political culture. Yet despite the autocratic structure, New France's inhabitants enjoyed a degree of freedom that stood in dramatic contrast to contemporary European peasants.

The governor general represented the crown's interest in the colony. His duties were a mixture of the ceremonial and functional. The governor was responsible for diplomacy, including relations with Native peoples, and he essentially supervised military affairs. New France's governors came from the nobility, and many had military expertise. The best example of a dynamic governor in the seventeenth century was Count Louis de Buade Frontenac, who gained a reputation as the "fighting governor" on both sides of the Atlantic. Self-assured and energetic, he ordered forts to be constructed in the Lake Ontario region. During his two terms as governor (1672–1682, 1689–1698), Frontenac expanded the French connections to the interior, galvanized the fur trade, and proved himself a fearful opponent as New France clashed repeatedly with the Iroquois and the English.

A second important council member was the bishop, the leader of the overwhelmingly Roman Catholic population in New France. Given the centrality of religion in shaping political and social events in contemporary France, the head of the Roman Catholic church in the New World became an essential ingredient of colonial governance. By design few Protestants lived in New France, and given the missionary impulse of several Catholic orders in the colony, the bishop potentially wielded a great deal of influence. Indeed, he often played a crucial function in shaping the course of civil affairs. Illustrative of the power that an aggressive and committed bishop could exercise was François de Laval. A seventeenth-century cleric, Laval created a parish system, established a seminary, and developed schools for arts and crafts. Although the bishop's impact on governing the colony faded over time, the church maintained a central role in determining political and social matters. For example, it became a major landholder in New France. One religious order, the Sulpicians, controlled vast portions of Montreal island.

The intendant, a bureaucratic position, rounded out the governing elite. Intendants controlled justice, finances, and even military matters because governors required their support to pay for troops and purchase supplies. In the late seventeenth century, intendants instituted a justice system based on a French model, the *coutume de Paris*. New France's first intendant after the colonial restructuring, Jean Talon (1665–1672), proved to be one of the most influential in the colony's history. Faced with the imperative of bringing settlers to clear land and develop agricultural settlements, Talon and his officers drafted town plans and sponsored a variety of industries to provide goods for colonial use, such as shipyards and a brewery. He attempted to improve the fisheries, timber production, and livestock development and sought to diversify the colony's agricultural output. Many of his designs to create lasting industries and villages were not successful in the long run; nevertheless, his contributions as an effective bureaucrat helped to increase the colony's population. In the hands of a skilled administrator, the intendant position wielded tremendous power.

The Peoples of New France

Given the rigors of surviving the transatlantic passage and adapting to life in the New World, New France appealed only to certain kinds of people. Historians have determined that while most colonists came from the French lower orders, they were rarely destitute. Many of the settlers came from Normandy and western France, while cities, especially Paris, provided soldiers and large numbers of the *filles du roi*, young women transported to New France at the crown's expense.

Many single males made their way to the colony for three-year terms of labor. For their promise to work, these *engagés* received passage both ways, modest wages, and room and board. The system was designed to attract some permanent settlers to the colony as well as to provide a temporary labor pool, but it lacked a requirement for the workers to remain in the colony once their terms had expired. Probably fewer than half the *engagés* remained in New France. Military officers and enlisted personnel were another important source of permanent settlers. Committed to protecting the fledgling colony, France regularly sent professional troops to New France for tours of duty. The most famous in the seventeenth century was the Carignan-Salières regiment. Over one thousand men from this contingent defended the colony, especially along the Richelieu River, to block the natural invasion route from Lake Champlain to the south. They also fought repeatedly with the Iroquois tribes, in particular the Mohawk. Administrators successfully encouraged some of the Carignan-Salières regiment to remain in New France.

Because of the large number of bachelor males, including the *engagés* and soldiers, French authorities devised a plan to bring women of marriageable age to increase the colony's population. The *filles du roi*, or king's daughters as they were called, came from orphanages or from poorer families. Authorities assessed the moral and religious character of each *fille du roi* before she left France. The plan enjoyed a degree of success. Most were married rapidly after their arrival, thanks in part to the money and goods, such as livestock, that the crown had provided for their dowry. Upwards to 1,000 *filles du roi* made their way to New France, and because of the large number of children whom farm families in New France typically produced, a significant number of French Canadians can trace their ancestry to these hardy women.

After an initial burst of energy bringing people to New France—the colony's population doubled from the 1660s to the 1670s—immigration slowed dramatically later in the century. As a result, many of Canada's French descendants can locate their ancestral roots in seventeenth-century New France. Almost 10,000 people called the colony home by the early 1680s. Even with the large families, the farmers and settlers of New France, called the *habitants*, enjoyed better prospects of living fuller and more healthy lives than did contemporary French peasants. Nevertheless, the rigors of life in New France—from clearing the forest, to braving the elements, and to coping with periodic attacks by Iroquois—should not be romanticized.

The Seigneurial System

One of the colony's most attractive features, certainly from a landless peasant's perspective in France, was the *seigneurial* system. Prompted by the crown, this land grant plan explains the settlement patterns of New France and the persistence of peoples in the New World. Some lively historical discussion circulates around the question of whether the system benefited or repressed the *habitants* and, given its design and language, whether it represented an attempt of the French elite to transplant the feudal system to Canada. Independent of these important considerations, few dispute the long-term significance of the *seigneurial* system for drawing settlers to New France, firmly rooting them to the soil and creating the environment for a distinct way of life in the North American hinterland.

Designed to delegate land-granting responsibilities from the crown to *seigneurs*, who held the responsibility for finding settlers, the system was contractual. The *seigneurs*, vassals of the crown, acquired large parcels of land to subdivide and distribute to tenant farmers. Although they technically controlled the land, they were bound to reserve for the crown certain trees for masts and shipbuilding and the subsoil for minerals. Their duties included constructing a manor house, building and maintaining a flour mill, overseeing judicial matters, and helping to sponsor a local religious presence in the form of a *curé* (priest). The *seigneurs'* chief responsibility, however, was to facilitate the settlement of habitants on subdivided land plots. Individual *seigneurs* ranged widely. Some (both men and women) came from the nobility, and some represented the ranks of the military officer corps. Their attention to their responsibilities also varied dramatically as the system developed. Some *seigneurs* lived on their domain and carefully monitored the development of their *seigneuries*, while others hired landlords to supervise their estates. A few *seigneurs* never set eyes on their holdings.

The *censitaires*, the official term for the settlers, were assigned parcels of land to farm. Typically narrow and long, these strips often fronted on the St. Lawrence River or other waterways for transportation. In return for their land grants, the *habitants*, as they preferred to call themselves, annually made modest cash and rental payments, the latter often in the form of produce. In addition, they could be called on to work for a few days a year building or maintaining roads. Virtually all male *habitants* served in the militia for most of their adult years. As evidence of the colony's attachment to the church, *habitants* were expected to tithe one-twenty-sixth of their annual crops to the Roman Catholic church.

While the system existed under an official framework, in practice there was great diversity in the relationship between *habitants* and *seigneurs* and in the relative strengths and weaknesses of individual *seigneuries*. Although some *habitants* became *seigneurs*, New France was not a place of genuine social mobility. The *habitants*, who preferred not to be called peasants, mirrored Old World peasant life in many ways. The relationship between power and the holding of land remained in place throughout the New France era, and although not particularly oppressive, the annual payments and the nature of farming on small plots of land meant that the *habitants* would remain essentially powerless and closely tied to the land. The system was based on a contractual arrangement, which afforded some protection to *habitants* and certainly was more equitable than the rights extended to French peasants.

Seigneurial settlements, clustered along the St. Lawrence River and its tributaries, gave the appearance of one continuous community. Given the hardships of traveling overland in the period, most *habitants* favored the front lots on river systems and displayed a reluctance to move deeper into the hinterland through back lots. Thus, the approximately 200 *seigneuries* by the early eighteenth century remained tightly clustered along the major water systems of New France, chiefly between Quebec and Montreal. The farming that took place on the plots was not sophisticated yet gave evidence of some crop rotation. *Habitants*, overwhelmingly devoted to growing wheat as their primary crop, also planted peas, oats, barley, rye, and corn (maize). Some of the more successful farmers exported wheat. New France clearly experienced a rhythm of life, with powerful official connections between church and state, tenant and landholder. Social distinctions remained important. New France's hierarchical society harked back to the Old World in many ways. Yet ample evidence suggests that *habitants* enjoyed some freedoms, aggressively asserted an independent streak, and regularly ignored state regulations or church edicts. In short, the peasants of the Old World were swiftly becoming the *Canadiens* of the New World (see "A Church Perspective on Women and Their Clothing" in the Documents section).

The Fur Trade

Agriculture by the eighteenth century outpaced the fur trade, yet the latter remained a central focus of New France and helped to set the stage for continental rivalry. The independent-minded French-Canadian *coureurs de bois*, originally encouraged by Champlain, became adept at avoiding governmental controls. These trappers and traders availed themselves of Amerindian technologies, guidance, and often partnerships. They used birchbark canoes, snowshoes, and toboggans and learned survival skills from Native peoples. Trapping was an attractive lifestyle to the offspring of many *habitants*, who engaged in the enterprise for part of a year or a portion of their life. With increased sophistication, large groups called *voyageurs*, often *engagés* working in teams, were contracted to bring furs out of the Great Lakes region and the deep hinterland. Furs, especially the beaver, were rapidly being depleted in the East.

Great rivalries marked the fur trade throughout the colonial phase. The English supplanted the Dutch traders of the Albany area after 1664, while in New France, Montreal became the most significant trading center as trappers filtered into the upper country of the West and North, called the *pays d'en haut*. Greater distances made the traders hard to regulate. Ironically, in spite of the fact that the trappers' activities were often technically illegal, the French dramatically extended their knowledge of the interior through their efforts. Forts and trading posts were built deep in the continent to facilitate and protect trade along the major water routes, an example of which was Fort Michilimackinac, at the narrow passage between Lakes Michigan and Huron.

Other factors made the fur trade empires complex and sharpened the imperial rivalry that would bring about the collapse of New France. Traders Médard Chouart Des Groseilliers and Pierre-Esprit Radisson, upset at having their furs confiscated for running afoul of regulations, offered their mapping and exploration services to the English and thereby provided the spark for the Hudson's Bay Company. Chartered by Charles II in 1670, the company received a vast territory, Rupert's Land, with drainage to Hudson Bay. At roughly half the size of present-day Canada, the grant encompassed diverse groups of Native peoples without their consultation. The Hudson's Bay Company immediately set up an intensely competitive fur trading dynamic in North America by offering an alternative system. The English traders relied extensively on Amerindians to bring furs to small posts, called factories, on Hudson Bay for processing and shipping to England. The other more traditional system, controlled in New France, relied on a lengthening overland route that used waterways and the Great Lakes. Traded in Montreal, furs passed out the St. Lawrence River on their way to Europe. The rivalry between the two systems persisted until 1821, when the companies finally merged into the Hudson's Bay Company.

Towns and Trade

Although New France had an overwhelmingly agricultural orientation into the eighteenth century, between one-fifth and one-third of the population lived in nonrural settings. Town life differed substantially from life in the *seigneuries*. Montreal, despite its roots as a religious bastion, rapidly became a thriving trading location thanks largely to the fur trade. Quebec City, the administrative capital, remained the largest town in New France. Even after the construction of a road between the two cities in the 1730s, various waterways remained important year-round transportation routes by boat or sleigh. French merchants controlled the bulk of the colony's trade, but on a local scale, merchants, including women who ran provisional and clothing businesses, maintained a robust livelihood. Although the extent and impact of the merchant class in New France continues to trigger intense debate among historians, clearly the colony's largest communities displayed some of the economic diversity that other colonial American cities experienced in the period. While limited manufacturing took place in New France, such as shipbuilding, the cities and towns basically served as trading, merchant, and financial centers.

A wide range of people inhabited the colony's cities. A Canadian aristocracy partook of social engagements that reportedly impressed European visitors. Merchants hawked manufactured goods and foodstuffs, such as rum and molasses, from France and its West Indian colonies. Cultural and social gulfs separated the comfortable townspeople from the *habitants*, reinforcing the sharp class distinctions of New France. Upwards of 4,000 slaves were present in the colony—both Amerindians from the Mississippi River region and people transported from the Caribbean. The upper classes owned most of the slaves, who were not extensively used for agricultural labor as was the case in the English colonies.

New France Before the Conquest: A Distinctive Society

Over several generations, the population of New France became *Canadien*, despite the French imperial model for growth and control. By the eighteenth century, the colony exhibited a unique culture and set of values. Thousands of colonists had successfully adapted to the North American environment. Most of the inhabitants were humble subsistence farmers, yet they enjoyed a freedom of movement and certain benefits within the *seigneurial* system. Moreover, at least for males, the opportunity to seek one's fortune in the fur trade provided an alluring alternative to wringing a living from the land. Even with its obvious class layering, the colony's society provided an essential component of the future Canada. Another important element, the English and their American colonial allies, had been affecting New France from the earliest moments of exploration. The centuries-long contest between the French and the English for North America would determine the continent's fate and irrevocably chart the unfolding of Canada's history.

Contest for the Continent

Various factors shaped the struggle for the continent, including imperial rivalry, competition for trade and furs, strategic command of ports and waterways, and the historic tension between the predominantly Protestant and relatively self-governing American colonies and the Roman Catholic and autocratically ruled New France. From the 1613 raid of a Virginia privateer on Port-Royal to the defeat of New France in the 1760s, colonial contests were thoroughly intertwined with titanic wars on the European continent.

Identifiable patterns underscored these engagements, which ranged from small raids to elaborate battles. Mercantilism, practiced by all major European powers at the time, implied a zero-sum rivalry. If your enemy or competitor had more possessions, then it was by definition richer or better positioned to trade and exert influence. Native peoples were triangulated into the European-based agendas from the earliest moments of contact. This dynamic in times of peace and war meant that Amerindians would be increasingly marginalized, despite the fact that they continued to outnumber whites in vast regions of Canada well into the nineteenth century. Moreover, colonial peoples, French and English alike, pursued their own agendas for defense or control over resources. The colonial struggles typically overlapped with wars on the European continent, although they generally had distinct names and a different chronological range of armed engagement. These wars were early illustrations of global conflicts. Finally, diplomats and militarists determined the territorial makeup of the New World through peace treaties in the Old World. Inevitably they did not have colonial interests foremost in their thoughts. As a result, grander imperial considerations subsumed colonial ideas. Before the most important wars are discussed, it is instructive to assess the relative strengths and weaknesses of the European powers and their colonial possessions.

New France: Strengths and Weaknesses

The French employed many strategies to maintain their possessions in the New World. They effectively used an extensive network of relationships with Amerindians. Their knowledge of the North American hinterland was far superior to that of their English rivals because of their extensive fur trading empire. In addition, the French maintained, or at least claimed, an expansive fort network that ranged from staffed enterprises to abandoned palisades. In the broadest sense, the French planned to keep English troops and American colonists hemmed in by the natural boundary of the Appalachian mountain chain that followed the North American spine.

The French could count on many advantages in periods of conflict. The military and militia command system was clearly designed and well staffed; virtually all males served in the militia. The typical French fighter, experienced in battle, used natural defenses and hit-and-run raids to harass the enemy. In addition, the French-controlled waterways that the English considered ideal invasion routes, such as the St. Lawrence River and the Lake Champlain/Richelieu River corridor, froze over for almost half the year and were thus relatively easy to defend. Algonquian allies, from the Mi'kmaq in the East to the Illinois in the Great Lakes region, provided formidable support in times of hostilities. American colonial dynamics also shaped events. The various colonies disagreed on a host of issues, and while their sporadic attempts to work together in a collaborative fashion become one of the important ingredients of the American Revolution, only the northernmost colonies of Massachusetts and New York earnestly supported the struggle to defeat New France.

The French also faced deficiencies and flaws in their colonial design, problems that would become more debilitating over time. For example, New France's population of roughly 50,000 in the mid-eighteenth century paled when compared with the almost one million American colonists. The colony had only a few key ports and cities for the English and their American allies to target for attack. In each of the four major conflicts, these allies repeatedly sought to capture the prizes of Quebec, Montreal, and the important French trading center and fort at Louisbourg. In addition, the English were generally in a more favorable economic position to wage war. Both the English treasury and the far more diverse and richer American colonies would have defining roles in bringing about a French defeat in North America.

To summarize, New France may have been prepared to fend off glancing blows and loosely coordinated series of attacks by the English and Americans indefinitely. But if the English devoted a great deal of attention to events in the colonial phase of their broader struggles, then the French would find themselves in a more precarious position. As events would have it, this scenario unfolded in the final war of conquest.

Colonial Wars to the Conquest

King William's War (1689–1697) broke out with a devastating Iroquois raid on Lachine, a community west of Montreal. Part of an ongoing struggle, the Iroquois attacks on settlements in New France blended with a general war between France and England, the War of the League of Augsburg. Count Frontenac, recalled by the French because of squabbles with his superiors, returned to New France when his military expertise was required. Teaming with their Algonquian allies, the French orchestrated brutal raids on several New York and New England communities. By the war's conclusion, the pattern of harassing skirmishes, with both sides using Amerindian allies, had been well established. In the contested zone, a fault line between the southern perimeter of New France and northern New York and New England, embittered peoples would not soon forget the massacres and torched villages. In addition, a fleet based in New England attacked Acadia's Port-Royal, and the British unsuccessfully laid siege to Quebec.

The uneasy peace was shattered a few years later with the War of the Spanish Succession between France and an alliance of European powers. In fact, French and English colonials had barely taken a pause from hostilities since the last dispute. Queen Anne's War (1702–1713), as the colonists dubbed it, saw a resurgence of bloody raids directed at small communities on both sides. Significantly, the English captured Port-Royal, which they renamed Annapolis Royal. A massive naval and ground attack on Quebec collapsed due to poor coordination and inclement weather in 1711, a remarkable piece of ill luck for the British given the extraordinary number of invading forces. The war's two largest battles, one successful for the British and the other a fiasco, pointed to the English and American advantage in these struggles. The capture of only a handful of key targets would be required to claim the prize of New France.

The point was clearly made at the Treaty of Utrecht, where the victorious British picked up territory in the New World that France had historically claimed. The Hudson's Bay Company forts that the French had seized during the conflict were returned, and France recognized English control over Hudson Bay, Newfoundland, and Acadia. France received the right to use Newfoundland's northern shore to land and dry cod. It also retained Ile Royale (Cape Breton Island), where it soon located a fortified trading center named Louisbourg. The fortress became an object of English and American desire in future wars. Remarkably, given the fact that neither side had the right to make such an agreement, the French also recognized English control over the domains of the Iroquois confederacy. The territorial shifting, due not to significant losses in North America but to French defeats in the European phase of the war, engendered resentful feelings in French Canada toward their imperial masters.

The French clearly considered the colony a pawn to be used in a larger context. In the years between this war and its successor, the French fortified existing forts and built new ones throughout the Great Lakes region and in the Mississippi River system.

King George's War (1744–1748), which grew out of Europe's War of the Austrian Succession, brought depressingly familiar raids along the New France–New York–New England border. It also saw the successful capture of Louisbourg in 1745 by an invading force of New Englanders, who targeted the French fort because it was a fishing and trading competitor and strategically guarded the entrance of the St. Lawrence River. At the Treaty of Aix-la-Chapelle in 1748, the English returned Louisbourg to the French in return for India's Madras. This time it was the British Americans' turn to be irritated that their imperial masters had traded a colonial-won prize in the greater interest of imperial schemes. The peace treaty was but an armed truce; both sides prepared for another struggle. For example, in 1749 the English established Halifax in their newly acquired Acadian possession to serve as a naval counterpoint to Louisbourg.

The Seven Years' War and the Conquest

The flashpoint for the final war between the English and French came along another dividing line between the empires in North America, the Ohio country. A youthful militia officer from Virginia, George Washington, clashed in 1754 with French forces and met defeat in a contest for control of the Ohio River. The engagement focused on the French Fort Duquesne, which was renamed Pittsburgh after its subsequent capture by the British. Two years later, the North American skirmishes merged into the European Seven Years' War (1756–1763). Going into this conflict, the French position was far more precarious. Its Amerindian alliances had eroded, and its overextended and undiversified empire looked like a poor match for the increasingly unified British American colonies. The French disadvantages erupted to the surface when an energetic English political administrator, William Pitt, devoted his attention to removing the French presence in North America permanently. Pitt focused the English military might on fighting the colonial phase of the war while his allies battled French forces in Europe. The plan, now crystallized after more than one hundred years of struggle, was to conquer New France.

The war went through two distinct phases. French successes at staving off superior English and American forces, with the great exception of losses in Acadia, marked the first. The second period, defined by swift and definitive defeats of the three crucial centers of French power in North America from 1758 to 1760 led to the Conquest. In the conflict's first phase, from 1754 to 1757, the British failed in several attempts to take French positions. At the same time, marauding bands of French Canadians and their Amerindian allies operated as far south as the Carolina colonies. Under the capable leadership of the Marquis de Montcalm, the French maintained a superior military posture. While power struggles involving Montcalm, the Canadian-born governor, the Marquis de Vaudreuil, and a corrupt intendant named François Bigot undermined their efforts, the French enjoyed several military successes. These included taking Fort Oswego on Lake Ontario, Fort William Henry in the upper Hudson valley, and the defense of Fort Carillon (later renamed Ticonderoga) below Lake Champlain. The sole important failure during the war's first phase was the capture of Fort Beauséjour, located at the head of Chignecto Bay in Acadia, in June 1755 (see "A Military Perspective During the Seven Years' War" in the Documents section).

The Acadian Expulsion

One of the most profound tragedies of the final conflict for imperial control of North America was the expulsion of most of the Acadian population, an event known as *le grand dérangement*. The French presence in Acadia, the region around the Bay of Fundy, was less structured and of greater ethnic complexity than in New France. Settled during the seventeenth century, Acadia developed a unique society that included aspects of French, Scots, and Mi'kmaq cultures. Acadians built dikes to reclaim salt marshes in an area with strong tidal action. They produced wheat and livestock and spoke a distinctive dialect. Although they were nominally affected by French governance, they engaged in a fitful trading relationship with

New England, especially Boston. Unfortunately, their location placed them in a dangerous borderland in the repeated wars for continental control.

After the 1713 Treaty of Utrecht, when much of Acadia formally fell under British control, the Acadians attempted to survive by maintaining a neutral status. For decades the British were relatively content to leave the Acadians alone. However, the establishment of Halifax in 1749, which introduced a formidable British military presence in Acadia as well as some settlers, and the beginning of yet another war increased the pressures on the neutral Acadians. By the early 1750s both the French and the English looked with a degree of suspicion on the group. New Englanders, especially those from Massachusetts, coveted the Bay of Fundy for its settlement and economic potential.

The Seven Years' War brought bad news to the region, including the capture of the garrison at Beauséjour, with some Acadian defenders in the fort, and a new English governor named Charles Lawrence. A soldier, Lawrence pressured the Acadians to take a stronger oath to support the British crown than the one they had typically agreed to since the Treaty of Utrecht. This new oath clearly indicated an allegiance to Britain and opened the distinct possibility of pressing Acadians into military service. Despite the ominous tone of Lawrence's new administration, Acadian leaders had no reason to believe that this phase of events would change the status quo that had been in place for decades. They judged incorrectly. Administrators in Halifax decided to remove the Acadian population in 1755.

During the deportation, mainly carried out by New England recruits, about 7,000 Acadians were forcibly rooted out and placed on ships. The initial plans for an orderly evacuation disintegrated as extended families were divided. Compounding the ordeal, many ships lacked adequate provisions. Farms and buildings were put to the torch to force Acadians off the land. More Acadians were rounded up and evacuated in subsequent years, but about 2,000 fled to the interior to avoid deportation. Acadians were scattered to all the American colonies, although many died on board ship because of insufficient supplies and disease. While some American communities struggled to incorporate the Acadians thrust into their midst, prejudice and glaring religious and cultural differences undermined their efforts. In addition, some migrated to Ile Royale and Ile Saint-Jean (Prince Edward Island).

Others resettled in New France. About 2,500 made their way to Louisiana over time. Skilled in draining the marshland of the bayous, they became the core of the state's Cajun population. There are now well over one million Acadian descendants in Louisiana.

After the war several thousand Acadians returned to their homeland to relocate in the present-day Maritime Provinces, particularly New Brunswick. Their distinctive culture and devotion to Roman Catholicism continued and perhaps was strengthened by their harrowing experiences. Generations of Acadians orally transmitted the memories of the deportation. The American writer Henry Wadsworth Longfellow, after hearing a version of the Acadian diaspora, crafted a poem in the 1840s. *Evangeline* received international attention; it also helped to kindle an interest in studying the history of Acadia and in coming to grips with the impact of *le grand dérangement* (see "The Acadian Experience" in the Documents section).

The Conquest

The second phase of the Seven Years' War, three bleak years for the French, led to the collapse of New France. Pitt increasingly devoted war materiel, men, and money to the enterprise. New France's shortcomings were progressively having an impact. A seemingly endless series of wars and dwindling resources took a toll on French-Canadian society, while a superior Royal Navy effectively blockaded the colony. The British in 1758 captured Louisbourg, the thriving French presence on Ile Royale, after a seven-week siege. The most important target, Quebec City, loomed as both a symbolic and strategic prize. Situated at the original site of an Amerindian settlement, Quebec possessed formidable natural defenses thanks largely to its towering heights. General James Wolfe, a young British commander, laid siege to the city, pounding the town with his artillery throughout the summer of 1759. In addition, he destroyed homes and communities along the St. Lawrence. Seizing an unexpected opportunity, he boldly maneuvered his men up a path north of the walled city, a direction that Montcalm's defenders did not anticipate. This permitted Wolfe to position about 4,500 of his men on the summit of the cliffs on fields known as the Plains of Abraham. Without waiting for nearby reinforcements, Montcalm met Wolfe in open battle in a European-style engagement on the Plains with a roughly equal force on September 13, 1759. About fifteen minutes of fierce battle sealed the fate of North America. Both generals died—Wolfe on the field and Montcalm the next day—and the city surrendered a few days later.

Despite the shocking loss of Quebec, the French did not capitulate. Indeed, a large French force returned to lay siege to Quebec in the spring of 1760, and a battle with even greater casualties was fought and won by the French at Sainte-Foy. Yet the crucial knockout blow came thanks to Pitt's grand design. Reinforcement ships that appeared when the ice let out of the St. Lawrence in the spring flew the British flag, not the French. A superior navy and attention to shipping more men and war materiel to North America helped to write the script for the continent's future. Montreal's defenders surrendered in September 1760 to superior numbers of British and American forces, providing an anticlimactic engagement in the struggle to capture New France.

The Treaty of Paris in February 1763 ended the Seven Years' War and brought a swift end to New France. France essentially retreated from the continent, retaining only the fishing stations of St. Pierre and Miquelon off the coast of Newfoundland. They remain French possessions to this day. France also received fishing rights on Newfoundland's north shore and kept several sugar islands in the Caribbean, including Guadeloupe and Martinique. Louisiana was granted to the Spanish in a separate arrangement. In a compressed series of moments, the British had their trophy: an immense territory ranging from Hudson Bay to the Gulf of Mexico, and the Atlantic seaboard to the Mississippi River system.

The Conquest's Impact

The Conquest, a seminal event in Canadian history, is laden with both pragmatic and symbolic meanings. On the practical side, the Conquest led to a new form of administrative control for the former New France. New British colonies were created out of New France and other North American possessions. Changes were forthcoming in the control of the fur trade system. Perhaps most profound, the governance of roughly 70,000 residents of New France presented a formidable challenge for the new British masters. *Canadiens* were a decidedly different population group. They spoke a foreign language, practiced Roman Catholicism, and adhered to distinct cultural traditions. Perhaps most problematic of all, they had been a fervent enemy of the British and Americans for over a century.

The symbolic aspect of the Conquest holds equal importance in understanding modern Canada. The Conquest, along with certain memories of New France and its demise, infuses history and politics to this day. The historical meaning of the Conquest varies sharply. The debate centers on the fate of the various components of New France—the *habitants*, elites, church, economy, and culture. Arguments range from pessimistic voices that maintain the British crushed—"decapitated" in the popular metaphor—New France's thriving bourgeoisie, to optimistic assertions that a more beneficial period emerged following the British victory, albeit after a protracted struggle. This more positive approach suggests that the relatively unenlightened *Canadiens* were guided into a new era of self-governance and economic diversity as a consequence of the painful Conquest.

Independent of these historical arguments, two points remain central to an understanding of the French-Canadian experience and the ways in which Canada's political and social development has been defined by the collapse of New France. The Conquest, as its name suggests, represented the defeat of a people. Equally important, many interpret the event as the utter abandonment of most of the French Canadians—many of New France's elite returned to France after the war—to their fate in North America without significant concern. To paraphrase a classic interpretation, the French imperial masters, after being at a disadvantage at the end of the Seven Years' War, chose to retain possession of some Caribbean islands instead of their vast northern holdings. Mindful of a flagging fur industry and limited prospects for colonial development in New France, the French chose "sugar over snow." The twin dynamics, defeat and abandonment, would be thoroughly woven into the social and political fabric of French Canada. Because it spawned challenges for linguistic, religious, cultural, and political survival, the Conquest shapes Quebec's relationships with its fellow provinces to this day. The emphasis on survival underscores a French Canadian ethos that is still alive and well, as evidenced by the phrase on the Quebec license plate: *Je me souviens*. I remember.

New France Becomes Quebec

The English, with their American allies, now had the prize that they had pursued for decades. It had taken four large-scale wars and scores of minor skirmishes to bring about the defeat of New France. What awaited now was a solution to the complex problem, at least from the British perspective, of administering its newly won possessions. Moreover, in the immediate future loomed questions concerning the colony's governance and economy, the fate of the Roman Catholic church, and the disposition of the inhabitants. Acadia's population had been deemed a manageable size for deportation, but removing over 70,000 French Canadians was logistically and practically impossible. The post-Conquest era until the mid-nineteenth century would see a series of administrative experiments and a strengthening resolve of both French Canadians and English-speaking Canadians to exercise more control over their lives in the larger embrace of the British Empire. In short, the two groups faced a thorny challenge to find a means to cohabit peacefully and successfully in a common administrative framework called British North America.

Chapter 4

British North America (1763–1850s)

Britain at the Helm

Momentous changes occurred for the peoples of British North America from the post-Conquest period until the mid-nineteenth century. At the same time, deep historical trends, defined by the different cultures and religions of European-based groups and Native peoples, continued to guide political, economic, and social developments. For the inhabitants of British North America, most of whom were clustered along the St. Lawrence River and the Atlantic coastline, life continued to present challenges. The British experimented with administering their conquered territories and an alien French-Canadian population. Appointed governors and administrators often clashed with popularly elected assemblies. Amerindians, who still vastly outnumbered whites, lost control of much of their territory and resources. Wars and violent upheavals continued to characterize colonial life. The American Revolution (1775–1783) triggered an out-migration of thousands of Loyalists, the Napoleonic conflicts provided a context for the War of 1812, and in the 1830s a series of rebellions broke out in two of the colonies. The definitions of two political entities in North America—one American and the other British North American—were more sharply etched as the result of conflict and diplomatic resolutions.

A bush farm near Chatham, Upper Canada, probably painted in 1838.

Source: Library and Archives Canada / Philip John Bainbrigge Collection / C-011811

The century after the Conquest witnessed a reformulation of existing colonial territory, sowed the seeds of Canadian political union, intensified the impulse for northern and western expansion, reinforced the exploitation of traditional staples, altered trading patterns, introduced new technologies and manufactures, and brought different immigrant groups to the colonies. On the eve of Confederation in the 1860s, British North America was inhabited by peoples with distinctive cultures, languages, and religions. Somewhat paradoxically, it had one foot firmly planted in the Old World of the British Empire and the other placed in the New World of North America.

The Quebec Experiment

Remarkably, considering the long struggle to remove the French imperial presence from North America, the British displayed some ambivalence about administering the former New France. A bloody struggle in 1763 with Native peoples led by Pontiac, chief of the Ottawa, presented a sobering reminder of the limitations of British control over the continent's interior. The Royal Proclamation of that same year, which created the colony of Quebec, also angered British American settlers because it created a vast region for Amerindians west of the Alleghenies. While the Proclamation promised popular representation for Quebec, it provided the context for assimilation of the *Canadiens*. Roman Catholics were prohibited from holding offices, and lacking formal recognition, the Roman Catholic church and the *seigneurial* system were left to wither.

Despite its intent, the Proclamation failed to achieve its goals on both the Canadian and American levels. The offensive Proclamation line added to a growing list of irritants that the American colonists used as rationales for breaking away from British control. In Quebec, the large number of anticipated anglophone settlers failed to materialize. Even Sir Guy Carleton, the colony's second governor, recognized the essential fact of New France's legacy: Quebec would forever remain the home of the *Canadiens*.

Accepting the flaws in their original plan, the British responded with a statute that led to dramatic consequences in both Canadian and American history. The Quebec Act, passed in 1774, was an adjustment in British policies in Quebec and a reaction to growing disobedience in the American colonies. Hailed by many as the guarantor of French-Canadian survival, the statute dramatically expanded the boundaries of Quebec to encompass the rich fur trading region of the Great Lakes to the Mississippi River. In addition, it recognized the *seigneurial* system, permitted the continued operation of the Roman Catholic church, and accepted Quebec's distinct civil laws. This was an important moment in Quebec's history. A group's cultural survival rests in part on the retention of its systems of landholding, religion, and law. Finally, the Quebec Act ignored the promise of the Proclamation of 1763 and established governance by a legislative council that would be appointed, not elected. Thanks to a special loophole, elite French Canadians could hold appointed positions after taking an oath. As historians have long argued, the act both facilitated the cultural survival of a people and ensured that Britain would remain firmly in control of Quebec.

The American Revolution

The whirlwind saga of the American war for independence, coming hard on the heels of the British conquest of New France, is yet another example of the intricate connections between the histories of Canada and the United States. Festering issues concerning trade, territorial expansion, taxation, and the quartering of troops underpinned the conflict that erupted in Massachusetts in April 1775. The Second Continental Congress, meeting after the outbreak of hostilities, viewed Quebec and Nova Scotia as natural extensions of the American colonies. However, Quebec turned down an invitation to combine forces in opposing King George.

The failure to entice either Quebec or Nova Scotia to join in the revolutionary enterprise meant that the "continental" design for breaking away from British control, implied in the name of the congress, would be partial. In Quebec many merchants relied on British trade. In addition, the *Canadiens*, who were relatively pleased with the rights extended in the Quebec Act, were understandably reluctant to fight alongside Protestant anglophones who had been their bitter enemies for over a century before the Conquest. The desire of most Nova Scotians to remain aloof dealt the Americans perhaps a more troublesome failure. Populated in large part by New Englanders since the 1713 Treaty of Utrecht and tied to the American colonies by family, cultural, and economic connections, Nova Scotia appeared ripe to Americans for joining the revolution. Instead, the dominance of the British naval and military presence at Halifax helped to control the region. The colony's scattered settlements, most of them along the seaboard, were exposed to frequent raids by American privateers. This did not engender good wishes on the part of Nova Scotians to the American cause. Finally, an intense religious revival movement, led by the charismatic American-born Henry Alline, drew the focus for many Nova Scotians to spiritual matters rather than worldly bickering over politics and trade issues. Therefore, a combination of factors created an environment in Quebec and Nova Scotia that allowed for an emphatic rejection of the American revolutionary impulse.

Nonetheless, American military leaders immediately turned their attention to capturing the strategic locations of Montreal and Quebec City. General Richard Montgomery entered an essentially undefended Montreal in the fall of 1775, then traveled down the St. Lawrence River to meet a contingent of soldiers led by Benedict Arnold, who had endured a grueling overland march through the interior of Maine to Quebec. A concerted attack on the fortress of Quebec in a snowstorm on New Year's Eve proved calamitous for the Americans. British forces killed Montgomery, wounded Arnold, and killed or captured over 400 Americans. The arrival of British reinforcements on ships in the St. Lawrence the following spring forced Arnold to abandon his position outside the city. Americans later withdrew from Montreal. The failed attempt to take Quebec was a serious setback for the American plan to deny the British control of the strategic St. Lawrence River. It also long stood as a reminder that Americans, in order to serve their purposes, could exploit the attractive water and land routes to attack Canada.

The American Revolutionary War had momentous consequences for Canadians. A combination of skill, fortune, and flagging British interest in waging war to keep the colonies in the empire led to some key American victories, including the crucial success at Yorktown in 1781. With the Treaty of Paris two years later, the republican experiment would be given free rein. By carving off the thirteen colonies, the United States left Britain with drastically diminished holdings in British North America a scant twenty years after the Conquest. In addition, the war triggered a migration of individuals who did not partake of the revolutionary fervor. To the Americans, these were the reviled Tories. To the British and Canadians, they were the Loyalists, a population group that would have far-reaching implications for Canadian history.

The Arrival of the Loyalists

The American revolutionary upheaval was a civil as well as political conflict. American colonists held a vast array of viewpoints, ranging from fervent support of the rebellions to opposition to the revolutionary impulse. The latter group, the Tories, was in turn a varied assortment of people. Those supporting the crown, perhaps one-third of the population of the American colonial population, included elites, merchants, soldiers, laborers, farmers, Amerindians, and blacks. Some actively fought for King George; some expressed reluctance to follow a treasonous path; some maintained British trading ties; some followed their pacifistic religious beliefs; and some were deemed traitorous by their neighbors. Discriminatory legislation targeted these Loyalists. Many lost their voting privileges, paid higher taxes, and had their property confiscated. Some were imprisoned. During and immediately following the war, tens of thousands of Loyalists relocated to British possessions in North America or to Britain itself. Most chose to relocate in the northern colonies, thereby forming one of Canadian history's most important groups.

The arrival of the Loyalists spawned two new political units in British North America. The largest contingent, ranging upward to 50,000, arrived in Nova Scotia. Many settled in communities along the Atlantic coast, on Cape Breton Island, and around the Bay of Fundy. The latter group, arriving from New York and assisted by Sir Guy Carleton, filtered into the fertile St. John River valley after landing at Saint John. By 1784 they successfully petitioned the British for a separate colony because of the great distance between their settlements and the Nova Scotian capital at Halifax. In addition, the Loyalists felt they had little in common with Nova Scotians, many of whom were of New England stock. The "Loyalist" province, New Brunswick, was created in a region that had been partially cultivated by the Acadians. This dispossessed group returned in growing numbers to settle in New Brunswick during the late eighteenth century. The mixture of Acadian and Loyalist peoples formed a unique place in Canada. Today, New Brunswick is the country's only officially bilingual province (see "One Loyalist's Perspective" in the Documents section).

The other significant concentration of Loyalists migrated into southern and western Quebec. Smaller in number than their Nova Scotian counterparts, these people carved settlements along the St. Lawrence River in western Quebec, the north shores of Lakes Ontario and Erie, the Niagara area, and near Detroit. Some of the land was purchased from Amerindians by Sir Frederick Haldimand, Quebec's governor. The Loyalists received land apportioned according to their civilian or military status, as well as supplies and agricultural equipment. Their numbers included about 2,000 Iroquois veterans of the Revolutionary War, who were settled on reserves. Life was hard for the Loyalists. The process of clearing land out of the wilderness, even for experienced farmers, was strenuous. Denied an elected assembly under the terms of the Quebec Act and wishing to live under English law and civil codes, the Loyalists brought pressures to create their own colony.

Britain's Constitutional Act of 1791, also called the Canada Act, divided Quebec into two provinces along the Ottawa River. Lower Canada, the more populous with approximately 100,000 *Canadiens* and 10,000 anglophones, lay to the east. The western Loyalist colony, Upper Canada, contained roughly 20,000 residents. The land grant systems, civil laws, and religious orientation of the two colonies reflected the traditions of the majority groups. Importantly, the Constitutional Act also provided for representative assemblies. While this was the first time such a system had been made available to the *Canadiens*, British control remained firmly entrenched in both provinces. The creation of Upper Canada—present-day Ontario— represented a physical, as well as symbolic, division of the French and English in British North America.

British North America at the Turn of the Nineteenth Century

In the late nineteenth century British North America consisted of the colonies and provinces of Newfoundland, Prince Edward Island, Cape Breton Island (part of Nova Scotia after 1820), Nova Scotia,

New Brunswick, Lower Canada, and Upper Canada. In addition, the British claimed a vast territory called Rupert's Land, which was controlled by the Hudson's Bay Company, and a largely unexplored territory that stretched to the Pacific seaboard and reached northward to the Arctic Ocean. Some of the boundaries between the United States and British North America were clearly defined, while others were poorly understood. British North Americans existed on the perimeter of the British empire by exploiting time-honored resources such as furs, timber, fish, and agricultural produce. They clashed periodically with an expanding United States, agitated for an improved form of representative government, and pushed relentlessly into Amerindian spaces to the west and north in the pursuit of furs and land.

An energetic collection of Scots, English, and American traders rapidly drove *Canadien* merchants from many businesses after the Conquest, but one illustration of a marriage of interests was the fur trade. Created in the 1780s and headquartered in Montreal, the North West Company used historic waterways and trails to bring furs out of the continent's interior. With the ratification of Jay's Treaty in 1795, an agreement between the United States and Britain, the Ohio Valley and lands below the Great Lakes were essentially opened to American settlement. As a result, the Nor'Westers, including *voyageurs* who traveled in specially designed canoes, aggressively developed a trade to the north and west of the Great Lakes. Some of the most famous western explorers in Canadian history, including Peter Pond, Alexander Mackenzie, Simon Fraser, and David Thompson, worked for the company.

The extension of the North West Company brought it into direct competition with the Hudson's Bay Company, especially in the vast region where the Canadian Shield gives way to the rolling prairies. Settlements and fur trading posts run by the opposing interests meant that whites and Native peoples would share an economic system as well as cultural ties. In the complex enterprise of trapping and processing furs, and then trading pelts for transportation to European markets, Amerindian women played an important role in cementing relationships and defining commercial patterns. Importantly, a group of mixed-blood descendants of Amerindian mothers and French-Canadian fur traders occupied the hotly contested space that both companies wanted to control. The Métis, who developed a unique culture, existed by trapping, farming, and hunting plentiful buffalo herds for food and clothing. They produced pemmican, a nutritious and portable food made of dried buffalo meat and berries, which rapidly became a staple for fur traders in both companies.

A great concentration of Métis lived near the confluence of the Red and Assiniboine rivers, the site of present-day Winnipeg. Both companies had posts in this Red River region. A philanthropist named Lord Douglas, the Fifth Earl of Selkirk, disturbed about the displacement of Scottish farmers to make way for sheep herding, sponsored the migration of Highlanders to Prince Edward Island, Upper Canada, and the Red River area. His largest grant, called Assiniboia and purchased from the Hudson's Bay Company, was also an important location for the Nor'Westers. Settlers arriving in 1812 triggered a series of conflicts involving representatives of the two companies and Métis, culminating in a massacre of Hudson's Bay Company workers at Seven Oaks in 1816. The incident led to a convoluted series of court actions in Upper Canada, with Lord Selkirk becoming personally involved. In 1821 the two companies merged under the title of the Hudson's Bay Company, thereby defusing corporate tensions. Nonetheless, the disparate mixture of peoples in the Red River—Métis, Amerindians, and whites—continued to define the region's evolution. Not forgotten, the settlements remained a beacon for British North Americans who aspired to develop the West.

The War of 1812

The Napoleonic struggles, a protracted series of conflicts between Britain and France that ebbed and flowed in the late eighteenth and early nineteenth centuries, ultimately helped to create tensions between the United States and British North America. Britain's superior sea power could effectively control the oceans, while Napoleon Bonaparte's armies and alliances effectively cut the European continent off from trade with Britain. The United States, alarmed by British orders to prohibit trade with the French and its European allies, as well as with French attempts to limit trade with the British, passed a series of embargo laws. The Royal Navy routinely stopped American ships on the high seas to interdict trade with the Continent.

In addition, it habitually impressed sailors from American ships who may or may not have been deserters from the British fleet. Young congressional representatives, known as the War Hawks, agitated for retaliation against the British for their purported assistance to Native peoples in their confrontations with Americans who were flooding into the interior. President James Madison's call for war in 1812 highlighted the key American grievances of the British blockade of free trade, impressments (forced conscription) of American sailors, and support of Amerindians in the interior of North America. Many argued that the United States declared war to get respect; thus, the War of 1812 (1812–1814) is still referred to as the "second American revolution" by a fair number of American historians.

With a superior British navy holding forth on the high seas, and to the delight of the American "War Hawks" who wanted to remove the British presence in North America, the only logical war plan entailed attacks on British North America. Whether the colonies were to be held as hostages to force the British to capitulate or to be absorbed by the United States remains a question of historical disagreement. Undisputed is the fact that Britain had most of its forces occupied in a massive struggle with Napoleon in Europe, so only a relatively small contingent of regular soldiers were positioned to defend British North America.

The war was a series of unmitigated military disasters for the Americans, with the surprising exceptions of naval victories on Lakes Erie and Champlain. An ill-advised attempt to mount an invasion from the west ended in a humiliating defeat of American forces at Detroit in 1812. In the fall of the same year, a battle in the Niagara region at Queenston Heights cost the British the life of a popular warrior and governor, Isaac Brock, but British forces with support from Canadian militia and Amerindian allies won an important victory. Repeated attempts by the Americans to attack the Canadas through the Niagara or by using the Lake Champlain/Richelieu River route met with formidable rebuttals. The Americans found a measure of success with small naval contests on Lakes Erie and Champlain and burned buildings in York (Toronto). Canadians remember the Americans being repelled at Beaver Dams, Châteauguay, Crysler's Farm, and Stoney Creek. One contest at Beaver Dams created a heavily mythologized heroine out of Laura Secord, who forewarned the British of an impending battle after hearing American officers discuss campaign plans at her home. A French-Canadian military leader, Charles de Salaberry, captured fame at the Châteauguay River. Thus, Canadians have a pantheon of heroic figures from the war, among them Brock, Secord, and de Salaberry.

With the American invasions failing dramatically, the war's final stages brought a series of attempts on the part of the British to attack the United States. Ironically, despite battle-seasoned troops pouring into British North America in the wake of Napoleon's defeat in 1814, the British fared no better at their invasion plans. They caused havoc in a campaign in the Chesapeake, including torching the White House, but were soundly defeated in their attempts to move down Lake Champlain, and they lost a stunning battle at New Orleans in early January 1815. Thanks to a lag time in receiving dispatches from Europe, the battle took place after a peace agreement had been signed in Ghent in late 1814. Americans, sobered by the painful rift between the states that the war had created and embarrassed by the inability of its forces to take the seemingly easy prize of British North America, were pleased to end the hostilities. The British returned territory it had captured from the Americans in Maine but refused to yield to the American demands that had triggered the conflict.

The War of 1812, as historian Charles Perry Stacey sardonically observed, was a conflict that eventually made everyone happy. It was not a contest of great global import. The British still consider it a minor nuisance during a more important struggle against Napoleon's attempts to master Europe. The Americans, despite the fact that they were politically divided and had compiled a dismal military record, found honor by standing up to the powerful British on the principles of trade and protecting the integrity of their citizens.

Canadians have their own interpretations of the War of 1812. Out of the American attempts to conquer British North America came embellished memories of the role played by Canadian militiamen. In fact, most of the war was fought by regular soldiers from England and Ireland. On a more practical level, the war helped to unify the two Canadas for defensive purposes and led to improvements in the movement of goods and construction of roads. Coupled with the recent American incursions during the Revolutionary War, the conflict reminded many British North Americans that the colonies lay open to attack and that Americans could not be trusted.

The British and Americans, in the war's immediate wake, worked to defuse tensions in North America and articulate their boundaries more clearly. In an attempt to demilitarize the Great Lakes, the Rush-Bagot Agreement of 1817 limited ship tonnage and weaponry on the Great Lakes and Lake Champlain. Although the treaty's spirit was sorely tested in the years after its signing and both sides continued to build forts along the boundary, it remained a centerpiece of the British and American resolve to avoid conflict in North America. The Convention of 1818 drew a boundary line along the forty-ninth parallel from the Lake of the Woods, west of Lake Superior, to the Rocky Mountains. A poorly understood and much disputed region, the lands west of the Rockies were left open to joint occupation. An important legacy of the War of 1812, therefore, was a more clearly etched border between the United States and British North America.

Rebellions in the Canadas

Despite the lessening of tensions between the United States and Britain after the War of 1812, a combination of factors created unrest in Upper and Lower Canada. A series of rebellions against British control broke out in late 1837 and lingered into 1838. The seeds of rebellion in Canadian history are both complex and much debated by historians. In both Upper and Lower Canada, reformers mounted aggressive campaigns to wrest control over colonial matters from the councils appointed by British governors. Canadian political elites, supported by powerful social and religious connections, symbolized autocratic rule. Called the Family Compact in Upper Canada and the *Château Clique* in Lower Canada, these groups held the lion's share of power. A historic reform impulse in Great Britain after 1832 to broaden access to political power provided another irritant for colonial reformers. It appeared that the British were reluctant to extend similar liberties to their colonies. In addition a sour economy in the 1830s, crop failures in Lower Canada, and mounting population pressures on the ancient *seigneuries* created widespread distress in British North America. Finally, colonial reformers admired the republic to the south. Few wanted to join the United States, but a number of reformers—and later rebels—wished to emulate some of the more democratic elements of American governance. In short, the

1830s brought together forces that laid a foundation for conflict. The rebellions were not preordained, but they were utterly shaped by the times.

Although there were fitful efforts to coordinate the rebellions in the two Canadas, they were quite distinct events. In addition to the problems already mentioned, disproportionately greater representation of British heritage citizens was a glaring annoyance to the relatively few French Canadians who shared the bounty of political power. Galvanized by the leadership of Louis-Joseph Papineau, an assemblyman and landholder, the reformers mounted a concerted effort to wrest control from the British. Their convoluted 92 Resolutions for change, issued in 1834, led to a harsh British response. In late 1837 a series of conflicts broke out between *patriotes*, a varied group that included a number of *habitants*, and forces representing the government. Although the *patriotes* fared well in one skirmish, they met resounding defeat at St. Charles and St. Eustache, communities lying to the east of Montreal.

Papineau and other leaders fled to the United States, and some of the leaders in 1838 made an unsuccessful attempt to set up a republic just across the border. In addition, some Americans established Hunters' Lodges, shadowy organizations that skirted the neutrality law of the United States by gathering money and arms to support the rebellions. The Lower Canadian rebellions were poorly orchestrated and easily crushed. Nonetheless, they were at times bloody and in at least one region along the Richelieu River they drew substantial support. A few leaders were hanged. Papineau and others sought asylum in the United States, and others were exiled to other British colonies. While support for rebellion was uneven, recent scholarship has drawn a compelling picture of a genuine effort on the part of the lower orders to address glaring class inequities in the province.

The Upper Canadian rebellions shared some of the dynamics of the Lower Canadian conflicts but were not as widespread or as intense. The rebellion's antecedents in Upper Canada were mostly political in nature. Representatives of the Family Compact, a small group of conservative elites, essentially held the reins of government. In addition, an inequitable land distribution system and the favored position of the Church of England angered Upper Canadians of more humble means or different Protestant denominations. A repressive governor in the 1830s, Sir Francis Bond Head, made an especially despised foil for the mounting reform forces. One particularly vociferous newspaper editor and politician, William Lyon Mackenzie, challenged elite authority and published a constitution for Upper Canada that mirrored the U.S. document. Skirmishes broke out in December 1837 near Toronto. Much like his French-Canadian counterpart, Mackenzie escaped and set up a tiny republic in the Niagara area. From this base, Mackenzie's group, periodically aided by sympathetic Americans, attempted to keep the rebellion alive by sponsoring raids into Upper Canada. British and militia forces easily tamped down the conflict by 1838, and Americans arrested and temporarily imprisoned Mackenzie. Like their neighboring compatriots, Upper Canada's rebels seemed dismal failures (see "Mackenzie's Call to Arms" in the Documents section).

Yet their actions helped to turn certain political tides in all of British North America. Upon hearing the news of the uprisings, echoes of an American revolt a half-century earlier, the British dispatched a political activist named John Lambton, the Earl of Durham and a small fact-finding team to the Canadas in 1838. After a relatively brief stay in Canada, Durham returned to England and drew up an extensive report. His recommendation to grant the British North American colonies more self-governance within the British imperial fold, a principle called responsible government, was an early statement of the confederation model that Canada would employ in 1867.

Equally important, but in a more negative vein, was Durham's assessment that French Canadians should be assimilated. As he famously observed, a central cause of tensions in British North America was the two "races" that were "warring in the bosom of a single state." Borrowing an old idea from Canadian anglophones, Durham suggested the political union of the Canadas in order to create more efficient government as well as an arena for French-Canadian assimilation. Durham's denigration of French Canadians backfired; it instead steeled the group to resist any means of assimilation. For example, a civil servant named François-Xavier Garneau published an extensive *Histoire du Canada* in the 1840s as a response to Durham's comments. Significantly, Garneau emphasized a survival theme for understanding the French-Canadian past.

Although responsible government was not immediately implemented, British Parliament passed the Act of Union that came into force in 1841. The legislatures of the two Canadas were combined in one colonial unit, now renamed Canada East (the former Lower Canada) and Canada West (the former Upper Canada). With equal numbers of legislators from each section, power still remained firmly in the hands of the governor and appointed councilors. Moderate reformers who had weathered the rebellions, including Robert Baldwin and Louis-Hippolyte LaFontaine, took control of the assembly in the 1840s. Over the course of several years Baldwin and LaFontaine created a partnership that bridged the cultural and language divide as they championed and eventually won the principle of responsible government. Despite the fact that French Canadians were now outnumbered in the combined province, programs defined by political orientation trumped exclusively ethnic considerations. Reformers and conservatives found ideological allies across ethnic lines. As a result, Durham's plan for assimilation, codified in the Act of Union, did not come to fruition.

Life in British North America

British North America grew dramatically with natural increase and immigration. At the Conquest, its population stood at 100,000; by 1851 British North Americans numbered almost 2.5 million. Predominantly French, British, and Amerindian in origin, the colonies increasingly absorbed people from other sources. The Loyalist exodus was but one of a series of migrations of peoples to the various provinces. Although Americans continued to arrive, most came from Europe, risking the dangers of crossing the Atlantic Ocean. People came alone and in family units. Many paid for their own passage, while others were sponsored by individuals and groups that wanted to resettle destitute Europeans to the seemingly open expanse of British North America.

Populated at the beginning of the period by Acadians, ex-New Englanders, Loyalists, Amerindians, and various British groups, the Maritime colonies received waves of immigrants from Europe and the United States. Scots, especially Highlanders, settled in large numbers after 1780 on Cape Breton Island, a separate colony that merged with Nova Scotia in 1820, and Prince Edward Island. Irish, both Protestant and Roman Catholic, made the passage to the Maritimes.

While the devastating potato famine of the 1840s triggered a mass migration of impoverished Irish, an event that has received a great deal of historical attention, in fact the Irish came throughout the period. New Brunswick received especially large numbers, particularly in the thriving port of Saint John and communities along the Miramichi River. Small pockets of Germans arrived, especially at Lunenburg, Nova Scotia. Blacks, coming first with the Loyalists and later from the American South and the Caribbean, also settled in Nova Scotia and New Brunswick. Newfoundland, considered an Atlantic—not Maritime—province to this day, was populated by both English and French peoples as a result of the protracted contest for control over the fishing colony in the sixteenth and seventeenth centuries. Tragically, following a series of grisly conflicts, the indigenous Beothuk became extinct by the early nineteenth century. Large numbers of Irish Catholics also came to Newfoundland, setting up tensions with English Protestants that underscored political and educational issues into the twentieth century.

Lower Canada's French-Canadian population grew substantially due to natural increase in the years after the Conquest, in part as a deliberate plan to ensure the group's survival. *Canadiens* referred to this process as the "revenge of the cradle." The colony received significant numbers of English, Scots, and Americans in the period. Loyalists filtered into Lower Canada, despite the efforts of British-appointed governors to get them to move west to populate tiny Upper Canada. The Irish came in large numbers, settling especially in Quebec City and Montreal, where they clustered along the river systems and scraped out a living. Montreal's population surpassed Quebec's by the 1830s.

Upper Canada's population, given its modest start as a Loyalist haven, expanded the most dramatically in this period. Early governors, in particular John Graves Simcoe, actively encouraged migration from both the United States and Britain as they developed roads and government agencies to support a growing populace. Some immigrants received assistance. For example, Colonel Thomas Talbot developed an extensive estate above Lake Erie, complete with roads and schools, that drew tens of thousands of settlers to clear the land and develop farms. Blacks reached Upper Canada from the United States. Many were fugitive slaves who traveled along the famous Underground Railroad. Some remained as permanent residents, while others returned to the United States when conditions improved after the Civil War. Irish Protestants settled in rural and urban Upper Canada, as did large numbers of famine Irish Catholics. English, Scots, Americans, and Dutch also came to the province. By midcentury, Upper Canada, with a population of just under one million, had become the most populous colony. Diseases such as smallpox and cholera, which reached epidemic proportions in the early 1830s, ravaged in particular the population of Upper and Lower Canada (see "A Perspective of Life in the Backwoods" in the Documents section).

Native Peoples

The Amerindians in all the British North American colonies were swiftly becoming outnumbered. Diseases, changes in diet, and a bloody history of conflict reaching back to the seventeenth century combined to decimate the numbers of Native peoples. Large tracts of land were relinquished through negotiations or absorbed by whites over an extended period. In the Maritime colonies, the Mi'kmaq and Maliseet saw land that had been reserved for them diminished by squatters. Their numbers declined precipitously. In Upper Canada, the process of selling land to whites accelerated. Tribes such as the Mississauga and Iroquois experienced shrinking numbers due to diseases such as smallpox, measles, and tuberculosis. In addition, incessant white encroachment pushed them out of reserve lands. The catastrophic diminution of a race of peoples, unfolding from the contact era, was well entrenched by the nineteenth century.

Religion and Education

Religion profoundly defined life for most British North Americans, as it did for virtually everyone else in the North Atlantic world in the nineteenth century. People quickly drew important distinctions between themselves and others based on religious beliefs and their identification with a particular denomination or sect. The overwhelming majority of British North Americans were Christians. Differences among the various Christian churches, however, often led to acrimonious disagreement and sometimes violent clashes. The Roman Catholic church embraced virtually all French Canadians, Acadians, and large numbers of Irish and Scots newcomers. In areas where the Irish and French Canadians lived in close proximity—Montreal, for example—separate parishes ministered to Irish and French Catholics. In Upper Canada, the Church of England, or Anglican church, enjoyed a position of favor thanks to generous clergy reserves granted in the Constitutional Act of 1791. A particularly elite denomination, it counted political representatives, civic leaders, and businessmen in its ranks. Methodist preachers on horseback, with strong American connections, literally cut their way into the backwoods of Upper Canada. Presbyterians, reflecting their Scottish roots, were dispersed throughout British North America. All of the denominations existed in the Maritimes, including a particularly vibrant Baptist organization that was a legacy of the Revolutionary War era's Alline movement.

Religion shaped the evolution of Canada's public and private educational systems. Formal schooling was traditionally accessible only to the rich, who could afford private tutors and sent their children to boarding schools. By the 1840s educational reforms were being explored in Upper Canada, largely due to the energies of Egerton Ryerson, a Methodist minister and reformer who believed that education should be open to all. Institutions of higher learning, with few exceptions, were directly linked to denominations. Many of Canada's premier universities and colleges trace their origins to distinct religious groups. Despite the introduction and modest growth of public schools during the nineteenth century, formal education essentially remained the purview of the more fortunate. Religious orientation continued to shape education as a complex system of denomination schools, later sponsored by tax dollars, became entrenched in every Canadian province. In the post-Confederation era, denominational schools became the focus of major political and cultural struggles.

Staples, Manufacturing, and Trade

Many British North Americans continued to make a living by working with their hands. They made a living from the soil, pulled fish from the sea, or hewed logs from the forests for markets in Europe. Newfoundland's trade remained focused on its connections with Britain and the Caribbean. After the War of 1812, the Maritimes' fishing industry prospered. A healthy trade with the West Indies also helped to underpin the Atlantic economy. The seemingly endless forests, especially in New Brunswick, helped to drive the greatest export industry of the period: timber and wood products. The availability of timber also supported a robust shipbuilding industry, and the sailing fleets of Nova Scotia and New Brunswick expanded. Cutting and processing timber enriched the economies of Lower and Upper Canada as well. The great rivers, such as the Ottawa, were used for floating logs to sawmills for processing. Farming remained largely at a subsistence level throughout British North America, with the exception of a modest export industry in wheat. The fur trade largely molded western development in the early nineteenth century. In sum, the development of staple products—fur, fish, agriculture, and timber—defined the livelihoods of most British North Americans.

Businesses, commercial enterprises, and manufacturers existed in the larger towns and cities of the colonies. Some industries made direct use of staple products, such as shipbuilding, flour milling, and potash production from timber ashes that was used to make soap. Manufacturing included textiles, leather products, paper, and glass. John Molson began making a beer in the early nineteenth century that would become one of the most recognizable Canadian trade names in history. Banking developed as one of Montreal's claims to fame, an industry that would remain vibrant well into the twentieth century. The commercial empire of the St. Lawrence, as historian Donald Creighton defined it, remained preeminent in defining Canada's economic growth. Although the cities became important trading, manufacturing, financial, and service centers, British North America retained a predominantly rural orientation throughout the nineteenth century.

Transportation: Roads, Canals, and Railroads

Waterways continued to be the best means of transportation into the early nineteenth century. British North Americans used steamboats, sailboats, and canoes on open waters. Sleds appeared during the winter months to move people and goods. Roads remained primitive and largely unpassable in inclement weather. By midcentury dirt, log, and gravel roads connected towns and farms throughout the colonies. John Molson introduced Canada's first steamship, the *Accommodation*, which plied the St. Lawrence after 1809. Canals became more important as technological improvements brought more steam-powered ships. The Lachine Canal near Montreal opened in 1825, followed four years later by the Welland Canal in the Niagara. A significant boost for commercial development, this canal allowed traffic to pass between Lakes Erie and Ontario. Unfortunately for the British North Americans, the opening of the Erie Canal through New York State in 1825 siphoned trade and shipping from the Great Lakes region down the Hudson River, thereby providing an incentive for New York's expansion. The flourishing trade along the Erie came at the expense of the developers who wanted the St. Lawrence River to be the natural outlet for goods from the continent's interior. The other important canal of the era, the Rideau, opened in 1832. Constructed to bypass the shared St. Lawrence borderland of New York and Upper Canada, it connected Lake Ontario to Bytown (Ottawa). Trading goods and potentially military supplies could then use the Ottawa River to reach Montreal.

The canal era was fairly brief because railroads rapidly eroded their usefulness in North America. Canada's first line was a small railway built south of Montreal in 1836, the Champlain and St. Lawrence Railroad. Enormously expensive to build and outfit with rolling stock, extensive railroad systems awaited a favorable combination of interests. Midcentury brought several of these factors, including economic necessity, technological improvements, and the financial support of governments and businesses.

Boundary Issues and Trade with the United States

The presence of the growing United States, felt dramatically during the War of 1812, continued to affect British North America's development. Although several treaties and agreements clearly defined large sections of the boundary between the British colonies and the United

States, the border in several areas remained disputed. The New Brunswick–Maine boundary was one of the oldest unresolved issues. When Maine became a state in 1820, land grants in the disputed interior became the center of attention. Loggers from New Brunswick and Maine clashed periodically in the area. Law enforcement and militia became involved as tensions rose during the "Aroostook War" in 1839, a mild confrontation that forced the issue to arbitration. Three years later, in the Webster-Ashburton Treaty, the boundary between Maine and British North America was clearly drawn. It left a crucial strip of land between the tip of Maine and the St. Lawrence River's south shore that linked New Brunswick to Lower Canada.

Similar problems unfolded in the vast expanse west of the Rockies that the Convention of 1818 had left open for joint settlement. Rival British and American fur trade empires, as well as American settlers in the Oregon Territory, agitated for a clear boundary. When the expansion-minded President James K. Polk incorporated popular rhetoric—"Fifty-four forty or fight"—to claim the northern boundary of the territory that encompasses most of present-day British Columbia, tensions increased. Talk of war rapidly gave way to negotiation as the United States entered hostilities with Mexico. The Oregon boundary settlement of 1846 continued the forty-ninth parallel to the Pacific Ocean; Britain retained Vancouver Island. The prospect of a Pacific terminus for western expansion appealed to many British North Americans by midcentury, thanks to the solidification of the forty-ninth parallel.

Other economic and political issues in the period suggested a closer relationship between British North America and the United States. In the wake of Britain's move to embrace free trade, which signaled a decline in colonial trade preferences, over 300 Montreal merchants suggested union with the United States in the Annexation Manifesto of 1849. Lacking widespread support, the movement swiftly collapsed. Nonetheless, a mounting desire to increase trade between the neighbors grew. The Reciprocity Treaty of 1854, negotiated by the British North American governor, Lord Elgin, dropped the tariffs on agricultural products, fish, timber, and coal. In addition, both Americans and Canadians received extended fishing rights in each other's coastal waters. Although the Americans terminated the agreement in 1866, it remained a positive model of trade cooperation that Canadians periodically revisited.

British North America at Midcentury

The British North American colonies by the 1850s had grown substantially. Their economies were still largely focused on the production and export of staples, buttressed by a new trade agreement with the United States. Following the tumultuous Rebellions of 1837–1838, the colonies achieved a form of self-governance called responsible government. At the same time, they remained strongly connected to Britain through both politics and trade. From the American Revolutionary War through various border disputes, British North America had resisted absorption into the United States.

The remainder of the nineteenth century would bring pivotal changes to the colonies: political union, renewed tensions with its neighbor, the emergence of aggressive imperialism on the part of world powers, and Canadian expansion into the continent's western and northern reaches. The colonial British North American framework, a legacy of imperial conflicts during the eighteenth century, would become reconstituted in a new political entity. The Dominion of Canada, enjoying a degree of autonomy yet still within the fold of the greatest imperial power of the nineteenth century, would now chart the destiny of a people.

Chapter 5

Confederation and National Expansion (1850s–1890s)

A Critical Juncture

Canadians experienced far-reaching changes in the second half of the nineteenth century. All of the existing British North American colonies, with the exception of Newfoundland, had joined a new Canadian political structure by 1900. Despite this unification, deep-seated political and cultural disputes between francophones and anglophones continued to fester, shaped by old themes of language and religion and new themes of provincial-federal tensions and education. Dramatic expansion into the West yielded new provinces in the interior and on the Pacific Rim; it also triggered violent confrontations between Native peoples and whites.

At the start of the period, British North America had some improved roads and canals but very few miles of railroads. By 1900 Canadians had completed a marvelous transcontinental railroad, and the plans for two more lines were underway. The vanguard of a wave of European immigrants had arrived. Thousands poured into the continent's interior to clear land and provide the muscle for a new industrial-based economy. A modest exporter in midcentury, Canada

A view of Yonge Street, one of Toronto's most important commercial thoroughfares, in the early 1890s.

Source: Library and Archives Canada / Andrew Audubon Merrilees Fonds / PA-166917

by 1900 was becoming one of the world's great producers of wheat and other agricultural products.

The United States, riven by Civil War and grappling with Reconstruction, quickly filled its own interior, decimated its Amerindian population, and pressed for expansion beyond its continental borders. All presented Canadians with formidable challenges for survival in the swiftly changing world of the late Victorian era.

The Impulse for Confederation

The political parties that developed in the British North American colonies presented a range of positions from conservative supporters of elite rule to reformers advocating more democratic self-governance within the context of the British Empire. Others promoted closer ties to the United States, but they failed to gather widespread support. Out of this complex political framework, coalition governments formed and fell. The most important political debate, one with roots in the late eighteenth century, was over colonial unification.

Reformers, with the modest support of British-appointed governors such as Lord Elgin, succeeded in establishing the principle of having colonial legislation originate from elected assemblies. In Nova Scotia the reformers under newspaperman Joseph Howe and politician James Boyle Uniacke created a ministry for responsible government in 1848. During the same year, Robert Baldwin and Louis-Hippolyte LaFontaine forged a political partnership—the "great ministry"—that reformed the political and judicial system of the Canadas. Prince Edward Island, New Brunswick, and Newfoundland soon followed. To many historians this expression of domestically controlled politics signified one of the cherished principles of Canadian development: the evolutionary emergence of a nation without a violent revolution.

Contemporary political parties focused on raising funds to pay civil servants, build roads, improve waterways, construct railroads, and develop educational systems. While politicians advocated ideas that reached across the political spectrum in all the colonies, the political landscape of the Canadas was particularly instrumental in providing a foundation for two of the country's most important modern parties. Tories, conservatives with ties to the Loyalists and the powerful Anglican church, continued to exert some influence in the period. Yet with the introduction of a more democratized principle of governance, the number of moderate reformers increased. Under the guidance of George-Étienne Cartier, a former rebel and railroad promoter, the *bleus* in Canada East brought together moderate reformers and Tories. A rising lawyer from Canada West, John A. Macdonald, organized a coalition with Cartier by the mid-1850s under the party banner of the Liberal-Conservatives. This party, the antecedent of the current Conservative Party of Canada, became the champion of colonial unification.

The other key political party to emerge in the mid-nineteenth century had closer ties to more radical reformers from the rebellions and people who advocated a form of governance that was closer to the American model. The *Parti rouges*, under the leadership of Antoine-Aimé Dorion, wanted to undercut the influence of the Roman Catholic church. The *rouges* formed a tenuous connection with reformers in Canada West known as "Clear Grits." George Brown, the Scots-born editor of Toronto's *Globe*, advocated the party's policies. The Grits supported universal male suffrage, the secret ballot, and elected representation based on population—popularly referred to as "rep by pop." Despite the fact that many Grits, including Brown, regularly criticized French Canadians, the 1850s saw attempts to join forces with the *rouges* in order to gain enough support to combat the Liberal-Conservative/*bleu* coalition. The Grits and *rouges* created the foundation of the modern Liberal party. Canadians still refer to the Liberals as the Grits, especially in print.

An impetus arose to seek a greater unification of the various colonies in British North America out of this complex political party development, an event called Confederation. Although British North Americans had discussed this idea periodically since the late eighteenth century, various factors account for the emergence of Confederation in the 1860s. A "Great Coalition" of key political figures, including Macdonald, Cartier, and Brown, sought an effective means to move beyond party differences and complicated procedural rules that had virtually crippled the passage of important legislation in the Canadas. The union concept overlapped with similar discussions taking place among politicians and newspaper editors in the Atlantic colonies.

Another feature that made union attractive was the desire on the part of political leaders, financiers, and railroad developers to expand into the West. Canadians had long known, and the Oregon controversy reinforced this point, that the forty-ninth parallel was an imaginary line that might not contain American Manifest Destiny indefinitely. The Red River settlement, for example, was most easily reached overland from St. Paul, Minnesota. The colony of British Columbia, a legacy of the Hudson's Bay Company formed in 1858, seemed an appropriate Pacific outlet to many British North Americans. Scientific expeditions in the late 1850s had determined that although a section of the prairies was semi-arid, vast expanses were suitable for settlement because of their potential for farming and raising livestock. Finally the Hudson's Bay Company, facing diminished markets in Europe and illegal trading that cut into its profits, was pressured into considering the sale of Rupert's Land. The time seemed ripe for British North Americans to obtain possession of the interior, but capital and leadership were necessary to bring the West firmly under the control of easterners.

Economic developments underpinned the discussion for colonial unification. Reciprocity with the United States, a fairly successful trading arrangement, was endangered by Britain's relationship with the Confederacy during the American Civil War (1861–1865). With Americans threatening to let reciprocity lapse, British North Americans envisioned the creation of a trading zone—or customs union—among the British colonies. Moreover, many of the individuals pushing for Confederation invested both financially and emotionally in the great vision of the day: railroads. After the development of short railroad lines in the 1830s, two of the most notable lines constructed before Confederation were the St. Lawrence and Atlantic and the Grand Trunk Railway. The former opened in 1853 as the first international railway; it connected Montreal with ice-free Portland, Maine. A bold endeavor sponsored by the Canadas to open rail traffic to the Great Lakes region, the latter ran into considerable difficulties. With bankruptcy and political tensions plaguing railroad developers, politicians such as George-Étienne Cartier desired a unified federal system to facilitate the construction of railroads that would fully interlink the eastern colonies and present an opportunity to open the West for settlement and economic exploitation. Crafted in the age of railroad development, Canada's constitution in 1867 included passages that addressed the completion of an intercolonial railroad.

Events in Britain provided yet another important motivation to develop a federal scheme in Canada. Endowed with the world's strongest industrial complex and largest commercial fleet, the British moved aggressively away from mercantilism and toward free trade in the nineteenth century. Canadian discussions about Confederation coincided with a relatively brief period called "Little England," during which Britons considered colonies expensive to protect and not cost-effective. British North America seemed to make the case for imperial detachment. Staples produced in the colonies could be easily obtained from other sources through international trade, and many British thought the time had come for the colonists to defend themselves.

Troubled relations with the United States provided the remaining essential impulse for Confederation. The debates for Confederation transpired during the Civil War, a grisly conflict that tore the fabric of the United States and strained Anglo-American relations. British North Americans mostly sympathized with the northerners and antislavery interests, and thousands volunteered to fight in the war. British public opinion divided in its support of the Confederacy, but for a time the desire to retain southern cotton to supply Britain's textile mills created tensions with the North. Actions on the high seas, including the damage inflicted by Confederate raiders such as the *Alabama* that had either been constructed in Britain or supplied in British North American ports, further aggravated relations between the British and the Union. Moreover, the integrity of the international border was sorely tested during the war. American deserters and draft evaders skipped across the border seeking refuge, and a dramatic raid from Canada East by Confederate raiders in 1864 to rob banks in St. Albans, Vermont, caused great anti-Canadian sentiment among northerners. With depressing familiarity, some politicians called for the seizure of British North America to remove a long-standing irritant. Although the crises eventually passed, the souring of Anglo-American relations suggested to British North Americans that a stronger federal union was needed for defensive purposes.

The Confederation Debates

The various political ideals, economic issues, international tensions, and nationalistic dreams combined to create the context for colonial unification in the 1860s. A planned meeting among Maritime political leaders to discuss a regional union took place at Charlottetown, Prince Edward Island, in September 1864. A contingent from the Canadas, spearheaded by Macdonald, Cartier, and Brown, seized the opportunity to forward their case that an even wider federal alliance of the colonies would be beneficial. Charlottetown's brief conference, which included eloquent arguments to meet again for a more comprehensive discussion, nevertheless continues to receive recognition as the birthplace of Confederation.

Delegates from each of the six British colonies east of Canada West hammered out the terms for Confederation a month later at Quebec City. With great dispatch, the representatives came up with seventy-two resolutions. One of the liveliest debates centered on the nature of the proposed union and the balance of power between the provincial and federal governments. The participants used the term Confederation to characterize their union plans. Their resolutions became the core principles embedded in the British North America Act of 1867. Heartened by their accomplishment, the delegates took the Confederation blueprint to their respective provinces for discussion and, with any hope, legislative approval. The provincial battles over the terms of the Quebec Conference resolutions absorbed the attention of British North Americans for the next two years (see "The Argument in Favor of Confederation" in the Documents section).

Opposition to Confederation

Champions of Confederation met staunch opposition in every colony. New Brunswick's political leader and key supporter, Samuel Leonard Tilley, met defeat in 1865 at the hands of an opponent who employed an anti-Confederation plank. Albert James Smith and his supporters articulated a classic Maritime viewpoint that persisted long after the Confederation era. They argued that the smaller provinces would suffer because of unequal representation. In addition, western development, a dynamic that would benefit the central Canadian provinces because of their geographical location, would do little to enrich the economies of the Maritimes. Tilley's government returned the following year, thanks to Smith's ineffective leadership and growing support for Confederation due to British pressures and a fortuitously timed series of Fenian raids. A brotherhood that included Irish Americans, the Fenians planned to wrest Irish independence from

Britain by attacking its British North American colonies. One attack on Campobello Island, just across the Maine border, was quickly repelled in 1866. Further raids occurred in the Canadas. Given their expressed objectives, the Fenians' attacks effected the opposite result. They inadvertently helped to drive the colonies, especially New Brunswick, closer to a political union for defensive purposes.

Opponents to Confederation in Nova Scotia used similar arguments to harass Charles Tupper, the province's strongest proponent. Influential newspaperman and politician Joseph Howe echoed the reservations of his New Brunswick counterparts by flippantly dubbing the proposals a "Botheration Scheme." Nonetheless, proponents of Confederation prevailed by promising to explore and incorporate changes that would be more favorable to the colony. Like their neighbors in New Brunswick, Nova Scotian assemblymen did not specifically accept the terms for Confederation.

The colony that most formally approved of Confederation was the one that stood to benefit the most from greater union: the Canadas. The most vehement opposition was expressed by Antione-Aimé Dorion and other *rouges*. Fearful that a greater union would subsume French Canadians politically and culturally, and unenthusiastic about being saddled with Maritime Provinces whose interests lay elsewhere, Dorion argued that a change of this magnitude deserved a popular endorsement. He preferred a plebiscite or an election directly targeting the Confederation issue. Proponents, especially Cartier, maintained that French-Canadian survival was best ensured in a broader union with protected language and civil rights. Dorion's plebiscite was not to be. The Canadian assembly voted overwhelmingly to approve the resolutions and move ahead with Confederation. Although French-Canadian representatives split on the issue, a majority approved the plans. Dorion and Cartier framed a contentious question that has been repeatedly asked throughout post-Confederation Canadian history: What is the most secure way to ensure language, cultural, and civil rights of French Canadians? To the defeated Dorion, as well as to modern separatists, the best means would not be through Confederation (see "The Argument Against Confederation" in the Documents section).

Prince Edward Islanders and Newfoundlanders rejected Confederation. With long-standing resentments over the control of absentee landlords who retained their positions with support from British administrators, anti-confederate Prince Edward Islanders found the proposal a thinly veiled attempt to replace London with a Canadian capital. Confederation still represented control from abroad. Additionally, and in support of the arguments heard in New Brunswick and Nova Scotia, they saw little political or economic advantage for the tiny island colony in Confederation. Newfoundland, with historic trading ties to Britain, demonstrated a modest support for Confederation among political elites, but the island colony's general population remained overwhelmingly apathetic. Prince Edward Island and Newfoundland turned their backs on the idea in the 1860s. They would join Canada later, when compelling circumstances made Confederation a more attractive proposition.

Thus, a change of governments in several provinces, coupled with formidable popular and political opposition, meant that Confederation garnered a clear vote of approval only in the Canadas. New Brunswick and Nova Scotia moved to the next series of meetings without a definitive vote on the idea and with hopes of improving the terms of Confederation. Late in 1866 delegates from the Canadas, New Brunswick, and Nova Scotia met in London to complete their discussions for union. With few changes, the British approved of the plans and agreed to submit them to Parliament for approval. Instead of calling the new entity the Kingdom of Canada, one of Macdonald's favorite ideas, the British persuaded the Canadians not to antagonize the United States by creating a "kingdom" on its northern border. One of the delegates offered a more neutral alternative, a biblical term from Psalm 72: dominion. From the same psalm Canadians borrowed one of the country's mottoes, *A Mari Usque Ad Mare*, translated as "from sea to sea." In March 1867, with precious little fanfare, the British Parliament passed the British North America Act (BNA Act). On July 1, 1867, the Dominion of Canada came into being.

The British North America Act: A Constitution for a Dominion

The BNA Act served as the constitution for Canada until 1982 and is thus a central document for understanding Canadian history. The Fathers of Confederation, as the conference participants are known, consciously designed a hybrid governing plan that combined the strengths of the British parliamentary system with the American constitutional idea of a clear division of powers. The BNA Act assumed that governance and traditions would be "similar in Principle to that of the United Kingdom" and that Canada would "promote the Interests of the British Empire." While the Fathers of Confederation liked the idea of a well-defined division of responsibilities between the federal and provincial governments, they also considered the U.S. Constitution deeply flawed. In the light of the Civil War, they believed it gave too much power to the states and the people. The BNA Act thus sought to tilt the balance of power in favor of the federal government.

The BNA Act was both pragmatic and conservative; it was emblematic of Canada's birth in a period of industrialization, technological developments, expanding markets, and a lively migration of population groups across boundaries. Whereas the U.S. Declaration of Independence trumpeted "life, liberty, and the pursuit of happiness," the Canadians nearly ninety years later promoted the ideal of "peace, order, and good government." Devoid of lofty language, the BNA Act got right down to the business of providing the new dominion a template for national development.

Much of the BNA Act was devoted to the distribution of powers and responsibilities. Executive powers resided in the crown, and Britain continued to appoint governors-general to Canada well into the twentieth century. The act provided for an appointed Senate based on regional representation, with the populous provinces of Ontario and Quebec most heavily favored. The name was borrowed from the U.S. upper house, but it more closely resembled Britain's House of Lords. The heart of the BNA Act was located in sections 91 and 92. The former articulated the powers apportioned to the federal government, including a House of Commons with powers of legislation and taxation, responsibilities for Native peoples, and the prerogative to disallow provincial statutes. Residual powers, meaning those not enumerated in the BNA Act, would be held by the federal government. Section 92 defined the powers granted to the provinces, which initially were Nova Scotia, New Brunswick, Quebec, and Ontario. The provinces also received the unambiguous right to govern education, which would become one of the post-Confederation era's most explosive issues. Importantly, some of the BNA Act's language would prove to be problematic. Provinces retained control of property and civil rights, for example, the definitions of which changed dramatically over time. As a recognition of Canada's two charter groups, French and English were deemed the official languages of Parliament and the federal legal system (see "The British North America Act" in the Documents section).

Importantly, the BNA Act left powerful connections intact between Canada and Britain. First, Canada's governing document was a British statute. Its legislation could be reviewed, held up, or disallowed by the British. Moreover, the BNA Act included no language for amendments. Changing the document, which was certainly envisioned and indeed accomplished many times over the years, was effected through requests submitted by the Canadians to British parliamentarians, who would then amend the BNA Act. Finally, the act included no machinery for developing an independent foreign policy, an essential characteristic of sovereign nations. Few Canadians in 1867 wished to sever the ties to the old colonial master. Although British troops were rapidly withdrawn from Canadian bases in the wake of Confederation, Canadians were comforted in the belief that Britain would protect their interests if their expansionist neighbor stepped out of line. Canada's foreign policy, as well as its sovereignty, would result from incremental changes. Therefore, the dominion was a unique creation in world history. Neither a sovereign nation nor a series of colonies, the new entity was a design for relative autonomy within the fold of a greater empire. New Zealand, Australia, and other former British colonies swiftly adopted the Canadian dominion model.

The spirit of the BNA Act and its impact on Canadian history have been the subjects of heated political and social debates since 1867. Federalists tend to view the act as a British statute, composed by Canadians, to create a strong federal government and subordinate the provinces in order to build a viable nation. Others, particularly provincial supporters and separatists, argue that the BNA Act was an agreement, or pact, between the provinces that left them in charge of important provisions. Some historians and politicians assert that it was a treaty between two European-based charter groups in Canada: the peoples of British and French heritage. Much more than an irrelevant discussion of dusty themes, the debate is often at the center of current political struggles. If the BNA Act was a pact between provinces that voluntarily agreed to join the Canadian endeavor, then individual provinces should be free to leave Confederation if they so choose. The pact concept essentially underscores the ideology of the separatist movement in Quebec, while the act concept forms the essence of the federalists' argument that the nation is not divisible.

Challenges for a New Dominion

The dawn of a new era broke on July 1, 1867 for almost 3.5 million people in North America. Cannons boomed, dignitaries delivered lofty speeches, and no doubt plenty of beverages flowed. The Fathers of Confederation and federalists, especially in the newly formed province of Ontario, probably celebrated the most. At the same time, sharply critical opponents promised to absorb a great deal of the newly elected government's attentions. To the surprise of few, Conservative John A. Macdonald emerged to lead Canada's initial Parliament, which gathered in the old lumbering and canal community of Ottawa. Relying heavily on his Quebec counterpart Cartier, Macdonald made a concerted effort, and thereby established a precedent, to appoint cabinet members from the country's various parties, regions, ethnic groups, languages, and religions. At the time this meant representatives from the Maritimes, Quebec, and Ontario; Protestants and Roman Catholics; anglophones and francophones; and French Canadian, English, Scots, and Irish. While the dynamic of appointing members from opposition parties would ebb and flow in the years after Confederation, the idea of maintaining a representative group of cabinet appointees would remain an essential ingredient for successful federal leadership.

The Conservatives had a majority in Canada's first federal government, but their opponents, soon to be named Liberals, were returned in great numbers as well. As the political period of the 1840s and 1850s suggested, profound differences divided the two parties. Broadly speaking, the Conservatives supported a strong federal union, ambitious western development, the protection of growing industries through tariffs, and railroad developers. Conversely, the Liberals were more inclined to champion provincial agendas, free trade, and the interests of working-class Canadians. Although politics were far more complex than this brief summary suggests, in the late nineteenth century the Conservatives generally fostered aggressive national expansion and economic development. Liberals, on the other hand, routinely questioned the wisdom of rapid territorial growth and what they interpreted as the heavy-handed power of Ottawa, inevitably wielded at the expense of provincial rights. The Conservatives essentially dominated the federal political landscape from 1867 to 1896, so much of Canadian history in the period reflected their interests.

The opposition to Confederation in Nova Scotia was over-whelming. With one exception, all of the federal members of Parliament elected in 1867 were anti-confederates. Led by the vociferous Joseph Howe, the "antis" protested being hoodwinked into Confederation without a clear vote or mandate. Some met with the British, some suggested seceding from Canada, and a few raised the possibility of joining the United States. Rebuffed by the British, who endorsed a closely knit dominion, the "antis" reluctantly struck a bargain with the willing federal government. Howe accepted a position in Macdonald's cabinet, the province received financial subsidies, and Ottawa promised to complete a railroad line connecting Nova Scotia and New Brunswick to Quebec. Opposition to Confederation diminished somewhat as a result, yet it remained a significant force in Nova Scotia's political landscape into the twentieth century.

The issues evident in Nova Scotia were also at work on Prince Edward Island, which turned its back on Confederation in 1867. With a population of about 90,000, many still struggling to extract themselves from a system of land tenancy, islanders generally opposed joining Canada on the grounds that it would ensure the province's permanent marginalization as the country developed. Economic misfortunes and railroad development problems quickly brought the colony to the brink of insolvency, making Confederation a more attractive prospect. Ottawa's offer to assume debts and provide subsidies, including cash to purchase farms from landlords and improved ferry services, became Prince Edward Island's hand-maid to Confederation in 1873. With both Nova Scotia and Prince Edward Island, financial incentives and transportation linkages to the rest of Canada trumped idealistic notions of joining a nationalistic enterprise. Only a handful of visionaries dreamed that continental expansion would be Canada's destiny.

Western Expansion

Whereas reinforcing Confederation in the East was achieved through skillful political maneuvering and more generous economic offers, expansion to the West was fraught with conflicts that on several occasions threatened to tear the bonds of the newly created dominion. Concerns about possessions and occupancy had been ongoing since the Convention of 1818. The West was immense; however, it was not a vacuum. It encompassed the Hudson's Bay Company's fur trading empire, the colony of British Columbia on the Pacific seaboard, the old Red River settlement, and thousands of Amerindians and Métis inhabitants. Americans, engaged in the post–Civil War Reconstruction era, were rapidly moving into the continent's interior. In addition, an expansion-minded secretary of state, William Seward, had purchased Alaska from the Russians at virtually the same moment of the dominion's birth. The decision to establish control over the West spurred the Canadian federal government into swift action.

Capitalizing on a discussion that predated Confederation, Macdonald's government entered into negotiations to purchase Rupert's Land from the languishing Hudson's Bay Company. The transfer was delayed due to mounting tensions in the Red River area, yet by 1870 Canada owned Rupert's Land as well as the former British possession, the North-West Territory. While this was an obvious coup for Ottawa in clearing the path for western development, the transfer of interior lands to the government without the assent of its population practically ensured that a struggle would ensue.

Tensions at Red River

The flashpoint for the struggle over control of the interior came at the settlement with a history of competition between white settlers and Native peoples, the earlier battleground between competing fur trade empires. Assiniboia, also known as the Red River settlement, centered around the old Hudson's Bay Company post at the confluence of the Red River and Assiniboine River. The locality was home to Métis, the "country-born" offspring of Scots and English trappers and

Amerindians, and people who arrived during the Selkirk and subsequent migrations. These groups carried on their lives according to their heritage and the environment. They hunted buffalo, trapped furs, raised crops, and traded. Many adhered to established Christian religions, particularly Roman Catholicism. They possessed an established culture—or rather cultures—which they clearly wished to keep intact.

When the federal government sent out a governor and surveyors in 1869, the initial signs of eastern control, local inhabitants non-violently blocked their entry. Spearheading the Métis' drive to maintain local control was Louis Riel, an articulate native of Red River who had been sent to Montreal for religious training. Riel's involvement in the tangled series of negotiations and armed resistance, both at Red River in 1869 and in the North-West Rebellion in 1885, makes him one of the most controversial figures in Canadian history.

The events that unfolded in 1869–1870 are variously labeled a "rebellion," "insurrection," or "resistance." Historians offer varied interpretations to explain the Red River conflict. Some blame the federal government, while others focus on the actions of the Métis and other indigenous peoples. Virtually all pay close attention to Riel's role in the struggles. Simultaneously, negotiations and armed skirmishes between representatives of the Canadian government and Red River residents unfolded. The Métis and other residents formed a provisional government, one purpose of which was to compose a list of rights to use as a basis for negotiating with Canada. At the same time, various official and unauthorized forces representing Canada and the peoples of the Red River sparred for control of strategic locations in Assiniboia. The capture of prisoners by the Métis, including a member of the ultra-Protestant Orange Order from Ontario, intensified the discord. When Thomas Scott was executed following a trial, the Red River crisis dramatically expanded. News of Scott's execution whipped up anti-Métis and anti-Catholic sentiments in Ontario. Conversely, the indigenous peoples' response to protect their culture and rights in the face of federal imposition struck a responsive chord among francophones in Quebec. Macdonald's government was now in a precarious position. With a strong desire to place a definitive Canadian stamp on the interior and clear divisions in sympathies emerging in the two largest provinces, the federal government was more open to negotiating an amicable resolution to the dispute.

The result was the Manitoba Act of 1870, which incorporated many of the ideas presented by the provisional government. Originally called the "postage stamp" province because of its shape and relatively diminutive size, Manitoba obtained federal representation, a provincial assembly, the assurance that French and English would be official languages, and the right to support separate schools through provincial taxes. The last two principles were embraced to placate French Canadians in Quebec as well as Manitobans. They also kindled intense political and social discussions well into the following century. Finally, the federal government retained rights to Manitoba's public lands and natural resources, a clear departure from the privileges enjoyed by the charter provinces. This federal control over resources, a contentious power, would be replicated as other western provinces joined Confederation. Federalists considered Manitoba's entry into Confederation an essential piece of the western puzzle. To send a signal to the United States and provide a show of force to impress locals, Canada ordered a military expedition to travel overland from Lake Superior to Manitoba in 1870. Fearing retribution, Riel fled to the United States before the troops arrived. Later elected a member of Parliament from Manitoba, he was prevented from taking his seat in the House of Commons because of a warrant for his arrest in Ontario. Riel voluntarily sought treatment at mental institutions in Quebec and later moved to Montana.

The North-West Rebellion

Many of the fears of Red River's indigenous and mixed-blood peoples were realized after Manitoba became a province. Migrants from eastern Canada flooded into the province, thereby changing its culture and economy. Many Métis migrated westward to the Saskatchewan River area in the North-West, an area inhabited by the Cree. From 1871 to 1877, seven treaties ceded land from Native peoples to the Canadian government in an immense area from the Great Lakes to the present province of Alberta and from the American border to the Nelson, Churchill, and Athabaska rivers. Although the specific terms of these numbered treaties varied, in general they incorporated reserve areas for Native peoples, promised government subsidies, and provided for certain Amerindian rights. The Indian Act of 1876 planned for the assimilation of Native peoples by subordinating tribes and offering full citizenship to Amerindians who left the reserves and relinquished their treaty rights. This created distinctions between status Indians—those still on reserves and in tribal units—and nonstatus Indians—who accepted citizenship and abandoned their special rights as Native peoples. In the early 1880s, with the increased migration of whites into the West and mounting evidence of the federal government's reluctance to adhere to the terms of its treaties, some Métis and Cree in the Saskatchewan River region took actions to protect their way of life.

Seeking experienced leadership, the Métis and Native peoples invited Riel to come to the North-West to galvanize their efforts. Riel and his closest supporters sought to replicate their relative successes in Manitoba by setting up a provisional government. The North-West of the 1880s, however, was unlike the Red River region of the 1860s. After 1873 a federally sponsored North-West Mounted Police—the forerunner of the Royal Canadian Mounted Police—maintained control in the area. In addition, the almost completed Canadian Pacific Railway (CPR) was primed to move reinforcements and supplies deep into the continent. With the Métis and Cree experiencing division in their ranks, conflict broke out in 1885.

The rebellion was marked by massacres and skirmishes throughout the Saskatchewan River region. Forces that served under Cree chiefs Poundmaker and Big Bear engaged in several battles with the Mounties and government forces. One grisly raid by Big Bear's followers at Frog Lake left two priests and at least seven whites dead. The Frog Lake episode, along with a number of other attacks on the part of the Cree, were quickly labeled massacres. Questions that still engender heated arguments among historians focus on the nature of these attacks and whether or not the Cree warriors were carrying out orders issued by Big Bear and Poundmaker. The Métis leader Gabriel Dumont pursued an effective campaign of hit-and-run raids on federal forces. Troop reinforcements and materiel sped west on the railway enabling the Canadians to crush the resistance. Chiefs Poundmaker and Big Bear were captured and sentenced to brief prison terms; both died soon after their release. Dumont made his way to the United States, where he later became a popular attraction in Buffalo Bill's Wild West Show. Eight Cree were hanged after the rebellion, an event that still stands as the largest public execution in Canadian history. The captured Riel was tried at Regina. With questions circulating about his sanity, a point that Riel emphatically denied during the proceedings, a jury found him guilty of treason. Appeals to Macdonald yielded postponements but ultimately no clemency. Riel was hanged in November 1885 (see "Louis Riel on Trial" in the Documents section).

The North-West Rebellion was the last large-scale resistance of indigenous peoples to Canadian control of the West. In a moment laden with symbolism, Riel's body was transported back to Manitoba for burial on the Canadian Pacific Railway, the last section of which was rushed to completion during the rebellion. With the North-West firmly in the hands of the federal government, the West was ensured for Canada's development. As with the Red River crisis of fifteen years earlier, the North-West Rebellion inflamed enduring passions in the East. Riel became a hero, if not a martyr, to Quebec's francophones. To many of Ontario's anglophones, he was a traitorous opponent of national development. The conflicting perceptions of Riel's role in history, borne of two western conflicts, illustrate the cultural, ethnic, and religious divides that characterized Canada into the twentieth century.

British Columbia Becomes a Province

Canada's desire to gain a foothold on the Pacific Ocean led Macdonald's government into negotiations with British Columbians. Negotiators representing the approximately 10,000 whites, the legacy of the fur trade and a brief gold rush, skillfully extracted the most favorable terms possible from the eager Canadians. In 1871 British Columbia officially entered Confederation following a number of promises from Ottawa. Most of them, such as absorbing the colony's debts and sponsoring a public works program, were fairly easily tackled. The biggest challenge would be to fulfill the commitment to link the province to eastern Canada with a railroad, making celebrations in Ottawa over British Columbia's inclusion short-lived. The headache of funding and constructing the Canadian Pacific Railway plagued Conservatives and Liberals for over a decade. Still, the overextended reach of the federal government seemed worth the risk. To many Canadians in the late nineteenth century, the country's survival without British Columbia seemed improbable.

Politics, The Economy, and International Affairs

Macdonald's Conservatives won reelection in 1872, largely on their successes in confronting Nova Scotia's anti-confederates and dramatically expanding the Canadian map in the West and North. To facilitate the movement of people into the interior, the government passed the Dominion Lands Act in 1872. The legislation, modeled on the American Homestead Act, created the machinery for issuing land—typically quarter sections of 160 acres—to homesteaders for a small fee and a requirement to construct buildings and plant crops. Intense bidding for the charter to construct the Canadian Pacific Railway led to an intertwining of the Conservatives and a company headed by Montreal businessman Hugh Allan. Canada's first serious political scandal erupted as information leaked that Conservatives, including Cartier, had received funds from Allan's company during the 1872 campaign in return for the transcontinental contract. The Pacific scandal led to Macdonald's resignation, the collapse of the Conservative government, and Canada's first Liberal administration in 1873.

For five years the Liberals, under the ineffective leadership of Scots-born Alexander Mackenzie, attempted to offer Canadians a stimulating plan for national development and keep an unruly coalition of former *rouges* and Grits together. To compound the government's problems, a general economic depression, felt on both sides of the Atlantic, coincided with its arrival. Work on the transcontinental railroad slowed to a crawl, and the U.S. Senate rebuffed the Liberals in their attempts to reestablish a reciprocal trade agreement. On the other hand, the Liberals altered the country's judicial structure and extended the vote to a wider range of citizens. The Supreme Court, created in 1875, labored for years to establish its role in the shadow of the still powerful British Privy Council. Liberals also introduced the secret ballot and expanded the electorate to include most non-Amerindian males. In spite of these positive changes, Mackenzie's government met defeat at the hands of a reinvigorated Conservative party in 1878.

A National Policy

Macdonald's Conservatives mounted a successful return to Ottawa by crafting and publicizing a plan called the National Policy. An interconnected scheme, the National Policy called for the construction of a transcontinental railroad, the protection of Canadian industries against less expensive imports, and the settlement of immigrants in the West to develop the land's agricultural potential. The Conservatives acted on the National Policy by adopting high tariffs on imports in 1879. This triggered angry outcries from consumers and people in the Maritimes and West, who claimed that tariffs unfairly favored the developing industrial heartland in Ontario and Quebec. The principle of raising the cost of imports so that Canadian-made goods would be more attractive led to mixed results. Some industries grew, including textiles, shoemaking, and agricultural machinery. However, the National Policy sharpened regional disputes and encouraged the development of American branch plants in Canada to sidestep the tariff schedules. Thus, the impact of this component of the National Policy on Canadian history remains debatable.

Few other events in Canadian history are more laden with emotional appeal than the construction of the Canadian Pacific Railway. Long envisioned as a way to encourage east-west growth and started as a result of a promise to British Columbia when it entered Confederation, the CPR's funding and construction led to woeful blunders and heady triumphs. Chastened by the Pacific scandal, Macdonald's Conservatives made the line's construction an imperative in the National Policy. The Canadian Pacific Railway Company, a joint venture that brought together an international cast of engineers, financiers, and workers, received the contract to construct the railroad. To create the most favorable environment possible, the government gave the company twenty-five million acres of land and economic incentives. Rising construction costs necessitated more government loans, imperiling Macdonald's government on several occasions. Nonetheless, under the guidance of a robust American engineer named William Cornelius Van Horne, tracks were rapidly laid across the prairies. The feats of blasting rock in the Shield, bridging countless waterways, and tunneling through the Rockies and British Columbian mountains made the CPR a world-class model. The railroad also came at a high human cost. By the time the last spike was driven at Craigellachie, British Columbia, in November 1885, hundreds of laborers, called navvies, had perished. Many of them were imported Chinese workers. When the CPR began service connecting Vancouver to Montreal, a national dream had become a reality.

International Issues in the Late Nineteenth Century

One of the oldest themes for understanding Canada's place in an international perspective is its triangular relationship with Britain and the United States. Although the War of 1812 led to negotiated boundary settlements and the virtual demilitarization of the Great Lakes, both sides constructed forts in the nineteenth century. The so-called Aroostook War and Oregon controversy reminded Canadians that they lived next to an expanding power. The end of the American Civil War in 1865 and Confederation two years later brought the almost complete withdrawal of protective British troops from Canada. The British North America Act consciously left the new dominion without the machinery to develop a distinct foreign policy. Most Canadians at the time assumed that their country would share the British Empire's destiny.

Nonetheless, the Treaty of Washington in 1871 signaled that the triangular relationship was changing dimensions. Desirous of harmony between their respective countries, British and U.S. representatives sought resolutions to thorny problems such as British payments for damages done by Confederate raiders such as the *Alabama*. A small contingent of Canadians, led by Macdonald, also attended the Washington conference. They came with their own agenda, which included fishing rights, boundary clarification, and restitution for Fenian attacks made from American soil. Canada's goals were pushed aside in the interest of improved Anglo-American relations.

The two larger powers agreed to a resolution for the *Alabama* claims, and the Americans received fishing rights off the Canadian coast and the permanent use of the St. Lawrence River. Macdonald, smarting from being rebuffed by British colleagues, returned to Ottawa with some tariff concessions by the Americans and the Canadian right to use three Alaskan rivers. Canadians learned a bitter lesson at the Treaty of Washington: the British would readily subordinate Canadian interests for broader concerns. At the same time, the Canadians were beginning to achieve American recognition, and the seeds of an international policy—perhaps independent of British imperial interests—were beginning to grow.

Late Nineteenth-Century Canada: A Nation of Contrasts

Canada in the late nineteenth century was still primarily a rural place, dominated by the extraction and processing of raw materials as it had been since the early colonial era. Yet it was undergoing rapid change. Its urban areas grew, assisted by railroad development, improved communications, and technological advancements. Immigrants and people from outlying settlements sought employment in the cities. Montreal and Toronto expanded their influence, while small towns such as Winnipeg, Vancouver, and Calgary saw their populations mushroom. In a land of many contrasts, great social and economic distances separated men and women, native-born and immigrants, Amerindians and whites, francophones and anglophones, Protestants and Roman Catholics, and workers and owners. With power still clutched firmly in the hands of relatively few elites, primarily those of English, Scots, and French-Canadian extraction, Canada survived the post-Confederation era to face the twentieth century.

Still part of the powerful British Empire, and sharing its only boundary with an expansive neighbor that was on the verge of becoming a global leader, Canada's experiences illuminated its European roots as well as its North American orientation. The second half of the nineteenth century, the era of Confederation and territorial expansion, whetted a national appetite for further growth and triggered debates on Canada's international position. Issues crowded the political and social landscapes, including the dividing line between federal and provincial responsibilities, education and language privileges, and the rights of women, workers, Amerindians, ethnic minorities, and immigrants. The approximately five million Canadians of the late 1890s looked forward to the next century. Perhaps, as their prime minister suggested, it would belong to them.

Chapter 6

A New Century
(1890s–1929)

Canada's Century?

Canada experienced tremendous change as it made the transition to the twentieth century. A greatly expanded nation after Confederation, it reached across the continent by the turn of the century. Its dominant political party had crafted the National Policy to protect its industry, build a transcontinental railway, and bring immigrants to the West. While the first two points of the National Policy were achieved, the last remained an essentially unfulfilled promise by the 1890s. Ever mindful of the burgeoning United States, which was becoming an industrial powerhouse, Canada sought to protect itself and compete as industrial capitalism became the favored economic model for the Western world. As a dominion, and thus technically lacking in the machinery needed to pursue a distinctive foreign policy, Canada struggled to navigate Britain's imperial schemes in Africa and Asia.

Domestically, political and social issues were underscored by contentious questions of linguistic and cultural duality. Although Quebec had joined Confederation, profound strains between francophones and anglophones dominated federal politics in the era. They shaped discussions of western development, education, immigration,

Multigenerational group of immigrants taken shortly after their arrival in Quebec, around 1911.

Source: Library and Archives Canada / Topley Studio Fonds / PA-010270

and British imperialism. Beset by a host of challenges, many Canadians nonetheless looked to the future with optimism. Prime Minister Wilfrid Laurier, whose administration bridged the two centuries, captured that spirit when he observed that the new century was to belong to Canada. With the tools of governance firmly in place and the expansive interior appearing ripe for development, Canada seemed poised to become a power. As it struggled with domestic tensions, the horrible drama of World War I, and the mixed blessing of postwar development, Canada in the period from the 1890s to the 1920s incrementally moved away from its European roots to favor a North American orientation.

Conservatives and Liberals

The Conservative plans for a National Policy remained in force during the 1870s and 1880s. Armed with constitutional tools including the right to disallow provincial statutes and the retention of residual powers, John A. Macdonald's government attempted to maintain federal supremacy. Yet the balance of power was tilting dramatically in favor of the provinces due in part to the British Privy Council, effectively the final arbiter in contentious court cases. In a series of decisions during the 1880s and 1890s, ranging from the control of liquor licenses to provincial boundary disputes, the Privy Council decided in favor of the provinces. These decisions effectively eroded the federal government's residual powers.

Also plaguing the Conservatives were two issues that strained the fragile bonds between anglophones and francophones. The Jesuits' Estates Act controversy pitted the pro-Catholic Quebec government against fervent Protestants in the Equal Rights Association. The 1888 statute provided financial compensation to Jesuits for property that had been confiscated in the eighteenth century. Macdonald's refusal to disallow the controversial act angered Protestants and Ontario Conservatives, who considered his actions a capitulation to francophone Catholics. An even more contentious controversy swirled around the Manitoba government's decision in 1890 to alter the Manitoba Act by making publicly funded schools nondenominational and abolishing French as an official language. Provincial rights advocates supported the changes, while francophones and Catholics protested and implored the federal government to overturn the legislation. Macdonald died in 1891, and his four Conservative successors struggled ineffectively to solve what had become a national problem. John Abbott, Macdonald's immediate successor, resigned in 1892 due to poor health. Nova Scotia's John Thompson died two years later on a diplomatic mission to Britain. Mackenzie Bowell became prime minister, but he was unable to inspire even his colleagues. Bowell acceded leadership in 1896 to Dr. Charles Tupper, a Father of Confederation, who faced defeat within the year to the Liberals.

Wilfrid Laurier, the new prime minister, had capitalized on the raging Manitoba schools question during the campaign of 1896 by promising a "sunny way" out of the dilemma. Unfortunately, the issue's tortured passage through various courts offered no clear guidelines. A lawyer by training, Laurier nonetheless brokered a compromise that kept the tax-based secular schools but allowed religious training at the end of the school day if a certain number of Roman Catholic students were enrolled. Similarly, provisions were included for some non-English training in French or other foreign languages. Few on either side of the debate were particularly pleased with the solution, but it clearly illustrated Laurier's negotiating skills. Denominational schools and language rights would continue to dominate both provincial and federal politics into the next century.

The Liberals embraced economic and social ideals that theoretically ran counter to the Conservatives'; nonetheless, Laurier's administration essentially adopted and modestly altered the principles of the National Policy. The new government faced a host of concerns, including domestic divisions, immigration and territorial expansion, international trade, and mounting British and American imperialism. Although it periodically sought a reciprocal trade agreement with the United States, Laurier's administration continued to protect growing Canadian businesses by instituting a scaled structure that essentially matched the tariffs of its trading partners. The Liberals also strengthened east-west linkages and prairie agricultural development by supporting the construction of two additional transcontinental railroads. The Canadian Northern Railway, chartered in 1899 with generous support of land and government subsidies, built a line that swept northward in the prairies and British Columbia and then terminated in Vancouver. The Grand Trunk Pacific, constructed by 1914, connected eastern lines at Winnipeg to Prince Rupert, British Columbia. These lines soon ran into severe financial difficulties. Still, for a time they boosted the economy and provided thousands of jobs for laborers. Thus, Laurier's Liberals reinforced two of the three elements of Macdonald's National Policy. The third component, improved immigration to populate the West, faltered under Conservative leadership. Perhaps ironically, this part of the plan succeeded spectacularly during Laurier's years in office.

Immigration and Western Expansion

The nationalistic plan to create a generation of new Canadians merged with the need to exploit the agricultural potential of the prairies. Modest immigration occurred in the post-Confederation era—for example, about 15,000 Chinese arrived to work on the Canadian Pacific Railway—yet a grand migration eluded the National Policy's proponents. Several factors combined to facilitate the fantastic influx that increased Canada's population in the early twentieth century. Recovery from an international depression in the late 1890s, the expansion of railroads and steamship lines, and improvements in farm machinery and crop strains made Canada an attractive destination for immigrants. Events outside the country also shaped the movement of peoples. Political, religious, and economic pressures, particularly in Eastern and Southern Europe, induced millions to leave their homelands. Canada capitalized on the dramatic announcement in the United States that its frontier was essentially closed for further settlement. Finally, populating the West became a priority of Laurier's government. Clifford Sifton, the interior minister, accepted the main responsibility for the endeavor. Aggressive advertising in Europe and the United States, touting the prairies as the "last best West," fancifully portrayed Canada as a flawless land of opportunity. As Sifton famously observed, he wanted hardy European "peasants in sheepskin coats" so that they would be prepared to endure the rigors of life on the land (see "Sifton's Rationale for Immigration" in the Documents section).

From 1896 to 1914 more than one million immigrants came to Canada's West. At the same time, Canadians migrated to the United States in large numbers, including tens of thousands of Quebecers who moved to New England in search of employment. Although many settled in cities, the bulk of the migrants from Europe and the United States rode the newly constructed rails to the West. Immigrants came from Britain, seeking economic opportunity while still secure in the empire's fold. Scandinavians, Germans, Russians, and Eastern Europeans arrived. All left indelible imprints of their culture, language, and architecture. Ukrainians, for example, constructed bloc settlements and Orthodox Catholic churches with distinctive onion-domed spires. Religious groups included European Mennonites, American Mormons, and the fiercely independent Russian Doukhobors. As a reflection of population growth, the provinces of Saskatchewan and Alberta entered the dominion in 1905. Echoing Manitoba's saga, a controversy over the nature of education and control of resources and public lands engendered bitter feelings. Nonetheless, by the eve of World War I, the Canadian prairies had become home to a tremendous variety of immigrants and two new provinces.

On many levels, this government-assisted migration was a phenomenal success. Immigrants provided muscle for industry and agriculture. They raised families, built communities, worshiped the religions of their forebears, established newspapers in their native languages, and attempted to keep elements of their culture intact. Over time, they also adopted and helped to fashion a Canadian outlook. This mosaic of peoples would later become one of the celebrated features of Canadian identity. Yet many Canadians viewed the rapid influx of non-English speaking peoples as a threat; they preferred Protestant immigrants from Northern and Western Europe. Nativist organizations, opposed to foreign influences, emerged in the late nineteenth century. The government instituted a head tax in 1885 to curtail Chinese immigrants. With the advent of a new minister of the interior in 1905, the government introduced more restrictive policies toward immigrants from Eastern and Southern Europe and limited the rights of Native peoples. In 1907 a riot broke out in Vancouver between Asiatic Exclusion League members and Japanese and Chinese residents. Concerned Canadians increasingly counted on strict laws to block certain immigrants and the educational system to play a key role in assimilation.

Canada and the British Empire

Britain rapidly abandoned its ambivalence toward colonies in the late nineteenth century, thereby touching off a spirited debate among Canadians about their country's role in the empire. In competition with other industrial and military powers, Britain aggressively sought possessions in Asia, the Pacific, the Middle East, and Africa. Canadian groups, consisting primarily of educated and professional anglophones, formed to support British imperial endeavors. The Imperial Federation League, for example, championed Canada's connection to the empire after 1884. A substantial number of politicians, including members of Parliament, joined these organizations. Although the empire had its tireless proponents, imperialism drew sharp criticism from other Canadians. One of the most eloquent empire opponents was Henri Bourassa, a member of Parliament from Quebec and editor of *Le Devoir*, an influential French-language newspaper. Bourassa and his supporters maintained that Canadians should not assist in the subjugation of Asian and African peoples. The heated debate between imperialists and anti-imperialists framed a larger question of Canada's future. Bourassa's Canada was North American in focus, and francophone rights were seen as analogous to those of other oppressed peoples in the world. Conversely, pro-imperialists defined Canadian nationalism through the dominion's connections to the empire. The popular professor and author Stephen Leacock, for example, argued that Canadians would be strengthened in both cultural and defensive dimensions by maintaining close relations with their counterparts in the empire.

A conflict that bridged the two centuries, the South African War (also known as the Boer War) illuminated the sharp domestic divide over the nature of Canada's commitment to imperial expansion. British designs to establish an extended African empire had already involved Canadians. Several hundred volunteers had been sent in the mid-1880s in a failed attempt to rescue the swashbuckling General "Chinese" Gordon, who was under siege in the Sudan. Later in South Africa, British attempts to shift the entrenched Dutch Protestant settlers known as Boers from their small homelands in the Orange Free State and the Transvaal touched off a brutal war that lasted from 1899 to 1902. These Boers used effective raiding tactics that stymied their opponents. When the British called on Canada to support the war, primarily by providing troops, it placed Laurier's government in a difficult position. Empire enthusiasts claimed that the war was an ideal moment for Canada to show its full support for Britain. Anti-imperialists argued that it would be inappropriate—even morally repugnant—to send Canadians to repress a minority group that was under British attack.

The war sorely tested Laurier's abilities as a compromiser. The government's solution was to raise and fund a modest volunteer force while allowing the British to recruit Canadians as well. Over 7,000 Canadians served in the hostilities, with disease claiming the majority of the nearly 250 casualties. The war's impact on Canada cut in two distinct directions. On the one hand, Canadian troops distinguished themselves in battle, and imperialists, while they may have believed Canada's contribution to be modest, were generally heartened. Conversely, the war had a divisive impact on Canadians, punctuated by a severe riot in Montreal. To many anglophones, Canada's place was at the side of Britain. To an equally dedicated group of francophones and anti-imperialists, Canada's interests should be North American in focus. The wounds created during the South African War, barely scabbed over, would be reopened in twelve years when Europe ran headlong into the most horrific armed struggle the world had ever witnessed: the Great War.

Canada and the United States

While questions of British imperialism loomed large, the United States continued to have a considerable impact on Canadian national development in the late nineteenth and early twentieth centuries. Tensions in the fisheries along both the Atlantic and Pacific coasts flared up periodically. At the same time, some Canadians, including English-born educator and journalist Goldwin Smith, maintained that Canada's destiny should be intertwined with that of its southern neighbor. The continental movement attracted few to its cause; still, the idea that the country's focus should be North American rather than European underscored much of the political and social debate in the period. Two episodes illustrated Canada's ambiguity in its interactions with the United States.

The boundary between Alaska's panhandle and Canada was a vaguely defined space. Following the Klondike gold strikes in the Yukon in 1896 that brought large numbers of people into the region, calls for an international tribunal to determine the boundary clearly intensified. When an arbitration commission met in 1903, the crux of the issue concerned the panhandle's width. Canada wanted water access through inlets from British Columbia to the Pacific. The United States envisioned a thicker panhandle that effectively landlocked northern British Columbia. In a classic example of his "big stick" foreign policy, President Theodore Roosevelt threatened force and charged the tribunal's three American members, including the secretary of war, to render a favorable decision. Two Canadian jurists and the British chief justice, Lord Alverstone, rounded out the commission. Alverstone sided with the Americans, thereby reinforcing bitter perceptions that Canada's interests were routinely sacrificed to improve Anglo-American relations. The Alaska boundary decision fueled Canada's drive to establish the machinery to pursue a more independent foreign policy. Coupled with the South African War, it led to the creation of the External Affairs department in 1909.

Trade issues pointed to another side of Canada's relationship with the United States, and they ultimately contributed to Laurier's defeat. The protective tariffs of the National Policy had helped manufacturers, but a growing number of Canadians wanted to reinstate a reciprocal trade agreement with the United States. Consumers, especially in the growing West, resented paying higher prices for tariff-protected products from Ontario and Quebec. Farmers also wanted a freer marketplace to export their goods. They dramatized their concerns by peacefully marching on Ottawa in 1910. The Americans, now under William Howard Taft's leadership, were in the midst of the Progressive era. Taft and some congressmen anticipated that a reciprocal trade agreement would be an important step toward Canada's annexation through economic means. The two countries hammered out terms that each planned to implement through legislation. The agreement covered many natural products, as well as some manufactured goods that farmers required. Congress promptly passed the appropriate legislation and waited for the Canadians to follow suit.

During the election of 1911, one of the most important in Canadian history, intense debate swirled around the reciprocity issue. Opponents to the trade plans targeted both economic and nationalistic themes. Many pointed out that the National Policy's tariffs had successfully created a favorable economic climate for industrial growth. Equally important, critics seized the moment to argue that reciprocity would lead directly to Canada's demise. Also shaping the election was the controversial Naval Service Act passed by the Liberals the year before. Under pressure from Britain, then in the throes of a grim competition with other nations to construct powerful naval fleets, Laurier's government created a small navy. Anti-imperialists deplored the initiative. Conservatives, on the other hand, belittled the fledgling "tin-pot navy." Under the leadership of Robert Laird Borden, they also mounted a withering attack by claiming that the passage of reciprocity would weaken Canada's ability to survive. Conversely, Laurier and reciprocity supporters asserted during the campaign that the agreement would strengthen Canada's economy and offer a greater chance to compete in international markets. Borden's nationalistic arguments carried the day. Following the Liberal electoral defeat, the reciprocity legislation did not pass in Parliament, so the agreement with the Americans collapsed. As the Conservatives settled in, however, domestic issues were rapidly overshadowed by the outbreak of Europe's "war to end all wars."

Canada and the Great War

The tragic events of 1914 to 1918 fundamentally altered Canada's relationship with Britain, deeply affected its political structure and economy, and widened the divide between francophones and anglophones on the issues of imperialism and conscription (compulsory military service). In fact, a considerable number of historians maintain that World War I was the most important event in modern Canadian history. Although this viewpoint might be disputed, there is little doubt that Canada in the 1920s was a radically different country from the one that Laurier governed in the opening years of the century.

The War Abroad

Canada was essentially unprepared for hostilities. Borden's failed attempt to raise millions for the construction of British battleships indicated that citizens were still divided on the issue of imperial support. Two years later, the swiftly moving events that unfolded in the wake of the assassination of the heir apparent to the Austro-Hungarian throne led to widespread European hostilities. Britain allied with the French and Russians against the Central Powers of Germany, Austria-Hungary, and the Ottoman Empire. Britain's declaration of war implicitly involved its extended empire. Lacking a distinct foreign policy and linked constitutionally to Britain, Canadians found themselves involved in a war that was not of their making.

Nonetheless, an emotional outpouring greeted the war news in Canada. Parades and political addresses illustrated a general enthusiasm for supporting Britain and France. The House of Commons gave its overwhelming and largely symbolic approval to the war and in the flush of the moment passed the War Measures Act in 1914. Broadly worded to encompass "war, invasion, or insurrection, real or apprehended," this statute gave Borden's cabinet extraordinary powers. During the Great War, it was used to direct the economy, steer men and women into jobs that the government deemed critical for the war effort, oversee the conscription of men into service, and detain and incarcerate people who by virtue of their ethnicity or ideas were considered threats to the state. With patriotic fervor, the ranks of the originally minuscule military of several thousand rapidly swelled. Troops flocked to unfinished camps, which were overseen by a zealous but incompetent minister of militia named Sam Hughes. These soldiers became the backbone of the Canadian Expeditionary Force. By the time the guns fell silent in November 1918, over 600,000 Canadians had served in the army. An additional 9,000 had enlisted in the Royal Canadian Navy, mostly for dangerous convoy duty protecting the steady stream of ships that plied the North Atlantic with men and war materiel. In addition, Canadian pilots comprised about one-quarter of Britain's Royal Flying Corps.

Although some Canadian soldiers served in the Mediterranean and in Russia, the overwhelming majority fought in the trenches along the Western Front that extended from the Swiss border to the

North Sea. In the dreadful battles along these lines, where generals continued to use antiquated tactics of having troops rush at one another to gain a victory, the casualties on both sides were staggering. Machine guns, artillery, and poison gas took a devastating toll. The Canadian Corps, under the command of British officers, performed admirably during the war and rapidly earned a reputation on both sides of the trenches as fierce fighters. Canadian soldiers were among the first troops to be victims of German mustard gas at Ypres in 1915 and suffered huge losses, yet they held their ground without protective equipment. They fought with distinction in the ill-conceived Somme offensive in 1916, which yielded more than one million casualties for a paltry gain of land. In April 1917 Canadian forces received international attention after they took Vimy Ridge in France, one of the most significant Allied victories of the war. Due to their performance in battle, the Canadian Corps finally received a Canadian commander later that year, General Arthur Currie. The country also received great attention due to the bold exploits of its pilots who served in the Royal Flying Corps. Ontario's Billy Bishop, for example, became one of the Allies' greatest aces, although the number of his victories may have been inflated in the interest of promoting the war effort (see "The Necessity for Victory" in the Documents section).

In the total context of a grisly war that claimed over seven million battle deaths by the armistice in November 1918, Canada's 60,000 casualties seem modest. Yet given its relative population size, Canada's losses were extraordinarily high. One soldier in ten who put on a uniform died during the hostilities. Canada's position in the British Empire and its international stature escalated considerably after 1914, changes wrought largely by the commitment of its fighting forces. Numerous monuments to the soldiers who served in World War I, dotted throughout the country, serve as a poignant reminder of the conflict's role in shaping Canadian nationalism.

The War at Home

The war's impact on the home front was equally important for shaping the country's history, for it touched all Canadians at some level. Women served as nurses, in various voluntary organizations such as the Imperial Order Daughters of the Empire, and in government-funded social services. Thousands of women entered the heavy workforce, including dangerous occupations such as manufacturing munitions. Eager to help in the war effort, women also wanted to break the long-standing obstacles to their presence in vocations outside of education, clerical work, and light factory employment. The country's economy expanded dramatically as it gained a major role in providing war materiel and foodstuffs for the Allied effort. Canadian factories churned out goods that ranged from clothing to ships. The war effort considerably boosted grain production and increased the market for minerals and timber products.

The federal government expanded its power during the war to orchestrate economic production. By 1918 it actively regulated everything from crop distribution to the right of laborers to strike. Under the leadership of the successful businessman Joseph Flavelle, for example, the Imperial Munitions Board became a model of efficiency. The war's legacy for Canada's economy was in fact two-edged. The furious expansion of its productive might, particularly in the East, edged the country closer to an industrial-oriented economy. There was little question that war was good for business and massive employment. Detracting from the glow provided by a flush economy was an increase in inflation, the institution of income and business profits taxes, and a rationing of goods and foodstuffs. Although a series of Victory Bond drives raised millions of dollars—over eighty percent of the total cost of the war effort—they ultimately placed the country in tremendous debt. The government also moved during the war to take control of the vast railroad networks that had been constructed in a bout of enthusiasm at the turn of the century. With western expansion peaking before the war, the Canadian Northern and the Grand Trunk Pacific soon faced bankruptcy. The government's absorption of these and other troubled railroads led to the creation of the Canadian National Railways by the early 1920s.

The war exacted its most severe domestic toll on Halifax, which served as a staging ground for convoys of merchant ships before they headed across the Atlantic. In December 1917 two ships collided in the city's harbor. In a devastating moment, the explosion of a French ship packed with munitions flattened a great portion of the city, created a tidal wave, and set off fires that ravaged the surrounding area. More than 1,600 perished, and thousands were wounded. The Halifax tragedy stands in history as the largest man-made explosion before the

United States dropped an atomic bomb on Hiroshima in August 1945. By the war's close, the lives of Canadians from all age groups, regions, and ethnic backgrounds had been irrevocably altered.

Conscription and the Union Government

Mindful of the country's divided opinion during imperial conflicts such as the South African War, Borden's government promised that the Great War would be fought exclusively by volunteers. The war lasted far longer than its supporters had originally anticipated, however, and by 1916 there was an alarming decline in the number of recruits. Convinced that the war effort was imperative for Canada's survival and that the level of the country's armed forces should be maintained despite the mounting casualties, Borden risked criticism and broached the idea of conscription. Opposition to the war had already been dealt with severely by the government. Upwards of 8,000 people had been interned under the terms of the War Measures Act, including German and Austro-Hungarian immigrants and radical dissenters. Nonetheless, the call for conscripts sparked intense opposition.

Conscription resisters included farmers, laborers, married men, and pacifists. Yet contemporaries focused primarily on opposition among French Canadians. The latter were still upset about Regulation 17, a provincial measure that eroded French language rights in Ontario's educational system before the war. Quebec was the traditional seat of the anti-imperial argument. Moreover, there was a widespread opinion that the protection of France, the old imperial master that had abandoned the *Canadiens* to their fate in North America at the Conquest, was not an endeavor that warranted the spilling of Canadian blood. In addition, the military discriminated against French-Canadian volunteers in a variety of ways. Still, the government forged ahead with the Military Service Act in the summer of 1917. The Conservatives also tried to broaden their political base to include Liberals who supported the war effort. An appeal to Wilfrid Laurier to join with the Conservatives to form a Union party failed. Other Liberals, however, embraced the idea (see "An Argument Against Conscription" in the Documents section).

With the machinery for conscription underway, Borden instituted plans to reformulate the government for the war effort. He called for an election in the fall of 1917 to have voters give approval to the newly constituted Union government, which included Liberal war supporters. To ensure a Union victory the government passed two statutes that extended the vote to women in the military and female relatives of servicemen, and prohibited the vote to conscientious objectors. By stacking the deck in favor of a pro-Union election, the government opened the franchise to selected women and inadvertently accelerated the campaign for female suffrage.

A Union victory in 1917 brought in a reformulated government that lasted until 1920. It also exacerbated relations between Quebec and the rest of the country. Without the support of Laurier and anti-imperialists such as Henri Bourassa, francophone Quebec voters roundly rejected the Union government and, by definition, conscription. Antidraft riots broke out in Montreal and Quebec City in 1917 and 1918. Conscription was a painful reaffirmation of the different visions that Canadians held for the country's future. To many anglophones and imperialists, the country's obligation was to support the British Empire at all costs. To most francophones and other war critics, Canada's proper destiny lay in North America. The call for conscripts yielded an extraordinarily large number of claimants for exemptions, mostly for farming or family hardship. In total, fewer than 25,000 conscripts made the journey overseas. Most historians agree that the negative cost of conscription in disunity far outweighed its positive results by replenishing the depleted military forces. The bitter memories of the conscription crisis had barely subsided before another global conflict reintroduced the question of whether Canadians should be required to serve in the military in a foreign war.

Peace and the Framework for a New World

The Great War highlighted contradictory impulses in Canada. Many historians have argued, for example, that the war acted as a bonding agent to give Canadians a sense of national purpose. Others maintain that Canadian national unity, both political and social, was damaged by the event. Various crosscurrents cleaved the country along ethnic, language, ideological, and class lines. Another paradox concerned the country's role in the empire. Undoubtedly Canada's military and domestic war efforts underscored its commitment to Britain. At the same time, the Canadian government consciously used the crisis as a platform to gain more autonomy in the postwar era.

A test for this approach came with the protracted peace talks that concluded the Great War and established a new world body, the League of Nations. Both British Prime Minister David Lloyd George and American President Woodrow Wilson originally opposed the idea that Canada and the other dominions should attend the negotiations as separate nations. Borden and the other dominion leaders, pointing to their casualties and America's belated entry into the war, prevailed in their arguments for separate representation. Consequently Canada attended the treaty meetings as both a separate country and as part of the British Empire's delegation. Although the actual impact of Canada's contribution to the peace process was negligible, these events were of utmost significance for two reasons. The principle that Canada deserved its own representation at the negotiations was an important leap forward in the country's evolution to become an independent nation. Canada also joined the League of Nations, an international body that had been the last of President Woodrow Wilson's Fourteen Points, which were designed to avoid another global conflict. Canada and over sixty countries joined the organization, although ironically the Americans declined after Wilson lost an acrimonious power struggle with the Senate. Canadians had reservations with the League's collective security clause; nonetheless in the 1920s and 1930s, the country participated in its deliberations and committees. Canada's active relationship with the League of Nations became an important training ground for its developing independence. World War I had thus wrought yet another change for the country by accelerating the political and popular resolve to seek a foreign policy independent of Britain's.

Women and the Vote

The war created a favorable environment for the final phase of the struggle for women's suffrage at the federal level. Women in early nineteenth-century British North America sometimes had access to the franchise because they held property or capital, but all the colonies by midcentury had passed legislation to restrict the vote to property-owning males. At the time of Confederation, only about one-fifth of Canada's males could vote. The struggle for female suffrage in Canada, part of an international impulse that included Britain and the United States, was linked to women's improved access to higher education and their activity in reform issues. After 1875 the Women's Christian Temperance Union, for example, targeted the prohibition of alcoholic beverages, but it also advocated women's suffrage and other reforms. The Toronto Women's Literary Club, formed about the same time by Dr. Emily Stowe, was really a forum for discussing women's suffrage.

Canadian women made the greatest suffrage inroads in the prairies during World War I. Due to the energies of articulate suffrage champions such as Nellie McClung, a Manitoban writer, the movement gained momentum in the 1910s. In 1916 Manitoba became the first province to open the franchise to women, followed quickly by the other western provinces. Ontario (1917), Nova Scotia (1918), New Brunswick (1919), and Prince Edward Island (1922) took the western provinces' lead. The combined impact of opening the franchise at the provincial level, coupled with the statutes passed by the Conservative government to ensure a Union victory in 1917, led to the national franchise for women in 1918. The province of Quebec, which no doubt responded according to its traditions and the conservative power of the Roman Catholic church, resisted the progressive impulse; it denied women the right to vote provincially until 1940. The federal election of 1921 witnessed Canada's first elected female member of Parliament, Agnes Macphail, an Ontario schoolteacher who endorsed improved conditions for farmers. Although women broke the suffrage barrier in most of the country by the 1920s, they continued to be a small minority of the House of Commons, the Senate, and other elected and appointed offices (see "A Case for Women's Suffrage" in the Documents section).

Canada in the Twenties: Roaring or Whimpering?

The experiences of Canadians from the end of the Great War through the advent of the Great Depression in 1929 varied substantially. On one level, the country emerged from the war a stronger nation, with a greater industrial base and expanding cities. At the same time, class

issues persisted as workers and farmers struggled to achieve rights
and gain protection from workplace abuses. Many sectors of the
economy flourished during the 1920s; others remained in the
doldrums. The two main political parties experienced important
leadership changes, while other parties formed to represent the
interests of groups that had become disillusioned with the Conservatives and Liberals. The economic and social divisions between
the regions appeared more sharply defined than during the war.
Applying the classic characterization of "roaring" to describe Canada
in the 1920s would be misleading. Yet much evidence suggests that
the decade was a strong and progressive one for Canadian national
development. Interestingly, the era's ambiguities are illustrated
perfectly in the behavior of its dominant political leader: William
Lyon Mackenzie King.

Postwar Political Themes

The immediate postwar era brought a watershed in political leadership
for both of the traditional parties, as well as a favorable climate for
constructing alternative parties. Robert Borden, exhausted and in
poor health, turned over the leadership of the Union government
to one of his cabinet members, the intelligent and prickly Arthur
Meighen. In the election of 1921 Meighen's party, renamed the
Conservatives, met a crushing defeat. Even the newly created
Progressive party sent more representatives to Ottawa than did the
Conservatives.

The Liberals mounted a victory in 1921 behind the leadership of
Mackenzie King, a party stalwart who had replaced Laurier when he
died in 1919. An effective compromiser, the grandson of the rebel
William Lyon Mackenzie would miraculously dominate Canadian
politics for the better part of three decades. King's life has been
heavily dissected, thanks primarily to his extensive personal journals,
yet he remains an enigmatic historical figure. Given to spiritualism
and receiving guidance from the afterlife, including his deceased
mother, King was poorly understood by Canadians in his own times.
His political survival skills, however, are in no doubt.

King's political scheme was frustratingly elusive for both contemporaries and historians who try to understand his uncanny

ability to remain in power. Moderation, sprinkled liberally with doses of obfuscation, seemed to be his watchwords. King deserves full credit, however, for his ability to retain the confidence of francophone voters. He regularly consulted his key Quebec political confidant, Ernest Lapointe, who held various cabinet positions until his death in 1941. The most identifiable Liberal programs of the 1920s were modest tariff reductions, the pursuit of an old age pension system, and increasing Canada's ability to act autonomously within the context of the British Empire.

The Liberals shifted their position to the left after the advent of the Progressive party, led by Thomas Alexander Crerar. The Progressives enjoyed a tremendous appeal in the West and Ontario among farmers and laborers. Their program, called the New National Policy, envisioned the active use of government to forward socialistic causes. These included lower tariffs, public ownership of utilities and railroads, and more direct democracy through the frequent use of referendums. One of King's initial success stories as prime minister was to lure many of the Progressives back to the Liberal party. By advocating tariff revisions, King effectively coopted the most powerful and unifying element of the Progressive party's plan.

In the wake of the election of 1925, by most accounts one of the least stimulating in the country's history, came political and constitutional crises that had far-reaching implications. With only modest accomplishments to celebrate, the Liberals barely lost to the Conservatives under Arthur Meighen. According to precedent, the Conservatives should have had the opportunity to form a government. Instead, the wily Mackenzie King orchestrated a series of parliamentary maneuvers to keep the Liberals in power with the help of the Progressives. This precipitated a convoluted and at times bizarre tussle between King and the popular governor general, Lord Byng. Byng's opposition to King's tactics, as well as the latter's desire to avoid a newly exposed scandal in his government, led to a dissolution of Parliament. Although Meighen had been prime minister for a brief period, Canadian voters were forced to return to the polls in 1926. King campaigned on the issue that the British-appointed Byng had overstepped his bounds and was trying to drag Canada back into colonial status. The Conservatives tried unsuccessfully to target the campaign on the scandal and King's dubious political behavior. The Liberals reversed their political fortunes in less than one year as they reclaimed control of the House of Commons in 1926, in large part because King had masterfully turned the event into a referendum on greater Canadian independence from Great Britain.

Temperance

A temperance movement that advocated the total or partial abstinence of alcoholic beverages, which had been growing during the nineteenth century, achieved a measure of success during and following World War I. Groups such as the Women's Christian Temperance Union lobbied to have legislation passed that would control the manufacturing and transportation of alcoholic products. A mixture of factors drove the prohibitionists, including urban problems, religion, and the perception that certain immigrant groups, such as the Irish and the Germans, abused alcoholic beverages. Motivated by patriotic messages that grains should be used for the war effort rather than in creating alcoholic beverages, all of the provinces, with the exception of Quebec, prohibited the sale of alcohol during the war. The federal government prohibited the manufacture, sale, and importation of alcohol in 1918, a measure that barely outlasted the war. By the 1920s the federal government and most of the provinces had abandoned their brief experiment with prohibition. Canada's production of alcoholic beverages continued apace in the 1920s, driven largely by a booming illegal trade to a United States that was engaged in the "noble experiment" of prohibition. The Bronfman family, for example, parlayed their Seagram Company into the world's greatest distillers largely by slaking a prodigious American thirst. Although Canada's prohibition experiment was short-lived, it illustrated a growing belief that government should be used to control the social behavior of individuals.

Workers and the Economy

Tensions among laborers and farmers had been building in Canada since the nineteenth century. Canadian workers echoed concerns that reached across national boundaries as industrial capitalism became entrenched in the Western world. Factories were typically dangerous and unhealthy places. Employees in the staples industries and manual laborers toiled long hours for low wages without health protections or benefits. Nineteenth-century labor organizations, such as the Knights of Labor, aggressively pursued the ideal of an eight-hour workday, legislation to protect workers' health and improve work environments, and the termination of child labor. While the Knights of Labor appealed to semiskilled and unskilled labor, various Trades and Labor Congress unions sought the support of more skilled workers. By the early twentieth century, the Trades and Labor organizations had been coupled with the powerful American Federation of Labor (AFL). Through the 1910s various labor organizations, ranging from the more conservative AFL to the radical unionists of the Industrial Workers of the World, known as the Wobblies, strove to draw workers into their ranks. Thousands of strikes erupted before and during the war, yet the federal and provincial governments were reluctant to pass meaningful legislation to protect the rights of workers. Laurier's government did create the Department of Labour and pass the Industrial Disputes Investigation Act in 1907, yet the statute essentially favored businesses.

Various labor struggles cropped up in the postwar era, thereby illustrating the complex labor-capital issues of the era. General inflation, the favored treatment of manufacturers, and rising unemployment led to a rash of strikes. During the most dramatic labor action, the Winnipeg General Strike of 1919, thousands of workers effectively shut down the city's services for weeks. Alarmed citizens, mindful of recent events that had transpired in Russia, incorrectly branded the general strike a pro-Bolshevik uprising. When the federal government intervened and the strike leaders were arrested, a violent confrontation broke out between the Royal North-West Mounted Police and protesting workers. The strike's collapse effectively undermined the recently formed One Big Union, a socialist-inspired movement of workers. Dramatic clashes, particularly in coal-producing regions such as Nova Scotia, continued in the 1920s, a reminder that deep class divisions existed in Canada.

Although their efforts lacked some of the high drama and bloodshed of the labor protests, farmers pursued similar agendas during the postwar era. With the perennial issue of tariffs weighing heavily on their minds and a downturn in the demand for the country's grain as the war came to an end, Canadian farmers sought relief in the political arena. Farmers' parties emerged in Ontario and the prairies. The Progressive party also drew heavy support from farmers for its goal of lowering the tariffs.

Sectors of the Canadian economy boomed in the 1920s, assisted directly and indirectly by provincial and federal governments that were eager to facilitate the country's expansion. Wheat production soared as the decade progressed, but competition with other grain-producing countries intensified as well. The paper and pulp industry, dominated by a few giant corporations, led the word in exports by the late 1920s. Spurred by improved hydroelectric production, Canada developed consumer industries and increased its capabilities to extract mineral resources such as nickel. The automobile industry burgeoned, as did the development of roads and services needed to serve an increasingly mobile society. Large chain stores, such as Eaton's, carried the most modern consumer goods, appliances, and fashions. The reliance on the export market to sustain the country's economy, particularly in the primary sectors of agricultural, mining, and timber products, would deliver a devastating blow to Canada when the Great Depression hit. But for much of the decade, a robust economy dominated. Indeed, the country crossed an important statistical threshold in the 1920s when its economy became more industrial than agricultural in total output and production.

Canadian Culture in the 1920s

Canada also became a nation in which more of its people lived in larger towns and cities than in rural settings during the 1920s. Its culture in the postwar era reflected a growing sense of national self-definition, often anchored to the cities, but just as typically embracing the country's rugged terrain and the grittiness of the Canadian peoples. Writers, editors, artists, radio employees, academics, and musicians combined to create a Canadian-defined culture. While some focused more on regions, such as Quebec or the Far North, many attempted to develop a sense of collective identity. Formed in the 1920s after the death of artist Tom Thomson, a collection of painters known as the Group of Seven created landscapes that have become some of the most recognizable paintings ever produced in Canada. Journals, both academic and popular, carved out respectable followings. Poets, fiction writers, and musicians, many operating in cities and university settings, authored and performed works that reached a broad audience. Periodicals such as *Maclean's, Saturday Night, Canadian Home Journal, Chatelaine*, and *Mayfair* scrambled to compete with American imports. A lobbying organization, the Magazine Publishers Association of Canada, brought few concrete results. In addition, the Aird Commission of 1928 recommended that a public broadcasting network would provide cultural unity for the country in the face of popular American radio stations. The Canadian Broadcasting Corporation was created in 1932 to achieve this end. Numerous writers and artists thus helped to fashion a Canadian identity in the 1920s, but they did so in the shadow of a more powerful, and thus threatening, American culture.

Canada and the Triangle in the Postwar Era

Canada's connections with the United States and Britain altered dramatically in the postwar era. In a milestone barely noticed at the time, the United States surpassed Britain as Canada's biggest trading partner and greatest investor in the 1920s. Two important events with the United States signaled a relationship that was becoming more bilateral and direct in nature. In 1923 Canada and the United States signed an agreement to regulate Pacific coastal fisheries. From both a global and American frame of reference, the Halibut Treaty was quite modest; nevertheless, it signaled an important step by Canada to formulate its own agreements without British intervention. The two countries also established formal ministries in each other's capitals in 1927. The forerunners of embassies, these ministries symbolized the historical linkages between the North American nations. Similar connections closely followed with France and Japan.

Canada's changing relationship with Britain in the postwar era was of equal import. Canadian input was instrumental during several British treaty negotiations involving Japan and other Western powers. When war tensions flared between Britain and Turkey in

1922, King's government dragged its heels in responding to the British call for support. Most important, the dominions and Britain formalized a new relationship. Meetings in 1926 between dominion leaders and British representatives yielded a key statement from the conference chairman, Lord Balfour. It recommended the formalization of "autonomous Communities within the British Empire, equal in status, in no way subordinate one to another in any aspect of their domestic or external affairs, though united by a common allegiance to the Crown, and freely associated as members of the British Commonwealth of Nations." This report became the basis of the 1931 Statute of Westminster, which created the Commonwealth and effectively gave the dominions, including Canada, the power to act independently in matters of foreign policy. The bonds to Britain remained durable, however, for the BNA Act remained a British statute. Thus, the 1920s witnessed alterations in the triangular relationship. By 1931 Canada had carved out a stronger bilateral relationship with its southern neighbor and entered into a more equal Commonwealth agreement with its former imperial master.

Canada Through War and Peace

The period from the late 1890s to the late 1920s brought sweeping changes to Canada. Tremendous physical and demographic expansion had finally created a country that was interconnected coast to coast. The crisis of the Great War had paradoxically forged a new sense of nationalism and combined purpose and simultaneously introduced disagreements about conscription that threatened to rend the national fabric along ethnic and language lines. The country faced traumatic adjustments after the war, yet many Canadians flourished in the expansive economy of the 1920s. Mainstream political parties attempted to build a common interest among Canadians for national development, while newer and issue-focused parties appealed to various regions and classes. Finally, Canada modestly joined the world stage as it reformulated its relationship with its most important partners, Britain and the United States. If, as some historians maintain, this was one of the greatest periods of national maturation and the formulation of self-identity for the peoples of Canada, it was also undeniably a time of stress and limited achievement in gaining a truly autonomous stature. The breathtaking financial crisis of 1929, which precipitated a massive economic depression that persisted for over a decade, would be a signal reminder of how closely interlinked Canada's fate had become with its neighbor.

Chapter 7

Trial of Nationhood: The Great Depression and the War (1929–1945)

Canada Comes of Age

Canada came of age in the period bracketed by the two world wars. The country's experience defied a simple characterization in the 1920s. A boom in certain sectors of the economy and an expanding middle class seemed to suggest that Canada was healthy and forward looking. Yet large numbers of Canadians, especially laborers and small farmers, scrambled to obtain essentials and agitated for increased rights by striking or participating in the political arena. In addition, Canada used its impressive wartime contribution as leverage to secure more control over its foreign policy. As the country incrementally pulled away from the British Empire in terms of trade, investments, and policies, it drew closer to the American economic and cultural orbit. Canada's largest trading partner by the end of the 1920s was the United States, and the country's traditional reliance on British investments to supplement its economic growth was shifting to American dollars.

The next two decades illuminated the implications of this changing relationship. An economic downturn, the deepest depression in Canada's history, strained the country's international relationships

Canadian soldiers arriving aboard a troopship for training in Britain, probably taken in 1940.

Source: Library and Archives Canada / Department of National Defence Fonds / C-064029

and created untold misery for its citizens. The contest between governments gained momentum during the Great Depression as the balance of powers shifted from Ottawa to the provinces. Caught up in the whirlwind of dramatic changes and relatively protected in North America by two oceans and a powerful southern neighbor, Canada in the 1940s would essentially reach full national status. The victory that followed another global conflict, this one even more horrific in magnitude than the Great War, was mitigated by another conscription crisis and the restriction of rights for certain ethnic groups. In the early Cold War years, Canadians would come to grips with their new status as a major world player as they grappled with the frightening prospect of international conflict in the nuclear era. From the collapse of the stock market in 1929 to the raging Cold War of the late 1940s, Canada endured a trial of nationhood.

A Global Depression

A series of jolts in the American stock market beginning in October 1929 kindled an economic collapse that reached far beyond the confines of New York, but it was not the only cause of the Great Depression in Canada. The country's economic growth after the war was born largely of export industries and the rise of consumer markets for items, such as automobiles and refrigerators, which an expanding middle class desired. Foreign trade and investment accounted for about one-third of Canada's income in the late 1920s. Many industries that forged the boom were entirely or partially owned by Americans. Stock prices reached exorbitant levels in Montreal and Toronto, just as they had in New York, driven by the unbounded enthusiasm of investors. Similarly, real estate and land speculation swelled. Exporters, particularly in wheat, increasingly pooled their produce and waited for the most favorable market prices to make their sales. Canada's growing reliance on trade with the United States and investment capital from Americans linked the country's economic fate to its neighbor's. As an old saying goes: when the United States sneezes, Canada catches cold. The events that followed the stock market collapse of 1929 illustrated the popular expression's wisdom. Although depressions had been a cyclical feature of economic life for Canadians as capitalism became entrenched, the magnitude of this downturn surpassed the others. Before the Depression's veil was lifted by the onset of another global war, Canadians would have spent a decade coping with the grisly realities of life during the "Dirty Thirties."

Within a year of the stock market crisis, Canada as well as a host of other countries interlinked by trade, markets, technologies, and investments, was mired in a depression. Prices declined sharply, foreign orders for Canadian minerals, wheat, and newsprint plummeted, and the country's trading partners erected high tariff barriers to protect their own industries. Virtually every economic monitor pointed to a shattered economy. The staggering statistics of the economy's free fall from 1929 to the mid-1930s, the Depression's nadir, would fill volumes. The country's national income decreased by almost one-half in those years. In the same period, the income generated by its crucial export industry dropped by about two-thirds. All sectors of the economy were hurt by the Depression: industry, banking, transportation, service, mining, forest products, fishing, and farming. All of the country's regions suffered, although some historians argue that the Maritimers were partially cushioned from trauma because their economy had been lagging since the dominion's creation. Perhaps they had less of a distance to fall in the deteriorating economy of the early depression years.

No other section of the country was hit harder than the prairies. The economic problems, coupled with dramatic climatic conditions and regular visitations by swarms of crop-devouring pests, created a disastrous scenario in Canada's grain belt. The fate of Saskatchewan's farmers during the depression became perhaps the starkest example of the misery inflicted during the Dirty Thirties. A relatively prosperous breadbasket in the 1920s, Saskatchewan experienced a farm income decline of about ninety percent in the space of several years. A series of severe droughts from 1933 through mid-decade, coupled with high winds, created the infamous dust bowl that reached from Texas to the Canadian prairies. Once-fertile topsoil, now bone dry, was picked up and swirled about. Some of the Depression's most alarming images were captured by the cameras of Canadians and Americans during the dust bowl years.

The shattering of Canada's economy, from Vancouver to Halifax, heralded difficult adjustments for virtually all of the country's inhabitants. The international scope of the collapse led to a profound loss of confidence in capitalism. With a crisis of such magnitude, Canadians looked to their federal and provincial governments for support and strategies to find their way out of the quagmire.

Governmental Responses to the Depression

Mackenzie King's government had been in power for most of the 1920s when the Depression hit. Like other government leaders, including U.S. President Herbert Hoover, King believed that the downturn was more political than economic in nature and that it would not last long. In one of his most famous utterances, he called the events a "temporary seasonal slackness." In fact, the Liberal government had made little progress in the 1920s to provide support for farmers and working people. The most significant piece of legislation in the category of social assistance was the Old Age Pension Plan, passed in 1927, which committed the government to paying half of a modest pension for people over the age of seventy. With that single legislative exception noted, Canada greeted the Depression without a substantial safety net of relief agencies for its citizens. A plan to have the federal government provide unemployment relief was decreed inappropriate by the Privy Council in 1925, thereby leaving the responsibility in provincial hands.

As unemployment mounted dramatically, Canadians turned to their communities and provincial governments for assistance. The magnitude of the crisis rapidly depleted provincial relief agencies, and in a much regretted and endlessly repeated comment, King declared in the House of Commons that he would not give "a five cent piece" from federal funds to help out Conservative provincial governments. Although he was specifically referencing the Tory provincial government in Ontario in his declaration, Canadians widely interpreted King's observation as proof of his insensitivity and lack of understanding of the despondency that people were already experiencing. Indeed King's actions, including cutting expenditures and balancing the budget, tended to aggravate the situation. With the country's economy spiraling downward while the prime minister made the situation worse, the time appeared ripe for the Conservatives to recapture the federal government.

Taking the lead in the 1930s elections was a feisty New Brunswick-born millionaire, Richard Bedford Bennett. A successful lawyer and businessman who had made his wealth in Calgary, Bennett deeply criticized the Liberals' inability to fix the Depression malaise. "Bonfire Bennett," as he was dubbed, effectively used the relatively new medium of radio to spread his message throughout the land. By promising to use protective tariffs to "blast" Canada out of the depression, a tactic used by economic nationalists in other countries, the Conservatives handily won a government that would be in power until 1935. The vanquished King noted in his diary that Bennett had made promises he could not keep and that the Conservative government would unravel under the strain of the Depression. On more than one occasion, King's predictions proved insightful. This was one such moment.

To his credit, Bennett worked tirelessly. He took on the responsibilities of several cabinet positions, including the external affairs portfolio. His stringent monetary policies guided his first years as prime minister. Following the lead of other nations, Canada raised tariffs in the early 1930s, which unfortunately served to deepen the Depression because so much of Canada's economy had relied on export trade. Tariffs provided modest relief to Ontario and Quebec, the seat of Canada's wealth, but they did little for the rest of the country. His attempts in 1932 to create preferential tariffs among Commonwealth members failed to gather enough support among the British, although it led to some modest improvements in trading items such as wheat and forest products. Funds to assist the unemployed were generated by the Unemployment Relief Act of 1932. The federal government provided close to $350 million for the unemployed and farmers by late in the decade, but given the magnitude of the crisis, the resources were woefully insufficient to provide comprehensive relief to a citizenry in dire straits.

Three institutions critical to Canada's economic and cultural development emerged in the traumatic depression years. During the 1920s radio became a popular and accessible form of entertainment for Canadians, as it did throughout the Western world. While radio stations spread across the country, most Canadians lived close enough to the U.S. border to receive their neighbor's transmissions. Many Canadians preferred to listen to popular American programs such as *Amos 'n' Andy* and *The Jack Benny Radio Program*. The idea of protecting Canadian-generated programs, first discussed by the Aird Commission in the late 1920s, spawned the forerunner of the Canadian Broadcasting Corporation (CBC) in 1932. The CBC was designed to provide cultural and information linkages that would span Canada's vast geographical terrain. In the 1930s *Hockey Night in Canada* with Foster Hewitt became a national fixture, combining the country's love for hockey and popular radio programming to attract a broad audience. While the power of the CBC to develop pan-Canadian cultural linkages would not come into full blossom until World War II, the impulse to use the era's dominant technology to provide a nationalistic tool to bind the country was rooted to the Depression years.

Second, the National Film Board was established in 1939 to resuscitate a fledgling Canadian film industry that had emerged in the 1920s. The explosive growth of American films presented Canadian filmmakers with a formidable challenge for survival. Making matters worse, Canadians sought employment in the world's emerging movie capital: Hollywood. The long saga of the drain of Canadian screen artists to the south began in the 1920s, starting with the irony that the great silent film star, Mary Pickford, nicknamed "America's sweetheart," was born and raised in Ontario. Legendary director Mack Sennett, another Canadian, heard Hollywood's siren song. The continuous line between Pickford and Michael J. Fox is a matter of deep concern for Canadians, who want to protect their culture and keep their talent. The creation of the National Film Board would prove to be a boon for Canadian filmmakers. It evolved into a great source of national pride when it sponsored award-winning films after World War II.

Finally, the Depression created a context for Bennett's government to establish the Bank of Canada. It began operation in 1935 as a private company but was nationalized three years later. The bank was envisioned as an overarching institution to provide a clearinghouse to regulate currency and maintain some fiscal control over other banks. These three creations, coupled with other governmental measures from the late 1910s and 1920s, demonstrated the federal government's impulse to manage banking, transportation, and cultural industries. The escalating degree of government involvement in the lives of Canadians elicited both positive reactions and angry objections. Despite the country's severe financial problems during the Depression, the 1930s saw an increase in federally controlled organizations.

Despite his diligence, Bennett received a great deal of criticism from a broad spectrum of Canadians. Facing an election in 1935, the Bennett government unexpectedly took a cue from the Americans and introduced a legislative barrage that was designed to alleviate the effects of the Depression. The package of laws, called the "New Deal," included measures to increase government's control over businesses and improve the plight of workers. Bennett's "New Deal" utterly failed to shift Canada from its predicament. Members of his own party, still deeply committed to conservative fiscal and social values, were deeply shocked by a plan that borrowed heavily from the left-leaning American Democrats. Equally important, social critics on the left considered the measures inadequate.

Stung by attacks from both political wings and now the brunt of "Bennettisms"—joke phrases wherein Canadians used his name to characterize their lives, such as "Bennett barnyards" for abandoned farms— Bennett faced the election of 1935 at a distinct disadvantage. His party lost in a landslide to the irrepressible Mackenzie King, who ran a campaign long on catchy slogans, such as "King or Chaos," but surprisingly short on a clear scheme for tackling the depression. Bennett's "New Deal" incentive disintegrated in the space of several years, undermined by a combination of legislative defeats and adverse court decisions. Bennett later moved to England, forever embittered that Canadians had so thoroughly intertwined the Depression's misery with his political career. King returned to the country's leadership in 1935 without a plan for reconstruction. In many ways, the human dimensions of the Dirty Thirties was the decade's most compelling story.

The Human Dimension of the Great Depression

Discussions of national economies and trade tend to mask the personal costs of an international depression. The human suffering created by a collapsed export market, decimated stock values, mounting unemployment, and weather catastrophes is virtually impossible to capture in a brief historical overview. Canada's unemployment figures reached tragic proportions. By the time the Depression reached its lowest point in 1933, more than one-fifth of the country's labor force was out of work. This needs to be considered in the light of unemployment figures that hovered in the low single digits before the 1929 crash. Particularly hard hit were industrial laborers, unskilled workers, and farmers. Regional figures in particularly depressed areas were even more dramatic. Without comprehensive unemployment protection, many Canadians were forced to turn to relief from municipalities and the provinces, as well as private charities. With their savings exhausted, thousands swallowed their pride and sought relief. They went on the "pogey," as it was bitterly called, to receive food and used clothing. The poignant stories of Canadians deeply scarred by the Depression emerged in many forms, including a rash of letters to Prime Minister Bennett from people seeking his assistance. In one such letter in 1935, an Albertan farm woman asked for a small loan from Bennett and offered her engagement ring as collateral (see "Letters from the Heartland" in the Documents section).

Growing resentment about the government's inadequacy in coping with the economic crisis merged with mounting popular fears of the growing numbers of unemployed. Many Canadians were especially concerned about young, single males, hundreds of whom were hitching rides on the railroads in a desperate search for employment. These considerations led the federal government to establish unemployment relief camps in 1932. They were run by the Department of Defence under the direction of General Andrew McNaughton, who achieved fame as a military leader and munitions expert during the Great War. Most of the two hundred camps were tucked far away from cities, women, alcohol, and the perils of radical ideologies. Men lived in military-style barracks and toiled at menial jobs clearing brush and building roads and airstrips. They earned twenty cents a day, hence the "Royal Twenty Centers" nickname. About 170,000 young men spent time in one of the relief camps in the four years of their existence. The plan to insulate the men from radical notions failed miserably, as the wretched conditions and austere lifestyle led thousands to join various communist-inspired unions to agitate for better treatment and pay. Thousands filtered from British Columbian camps to occupy public buildings in Vancouver in 1935.

Tensions mounted, leading panicky citizens to conclude that a revolution was at hand. About two thousand relief workers hopped the Canadian Pacific Railway to head east to meet with government leaders. The so-called On-to-Ottawa Trek got as far as Regina, where tempers flared and eventually degenerated into a bloody clash between the workers and police. Over one hundred trekkers were arrested, and Bennett unwisely fanned the tensions by suggesting that the protest was inspired by "reds." The episode highlighted the class divisions in mid-Depression Canada and helped to sour many voters on Bennett's style of governance. Despite the claims of the alarmists, the country was far from the brink of a revolution or class warfare. Nonetheless, the Depression clearly opened the floodgates for parties outside the political mainstream that appealed to Canadians on the left and the right.

Political Storms: Left, Right, and Center

Many of the ideals expressed by critics of the centralist politics of both the Conservatives and Liberals reached back into the nineteenth century. The high drama of the Depression and the failure of the two main parties to offer substantial relief and imaginative solutions to move the country beyond the crisis created an opportunity for other parties to mount formidable challenges at both the federal and provincial levels. Moreover, the Depression served to intensify the struggle between the federal government and the provinces, especially the powerful and largest provinces of Ontario, Quebec, and British Columbia. Overall, the changing political agendas during the depression helped to shift the mainstream parties to the left. They also sharpened questions regarding which powers should be controlled by the federal or provincial governments.

A mixture of laborer- and farmer-oriented leaders, many of whom had political roots in the Progressive party, met at Calgary in 1932 to address the need for substantial social and political changes in the country. An academic organization spearheaded by historian Frank Underhill, the League for Social Reconstruction, agreed to put together a comprehensive platform. The group met the following year to approve the Regina Manifesto and adopt a new name: the

Co-operative Commonwealth Federation (CCF). Boldly left leaning, inspired by social consciousness and a belief in the replacement of the capitalist system, the manifesto forwarded a socialist program for the country. It called for centralized government control over economic planning and banking, the public ownership of transportation, communication, and natural resources, and a comprehensive plan for unemployment insurance, national health care, and slum clearance. In sum, it expressed a classic socialist ideal of using the government to create a socially just and classless environment for Canadians (see "The CCF Platform" in the Documents section).

The widespread damage inflicted by the Depression meant that the party stood a good chance of capturing votes at the next election. Led by James Shaver Woodsworth, a Methodist minister and labor supporter, the party captured seven seats in the House of Commons in 1935 and thereafter became a vigorous political force in the western provinces. To many voters in Quebec and the Maritimes, the CCF was too radical. Although it never gained enough members of Parliament to lead the federal government, it undoubtedly shaped politics by promoting its social programs and ideas of the positive use of state stewardship. For example, Tommy Douglas became Saskatchewan's CCF premier in 1944, and his government designed the prototype of national health care that the federal government adopted in the 1960s. The CCF joined other labor forces in 1961 to become the New Democratic party (NDP), the predominant leftist political organization to this day in Canada.

The Depression also prompted a global search for political panaceas, or quick and simple solutions for the complex problems of the era. The rise of Alberta's Social Credit party provides the strongest Canadian example of this dynamic. Under the leadership of a high school principal and Baptist preacher, "Bible Bill" Aberhart, the party adopted a program developed by an eccentric Scots engineer named C.H. Douglas. The principle of social credit, rejected by virtually all contemporary economists, proposed to save the capitalistic system by having governments control prices and provide periodic payments to its citizens. Through an effective use of radio, Aberhart and his party gained control of the province in 1935. Legislative attempts to implement a monetary dividend of $25 a month for each citizen and other Social Credit ideas were rejected by the federal government and various courts. Nonetheless, the party remained in power for a quarter-century. Over time it migrated to British Columbia, where it evolved to become an extremely conservative party.

The Depression also provided an environment for strong, and often repressive, political behavior in other provinces. Historical inequities in Quebec, with a tradition of anglophone control over businesses and investments, reached a crescendo during the traumatic Dirty Thirties. Weaving together aspects of French-Canadian nationalism, conservative politics, Roman Catholicism, and anti-communism, lawyer Maurice Duplessis became Quebec's premier in 1936 as the leader of the Union Nationale party. A chorus of French-Canadian nationalist voices, gathering force since the appearance in the 1920s of *L'Action française*, a journal spearheaded by the cleric and historian Lionel Groulx, advocated francophone cultural survival in Duplessis's Quebec. The social messages used in campaign rhetoric swiftly disappeared, however, and under the strong arm of Duplessis, *le chef*, the Union Nationale passed restrictive laws against communists and repressed laborers and unions. Similarly, Ontario's Liberal premier, Mitchell Hepburn, used special police forces, nicknamed "sons of Mitches," to crush strikes. Ontario witnessed over one hundred strikes in 1937 alone, the most comprehensive of which involved General Motors in Oshawa. Combined, these feisty political activities in several of Canada's largest provinces mounted a formidable assault on the federal government's powers during the 1930s, especially after King's return in 1935. Thus, the Depression had yet another important impact on Canada: economic turmoil and social dislocation severely tested the federal-provincial bonds of nationhood.

In response to these problems, Mackenzie King charged a commission with making recommendations for improving governmental relations. Formally named the Royal Commission on Dominion-Provincial Relations, but popularly known as the Rowell-Sirois Commission after its key members, it reported in 1940 on the state of political affairs in Canada. Casting the report in the harsh light of the Depression and recent history, the commissioners concluded that residual powers, so clearly given to the federal government in the British North America Act in 1867, had shifted to the provinces largely as a result of court decisions. Moreover, the commissioners identified acute regional inequities and found the provinces shockingly ill prepared to pay for social programs and education. The commission's recommendations to restore constitutional powers to the federal government, largely by having Ottawa take on provincial debts and distribute taxes to the provinces to run social services, were emphatically rejected by several provinces. World War II was underway when leaders from the federal government and the provinces met at a stormy conference in 1941. While much of the Rowell-Sirois Report was shunted aside in the heat of an intensifying war, it cast the tensions between the federal and provincial governments in sharp relief. The design of having the federal government return taxes to the provinces, usually in the form of grants, would be implemented in the 1940s. In addition, the report's message that Ottawa should have a role in maintaining a degree of social and economic equity for Canadians, independent of the relative health of the individual provinces, would come to fruition after the war.

Another Global Conflict

It is widely recognized that World War II cured the Depression. Certainly the notion holds great merit in Canada's case. Widespread human suffering, ongoing class divisions, glaring regional inequities, and political confrontations characterized a troubled decade for Canada. Events rooted to the flawed solutions for global reconstruction after World War I led to the rise of fascist and militaristic regimes in Germany, Italy, Spain, and Japan. Clashes in the Pacific and Europe gathered force in the early 1930s and mushroomed to become a global war by 1939. Once again Canadians found themselves swept up in events over which they had little control. Unlike the Great War, however, when Canada automatically found itself involved because of a decision made in Britain, this time the country would make an independent determination to join the conflict. Nonetheless, in September 1939 Canada found itself again in a war for which it was poorly prepared. The consequences of fighting World War II on the side of the victorious allies would be far-reaching. For a country crippled and humbled by the Depression, Canada remarkably became a leading economic and global power in the 1940s. World War II indeed dealt a lethal blow to the Depression; it also give birth to the

Cold War and thereby altered Canada's history in almost unimaginable ways.

Canadian Foreign Policy before the War

In the wake of World War I Canada demonstrated an ambivalence in its role in international affairs. By joining the League of Nations, establishing missions in the United States, France, and Japan in the late 1920s, and obtaining Commonwealth status in the Statute of Westminster, the country incrementally took a foreign policy path that was distinct from Britain's. Canada played a modest part in the League of Nations, preferring instead to lean toward isolationism. As Senator Raoul Dandurand remarked in a speech to the League in 1925, Canadians "live[d] in a fire-proof house, far from inflammable material." Mackenzie King, who consistently fixated on national unity, expended little energy in cultivating Canada's influence abroad. Canada did, however, add its signature to the Kellogg-Briand Pact of 1928. Signed by over sixty nations, it essentially outlawed war as an instrument of foreign policy. Significantly, a Canadian-born academic at Columbia University contributed to the idea. James T. Shotwell also moderated the Carnegie Endowment for International Peace, which published in the 1930s and 1940s a celebrated series of scholarly studies on the Canadian-American relationship. Thus, Canada into the Depression years championed peaceful relationships with other countries and explicitly tried to avoid conflict.

Events in Europe, Africa, and the Pacific forced Canada to adjust this stance, but it sent mixed messages about its international role. When the Japanese invaded Manchuria in 1931, an overt act of aggression that eventually led to general warfare in the Pacific, Canada supported the League's refusal to provide aid to China. Four years later, another international crisis involved Canada when Italy's fascist dictator, Benito Mussolini, made plans to invade the African nation of Ethiopia. When the League discussed sanctions against Italy, Canada's representative pushed for adding oil to the list. Dubbed the "Canadian Resolution," Dr. W. A. Riddell's proposal briefly put the country in the forefront of explosive events. However, Mackenzie King, freshly reinstalled as prime minister, failed to support both Riddell and his measure. Among other issues, King feared dividing public opinion on the issue because many Quebecers supported Mussolini's Italy.

Unfortunately, the 1930s did not paint a favorable portrait of Canada's official actions as developments in Europe soured. When Jews fled the German fascists after Adolf Hitler took power in 1933, Canada became one of the world's most inhospitable countries for receiving the diaspora. As one key policymaker summarized Canada's policy toward accepting Jewish immigrants, "None is too many." Jewish immigrants to Canada numbered only about 4,000. Mexico, in contrast, took approximately five times that figure in the same period. Anti-Semitism in both language and behavior was evident throughout the country, but it was particularly poignant in Quebec. It was noticeable in the French-Canadian nationalist movement, and Duplessis's government and the Roman Catholic church made frequent references disparaging Jews. Small pockets of fascists and pro-Nazi groups were active in Canada. These organizations assiduously worked to counteract a modest number of communists, many of whom were immigrants from Finland and the Ukraine with vivid memories of mistreatment at the hands of the Russians before the revolution and the Soviets thereafter.

When the Spanish Civil War broke out in 1936, over one thousand Canadians volunteered in the Mackenzie-Papineau battalion to fight with the Republicans against General Francisco Franco's forces, which were supported by Hitler's Nazis. As was the case with many world leaders, King met with Hitler in the 1930s but failed to grasp the magnitude of the Nazi agenda. On one occasion King observed that the German leader was a "simple sort of peasant, not very intelligent and no serious danger to anyone." Apparently Dandurand's "fire-proof house" was still a compelling image for many Canadians. In the late 1930s Canada's impact on international events was negligible. Deeply divided over the tragic events unfolding abroad and led by a prime minister who was reluctant to take a clear position in world affairs, Canadians remained mired in depression.

The only foreign connection that was strengthened in the years preceding the war was with the country's neighbor. A trade agreement in 1935 improved relations with the United States, as did the charismatic president. Franklin D. Roosevelt's family had a cherished summer home in Campobello, New Brunswick, and he was genuinely fond of Canadians. Similarly King worked well with Americans, having spent time in the United States for educational and professional reasons earlier in his career. In 1938 Roosevelt assured an audience at Queen's University in Kingston, Ontario, that his country would not stand "idly by" if Canada was attacked. The speech prompted an immediate reply from King, who promised that Canadian space would not be used by a foreign power to invade the United States. Thus, Canadians and Americans reached an informal understanding for a united defense of North America before the outmatched Polish forces were surprised by Hitler's mechanized army on September 1, 1939. This symbolic agreement would be transformed into a formalized defense relationship during the war.

Canada at War

Canada entered World War II in 1939 utterly unprepared for a major conflict. Along with other people around the globe, Canadians had hoped that the 1938 Munich Agreement that gave Germany control over part of Czechoslovakia would pacify Hitler enough to avoid war. Germany's outrageous attack on Poland in September 1939, after signing a nonaggression pact with the Soviets, brought Britain into the war within days. Canada declared war on Germany on September 10, 1939, one week after the British did. The delay was largely symbolic because few Canadians thought the country would or should remain detached from the conflict. Nonetheless, it illustrated Canada's essential sovereignty after the Statute of Westminster. Only three parliamentarians opposed the country's participation, including the pacifist J. S. Woodsworth. The government immediately invoked the War Measures Act, the crucial device used to control the military and economy during the Great War. For the second time in the century Canada found itself embroiled in a global war not of its making, yet one that would irrevocably change its destiny.

The country went through distinct phases of commitment during the war. Although there was an initial outpouring of support and recruiting agencies swelled with men, many of whom were unemployed refugees of depression hard times, Canada did not go into the war with the same unbridled patriotic vigor that had been apparent in World War I. For the first fall and winter, after the rapid defeat of Poland, the European theater settled into what observers cynically called the "phony war." This first phase was dominated by King's plans for Canada's "limited liability" and an "unspectacular" effort to supply the British. At the war's outset the country had fewer than a combined 10,000 personnel in the navy, air force, and army. Symbolic of the limited liability idea was the creation of the British Commonwealth Air Training Plan. Canada, physically removed from events in Europe, constructed, staffed, and paid over half the cost of a flight crew program. During the war, over 130,000 Allied airmen received training in Canada, which proudly assumed the nickname "aerodrome of democracy." While the vanguard of the Canadian army reached Britain in late 1939, the country originally planned to play a supportive role.

The phony war concept evaporated rapidly in the spring of 1940, giving way to images of blitzkrieg and the breathtaking collapse of Denmark, the Netherlands, Belgium, Norway, and finally France. By the fall of 1940, with Britain barely staving off German air attacks, Canada had become the most significant partner in the Allied effort. The notion of Canada's limited commitment for a brief conflict was unceremoniously abandoned. By the war's end in 1945 over one million Canadian men and women had put on uniforms to battle the combined German and Italian forces in Europe and to defend Canadian territory. To a much lesser extent, Canadians fought in the Pacific after the country declared war on Japan following the surprise attack at Pearl Harbor in December 1941.

Canadians would see service in such far-flung places as the West Indies, Iceland, Hong Kong, Southeast Asia, and Alaska. The Royal Canadian Navy, active in several oceans, found its greatest task in protecting Allied supply convoys from German submarines in the dangerous waters of the Atlantic. But by far the greatest Canadian military contribution came with the battle to liberate Europe and defeat Italy and Germany. Under the command of General Andrew McNaughton, Canadian troops gathered and trained in Britain. They were used to test the German defenses of Western Europe at Dieppe in August 1942, a disastrous event that left 3,000 Canadians killed, wounded, or captured on the beaches of France. Dieppe spawned angry claims that Canada's infantry had been used as fodder for a poorly conceived mission. German propagandists, in the meantime, used dramatic pictures of the Canadian dead to show the impenetrability of their "fortress Europe."

Canada's major infantry commitment came during the campaign to liberate Western Europe. Canadians served as part of the British forces in the protracted battle to defeat Italy beginning in 1943. They were also critical participants in the greatest amphibious assault in history during the Normandy invasion on June 6, 1944. Juno Beach, one of five Allied landing sites, was a Canadian responsibility. Bloody fighting shadowed Canadian troops in capturing Caen, moving up the coast to Belgium, and taking the Scheldt estuary near Antwerp. As the war reached its closing days in the spring of 1945, Canadian soldiers liberated part of the Netherlands and crossed the Rhine River into Germany. While the ground fighting took place, the Royal Canadian Air Force suffered and inflicted extensive casualties in a relentless bombing campaign of German factories and military targets. Germany surrendered in May. The Japanese sued for peace three months later following the destruction of Hiroshima and Nagasaki by atomic bombs. After six years of unimaginable carnage, World War II drew to a close (see "A Portrait of the Fighting Forces" in the Documents section).

Although some historians quibble about Canada's relative impact on the war in a global comparative framework, few would dispute the assertion that the country's military contribution during the hostilities was nothing short of extraordinary. For a country of nearly eleven million, over one million men and women were in uniform at some point between 1939 and 1945. Of those, roughly 750,000 served in the army, 250,000 in the Royal Canadian Air Force (the fourth largest Allied air contingent by the war's end), and 100,000 in the Royal Canadian Navy. Of Canada's nearly 100,000 casualties, close to 42,000 lost their lives. As was the case in World War I, Canada's casualty figures pale when placed alongside those of most of the other belligerents. The Soviet Union, for example, lost about twenty million people, and the extermination of over six million Jews by Germany's Nazi regime set a ghastly record in world history for a nation's deliberate attempt to annihilate another group. Canada's unswerving dedication to the war effort is also widely recognized by historians. The country was Britain's strongest ally before Germany attacked the Soviet Union in the summer of 1941 and the Americans entered the war later that year. However, the use and behavior of Canadian forces during the war has been the subject of some fairly recent controversy. *The Valour and the Horror*, a television program shown on CBC in the 1990s, called into question the almost mythical image of Canada's noble fighting forces during the war. This contentious series, which drew angry responses from veterans and others, indicates that after a half-century, the nature of Canada's role in this most costly of human wars has not achieved a final agreement.

The Home Front

Mackenzie King and his Liberal government faced enormous political challenges at the war's outset, especially from two of his political enemies. Maurice Duplessis, Quebec's premier, was vocal in his skepticism of Canada's obligation to support the war. Conversely, Ontario premier Mitchell Hepburn claimed that the country was not doing enough to support Britain. King swiftly worked to defuse these critics. By enlisting the support of the influential cabinet member, Ernest Lapointe, the federal government helped the Quebec Liberals defeat Duplessis's Union Nationale in the fall of 1939. Then King called a federal election in 1940. During the campaign he promised not to implement a forced conscription of soldiers. After soundly defeating his opponents set to the task of assembling an especially able wartime cabinet. Notable was the American-born minister of munitions and supply, C. D. Howe, who was given the daunting challenge of managing the country's production efforts.

Insatiable Allied demands for the resources that made Canada famous—wheat, ore, fish, timber, and a host of minerals crucial to the war effort such as nickel, lead, aluminum, copper, and uranium—helped to break the Depression's grip almost overnight. Canada's industrial output surged. Factories produced airplanes, tanks, weapons large and small, and personal equipment for soldiers. Unemployment, which was such a shattering and emblematic characteristic of the Depression, virtually disappeared; remarkably, employers found themselves facing a shortage of workers in some sectors of the economy. Inflation rose and the government instituted wage and price controls. A multitude of wartime agencies monitored virtually every facet of production and distribution. Rations on items from sugar to gasoline became a wartime necessity and kindled a black market. The National Selective Service, instituted in 1941, controlled the movement of workers, women and men alike, and kept people in certain jobs that were deemed critical to the war effort. Canada used only about one-third of its production during the war. Its Allies consumed the rest.

The country's gross national product and industrial output nearly doubled during the war years. Labor tensions, however, accompanied the effort. Strikes plagued the wartime industries, shaped by concerns over wages and working conditions. In 1944 a government order-in-council, referred to as PC 1003, proclaimed that Canadian workers would have the right to organize and bargain collectively. This helped to bring down the frequency of strikes during the remainder of the war. Agricultural output increased on an equally dramatic level, with farm income doubling from 1939 to 1945. To pay for the war, the government raised taxes. It also borrowed heavily, as Canadian citizens turned out their pockets in a number of Victory Bond drives that generated about $12 billion. Canada loaned Britain several billion dollars during the war and essentially gave their former imperial masters about $1 billion to purchase Canadian products. Thus, while people made personal sacrifices on the home front, the war brought about a dramatic improvement in the country's economy.

Women and the War Effort

Canadian women were profoundly affected by the war. Single women had long been part of the workforce, generally in low-paying jobs such as teaching, secretarial work, service jobs, and retail employment. The thousands of men drawn into military service, coupled with a supercharged economy, created employment opportunities that had been practically nonexistent before the war. Single and then married women poured into factories that produced everything from tanks to canvas pouches for soldiers. The country's version of "Rosie the Riveter" was the "Bren gun girl," named after a light machine gun. Over one million women worked full time in factories and businesses by 1944, and at least another million toiled on farms and in part-time jobs. In addition, women served in the military and in the nursing corps. Close to 50,000 women enlisted in the armed forces: the Canadian Women's Army Corps, the Royal Canadian Air Force Women's Division, and the Women's Royal Canadian Naval Service. Although they received unequal treatment in the service, women nonetheless fulfilled critical duties. Female pilots ferried planes, for example, thereby releasing male crews for combat duty.

The dramatic influx of women into new sectors of Canada's economy forced changes that lasted beyond the war years. In 1944, largely as a response to the considerable number of women in the workforce, the government instituted the Family Allowance Act. The "baby bonus" provided a modest monthly payment to Canadian mothers with children under sixteen years of age to ensure a basic standard of food, clothing, and shelter needs. It also survived the war. The government's propaganda machinery, after initially encouraging women to do their bit for the war, signaled that they would have to make their jobs available to returning men in peacetime. Thousands of women lost their jobs as a result of deliberate policy and economic restructuring after the war. The percentage of women in the Canadian workforce did not return to wartime levels until the 1960s. Nevertheless, the wartime commitment of women helped to construct a platform for the postwar feminist movement. From raising money in bond drives to sacrificing their lives in military service, women were a key component of Canada's successful war effort.

Conscription Again

With a generation of Canadians having direct memories of the conscription tensions during World War I, the onset of another conflict brought immediate concerns about repeating the problem. Mackenzie King, ever the conciliator, repeatedly pledged not to move to conscription. Individuals and groups across Canada, particularly large numbers of French Canadians, were opposed to the idea of an enforced draft. Reasons for their lack of support for the war effort included resentments of Borden's actions during World War I, France's desertion of *Canadiens* at the Conquest, and sympathy in Quebec for at least some of the programs of the fascist governments in Italy and Germany. On the other hand, war proponents such as Arthur Meighen wanted to maintain a large military—through a draft if necessary.

Wartime events forced King and his government to consider conscription. The National Resources Mobilization Act (NRMA) of 1940 created the machinery to register and call up men for the defense of Canada. About 60,000 of these "Zombies," as they were cruelly nicknamed after the living dead characters in popular horror movies, were called into service. In 1942, as Allied war casualties rose, the government held the second national plebiscite in Canada's history to release King from his pledge of no conscription. The results perfectly illustrated the country's historic divisions. In eight provinces and the territories, voters overwhelmingly released the government from its pledge. Almost three-quarters of Quebecers, in contrast, voted to hold the Liberals to their promise. Even with clear national support, King did not move immediately to conscription. Instead he uttered perhaps his most famously ambiguous explanation for a policy: Canada would have "not necessarily conscription, but conscription if necessary." But the war ground on and casualties mounted. Late in 1944, after an unsuccessful appeal to NRMA soldiers by the popular General McNaughton to go overseas voluntarily, the government finally issued the orders. Of the approximately 2,500 NRMA soldiers to reach the front, sixty-nine were killed.

The conscription crisis was not as severe as it had been during World War I, thanks in great part to King's demonstrated reluctance to institute a draft. Nonetheless, the issue divided Canada along an old fault line. Many French Canadians viewed the event as another example of governmental insensitivity, while a number of anglophones considered the resistance to support the Allied efforts as more evidence that French Canadians were not fully "Canadian." Depending on one's interpretation, the conscription issue during World War II is an example of a government bending over backward in an effort to appease all sides or yet another illustration of Ottawa's tyranny.

Japanese Canadians

Few would dispute the war's impact on certain ethnic groups in Canada, especially those with blood ties to the country's enemies. The government, using national security as the rationale, detained and incarcerated hundreds of German and Italian Canadians during the war. But by far the most dramatic example of the removal of basic civil rights in wartime was the treatment of Japanese Canadians, which in many ways was similar to the plight of Japanese Americans.

The humiliating defeat of Canadian soldiers sent to defend Hong Kong in December 1941, coupled with a deep-seated suspicion of Asian peoples, brought anti-Japanese sentiment to a head in early 1942. After invoking the overarching theme of national security, and remarkably acting against the advice of the military and RCMP, the federal government forcibly removed over 20,000 Japanese Canadians from British Columbia. The majority were Canadian citizens; many claimed Canada as their birthplace. Stripped of their property, farms, and fishing fleets, the Japanese Canadians were relocated to interior locations. Many were placed on farms so that the owners could exploit their labor. At the war's end, thousands were prevented from returning to their original homes in British Columbia. In addition, the government actively sought the deportation of Japanese-born Canadians until 1947. Some made the passage to Japan rather than remain in Canada's hostile environment. Not until the late 1980s did the Canadian government offer an apology and some financial compensation to the victims and their families for this harsh and indefensible wartime injustice (see "A Japanese-Canadian Perspective" in the Documents section).

Relations with the United States

The war strengthened Canada's military and economic relations with the United States, largely because of the positive working relationship of the countries' leaders. In August 1940 King and Roosevelt, meeting in Ogdensburg, New York, agreed to form a Permanent Joint Board of Defense. While it lacked clear definition at the time, the agreement suggested that the two North American nations needed to coordinate their defensive efforts. A conference the following year at Hyde Park, New York, yielded a proposal to let Canada operate as part of the United States Lend-Lease program to provide aid to Britain. The Hyde Park agreement also set in motion plans to coordinate the wartime industries of both countries. Importantly, these agreements were reached before the United States was officially at war. Once the United States became involved in December 1941, Canada assumed a junior partner role in the Allied relationship. For example, Canada sponsored two important meetings between Winston Churchill and Franklin Roosevelt in Quebec in 1943 and 1944, but on both occasions King's essential function was that of host. U.S. pressures to build an Alaskan highway and oil pipeline through Canadian territory during the war reinforced old concerns about protecting the nation's sovereignty. Yet on the whole, the war created bonds between the two countries that firmly shaped Canada's history during the Cold War.

Canada in the Immediate Postwar World

Canada at the war's conclusion scarcely resembled the depression-wracked country of 1939. Thanks to its industriousness and location in North America where it had escaped the catastrophic destruction that had laid waste to much of Europe and the Pacific, Canada emerged from the war one of the strongest and richest countries in the world. Britain, with its empire severely diminished, saw its power to control and shape Canada's foreign relations drop precipitously during the war. Correspondingly rising in importance was the United States, newly christened a "superpower" in the new and terrifying contest called the "Cold War." Canada was one of the founding members of the United Nations, an organization created in 1945 to replace the defunct League of Nations. In the early growth years of the UN Canada served on various committees, including the important Relief and Rehabilitation Administration. In the unfolding decades after the Second World War, Canada would be an instrumental leader among a group of middle-power nations that sought influence in molding the modern world. The first spy case of the postwar era broke out in Ottawa—not in Washington—in September 1945, when a Soviet embassy clerk named Igor Gouzenko defected. Canadians reluctantly realized that their country was going to be part of the Cold War and that their future seemed destined to be intertwined with their colossal neighbor.

Chapter 8

Cold War Canada
(1945–1960s)

A New World

The Great Depression and a second global conflict profoundly changed the country. A relatively modest member of the new British Commonwealth in the early 1930s, Canada fashioned itself one of the world's strongest nations by 1945. As the nation neared the half-century mark, it faced contradictory impulses that still persist. It was well on the path to creating a strong international presence as a judicious middle power, while domestically its government continued to construct one of the world's most comprehensive social systems to ensure a reasonable quality of life for all Canadian citizens. At the same time, persistent strains between anglophones and francophones, now focused overwhelmingly on the relationship between Quebec and Canada, would threaten to stretch the bonds of nationhood to the breaking point. Canada's social and political landscape in the next half-century would be complex and periodically contentious.

Overshadowing Canada's development in this period was the Cold War, the defining dynamic in global history from the close of World War II until the early 1990s. Canada's ideological orientation

A remarkable photograph taken in 1967 of four Liberal politicians, all of whom would serve as prime minister during their careers: (left to right) Pierre Elliott Trudeau, John Turner, Jean Chrétien, Prime Minister Lester B. Pearson.

Source: Library and Archives Canada / Credit: Duncan Cameron Fonds / PA-117107.

as a Western democracy, with its historic ties to Britain and the United States, placed it in the forefront of nations that acted as a counterweight to the Soviet Union and its often reluctant allies. Importantly, geography placed Canada directly between the competing superpowers when a polar map projection was employed. Cold War strategists on both sides grasped the fact that the quickest way to strike the enemy was by sending bombers or missiles over the top of the world. While Canadians initially supported American initiatives to contain Soviet influence, the nation's precarious location shaped not only its emerging foreign policy, but politics, the economy, and social developments as well. Much like the all-embracing effects of both world wars, the Cold War would reach deep into the lives of Canadians and cast a shadow that reached beyond strictly international considerations.

Political Changes in the Late 1940s

Mackenzie King added to his remarkable political career by successfully leading the Liberals to another victory in 1945, but the war and advancing age had taken their toll. He retired in 1948, leaving the Liberal party in the hands of a lawyer who at Ernest Lapointe's death in 1941 had become his most trusted Quebec confidant. Louis St. Laurent, a widely respected politician and now the country's second French-Canadian prime minister, would lead the Liberals to another resounding win in 1949. One year later, King died, bringing to an end one of the most extraordinary of Canadian lives. A man who had dominated politics for almost three decades, King was the ultimate conciliator. As a popular expression goes, he succeeded because he divided Canadians the least. With the exposure of King's intensely private diaries after his death, the personal life of a spiritual and conflicted bachelor would become fodder for lively historical assessments. For contemporaries, however, Mackenzie King was rarely idolized, sometimes despised, and always elusive. Under St. Laurent's leadership and prodded by parties on the left that were gathering strength, the Liberal government took on more of an activist role in defining—and theoretically improving—the lives of Canadians.

1949: A Remarkable Year

Several unconnected events in 1949 illustrated that Canada was undergoing fundamental transformations in the postwar era. The country's sovereignty and territory increased. Dominion, a term that suggested historic linkages to Britain, was formally removed as part of Canada's title. Also in that year Canada stopped sending court cases to the British Privy Council, thereby making its Supreme Court the final arbiter of judicial matters. Newfoundland, which had voluntarily returned to a form of British colonial status during the 1930s due to severe economic distress, became Canada's tenth province in 1949 after a series of negotiations with Ottawa and two controversial referendums. Thanks largely to the energies of Joey Smallwood, a journalist and union organizer, the confederation forces barely prevailed over groups that wanted Newfoundland to remain close to Britain or join the United States. The votes triggered great opposition, but Britain was glad to be divested of the responsibility of protecting the island in the developing Cold War. Canadians were relatively pleased to embrace the new province, for it strategically guarded the mouth of the St. Lawrence River. Confederationists in Newfoundland were content to avail themselves of the social programs that Canada had to offer. Newfoundland joined the country with Labrador as part of its jurisdiction as a result of a controversial boundary settlement made in 1927. Quebec, the only province that physically borders Labrador, continues to dispute the decision. Finally, a career diplomat named Vincent Massey was appointed Canada's first native-born governor general in 1952. Coupled with the events of 1949, this further strengthened Canadian sovereignty in the postwar era (see "Smallwood's Argument for Confederation" in the Documents section).

The Postwar Economy

Canada emerged from World War II physically unscathed, militarily strong, and economically vibrant. Yet it rapidly dismantled its military forces and its economy struggled to make the transition from wartime production to a consumer-oriented environment. Although it was now one of the world's leading industrial countries, Canada's export market in the postwar era still relied mostly on primary products, as it had since colonial days. The rest of the world, and especially the United States, needed its newsprint, wheat, forest products, and minerals. The development of oil and natural gas production in Alberta and British Columbia led to the construction of several pipelines to provinces that increasingly were dependent on petroleum products for heating and transportation. With Britain's economy crippled by the war, foreign investments in Canada increasingly shifted from British to American capital. Similarly, trade with the United States accelerated. The construction of American branch plants continued apace, further intertwining the economies of the two countries. As the U.S. government developed its successful Marshall Plan to resuscitate a shattered Western Europe and thereby cultivate allies, Canadians were able to tap into the system by having Europeans buy their goods with Marshall Plan funds. The two-edged sword of this dynamic was becoming a Canadian fixture. While the producers of export goods benefited, even the modest attachment of Canadian businesses to the plan suggested another step toward economic integration with the United States. In addition Canada in 1947 became part of the General Agreement on Tariffs and Trade (GATT), an international accord that was designed to foster trade by lowering tariffs.

The expanding economy created a boon to organized labor. By 1950 about thirty percent of the country's workers belonged to a union. Age-old considerations, including the improvement of wages and working conditions, motivated men and women to agitate for changes. Empowered by winning the right to strike and collectively bargain during the war, labor groups in the postwar era engaged in some of the most contentious strikes in Canadian history. Strikers included Nova Scotian fishermen, Ontarian automobile employees, and British Columbian longshoremen. The formation of the Canadian Labour Congress in 1956, which brought former competing unions together in a fashion similar to the momentous American Federation of Labor–Congress of Industrial Organizations (AFL-CIO) merger a year earlier, served to alleviate problems within the ranks of organized laborers. A particularly dramatic strike among asbestos workers in Quebec helped to shift public opinion away from supporting big business and harsh management; it also served as an important antecedent of the eventful "Quiet Revolution" of Quebec's cultural and political values in the 1960s.

Politics: Liberal Style

St. Laurent controlled Parliament until 1957, reflecting widespread voter approval to continue Liberal policies as well as the inability of Conservative leaders to draw together their supporters from across the country. To improve the lives of Canadians, St. Laurent's government built on a social platform that had been incrementally developed since the 1920s. It already included the modest pension plan of the late 1920s and the unemployment insurance and Family Allowance Act of the war years. The Liberals instituted a fuller old age pension scheme in 1951 and passed a hospital insurance plan in 1957. Designed to work in tandem with cooperating provincial governments to pay a portion of the bills for hospital patients, this controversial plan was a major step toward a comprehensive national health care program.

Other important initiatives, designed to improve the postwar economy, involved transportation and the movement of products to markets. One of the oldest dreams in Canadian history, the development of a comprehensive lock system that would open the Great Lakes to oceangoing vessels, became a reality in 1959. The international construction project, supported by both Canadian and American funds, permitted the movement of grain, iron ore, and coal into and out of the continent's interior by using the St. Lawrence River. Queen Elizabeth, President Dwight Eisenhower, and newly elected Prime Minister John Diefenbaker gathered to celebrate the inauguration of the St. Lawrence Seaway, a technological marvel of its time. In addition, construction began in 1950 on the Trans-Canada Highway. When it opened in 1962, its almost 5,000 miles of road linked the East and West coasts, with additional sections in Newfoundland and Vancouver Island. Both projects, particularly the latter, instilled a great deal of pride among Canadians. Yet another plan to improve economic development was the construction of a pipeline that would bring Alberta natural gas to central Canada. At great political cost, the Liberals pushed the controversial Trans-Canada Pipe Lines bill through the House of Commons. Concerns about American funding behind the project, the government's heavy-handed maneuvering to pass the legislation, and the perception among many Canadians that the pipeline would benefit only certain regions combined to give the Conservatives an opportunity to bring an end to the Liberal dynasty that had dominated federal politics for decades.

The Conservative Plan: Diefenbaker's One Canada

The election of 1957 brought the Conservatives into power and ushered in a decade of exceptional political turmoil. Under the leadership of a Saskatchewan lawyer named John George Diefenbaker, the Conservatives fanned the embers of postwar Canadian nationalism. Diefenbaker's populist speeches invoked images of a unified country—"One Canada"—with an emphasis on social and legal equality for all Canadians. Coupled with a dash of anti-American rhetoric and the intriguing idea of developing the North, his messages captured the interest of Canadian voters. Confident in his mounting popularity, Diefenbaker called an election the following year that delivered a sweeping victory to his party. In 1958 it appeared that the Conservatives had found the right combination of political rhetoric and programs to unify the country and ensure Canadian sovereignty as the Cold War intensified. The Conservatives passed the Agricultural and Rural Development Act to alleviate rural poverty and created the National Productivity Council to improve cooperation between management and labor. Plans were also developed to build roads and airfields to gain access to the remote, vast resources of the Northwest and Yukon territories.

Although Diefenbaker's economic and social programs were partially successful, they also aroused significant opposition. The Conservatives passed in Parliament the Bill of Rights in 1960, a measure that the prime minister considered one of his greatest accomplishments. Consciously modeled on the U.S. design, it promised all Canadians "life, liberty, and personal security," as well as the freedom of religion, speech, assembly, and the press. Some of Diefenbaker's policies were molded by the Royal Commission on Canada's

Economic Prospects. The lengthy Gordon Report, as it was called, can be distilled into two basic observations. With tremendous detail it characterized the Atlantic region as an economic backwater of Canada. While it recommended support for the region's rural communities and fishing industries, it also suggested that a number of people from the four eastern provinces would have to relocate to other regions to find employment. The Conservatives responded by financially supporting the diversification of manufacturing in textiles, forest goods, and fishing products. At the same time, the report's suggestions concerning relocation energized fierce opposition among gritty Atlantic residents who shared generational attachments to the land and sea. The Gordon Report also raised concerns about foreign investment, particularly from the United States. This fueled the Conservative government's deep distrust of U.S. economic and political agendas.

Despite the popular appeal of Diefenbaker's message in the late 1950s, his programs and leadership style led to a series of domestic and foreign policy scrapes that rapidly eroded his government's support. His One Canada impulse discouraged people from highlighting their ethnicity, such as identifying themselves as French Canadians or Icelandic Canadians. Many Canadians considered this a covert assimilation policy. Moreover Diefenbaker's energetic pro-British stance, illustrated by his tour of Commonwealth countries in 1958 and his notorious lack of sensitivity to francophone interests, made him immensely unpopular in Quebec. Even his cherished Bill of Rights was interpreted by many as a federal impingement on the prerogatives of provinces, which were constitutionally responsible for civil rights. Finally, rising inflation and unsettling fluctuations in the Canadian dollar created political troubles for the Conservatives. Diefenbaker's attempts to shift a percentage of trade from the United States to Britain failed. In addition Canadians widely criticized his plan to peg the Canadian dollar to the American dollar at $0.925; they nicknamed it the "Diefenbuck."

Savaged by a Liberal opposition led by Lester Pearson and routinely excoriated in the press, Diefenbaker entered a political tailspin that was heavily determined by domestic themes. But it was in the overarching developments of the Cold War that Diefenbaker found his greatest challenges. Paradoxically, he lost power on the assumption that Canada's foreign policy should not be too closely aligned with that of the United States. Despite a growing sense of nationalism during the Cold War, a large number of Canadians would reach different conclusions and send Diefenbaker to defeat in 1963. To his supporters, this signaled that Canadian nationalism and sovereignty were at risk. As Professor George Grant argued in a classic pessimistic statement in 1965, *Lament for a Nation*, Canada's essentially conservative impulse had succumbed to American liberalism. Grant and others believed that this foreshadowed the end of Canadian nationalism.

The Middle Power Ideal

Canada pursued an international policy in the postwar era that was plagued by a fundamental contradiction. In the early years of the Cold War, as the United States and the Soviet Union used their extraordinary powers to define their alliances and engage in a nuclear arms buildup, Canada found itself in the position of being one of the former's most dedicated allies. At the same time, Canadians voiced concerns about maintaining their sovereignty. The apparent solution to this dilemma in the late 1940s and 1950s was to cultivate a middle power status. This "functional" ideal, formulated by a diplomat named Hume Wrong during World War II, suggested that each country should exercise powers relative to its capacity. Thus, Canada, as a strong country with a tremendous ability to produce food, raw materials, and industrial goods, should have more influence in determining the course of the war than smaller powers. Although the functionalist model did not blossom during the war, it shaped a conviction that was shared by an overwhelming number of Canadian diplomats and foreign policy strategists in the postwar era. St. Laurent's head of external affairs, Lester Pearson, was a career diplomat who embodied the middle power notion and became one of the chief architects of Canadian foreign policy in the early Cold War era.

The ideal of Canada playing an influential geopolitical role as the largest powers sorted out European and Pacific matters showed up immediately in the discussions that led to the creation of the United Nations. Canadians spearheaded the inclusion of Article 44, which stipulates that when the Security Council decides to use force, it should include in the decision-making process all nations expected to make military contributions. Canada was also instrumental in forming the North Atlantic Treaty Organization (NATO) in 1949 with eleven other countries, the single most important Cold War measure among Western nations to counteract the power of the Soviet Union and its allies. A little-known Canadian proposal in the NATO agreement, Article II, attempted to reinforce economic linkages among the treaty members. The treaty's collective security principle, however, remained NATO's most important function throughout the Cold War. Canada's commitment of forces to NATO would vacillate over the years, and this lack of consistency would often cause friction with its more earnest partners.

Korean War

The country's sovereignty dilemma was sorely tested the year after NATO's inception. Troops from North Korea invaded South Korea in an attempt to unify the divided country in June 1950. A legacy of World War II, with the Soviet Union exerting influence in North Korea and the United States establishing a strategic alliance with South Korea, the conflict became a test of Canada's ideals and foreign policy aspirations. The UN, largely at the insistence of the Americans, committed forces to assist the South Koreans. Canada's government decided to contribute a modest military contingent to the UN forces, which in fact were overwhelmingly American in composition. The Igor Gouzenko spy affair, a deep-seated suspicion of communist ideology, and a fear that the Soviet Union would extend its power throughout the world if left unchecked, generated favorable public sentiment for sending troops and materiel to assist in the war effort.

For the three years of the Korean War, Canada contributed about 22,000 infantry that served as part of the Commonwealth forces. The Royal Canadian Air Force and Royal Canadian Navy were also used in support. Just over three hundred Canadians died in the war. Canada's military expenditures rose dramatically during the conflict. In 1953 the country was spending about 7.6 percent of its GNP on defense, the highest proportion of the budget devoted to the military in peacetime to that point in the country's history. Along with most of the world's inhabitants, Canadians were terrified when General Douglas MacArthur's astounding campaign through North Korea to the Chinese border threatened to expand localized hostilities into a larger world war. As the war settled into a stalemate along a ragged demilitarized zone at the thirty-eighth parallel by 1953, Canadians were reminded of the precarious line they walked by supporting American policies in the Cold War.

Suez and Peacekeeping

Pockets of international tensions, some of which mushroomed into armed conflict, belied the term Cold War in the late 1940s and 1950s. One such clash led to the formulation of an idea that seemed to capture perfectly the essential ingredients of Canada's foreign policy aims. The nationalistic Egyptian president, Colonel Gamal Abdel Nasser, seized a strategic and economic conduit of immeasurable importance in 1956, the Suez Canal, prompting military intervention on the part of Britain, France, and Israel. The Americans were opposed to the actions of their allies, yet events in the Middle East threatened the balance of power because of Nasser's support from the Soviets. Meanwhile the UN worked feverishly to avoid an escalation of hostilities. The Canadian delegation, led by Lester Pearson, largely designed the idea of inserting a UN peacekeeping force between the belligerents to facilitate a truce. While Nasser balked at the idea of using Canadian forces in the peacekeeping efforts because they looked too British, the plan yielded a multinational force under the auspices of the UN that successfully defused the regional tensions enough to avoid war.

In recognition of his labors, the Nobel committee offered its prestigious Peace Prize to Pearson in 1957. At the same time, Canadian Conservatives criticized the Liberal government for neglecting to support Britain in its hour of need. Yet the peacekeeping idea became a standard feature of the Canadian middle power ideal thereafter. In over thirty countries around the world, including the Congo, Cyprus, Cambodia, and Haiti, Canada has contributed to peacekeeping missions. Canadians have displayed a great deal of pride in this effort, as evidenced by the peacekeeping monument near the National Gallery in Ottawa.

Continental Defense and Relations with the United States

Despite Canada's desire to extend its multilateral relationships, it never escaped the compelling gravitational pull of its neighbor. While Canadians sold wheat to China and the Soviet Union, marketed its Candu nuclear reactors to various countries, and made substantial contributions to less fortunate nations as a participant in the Commonwealth's Colombo Plan of the 1950s, the country's trading relationship grew ever tighter with the United States. Diefenbaker's suspicion of all things American and desires for a closer association with Britain clashed with the realities of Canada's economic relationship with the United States and diminished strategic options as the Cold War deepened. Politics and foreign policy intermeshed during the height of the Cold War.

Following the spirit of the Ogdensburg agreement during World War II, and with the world's attention shifting to nuclear weapons carried by bombers or delivered by missiles, arguments to strengthen the defenses of the continent's northern perimeter became more acute. The plans for the North American Air Defense Agreement (NORAD) of 1957, started under the Liberals and approved by the newly elected Conservatives, intertwined the defensive network of Canada and the United States. In emergencies, Canadian forces were to act in tandem with U.S. forces to repel attacks. The command structure, with an American in charge and a Canadian in the subordinate role, illustrated the unequal relationship. During the 1950s three defensive perimeters of radar stations were constructed, largely with American dollars and mostly in Canadian territory. The most famous was the Distant Early Warning (DEW) network that fanned across the Arctic. To Canadian nationalists, the NORAD agreement represented an erosion of the country's sovereignty. The NORAD technology was outdated almost immediately after the construction of the radar sites. Submarines armed with multiple nuclear missiles, plying the waters off the Pacific and Atlantic coasts, would quickly become the most likely source of attack. NORAD was a testament to the bomber and intercontinental ballistic missile capabilities of the early Cold War era.

Tensions with Canada's growing dependence on the United States were also cast into relief with Diefenbaker's 1959 cancellation of plans to construct and market a Canadian-built supersonic fighter plane. Started under the Liberals, the Avro Arrow project was to be a Canadian contribution to improved Cold War weaponry. Thus, the Arrow engendered pride among Canadians as an example of the country's capabilities as a technological leader in the 1950s. Yet the design was riddled with technological glitches and rising production costs. Diefenbaker's decision to cancel the project might have made excellent practical and economic sense, but it was deemed a blow to Canadian pride and shattered hopes for a modest independence in the military hardware industry. The purchase of American F-101 fighters for the Canadian Air Force after the Arrow's demise further illustrated the country's reliance on American arms in this period.

Events of late 1962 and early 1963, clustered around Canada's relationship with the United States and governed by the tides of the Cold War, irrevocably weakened Diefenbaker's government. The young American president, John F. Kennedy, and the prime minister disliked one another from their initial meeting. With personal styles and political beliefs that stood as almost polar opposites, the leaders of the two countries stumbled into events circulating around the growing relationship between Cuba and the Soviet Union. After discovering ballistic missile sites in Cuba under construction with Soviet technology and hardware, Kennedy in October 1962 announced a quarantine of the island to force the Soviet Union to withdraw its support. For a tense week in October, the world seemed poised on the precipice of a nuclear war.

Angered that it had not been consulted by the Americans and instead ordered to put its forces on military alert, Diefenbaker's government delayed in responding to the crisis. According to the terms of the NORAD agreement, the Conservatives had a point. The event widened a divide in Diefenbaker's cabinet between the cautious minister of external affairs, Howard Green, and the hawkish minister of defense, Douglas Harkness, who called for unequivocal support of the Americans in a moment of urgent need. Fortunately the Soviet premier, Nikita Khrushchev, rapidly backed down and agreed to dismantle the ballistic missile sites, but Diefenbaker's actions exposed Canada's unrelenting predicament in the Cold War. The prime minister assumed that Canadians would support this modest show of independence by not demonstrating a knee-jerk response to American demands. Instead many Canadians were embarrassed by what they viewed as a failure to own up to their obligations in an extraordinarily tense moment (see "Diefenbaker and Nuclear Weapons" in the Documents section).

The point was repeated within months when Diefenbaker's government refused to arm recently completed Bomarc missile sites in Ontario and Quebec with nuclear tips, a stipulation of the original agreement from 1959. Swayed by the antinuclear arguments of Green and others, Diefenbaker again counted on popular support to send a clear signal that Canada was not to be America's nuclear toady. The reneging backfired. Early in 1963 Harkness resigned, the U.S. State Department issued statements criticizing Canada's waffling and lack of commitment to North American defense, and Diefenbaker faced an unhappy electorate. In the spring of 1963, after rapidly reversing his antinuclear stance, the Liberal party leader, Lester Pearson, led his forces to a victory. Diefenbaker's popularity had suffered due to many issues, including a public dispute with the Bank of Canada over monetary policy, but Canada's relationship with the United States proved to be one of the most decisive factors. One of Pearson's first formal acts was to arm the Bomarc missiles with nuclear tips. Canada would have nuclear weapons on its soil until 1984. The Cold War's complexity and Canada's particular challenge of trying to be a special partner and steady ally of the United States, and yet not a passive extension of the growing American empire, affected the country's politics and social landscape. Pearson's Liberals would wrestle with the same bilateral dynamics that had contributed to Diefenbaker's defeat.

Life in Cold War Canada

Like many other nations in the aftermath of World War II, Canada's population expanded dramatically with natural increase and immigration. With a population of twelve million in 1945, it soared to over eighteen million by 1961. In less than two decades, Canada experienced an increase of nearly fifty-five percent. A large part of this growth can be attributed to a baby boom in the postwar era, with young couples marrying fairly young and having several children. The school population more than doubled in the years after the war until the early 1960s. At the same time, the number of educators in primary and secondary schools increased at a similar rate. The burgeoning population of young created a compelling need to enlarge the capacity of Canada's colleges and universities by the 1960s, when baby boomers started coming of postsecondary education age. Importantly, as the percentage of young in the population rose, it stimulated various dynamics that shaped the country's political, social, economic, and cultural development in the second half of the century.

The cities of Toronto, Montreal, and Vancouver grew rapidly as a result of internal migration and immigration. The urbanization trend that had been mounting since the nineteenth century, and statistically achieved in the 1920s, accelerated in the postwar era. Despite the realities of vast spaces and ideals of enthusiastically embracing the northern environment, modern Canada became one of the most urbanized nations on earth. Correspondingly, suburbs mushroomed. Improved roads, railway lines, and subway systems interlinked the expanding cities to bedroom communities. After 1946 shopping centers became one of the hallmarks of the suburban lifestyle. Canadians, clearly hungry for consumer products after the long hiatus of the Depression and wartime rationing and self-denial, purchased homes, automobiles, and washing machines. Increasingly that mesmerizing box known as the "electronic hearth"—television—made its way into Canadian homes.

Immigration

The postwar era spawned a massive international migration that brought immigrants to Canada in numbers that had not been witnessed since Laurier's administration in the early twentieth century. From the close of the war until 1957, over 1.5 million people immigrated to the country; from 1946 to 1966, the figure would reach 2.5 million. The patterns of immigrations fundamentally changed Canada's ethnic composition. Despite the overarching national image of exceptional tolerance, racial, cultural, and religious tensions accompanied this process. The immigration policy of the various postwar governments into the 1960s clearly favored Europeans while it deliberately limited the numbers from Asia, Africa, and the Caribbean. Unlike during the Sifton era, when sturdy peasants were solicited to populate the prairies, government immigration officials in the postwar period favored skilled people who could contribute to the expanding economy. British, Italians, Germans, Dutch, and Poles came pouring out of a shattered Europe. Numbered among the waves of newcomers were Jewish survivors of the Holocaust, thousands of British war brides who accompanied returning veterans, and over 35,000 Hungarians who escaped an unsuccessful uprising against Soviet authority in 1956.

Ontario and Quebec were the favorite destinations of these immigrants, many of whom sought employment in factories, helped to build the suburbs, and extracted minerals from mines. At the same time hundreds of thousands of Canadians migrated to the United States, lured by economic and professional opportunities that many perceived were not readily available in Canada. This "brain drain" siphoned away well-educated, professional, and talented Canadians to work in occupations as varied as newscaster, artist, engineer, and university professor. The ebb and flow of large numbers of people painted a portrait of an expanding and increasingly multiethnic North America. Another shift in immigration policy during the 1960s increased the numbers of people from underrepresented ethnic groups, quite literally changing the face of the average Canadian.

Articulating a Canadian Culture

Canada's strengthening relationship with the United States, underway throughout the twentieth century, touched the lives of ordinary Canadians in various ways. The growing power of the U.S. economy also meant that its cultural industries would extend beyond its borders. The proliferation of American culture throughout the twentieth century, and especially after World War II, became a subject of concern for virtually every nation on earth. For Canadians, an emerging American "cultural imperialism" presented a particular challenge, despite the development of the CBC in the 1930s and a governmentally supported national film industry. Quite literally the border was and remains porous. Most Canadians lived within one hundred miles of "the States," placing them within easy reach of printed material, radio, and television. Individual Canadians chose to purchase American literature, tune in an American radio station, or watch a favorite television program about a mythical California family. Yet many individuals were sufficiently concerned about clearly defining and protecting a Canadian culture in the postwar era that they turned to the government to increase its support in the enterprise.

The St. Laurent government charged an investigative body to look into the problem in 1949. Two years later, the Royal Commission on National Development in the Arts, Letters, and Sciences published its findings. Vincent Massey, a diplomat with experience in both the United States and Britain, chaired the exhaustive study. The Massey Report found that Canadian culture was on the fringes of society; it argued that more citizens should incorporate it into their lives and that the government should have a key role in nurturing it. Leaping off the report's pages was a fear of "mass culture," a reference to the influence of American media. The warnings were clear. Canadians should deliberately encourage and protect their own culture and education; otherwise, they would become overwhelmed by an invasive American or international culture. Determining what is distinctively Canada, long a subject of debate, would continue to receive the attention of zealous defenders of Canadian culture and critics who found the exercise frivolous or wasteful (see "Recommendations of the Massey Report" in the Documents section).

Although the government had strong reservations about becoming a patron of the arts, the Massey Report created a wellspring of governmental largesse to support the country's cultural industries, education, and heritage over the next decade. The CBC and the National Film Board received an infusion of capital in the 1950s. National television broadcasting began in 1952. Popular Canadian programs, including *La famille Plouffe* and *Music Hall*, entertained Canadians and carved out a niche in the face of an onslaught of American-made shows. A National Library was created the following year; it would be closely linked to an older organization that also grew in the postwar era, the Public Archives of Canada (now coupled with the library and renamed Library and Archives Canada). The Canada Council, created in 1957 with an infusion of inheritance taxes, provided grants to arts organizations, funding for universities, and scholarships and loans to students. By the 1960s Canadian theater productions, ballet schools, and artistic programs had created a respectable community of artists across the country. Supported by a combination of government agencies and private patrons, a cultural industry carved out a role for itself. For example, one of the world's most famous Shakespearean festivals began annual productions in Stratford, Ontario, in 1953. At the same time, the small cultural industry was beleaguered by the overwhelming volume of American material as well as constantly fending off critics who argued that the function as steward of the arts represented an inappropriate intrusion of government. In many ways, the expansive role of government in the wake of the Massey Report foreshadowed the creation of the social and medical networks of the 1960s. A growing number of Canadians believed that their federal and provincial governments should be the first line of defense for maintaining and defining a distinctive Canadian culture.

A "Quiet Revolution"?

Antecedents to Change

Following the Conquest, Canada's francophone population, particularly in Quebec, struggled to maintain its cultural identification, preserve its language, and protect its civil laws. From the eighteenth to the mid-twentieth century, *la survivance* was characterized to a large extent by memories of an agrarian past, devotion to Roman Catholicism, the active defense of the French language, and conscious efforts to resist assimilation. For most of this period, political, church, and social elites took charge of the task and defined the terms of francophone identity in North America. Challenges came in the form of Canada's western expansion after 1867, which was essentially a nonfrancophone enterprise. Further problems came with the loss of approximately one million people from 1840 to 1940 as people migrated from Quebec to the United States, especially New England, in search of employment and economic opportunity. Illustrated by the anti-imperialist stance of Henri Bourassa and the nationalistic arguments of Lionel Groulx, Quebec's francophones by the twentieth century lived in a society that cherished certain memories. The past was punctuated by repeated official and unofficial attempts to assimilate francophones and colored by the triumphant will of the group to survive against overwhelming odds.

Changes that accompanied the Depression and World War II altered the ways in which francophones defined their position in Canadian society and ultimately led to a fundamental reorientation of political and social power in Quebec. The province during the mid-twentieth century was swiftly becoming more urban and industrial in nature. As the population in rural areas declined precipitously during and after the war, cities such as Montreal burgeoned. Quebec families grew robustly, creating a provincial baby boom. In addition, a growing number of nonfrancophone immigrants—Italians, Greeks, Poles, and Germans—came to Quebec after the war. Technological changes, especially the encroachment of anglophone media, chipped away at French Canada's traditional culture.

The most immediate root of the changes of the 1960s was the end of the political dominance of *le chef*. Maurice Duplessis's Union Nationale, outmaneuvered by a combination of federal and provincial forces at the outset of World War II, returned to power in 1944. Duplessis ran Quebec in an old-style political fashion. Patronage and excessive control were the hallmarks of his premiership. A gulf separated Duplessis's promises and his actions. Allegedly he championed political and social reforms, and he successfully appealed to French-Canadian pride. He courted business investments from outside the province, especially from Americans. His government was particularly repressive concerning communists and labor unions. The Padlock Act of 1937, which was found unconstitutional two decades later, outlawed the publication of communist literature and imposed stringent sentences on offenders. A sensational strike of asbestos workers in 1949, which divided politicians, Roman Catholic church officials, journalists, workers, and students, is generally considered evidence that Duplessis's repressive regime was beginning to unravel. *Cité Libre*, a paper founded by journalist Gérard Pelletier and law professor Pierre Elliott Trudeau, promoted modern democratic ideals, liberalism, and individual rights. The emergence of *Cité Libre* and other journals that were harshly critical of older French-Canadian ideals and elites helped to channel an intense debate over the future of Quebec's francophone society. Duplessis kept control of the province until his death in 1959, but his Union Nationale successors failed to maintain the party's impetus. With the election of a Liberal government in 1960, the province underwent a staggering transformation that ultimately stretched the bonds of Confederation to the breaking point.

The Quiet Revolution

The events of the early to mid-1960s fundamentally reconfigured the definition of French-Canadian survival and put in motion political forces dedicated to the permanent alteration of Quebec's relationship with the rest of Canada. The election of Liberal Jean Lesage in 1960 served as a catalyst for a movement that journalists referred to as the "Quiet Revolution." Based on a combination of demographic, economic, cultural, and political ingredients, *la revolution tranquille* radically transformed Quebec. It shifted from an essentially conservative society, steeped in Roman Catholicism and focused on a pessimistic interpretation of the francophones' lot in Canadian history, to a more modern and forward-looking place where the state assumed a proactive role in determining the future and protecting the special rights of French Canadians. Some historians think of the Quiet Revolution as a societal catharsis. It was indeed a mixture of heated intellectual and emotional discussions that ultimately left few stones unturned. Critics questioned Quebec's traditions, economy, arts, education, and religion. By the end of the 1960s, francophone Quebecers were calling themselves *Québécois*, implying a French-Canadian nationalism that was now rooted to the province.

Although Jean Lesage did not create the Quiet Revolution, he presided over it. The Liberals attempted to corral the various threads of the movement, and an activist state became the hallmark of modern Quebec. Lesage's political refrain of *maîtres chez nous*— masters of our own house— struck a responsive chord to millions of Quebecers who wanted the government to lead the province into the future and protect francophone rights. One of the centerpieces of the new Quebec was the government's investment in developing hydro-electric energy. Under the leadership of the natural resources minister, René Lévesque, the Liberals built Hydro-Québec into a government monopoly by absorbing private hydroelectric power companies. The success of Hydro-Québec, with French as its business language and francophones as its engineers and workers, encouraged people to conclude that French-Canadian survival would be achieved by developing industries and resources in a francophone environment. Over time, however, other corporate efforts to replicate the successes of Hydro-Québec, such as a steel company named Sidbec, were not as financially successful.

One of the most far reaching of the Lesage government's measures was revamping the province's educational system from grade school through the university level. Charged by the government to assess education, the Parent Commission reported its findings from 1963–1966. It suggested a separation of church and state, the creation of a government ministry of education, and a more inclusive system of higher education that incorporated vocational and technical training in addition to traditional academic subjects. As a result, the province experienced an educational revolution in the 1960s that produced tuition-free high schools and an expanded public university system, the Université du Québec. Religious influences in education eroded, replaced in many cases by scientific and technical courses. Many of Quebec's current political, economic, and social leaders came of age in this expansive period of educational growth.

Finally, during the height of the Quiet Revolution, Lesage's Liberals engaged in bitter struggles with the federal governments of both Diefenbaker and Pearson to extract more provincial rights and responsibilities. While a minority of *Québécois* were advocating separation of the province from Canada at this point, a growing number of people wanted more freedom to exercise control over social programs as a way to ensure French-Canadian survival. The clashes with Ottawa focused on revenue sharing, because the federal government collected the bulk of the country's taxes, and the operation of social agencies. For example, the Lesage government insisted that Quebec run its own pension plan after Pearson introduced measures to construct a federal plan in 1963. While these changes empowered Quebec's government, they also brought negative side effects. Taxes increased, the debt rose, and the province developed a cumbersome bureaucracy that was much criticized by the mid-1960s.

The Quiet Revolution cut paths in many directions, so summarizing its impact in a definitive fashion is problematic. Clearly the period under Lesage's tutelage from 1960 to 1966 was one of intense, exciting, and sometimes frightening debate and change. In less than a decade Quebec underwent a cultural metamorphosis that created a highly secularized society out of one of the world's bastions of

Roman Catholicism. Even Pope John Paul II would criticize the new Quebec as a "de-Christianized society." The provincial birthrate also declined sharply; by the end of the decade, it was the country's lowest. A better-educated and professional citizenry probably wanted to devote its energies to building careers and modernizing Quebec instead of raising the large families of earlier generations. A form of Quebec nationalism, based on ideas that reached back into the early decades of the twentieth century, was given a clearer voice during the Quiet Revolution. Mounting tensions between Quebec and Ottawa helped to refine a political movement that called for the province's removal from Confederation. Finally, the Quiet Revolution helped to spawn small militant groups that tried to expedite, through threats and even violence, the province's independence from Canada. Thanks to the whirlwind events of the Quiet Revolution, *les Canadiens*, an expansive term that encompassed francophones across the country, had all but disappeared. It had been replaced by *les Québécois*, a self-identification that hinted at increased sovereignty or separation for the province of Quebec (see "A Voice of the New Quebec" in the Documents section).

Capitalizing on a general sense of exhaustion and disillusionment, the Union Nationale returned to power in 1966 under the leadership of Daniel Johnson. Many supporters of the Quiet Revolution were losing their enthusiasm, rural voters wanted to counteract a movement that had been primarily urban and intellectual, and Lesage's Liberal government was under attack for its high taxes and spending habits. While there is some disagreement as to when the Quiet Revolution came to a close, the resurgence of the Union Nationale clearly indicated that the most intensive period of change was in temporary retreat. In the 1970s, however, the movement for Quebec nationalism would come into full blossom: a stepchild of *la revolution tranquille*.

Canada in the Mid-1960s: A Tumultuous Time

The advent of the Cold War, the embers of which can be found in the ashes of World War II, signified momentous adjustments for Canada. The war helped to position the country as one of the world's leading democracies and industrial powerhouses. Geographically sandwiched between the emerging superpowers, Canadians deliberately fashioned an international role based on a middle power principle. With financial and trade linkages to Great Britain redefined because of the war, Canada's North American focus became magnified. In 1963 Pearson's victorious Liberals capitalized on Diefenbaker's failed attempts to disentangle Canada from American defensive, economic, and cultural influences. Canadians were ambivalent about their relationship with their superpower neighbor, and events after the mid-1960s would only intensify that uncertainty.

On the domestic front, the historic tensions between anglophones and francophones that had served to define so much of Canadian history continued apace. Importantly, the battleground became more sharply clarified as a contest between a self-assured Quebec and the federal government. On another level, the influx of immigrants in the postwar era profoundly altered Canada's ethnic composition. An increasingly urbanized and industrialized society after the war, the country would slip into a global postindustrial environment by the 1980s. The federal and provincial governments would expand their powers considerably, creating collectively or individually a vast network of social and medical programs. The next two decades would bring the clearest articulation yet of Canadian nationalism, illustrated by a new constitution that effectively completed the protracted process of gaining sovereignty from Britain. At the same time, events in Quebec kindled a provincial variation of nationalism that threatened to dissolve the bonds of Confederation. Hard on the heels of these events came trade agreements with the United States that led many Canadians to believe that their country's chances for survival into the twenty-first century had been severely diminished. In sum, one of the most eventful periods in Canadian history loomed on the immediate horizon in the mid-1960s.

Chapter 9

One Nation or Two?
(1960s–1984)

Competing Nationalisms

During the 1960s Canadians experienced a period of intensive nationalistic feelings that seemingly moved in opposite directions. To improve the quality of life for all Canadians, Liberal governments under Pearson and Trudeau passed legislation for medical coverage, welfare programs, pension plans, and unemployment insurance. These social measures became a bedrock ideal of the new Canadian state, but they also raised troublesome questions of how to pay for the expensive services and control the government's mounting debt. Yet even to the critics of the Liberal mandate, the notion that Canada boasted a superior quality of life with a government that cared for every one of its citizens became an essential ingredient of nationalistic pride. Illustrations of Canada's maturation included the adoption of a new flag in the 1960s and the creation of a constitution to replace the BNA Act in 1982. With Americans mired in political upheavals and a seemingly intractable war in Vietnam, Canadians felt that their country had developed a superior model of governance that struck the right balance of individual rights and governmental stewardship.

While Canadians justifiably trumpeted their country's accomplishments, the Quiet Revolution led to a celebration of nationalistic pride in Quebec. By the 1970s a growing political movement, the

Fireworks display on Parliament Hill in Ottawa during the Centennial celebration of 1967.

Source: Library and Archives Canada / Malak Karsh / C-027286

Parti Québécois, dedicated itself to seeking a fundamental restructuring of the relationship between Quebec and Canada. A series of Quebec legislative measures designed to ensure that French would become the language of politics, work, and education prompted intense discussions and widened divisions between anglophones and francophones. The political agenda to explore separation culminated in a referendum in 1980. Voters rejected the sovereignty proposal, but the issue remained alive. Other groups and regions in Canada also agitated for more representation and rights. They maintained that the francophone-anglophone debate received a disproportionate share of the nation's focus. Thus, Canada from the mid-1960s to the early 1980s was an immensely complex place. Its many strengths notwithstanding, competing social, political, class, and ethnic identities repeatedly threatened to unravel the skein of nationhood.

The Liberals and the Social State

Lester Pearson's promise to bring "sixty days of decision" to tackle the complex economic and social issues that had been pestering the country under Diefenbaker's leadership helped to bring the Liberals into power in the spring of 1963. Pearson brought tremendous diplomatic experience to his new job as prime minister. He had served as president of the General Assembly of the United Nations in the early 1950s and garnered a Nobel Peace Prize for his peacekeeping efforts during the Suez crisis of 1956. His stewardship of Canada until 1968 would sorely test those skills in both domestic and foreign policy issues. Tricky political crosscurrents of nationalism, regionalism, and Quebec's uneasiness, in addition to maintaining a close but not intertwined relationship with the United States, meant that Pearson and the Liberals would enjoy only marginal successes.

The rapid changes brought about by industrialization and the interconnected trade patterns of the postwar world deeply affected Canadians. The country's explosive population growth, through both natural increase and immigration, contributed to a climate for social reform. In the 1960s the Canadian government aggressively developed a broad range of social programs. The Economic Council of Canada, created in 1963, created a think tank to explore economic policies for both domestic and international markets. One of its first recommendations was to identify the need for a well-trained and skilled workforce to compete in the intensely competitive postindustrial environment. Many observers considered the Economic Council to be one of the best innovations of the Pearson era.

The social and medical network of modern Canada became a reality in a wave in far-reaching legislation passed in the 1960s. As sociologist John Porter argued in a landmark work published in 1965, *The Vertical Mosaic*, great distances separated the country's class and ethnic groups. Anglophones of British heritage, Porter maintained, were clearly at the top of the economic and social hierarchy. Many agreed that Canada had disturbing gaps between haves and have-nots, and they wanted the government to ensure that all Canadian citizens reached a threshold of basic services. The Canada Assistance Act, passed in 1965, provided for welfare assistance to help the needy, offer child care funds, and fund training projects to help the unemployed become marketable. The act placed the federal government squarely in the position of stewardship. It attempted to draw the responsibility of assisting society's underclass away from provincial governments and private charitable organizations (see "The Underside of Canadian Society" in the Documents section).

The crowning achievement of the Liberal social mandate was the creation of a comprehensive medical plan. Modeled directly on the Saskatchewan program developed by Tommy Douglas's CCF party, the Medical Care Act came into effect in the mid-1960s. According to the Medicare terms, the federal government would share with the provinces medical costs for every citizen. By 1972 all of the provinces and territories had agreed to the proposal. Although the medical profession vehemently opposed its implementation and various provinces complained that they were being coerced because it was almost impossible to refuse the federal government's offer to pay half of its costs, the comprehensive medical plan had become a Canadian institution by the 1970s. Expensive and varied in the quality of its coverage and treatment, Medicare nonetheless became a source of pride as it expanded the role of the federal and provincial governments.

Other stewardship plans followed with an avalanche of legislation. The Canada Pension Plan of 1965 created a universal pension scheme for working Canadians at the retirement age of sixty-five. Contributions from the government, employers, and individuals paid for the benefits. Measures to improve unemployment insurance, create student loans, and provide low-income housing assistance also passed the House of Commons. By the 1970s Canada's government had created a comprehensive social network that rivaled those of socialist countries. Citizens rapidly found that these programs came at a great cost. The tax burden for individuals and businesses rose; the federal debt increased substantially. Moreover, the vast social apparatus became a political hot potato. Individuals generally supported the programs, but larger provinces such as Ontario and Quebec regularly complained that their powers were being usurped by the federal government.

Canadian Nationalism Triumphant

Canadian national pride soared in the 1960s, despite rising dissatisfaction in Quebec. A new national flag, with a maple leaf design, was raised in 1965 after a contentious parliamentary debate. Another source of positive national self-esteem was Montreal's Exposition in 1967, which was designed to showcase the city as well as to celebrate the centennial of Confederation. The brainchild of Jean Drapeau, Montreal's mayor, Expo '67 absorbed tremendous resources, kindled labor disputes, and ran into staggering cost overruns. Remarkably, given its manifold problems, Expo '67 was a shining moment for both Canadians and *Québécois*. The rosy glow dissipated rapidly, however, when French President Charles de Gaulle appeared to give approval to Quebec's separatist movement when he proclaimed to an emotional crowd: *"Vive le Québec libre!"* Angry federalists pointed out that Quebec was free and did not need liberation. While this centennial event was bittersweet, most Canadians fondly remember it.

The federal government moved on other fronts during the 1960s to liberalize the country's laws. In an attempt to promote "co-operative federalism," Pearson placated the provinces by paying attention to their fiscal and social needs. Perhaps the most important response to this ideal was the Royal Commission on Bilingualism and Biculturalism. Over the course of several years, the commission studied the historic divisions between "the two founding races," meaning francophones and anglophones. Its most important legacy was the Official Languages Act of 1969, which guaranteed Canadians the right to receive federal services in either French or English. Over time civil servants would have to display competency in both official languages. Bilingually labeled consumer products and advertising followed suit. With Acadians comprising approximately one-third of its population, New Brunswick became the only officially bilingual province in 1968. The adaptation of bilingualism drew mixed responses. Canadians considered their language policy evidence of the country's tolerance, and within a generation language immersion programs became a booming industry. However, the cost of bilingualism's implementation, from printing expenses to ensuring that government agencies fielded bilingual staffs in overwhelmingly unilingual areas, became a brunt of criticism. Few dispute the claim that the government's move to embrace bilingualism and biculturalism left an important legacy, and while it ameliorated some of the tensions with Quebec, it continues to be a matter of some debate over forty years after its inception.

Other commissions and government actions redirected the country in the 1960s. Capital punishment was discontinued, except in cases involving the murder of police or prison officers. Labor laws were liberalized, including the right of civil servants to collective bargaining. Strikes by civil service workers, such as employees of Canada Post, periodically disrupted life and led to great public resentment. Women's rights also expanded in the decade. The Royal Commission on the Status of Women, charged in 1967, took three years to address family issues, employment, and education. It contributed to the formation of the National Action Committee on the Status of Women (NAC) in 1971, an overarching organization for hundreds of women's groups. In addition, immigration laws after 1967 were changed. Strict consideration of geographic origin or ethnicity shifted to a point system that weighed a prospective immigrant's educational level, work experience, and financial resources. In sum, Liberal policies under Pearson and then Trudeau constructed an enormous social network and a more open political environment to accommodate the specific needs of various groups and regions. Yet these changes in the 1960s did not eliminate the country's problems. In some cases, it magnified them.

Bilateralism or Multilateralism?

The deepening Cold War in the 1960s produced a particularly troublesome series of circumstances for Canada's governing officials and foreign policy experts. Canadians sensed, as did their political leaders, that the country's most important foreign relationship had become its bilateral trade and military alliance with the United States. At the same time, Pearson wanted to maintain Canada's visibility in the UN and NATO. Diplomats presented Canada as a fair-minded middle power, one with a special relationship with the United States but not under its control. Canada cultivated its linkages to other Commonwealth countries in the postwar era as Britain's aging empire was rapidly dismantled. Relationships with these countries rested on modest trade agreements and cultural events, such as the Commonwealth Games of athletic competition held every four years.

Canada's peacekeeping efforts in a world riddled by regional conflicts became perhaps its most notable international role. The country sent peacekeepers to over thirty hot spots from the Suez crisis in 1956 to the turn of the century. In one protracted mission, for example, a generation of Canadian troops served as a buffer to keep hostile pro-Greek and pro-Turkish elements separated in Cyprus. Canada was also invited to be on the International Commission for Supervision and Control (ICSC) in 1954. The three-nation group (Poland and India were the other two) was charged with overseeing a cease-fire and monitoring elections in a war-ravaged and divided Vietnam. Deteriorating events and a growing U.S. military presence in South Vietnam meant that Canada, as the Western representative on the ICSC, would increasingly support the interests of the United States.

Canada and the United States developed a more favorable relationship after the sour Diefenbaker-Kennedy years. They signed the Autopact in 1965 that decreased duties on cars, trucks, and parts. As a result, the automobile industry became the largest trading sector between the two countries. Plants on either side of the boundary used parts made in the other country, thereby interweaving the automobile manufacturing system in North America. Another sign of bilateral cooperation emerged in an important 1965 report, *Principles for Partnership*. The authors, Canadian diplomat Arnold Heeney and his

American counterpart Livingston Merchant, argued that the two countries shared similar outlooks and should seek peaceful and mutually beneficial economic and diplomatic relations. While in hindsight *Principles for Partnership* seems almost naively optimistic, it illustrated a powerful desire in the mid-1960s for the two countries to avoid divisive issues.

The developing U.S. involvement in the Vietnam conflict placed Canada in an uncomfortable and sometimes compromised position. As the French failed to reassert their imperial control over Vietnam after World War II, the United States stepped into the breach. U.S. participation in the war escalated in the early 1960s, first with President Kennedy's military advisers and then with President Lyndon Johnson's combat troops after the congressional Tonkin Gulf Resolution in 1964. Although Canadian representatives worked to provide a communication link between North Vietnam and the United States in this period, Canadian industries were already making millions producing goods that would be used for the American war effort in support of South Vietnam. This fact was not firmly grasped by contemporaries. Moreover, the American impulse to contain the spread of communism received a great deal of support among Canadian citizens and leaders. Yet the intensity of Johnson's bombing campaign, known as "Rolling Thunder," threatened to expand the localized conflict into a regional war that would engulf all of Southeast Asia. In a speech at Philadelphia's Temple University in 1965, Pearson suggested that a temporary halt in the bombing could bring beneficial results by giving the North Vietnamese time to consider peaceful reunification ideas. The mild criticism of U.S. foreign policy triggered a remarkable diplomatic incident. In a meeting following the speech, a livid Johnson grabbed Pearson's lapels and berated him for questioning American war tactics while he was a guest in the United States. Badly shaken by the episode, Pearson publicly threw his support behind the bombing.

The relationship between the two countries would continue to be strained as the war raged and the number of U.S. combat troops grew and bombing missions escalated into the late 1960s. As thousands of Canadians voluntarily joined the American military to fight in Vietnam, approximately 125,000 draft evaders and some deserters crossed the border from the United States to Canada. By the late 1960s, Canada's ambivalence toward the Cold War was showing.

Its earlier attempts to be a special partner of the United States were shopworn, largely because of the brutal and seemingly insoluble nature of the Vietnamese conflict. Canada was still one of the world's leading sources of peacekeeping forces. At the same time, Canadians were questioning the wisdom of supporting bloody regional conflicts that grew out of the larger struggle between superpowers during the Cold War.

Trudeaumania

Pearson's resignation announcement in 1967 led to a flurry of activity to seek an appropriate replacement to be the Liberal prime minister. An eligible bachelor of comfortable wealth, Minister of Justice Pierre Elliott Trudeau seemed an ideal choice. Quebec's fluently bilingual Trudeau, of French-Canadian and Scottish heritage, relished the chance to lead the country. Intelligent and sharp witted, Trudeau carried educational credentials from the finest institutions in Canada, England, France, and the United States. After replacing Pearson, Trudeau handily won the federal election in 1968 against the Conservative forces of Robert Stanfield. "Trudeaumania," stemming from the new prime minister's promises to create a "just society," caught the imagination of a significant number of Canadians. The bridge from the aging cold warriors to the baby boomers seemed to have been constructed.

Trudeau's Liberal governments from 1968 to 1979 and from 1980 to 1984 were heavily stamped by his political philosophy and anti–Cold War perspective. A devoted federalist, Trudeau believed that the government had a responsibility to ensure basic rights for all Canadians. In his estimation, no individual, group, or province deserved special treatment. In international affairs Trudeau emphasized a greater degree of Canadian sovereignty, trade, economic aid to developing countries, and a partial withdrawal from Canada's military obligations in alliances such as NATO. Plagued by an ailing economy and forced to confront a mounting separatist movement in Quebec, Trudeau during his years in office inspired many Canadians to devoted loyalty. At the same time, his reputation as an abrasive leader fueled an intense hatred among the opponents to his vision for Canada.

Like other countries during the late 1960s and 1970s, Canada's economy foundered as inflation, the consumer price index, and unemployment rose. Trudeau expanded federal powers to grapple with these issues. The Department of Regional Economic Expansion (DREE), formed in 1969 to assist economic expansion in regions with high unemployment, such as the Atlantic provinces, was one example. DREE enjoyed some success in building roads and improving municipal services, and until it was disbanded in the early 1980s, it was an illustration of a federal agency that attempted to provide some balance between Canada's have and have-not regions. International trade patterns were partially responsible for the country's economic woes. The rising power of the Organization of Petroleum Exporting Countries (OPEC) in the mid-1970s contributed to the problems because Canadians were becoming increasingly dependent on oil for business and recreation. Another blow came when President Richard Nixon's government instituted a special American tax on imports in 1971 and failed to create a special category for Canada.

After almost losing an extremely close election in 1972, Trudeau developed plans to pursue a third option in trade policy. Instead of maintaining the status quo or drawing closer to the United States, Canada would attempt to boost its international trade. Markets in the Pacific Rim were especially attractive, and in 1970 Canada formally recognized the People's Republic of China. Following the Gray Report, a scathing critique of foreign investment's negative impact on the country, the Foreign Investment Review Agency (FIRA) was formed in 1973. Americans owned almost a quarter of Canada's assets, and two-thirds of Canada's foreign trade was with the United States. FIRA created an expensive bureaucracy to review outside investments; it theoretically blocked funds if they did not prove to be of "significant benefit" to Canadians. But as its critics pointed out, it accepted over ninety percent of the potential funds and utterly failed to alter the directional patterns of foreign investments. A testament to the fear that only negative results would come of a closer economic relationship with the United States, FIRA would be fundamentally revamped when the Conservatives came into power in the 1980s.

Following an election in 1974, during which the losing Conservative Robert Stanfield proposed wage and price controls, the country's economy soured even more. With global prices skyrocketing for OPEC oil, plans to have western Canada's oil production offset eastern Canada's reliance on petroleum imports became more imperative. The year after the election, despite his criticism of Stanfield's plans, Trudeau instituted wage and price controls. They were designed to reduce the country's inflation, which stood at over ten percent. Parliament created Petro-Canada the same year. A crown corporation, meaning it was government owned, it was designed to foster western and northern oil production and negotiate trade with foreign producers. Despite its initiatives, Trudeau's government struggled. Alarming federal deficits, due to expensive social and medical programs created in the 1960s and a weak Canadian dollar, signified an economy in extreme duress. With a federal election pending in 1979, the Liberals seemed ripe for defeat.

Trudeau's Foreign Policy

In many ways Trudeau's foreign policy represented a profound rejection of some of the Cold War's most cherished guiding principles. While most of his counterparts in the United States and Western Europe remained devoted to blocking Soviet expansion and as the United States became increasingly mired in the Vietnam War, Trudeau's government deliberately sought to weaken Canada's economic and cultural attachments to the Americans. Following a rancorous debate late in Pearson's administration, the government unified the military forces into a single organization in the Canadian Forces Reorganization Act of 1968. Even skeptical of Canada's established peacekeeping role, Trudeau tried to implement a foreign policy that was defined by "caring" relationships. The Liberals in 1970 published a series of glossy pamphlets for public distribution called *Foreign Policy for Canadians*. The booklets highlighted trade and humanitarian aid. Much to the chagrin of fellow NATO members, Canada decreased its already modest military presence in Europe by about half. Trudeau's priorities were to protect Canadian sovereignty rather than to participate aggressively in the Cold War containment of the Soviet bloc.

Profoundly affecting the Liberal government's policies was a frosty relationship with the new U.S. president, Richard Nixon.

While maintaining Canada's commitment to the defense of North America under the auspices of NORAD, Trudeau was especially apprehensive about American participation in the raging Vietnam War. Along with the thousands of draft evaders came Americans who were critical of their country's foreign policy. These migrants—many of whom were professionals, teachers, and students—considered Canada a peaceful and enlightened refuge. A flurry of articles and books by academics and journalists in the late 1960s and early 1970s, including *Close the 49th Parallel, Etc.*, *The Star-Spangled Beaver*, and *Silent Surrender*, showcased a deep-seated antagonism to America's economic and cultural impact on Canada. Trudeau attempted to capture this popular sentiment to support his programs to redirect some of the country's trade away from the United States. Yet while this process was unfolding, alarming political and social events in Quebec captured an increasing amount of the federal government's attention. By the 1970s Trudeau had become consumed with combating a surging nationalistic movement in his home province (see "Keenleyside's Letter" in the Documents section).

Quebec and the Question of Sovereignty

The Quiet Revolution created a climate for French-Canadian nationalism. After the loss of Jean Lesage's Liberals in 1966, the Union Nationale returned to power until 1970. Their ineffective governments, led first by Daniel Johnson and then by Jean-Jacques Bertrand, failed to tackle Quebec's mounting economic and social pressures. Despite the federal government's embrace of official bilingualism after 1969, the stage was set for a contest between a Trudeau vision of federalism, which rested on individual equality and no special status for any one group or province, and a *Québécois* sense of distinctiveness and pride. Riots in the late 1960s during Quebec's nationalistic celebrations on Saint-Jean Baptiste Day (June 24), violent strikes, and angry student gatherings in Montreal illustrated the most recent phase of historic divisions between anglophones and francophones. The return of Quebec's Liberals in 1970, under the leadership of a young economist named Robert Bourassa, aroused hopes that tensions would dissipate. Instead,

Quebec immediately stumbled into one of the thorniest political moments of its history.

After its inception in 1963 a militant wing of separatists, the *Front de libération du Québec* (FLQ), directed a campaign of harassment and violence against agencies of the federal government and Quebec's anglophone community. Under the guidance of Pierre Vallières, the author of a scathing statement of injustices directed against franco-phones entitled *Nègres blancs d'Amérique* (translated as *White Niggers of America*), the FLQ was responsible for hundreds of bombings during the 1960s. These ranged from attacks on mail-boxes in Montreal's anglophone Westmount to the Montreal Stock Exchange, where over two dozen people were injured. A tiny organization comprising even smaller subgroups, called cells, the FLQ demanded and received attention from Canadians. Its goal was an independent Quebec.

In early October 1970, soon after Bourassa became premier, the FLQ kidnaped the British trade commissioner in Montreal. For James Cross's release, it demanded and received permission to read its manifesto on Radio-Canada, the French-language component of the CBC. Days later another FLQ cell kidnaped the provincial minister of labour, Pierre Laporte. Despite an initial outpouring of sympathy for the kidnappers from nationalist elements in Quebec, Bourassa asked Ottawa for military support. Citing an "apprehended insurrection," Trudeau's government invoked the War Measures Act. Thousands of soldiers appeared on the streets of Montreal and Quebec City, creating disturbing images of public disorder that had become commonplace in American and European cities in the 1960s. Over four hundred people were detained; most were soon released. Officials discovered Laporte's body in the trunk of a car, one of the few political assassinations in the entire scope of Canadian history. The urgency passed by December when Cross was released and a number of FLQ members were arrested or escaped to Cuba. The October Crisis shaped the country's future in several ways. While the Canadian public overwhelmingly supported the use of the War Measures Act, the prime minister's actions angered Quebec nationalists and defenders of civil liberties. They pointed out that Trudeau's behavior was hypocritical in the light of his promotion of individual freedoms. Nonetheless, both federalists and separatists were unified in their rejection of political violence. The October Crisis helped to clear a path for people who believed that Quebec's independence should be won by democratic means, not through violent revolutionary tactics.

Bourassa, whose image was tarnished by his reliance on federal forces to cope with the October Crisis, tempered the concerns of *Québécois* who believed that an erosion of language and culture would lead to assimilation. In 1974, Bill 22 passed Quebec's National Assembly with Liberal support. It ensured that French would be the language of government and the workplace in Quebec. For educational purposes, nonfrancophone children would be permitted to learn in a non-French environment if they could demonstrate competency in another language. The bill ultimately pleased few. Many francophones wanted stronger measures, while anglophones found the bill, especially in the light of federal bilingualism, a reprehensible curtailment of their rights. The modern Quebec nationalist movement was making the protection of French one of its core issues. A 1976 strike of Canadian air traffic controllers who wanted English to be their exclusive work language further convinced *Québécois* that their language and culture needed to be maintained, and the most fitting locus of that preservation would be Quebec. Even plans to hold the 1976 summer Olympic Games in Montreal could not reinvigorate a sense of Canadian nationalism that included Quebec. As a result of the Quiet Revolution and the stresses of the 1960s and 1970s, *Québécois* had linked the survival of Canada's francophones exclusively to the province of Quebec.

The Parti Québécois and Sovereignty-Association

The political legacy of the rising tide of nationalist spirit in Quebec was the formation of a political party dedicated to rearranging fundamentally the province's relationship with Canada. The Parti Québécois (PQ) gathered smaller nationalist groups under the banner of a single party in 1968 with a platform to seek independence from Canada. A former Liberal in the Lesage government, René Lévesque, emerged as the PQ's leader. Lévesque, a bilingual war correspondent and television commentator, was both popular and persuasive. Although he personally lost elections in the early 1970s, his party gathered strength. Bourassa's growing unpopularity, caused by his scandal-ridden Liberal government and Quebec's economic woes, eventually gave the PQ a chance to win power in 1976. The new government that settled into control in Quebec City sent shivers down the spines of Canadians, essentially because the PQ had been elected with a promise to negotiate a new relationship with Canada. The PQ believed that Quebec was already a nation. What it lacked was the sovereignty to pursue its own destiny.

The PQ swiftly implemented the ideals of the Quiet Revolution. Legislation poured out of Quebec City, including measures to create no-fault automobile insurance, curtail corporate donations to political parties, and reform labor laws. In 1977 the PQ passed Bill 101, the Charter of the French Language. According to its terms, children could receive public education in English only if one or both of their parents had been educated in English in Quebec. Effectively the bill was designed to force immigrants and Canadians who had migrated from other provinces to adopt the francophone culture. Bill 101 also mandated that larger businesses carry on their entire work in French and insisted that store and public signs be in French. Nationalistic *Québécois*, believing that it adequately protected Quebec's language and culture, cheered the legislation. Not surprisingly it aroused fierce resentment among nonfrancophones. The emergence of the PQ and the passage of Bill 101 prompted an out-migration of anglophones, many of them young and well educated. An estimated one-seventh of Quebec's anglophone population had relocated to other Canadian provinces by the mid-1980s. Similarly, a flight of large corporations followed the law's passage. The most sensational example was Sun Life, one of the world's largest insurance companies, which relocated to Toronto. More than any other legislative measure of the PQ government, Bill 101 indicated that separatists were aggressively protecting francophone culture and French. A bigger event awaited, however. A popular referendum on the PQ's idea of sovereignty-association, promised in the election of 1976, would be a chance for separatists to alter Quebec's relationship with Canada. Federalists, on the other hand, had their own plans to defuse the PQ's agenda.

Trudeau's Travails and the Clark Interlude

By 1979 Trudeau's Liberals were in desperate trouble. A bloated bureaucracy struggled to maintain numerous social and medical programs. The country's economy was plagued by rising oil prices and inflation, issues that had helped to seal the fate of the hapless American president, Jimmy Carter, in 1980. Once the object of a devoted following, Trudeau was now considered by many Canadians an aloof or even dictatorial leader who invited confrontations with opponents in Parliament and the provinces. Westerners, following the leadership of forceful premiers such as Alberta's Peter Lougheed, agitated for more provincial control over resources and improved regional economic development. The rise of a strong West with political clout was illustrated by the selection of a young Albertan, Joseph Clark, to lead the Progressive Conservatives in 1976. The choice of a relative unknown, obviously unseasoned in both domestic and foreign policy issues, did not prevent the Conservatives from ousting Trudeau in 1979.

The opportunity that the Conservatives had long dreamed of proved to be fleeting, however, as the new prime minister failed utterly to survive the cruel test of the media's glare. Dubbed "Joe Who?" by an mostly unfavorable and skeptical press, Clark wanted to institute a Conservative program that included a rethinking of Canada's enormous social structure. His election slogan to create a "community of communities" suggested a sensitivity to the complex political and social variations in the country's regions. One of his most dramatic plans was to privatize government-owned Petro-Canada, which to Conservatives represented an inappropriate government activity and misguided use of taxpayers' funds. Yet Clark's inexperience proved politically fatal. A major foreign policy blunder of proposing to move Canada's embassy in Israel from Tel Aviv to Jerusalem touched off an international firestorm. Opposition in Canada forced the Clark government to scrap the idea. When his budget proposal called for an increased gasoline tax of eighteen cents per gallon to help pay down the deficit, his government failed to receive Parliament's approval. Less than nine months after reaching power, the Conservatives lost power to Trudeau's resurgent Liberals. Assessments of the brief Clark interlude tend to vary considerably.

Some highlight Clark's lack of experience. Others believe that his rise to power was premature. A conservative movement would fundamentally reconfigure Canada's economy and relationships, especially with the United States, starting in the mid-1980s under Brian Mulroney. Remarkably, given the harsh treatment that he received in his moment of leadership, Clark would later return as a respected external affairs minister in Mulroney's cabinet.

Canada's voting patterns in the 1980 election that brought Trudeau back into power painted a stark image of a deeply divided country. The Liberals were virtually without members from the West, yet they almost swept Quebec. The New Democratic Party (NDP) failed to pick up seats east of Ontario. The Atlantic Provinces and Ontario were more mixed in the political affiliations of their members of Parliament. Trudeau promised voters that this would be his final stint as prime minister. In 1980 his government introduced a National Energy Program (NEP), which was designed to boost Canada's share of its energy revenues by decreasing foreign ownership, especially American. The NEP drew negative responses from the western premiers, especially Alberta's Lougheed, who complained that it was another example of the federal government's meddling in provincial matters. In hindsight, the NEP was one of the last gasps of a protracted legislative effort to reverse the trading and investment trends that had so intricately fused the economies of Canada and the United States since the late nineteenth century. Trudeau's successor, Brian Mulroney, would find common conservative ground with his American and British counterparts and all but silence the anti-American voices from the 1970s.

Quebec's 1980 Referendum

The Parti Québécois, in the meantime, geared up its political machinery and moved toward a referendum. Guided by modern polling techniques, the PQ backed off on its original plan to seek total independence when it determined that such a proposal would fail to draw widespread support. Instead, it worked out a scheme to reformulate its relationship with the rest of Canada based on a more qualified sovereignty-association. This "new deal" would sever the constitutional links to Canada. Quebec would thus gain full control over its taxes, laws, and foreign relations. Yet Lévesque's government also proposed to maintain certain connections with Canada, including a common currency, free trade, defense agreements, and open borders. The Liberals, in a "new federalism" program spearheaded by Claude Ryan, offered *Québécois* an alternative suggestion. They promised to work with the federal government to develop a new constitution, change the Senate, and create a federal council to improve federal-provincial relations. In May 1980 Quebec adults went to the polls to respond *oui* or *non* to a question that would give the PQ permission to enter into discussions with the federal government on its terms of sovereignty-association. It was not a vote on separation. Even if the federal and provincial governments agreed to make substantial changes in the future, Quebec's voters would have to give their approval in another referendum. Sixty percent of the voters responded *non*. A greater disappointment for the PQ, however, was the fact that just over half of the province's francophone voters rejected their proposal. Perhaps the best news for the separatists was that younger and better educated voters, the heirs of the Quiet Revolution, were heavily in the *oui* camp (see "Perspectives of History and the Sovereignty-Association Question" in the Documents section).

The sovereignty-association question failed for several reasons. Trudeau promised during the campaign, largely through a popular Liberal named Jean Chrétien, that if voters rejected the PQ proposal, then the federal government would work out a new constitutional arrangement with all the provinces. The Liberal opposition in Quebec was fairly effective in exposing the ambiguities of sovereignty-association and convincing voters that there was no guarantee that Canadians would agree to the "association" part of the proposal. Finally, the watered-down question angered hard-core separatists who wanted total independence from Canada. In spite of the referendum loss, Quebec's voters overwhelmingly returned the PQ to power in 1981. Ironically, the PQ's platform included the same plan to seek sovereignty-association. Baffled by this mixed message from voters, Lévesque shelved the separation agenda and turned to Trudeau's federal government to make good on its promise to revamp the constitution to make the provinces more important players in Confederation.

A New Constitution

Discussions about making fundamental changes to the BNA Act, Canada's constitution, were almost as old as the document. It remained a statute of British Parliament after 1867. Conferences dedicated to this topic had taken place periodically during the twentieth century. Much of the debate focused on the balance of powers between the federal and provincial governments, in particular taxation and spending rights and the control of social, medical, and educational programs. In addition, the details of amending a new constitution proved a troublesome issue. Discussions to create an amending formula that was acceptable to all ten provinces collapsed in 1964 after Quebec retracted its initial support. In 1971 the so-called Victoria Charter grew out of a federal-provincial conference. It included material on language rights and reforming the Supreme Court, as well as new amending principles. When Quebec once again signaled its displeasure, the Victoria Charter collapsed.

Trudeau was determined to give Canadians a new constitution after he returned to power in 1980. After promising Quebec voters substantial constitutional revisions during the 1980 referendum campaign, his government gathered the country's provincial leaders to determine how to "patriate" the constitution. Trudeau received strong support of his plan to craft an exclusively Canadian governing document from only two premiers, Bill Davis of Ontario and Richard Hatfield of New Brunswick. The tricky negotiations opened up questions of the legality of the proceedings. In 1981 the Supreme Court determined that the provinces enjoyed traditional "conventions," meaning customary rights. This suggested that their input in such grave matters as altering a constitution should be recognized and accepted. At the same time, the Supreme Court pronounced that the federal government had the power to request a new constitution. While both sides found solace in the equivocal decision, the prime minister pushed ahead to complete the process of constitutional patriation.

In November 1981, after feverish negotiations that brought nine of the ten premiers into an agreement on the terms for a new constitution, Trudeau presented a legislative package to the British Parliament. René Lévesque, angered at what he considered the denial of Quebec's unique rights in the bargaining process, refused to sign the agreement. Some Native peoples and women's groups, disappointed that their rights were not adequately protected, also objected to the proposal. The British Parliament passed the Canada Act in March 1982 after representatives from Quebec and the First Nations unsuccessfully made their cases to derail its approval. The Canada Act formally removed the BNA Act as a British statute. The following month, at a ceremony in Ottawa with Queen Elizabeth in attendance, Canada's Constitution Act became law. Conspicuously absent during the celebration was a delegation from Quebec. Other protesters formed part of the backdrop on the chilly day when the document was signed, a dramatic reminder that the country still faced considerable domestic challenges. Nonetheless, after 115 years, a constitution resided in Ottawa. Keeping only its ties to the British monarchy, Canada had finally achieved complete autonomy.

Constitution Act (1982)

The Constitution Act gave Canadians a document that was both familiar and new. Many parts of the BNA Act, including its amendments since 1867, were used as a foundation for the new Constitution. The most important additions were amending formulas, the Charter of Rights and Freedoms, and some expanded rights granted to the provinces. The thorniest issue of determining an amendment procedure yielded a complex range of possibilities that followed a scale of importance. For crucial matters it would take agreement in Parliament and all of the provinces to effect a change. These "entrenched" aspects of Canadian government that cannot be altered by legislation alone are the linkage to the British monarchy, the Supreme Court, and the amendment rules themselves. Non-entrenched terms could be modified by the assent of seven of the ten provinces, as long as the seven represented at least half of Canada's population. As one of their concessions, provinces could legally opt out of certain constitutional requirements. Since 1982 provinces can—and have—invoked the "notwithstanding" clause to avoid aspects of the Constitution that limit their powers, causing concern among a large number of Canadians. Finally, measures that address the operation of Parliament could be changed in the House of Commons without provincial approval. The complicated amending formulas are indications of the various compromises made during the negotiating process to gain the support of most of the provinces.

The most innovative component in the new Constitution was the Charter of Rights and Freedoms, a statement analogous to the U.S. Bill of Rights yet far more inclusive. The Charter guarantees Canadians equality, freedom of thought, legal rights, and religious freedoms. The principles to "life, liberty and security" are enshrined, as are English- and French-language rights in all agencies of government and Parliament. Significantly, the Charter ensures rights "without discrimination based on race, national or ethnic origin, colour, religion, sex, age or mental or physical disability." The Charter is thus one of the most progressive constitutional documents in the world, and almost thirty years after its adoption its implications are still being sorted out in Canada's various court systems (see "Charter of Rights and Freedoms" in the Documents section).

"Patriated" after fierce political wrangling, the Canadian Constitution of 1982 stands as a monument to the efforts of Trudeau and a handful of dedicated advisers, including future Prime Minister Jean Chrétien. They pushed the constitutional agenda through to completion in the face of significant opposition among the premiers and various groups. Nevertheless, the new Constitution has instilled pride among many Canadians for its progressive and inclusive language. In addition, the events of 1982 finally created a sovereign country, with only the most symbolic of linkages to the British monarchy remaining. By conscious design, the Constitution places the federal government in the foreground to protect the rights of individual Canadians.

On the other hand, the Constitution met intense opposition from one province and various groups. Already disturbed by Trudeau's blunt negotiation methods, *Québécois* resented the new Constitution because in their estimation it denied Quebec a traditional veto in deciding matters of state. Moreover, they believed that it did not adequately ensure that Quebec's distinct needs and culture would be protected. Women's groups, although pleased with the inclusion of language guaranteeing gender equality, also had concerns with the Constitution. Most problematic was the legal capability of provinces to opt out of some of the Constitution's terms, thereby potentially restricting women's rights in social services and the workplace. First Nations also had severe reservations with the Constitution. Although it entrenched the "existing aboriginal and treaty rights" of Native peoples, First Nations wanted more expansive language to protect their particular rights. In sum, the Constitution left certain groups and one province convinced that it fell short of addressing their specific needs. Thus, the fundamental tensions between the powers of the state, the special rights of groups, and the guaranteed rights of individuals were not solved by the Constitution Act of 1982. In many ways, they were given new life.

The Close of the Liberal Era

The constitutional process drained the energies of Trudeau and his Liberal government. Few other leaders in Canadian history have left behind such conflicting interpretations of their successes and failures. In Trudeau's case, the issue is compounded because the events are too recent to have drawn enough objective analysis. Trudeau still casts a shadow across the country, even after his death in 2000, and few Canadians are ambivalent about his memory. To his detractors he was a hypocritical politician who talked about guaranteeing individual rights while invoking the stringent War Measures Act. His "just society" was elusive; his government enthusiastically ran crown corporations such as Petro-Canada and attempted to control the marketplace by instituting the National Energy Program. To his supporters, Trudeau's style skillfully captured the essence of the complicated political, social, and economic landscape of Canada from the late 1960s to the mid-1980s. Trudeau's Canada, they argue, was riven by regional, provincial, racial, and class divisions. A divided country was not of his making; nonetheless, he protected basic individual rights and at the same time maintained a strong federal government to ensure Canada's national survival.

A sweeping reversal of national focus occurred after Trudeau's retirement in 1984. His government left a deficit of $30 billion and a national debt of almost $150 billion. The unemployment rate hovered around eleven percent, the highest since the Great Depression. Taxes had increased substantially, largely to pay for expanded social and medical services. Following Trudeau's resignation, the Liberals chose John Turner to be leader over Jean Chrétien. Turner became prime minister in June 1984. A former Liberal cabinet member who had been in the business world for years, Turner supposedly had sufficient distance from the unpopular Trudeau to weather a leadership change. He prematurely called an election in September 1984, hoping to receive popular approval. Instead the election turned into a shattering rout at the hands of a reinvigorated Progressive Conservative party under the leadership of Brian Mulroney, a Quebec lawyer and businessman with little political experience. The devastating Liberal losses, interpreted by many as a backhanded slap at Trudeau, ushered in a decidedly new era. Part of an international veer to the right in the 1980s, Mulroney would preside over an expansive economy. He would also intermesh the country, perhaps closer than ever before, with its neighbor.

The End of Cold War Canada?

The Cold War lingered into the 1980s, but it barely survived into the next decade. With breathtaking speed and few predictions, Germany moved toward reunification and the Soviet Union dismantled. Canada's attempts to adjust to extraordinary pressures during the height of the Cold War, when the United States achieved superpower status, rapidly became a distant memory. The "global village," a term popularized by Canadian intellectual Marshall McLuhan, seemed to materialize overnight. The globalization of business practices, technological interconnections, and a generic international culture threatened to expunge the few remaining characteristics that made Canada unique. The country in the late 1980s and 1990s endured the strains of union. The powerful West barely resembled the lagging Atlantic region. Quebec still refused to sign the Constitution, yet for most practical purposes it behaved as if it were a fully integrated province. Shifting immigration patterns fundamentally altered the country's ethnic composition. Resurgent Native peoples demanded and received more self-rule. Thus, Canada in the 1990s entered perhaps its most contradictory era. Repeatedly identified as the best nation on earth by the UN, the country lumbered through a series of abortive efforts to bring Quebec firmly back into the Confederation fold. By the turn of the century, most Canadians suffered mightily from secession fatigue, caused by endless discussions about the country's and Quebec's futures and the perennial threat of dismantlement. In many ways, Canada on the eve of the twenty-first century embodied the strengths and weaknesses of a modern nation-state.

Chapter 10

Late Twentieth-Century Canada (1984–2000)

The Challenges of Nationhood

From the 1980s to the turn of the twenty-first century Canada faced the challenges of a mature nation in the modern world. The accelerating globalization of economies, trade, and culture placed the country at a crossroads. After a second referendum on separation in Quebec in the mid-1990s, polls indicated that almost one in three Canadians and one in two *Québécois* assumed that by 2000, the country's current form would cease to exist. Moreover, traditional divisions between francophones and anglophones increasingly became an unsatisfactory way to understand the pivotal issues that underscored the country's political and social debates. By the late twentieth century, Canada had become a truly multicultural society. To cite only one example, Toronto, known in the nineteenth century as an anglophone and Protestant bastion, had become one of the most ethnically diverse cities on earth by 2000.

Canada remained firmly entrenched as one of the world's economic powerhouses, yet various factors drew the country even closer into the American orbit. By the 1990s the strident suspicions of American intentions that had been voiced by John Diefenbaker and Pierre Trudeau seemed to be curious sentiments from the past. Indeed, Canada had become part of an international arena where crucial

A drilling platform being towed to the Hibernia oil field, taken above Trinity Bay, Newfoundland, in 1997.

Source: Associated Press / Jonathan Hayward

decisions that affected the country could be made in London, Tokyo, or New York as easily as in Toronto, Montreal, or Vancouver. At the end of the Cold War, Canadians searched for new meanings and roles in a world riddled by localized and bloody struggles, but at least for the moment relieved of the prospect of a superpower nuclear confrontation. Canada would not be alone in experiencing growing pains and coping with a confusing array of directional signals about where to head in the future. Undeniably some of these issues were unique, molded in large part by the country's complex history. Yet in other important ways the "best nation on earth" had become the global equivalent of "every country."

The Conservative Impulse

Canada experienced one of its most dramatic changes ever in political orientation after the collapse of the Liberal mandate in 1984. The resounding return of the Progressive Conservatives under Brian Mulroney, a fluently bilingual lawyer and businessman from Quebec, was comparable to the right-wing movements that swept many other Western democracies in the 1980s. British Prime Minister Margaret Thatcher and U.S. President Ronald Reagan were models of the new conservatism. Mulroney's party ran a campaign that promised spending cuts and negotiations with Quebec so that it would agree to the new Constitution. Significantly, and in contrast to the tough social policies of Thatcher and Reagan, Mulroney and many other Conservatives understood that most Canadians valued their expansive social and medical programs. Nonetheless, privatization became a watchword of the new order, and adamant Conservatives wanted to cut into the social network to help bring down the deficit.

A full plate of problems awaited the newly installed Conservatives. With unemployment soaring to over eleven percent, a crippling inflation rate, and a frightening deficit, the government attempted to implement radically different fiscal policies. Emblematic of the new direction was the revamping of Trudeau's Foreign Investment Review Agency (FIRA). Born of the idea that the price for indiscriminately accepting investment capital was not worth the dilution of Canadian sovereignty, FIRA was given a mandate that was the polar opposite of its initial spirit. Later called "Investment Canada," it encouraged foreign investment. Similarly, the National Energy Program, the bane of westerners who considered the program an example of improper federal interference, was essentially gutted.

Although Mulroney prided himself on his negotiating skills, his administration swiftly resembled some of the scandal-ridden governments of his predecessors. Two issues during his years in office from 1984 to 1993 absorbed the bulk of his government's energies. Attempts to improve relations with Quebec dominated his domestic endeavors, and free trade discussions with the United States and later Mexico overshadowed his foreign policy. The failure to come up with a workable proposal to bring Quebec's signature to the Constitution and the success in intertwining the economies of Canada and the United States became Mulroney's legacy. Interestingly, his actions placed him on a trajectory that was similar to that of recent leaders such as Diefenbaker and Trudeau. Mulroney's politics and personality combined to explain his plummet from enjoying overwhelming popular approval to becoming one of the most reviled political figures in the entire scope of Canadian history.

A Distinct Society?

Mulroney sought a federal reconciliation with his native province, and René Lévesque's retirement in September 1985 led to a chain of events that opened the door to discussions on Quebec's position in Canada. Lévesque's replacement, Pierre Marc Johnson, promptly lost an election to the resurgent Liberals. Remarkably, given his low level of popular support when he was ousted in 1976, Robert Bourassa became premier once again. With the separatist Parti Québécois no longer in power, the conditions for a dialogue had improved. In spring 1987 Mulroney and the ten provincial premiers engaged in a series of meetings in Ottawa and at a nearby government retreat at Meech Lake. After marathon sessions the so-called first ministers came up with a list of proposals that, if the provinces and federal government gave their approval by June 1990, would ensure Quebec's agreement to the Constitution. The Meech Lake Accord suggested innovations in choosing Supreme Court justices and senators, changes in the Constitution's amendment procedures, and expanded language for provinces that wished to use the opting-out clause. Most important, it included a phrase that became the key sticking point for its opponents: Quebec would be recognized as a "distinct society."

The battle to pass the Meech Lake Accord in Parliament and the legislatures of the ten provinces broke out immediately. Proponents argued that the accord was reasonable and necessary to bring Quebec back into the Confederation fold. Opponents ranged widely in their viewpoints. Staunch federalists such as former prime minister Trudeau claimed that the accord would erode the powers of the federal government. Quebec separatists maintained that it did not adequately protect the province's special needs. Other groups, including First Nations, pointed out that they also deserved the constitutional protection of their distinct rights. Opponents were in general agreement that the process of having a handful of politicians, all white males, determine the country's future was fundamentally flawed.

Several events undermined and ultimately defeated the accord. In 1988 the Canadian Supreme Court agreed with several Quebec court decisions and found parts of Bill 101, Quebec's key French-language law, in violation of the Charter of Rights and Freedoms. Bourassa's government angered anglophones by invoking the Constitution's notwithstanding clause and passing Bill 178. This complicated sign law reinforced the use of French in businesses and permitted bilingual signs inside stores only if French remained prominently displayed. In addition, the weakness of having the first ministers complete the nation's business was exposed when several of the premiers who had been at Meech Lake lost their next elections. The new leaders in New Brunswick, Manitoba, and Newfoundland, for example, stated that they were not bound to the accord's terms. Ultimately the Meech Lake Accord collapsed in 1990 because of its built-in termination clause. Manitoba and Newfoundland failed to ratify it. Elijah Harper, a Cree member of the Manitoba legislature, received national attention by blocking the accord vote on a procedural issue because Native peoples had been excluded from the negotiations.

As a tribute to the dedication, or perhaps the obstinance, of the Mulroney government, the country was given another chance to solve the constitutional dilemma. A series of meetings transpired from 1991 to 1992 between federal and provincial ministers, as well as representatives from First Nations and other interest groups. These sessions symbolically ended in Charlottetown, Prince Edward Island: the birthplace of Confederation. The intense negotiations produced a more complex package of proposed constitutional changes than did the Meech Lake Accord. Westerners pushed for a reformulated "Triple E" Senate, meaning equal, elected, and effective. Given the body's traditional composition, Ontario and Quebec received the most senators, while western provinces were entitled to fewer senators than some of the Atlantic provinces. Native peoples insisted on the inclusion of the "inherent right to self government," the meaning of which was ambiguously defined. Importantly, the agreement borrowed from the Meech Lake Accord in describing Quebec as a distinct society. The meaty Charlottetown Accord, as it was called, was duly printed in both official languages and distributed to Canadian citizens.

The package was put to a national referendum on October 26, 1992, only the third such event in the country's history. Supporters included the leaders of the three major political parties, all the premiers, and a host of influential business, labor, and cultural activists. The opposition also varied. Many *Québécois* argued that the proposal did not go far enough to ensure Quebec's rights. First Nations were divided on the issue. Other groups wanted more assurances to protect their rights. Many Canadians had grown to despise Mulroney's initiatives, including the immensely unpopular Goods and Services Tax (GST), so they responded negatively to his latest plan to bind the wounds of Quebec and Canada. Almost fifty-five percent of the country's voters rejected the proposal. It received a favorable majority in only three of the Atlantic provinces and Ontario. Exhausted by years of discussions, cynical about the process, and frustrated by the constant threat of dismemberment, Canadians seemed to retreat from the issue after the failure of the Charlottetown Accord. As of 2000, Quebec has not signed the Canadian Constitution under which it effectively operates.

Going with the Flow: Free Trade

The other major initiative of Mulroney's Conservative government was driven by economic forces that had been developing since the nineteenth century. Despite the attempts of various governments to alter the patterns, Canada's economy by the 1980s was intricately tied to American markets and investments. Eighty percent of Canada's exports went to the United States, and about seventy percent of its imports came from the same country. One out of three Canadian workers earned a living that was defined by trade with Americans. Thus, there were compelling reasons to strengthen economic linkages. Mulroney and Reagan, already in agreement on many ideological issues, met in Quebec City in 1985. During this so-called "Shamrock Summit" the two leaders shared stories of their common Irish heritage and set the symbolic stage for a discussion about dropping the remaining tariff barriers between the two countries.

Negotiators from Canada and the United States delivered a massive free trade proposal in 1987. Running to three thousand pages, it called for the removal of tariffs within ten years of the proposal's acceptance by both parties. The Liberal-dominated Senate balked at the agreement, forcing the issue onto center stage during the 1988 elections. The campaign of that year in many ways evoked images of the 1911 reciprocity election, with the important exception that the political parties had reversed roles. Opposed to free trade were protected businesses and staple producers, laborers who feared losing their jobs, and people who were concerned that the country's sovereignty would be eroded as a result of the agreement. As key Liberal opponent John Turner famously proclaimed during a free trade debate, Mulroney's plan had "sold out" Canada (see "An Argument Against Free Trade" in the Documents section).

Despite these alarmist sentiments, Canadian voters returned the Conservatives to a second government. With the electorate's apparent approval, the agreement was implemented in 1989. Virtually all of the tariff barriers between the two countries would be dismantled by the turn of the century, with the exception of protections for Canadian cultural industries and selected agricultural products and resources. Plans to clarify a dispute resolution mechanism fell through, however, and the important issue of government subsidies to industries remained unresolved. Negotiations to include Mexico in a similar trade arrangement began immediately. In 1993 the three countries formalized the North American Free Trade Agreement (NAFTA). Since their implementation, free trade and NAFTA have received mixed reviews. Many

Canadians blame job losses and ailing sectors of the economy on the agreements. Others claim that business is booming without tariffs. By the turn of the century some trade disputes remained unresolved, such as a particularly tense series of charges and countercharges about national subsidies in the softwood industry. Although the long-term impact of the agreements awaits a future generation's assessment, they clearly boosted the already strong trade relationship between Canada and the United States at the close of the twentieth century. In 1997 eighty-one percent of Canada's exports headed to its neighbor, and seventy-six percent of its imports poured across the American border.

Canada and the World at the Turn of the Twenty-First Century

By the 1990s Canada had achieved a stature as one of the world's greatest democracies and economic leaders. Two world wars, Cold War alliances, and global trading patterns had increased the country's potential markets for its numerous primary materials. Yet developing countries, many of them also rich in resources such as forest products and minerals, aggressively competed with Canadian producers. Canadians struggled to adjust to the new realities of the "post" era: the post–Cold War and postindustrial environments thoroughly reshuffled the international deck. Traditional Canadian concerns about protecting the country's sovereignty were grafted onto modern ideals of trade without boundaries and corporate mergers.

In many ways, the architects of Canada's middle power ideal during World War II would have been pleased by the country's global position a half-century later. A founding member of the UN, the country had served on the Security Council and been active on organizations such as the World Food Program and the Children's Fund. Its cultivated role as a reliable peacekeeper since the 1950s had been the source of tremendous national pride. Canadian peace-keepers had served in over thirty separate missions in the Caribbean, Central America, Africa, the Middle East, Asia, and the Pacific. Tragically, on an assignment to Somalia in the 1990s some Canadian soldiers tortured and murdered a young Somalian. Televised pictures of the victim and the resulting scandal sullied the country's peacekeeping image and reminded Canadians that their troops were not immune from committing atrocities. Canadian forces also provided modest support in attacking Iraq after it invaded neighboring Kuwait in August 1990. The Gulf War was mostly a United States' undertaking that was essentially designed to protect the flow of oil from the Middle East, but it was authorized by the UN Security Council. Canada sent three ships and a squadron of fighters to join an international force in the troubled region. When some Canadian pundits cynically pointed out that an extraordinary proportion of the country's military had sailed off to the Middle East, they were not far off the mark. By the late 1990s the Canadian armed forces numbered about 60,000 active personnel. In the post–Cold War era, Canada's military had become minuscule. In 1995 tensions flared when a Canadian naval vessel fired a shot over the bow of a Spanish trawler that had been taking fish in protected offshore waters. Fisheries minister Brian Tobin, a feisty Newfoundlander, achieved popular fame as "Captain Canada" by staunchly and at times belligerently defending the country's interests in negotiations with Spanish diplomats.

Canada maintained connections to a number of international organizations besides the UN in the closing decades of the twentieth century. It remained a member of NATO and continued to staff a small military contingent in Europe, but its role in the alliance diminished significantly after the Cold War ended. In 1980 the country belatedly joined the Organization of American States (OAS), an association with roots in the nineteenth century that was designed to promote hemispheric relations. Canada remained an important part of the Commonwealth, the fifty-four countries that evolved from the former British Empire. Commonwealth activities included financial programs, educational exchanges, and sporting events. Similarly, Canada actively contributed to La Francophonie, an organization of French-speaking countries that encourages cultural and economic linkages between its members.

A participating member of the General Agreement on Tariffs and Trade since the late 1940s, Canada also fostered international trade. Besides its partnership with the United States and Mexico, Canada traded heavily with Japan, the United Kingdom, Germany, South

Korea, China, France, and Taiwan. In the mid-1980s it became a member of the G7, a seven-country organization of the world's wealthiest nations that met regularly to promote its interests in expanding global markets and investments (there are now twenty members of the G20). According to rankings provided by the UN and the World Bank, at the close of the century Canada was one of the leading countries in wealth, per capita income, industrial production, and rate of annual growth. These kinds of statistics, while important, tended to mask class, ethnic, and cultural issues that deeply affected Canadians. Although the number of wealthy Canadians had grown in the recent past, the gap between rich and poor remained.

Canada and the United States: Defense and Sovereignty Issues

Canada's relationship with the United States by 2000 was perhaps as close as it had ever been. The NORAD agreement was still in force, but "Aerospace" had replaced "Air" in its title to reflect Ronald Reagan's Strategic Defense Initiative (SDI). Nicknamed "Star Wars" by its critics, SDI sought to develop and deploy laser technology to provide an impenetrable defensive shield over North America. In the mid-1980s, plans were underway to supplant an antiquated Distant Early Warning system by a North Warning System. Thus, even without the intense pressures of the Cold War, and with questions about the nature of defense and deterrence on the cusp of the twenty-first century begging answers, the military linkages between Canada and the United States remained tightly interlocked.

Nonetheless, sources of tensions persisted in the relationship. Environmental issues, for example, continued to cause concern among Canadians and Americans. Acid rain was perhaps the most publicized of these irritants. Formed by poisonous emissions from massive fossil fuel-burning plants and the exhaust from trucks and automobiles, acid rain profoundly affected the environment of eastern Canada and the United States. Canadians were tenacious about identifying the problem and seeking solutions in the 1970s and 1980s, while the American governments of Reagan and George Bush neglected to enforce existing laws such as the Clean Air Act of 1971.

Well into the 1990s the issue remained unresolved, although the Canadian Environmental Act of 1988 created stringent guidelines to protect the country's environment. Similar environmental concerns festered as the century turned. The most publicized involved the pollution of joint waterways, dwindling fishing stocks in the Atlantic and Pacific oceans, and the potential for oil spills by supertankers.

Territorial claims also proved to be troublesome. Canada was instrumental in moving its sea boundaries to 200 miles in 1977. The United States and Mexico followed suit, making vast areas of North America's coastal waters contested zones. One dispute, the Gulf of Maine case, was resolved in 1984. It involved fishing and oil and gas development rights in the rich fishing grounds of the Atlantic Ocean's Georges Bank. The sea passage through the Arctic islands presented another thorny issue. While the Americans did not dispute Canada's claim to the islands in the Arctic archipelago, which Britain transferred to the dominion in 1880, they considered the waters surrounding the islands an international space. In 1969 an American oil tanker, the *Manhattan*, made the Northwest passage. The icebreaker *Polar Sea* made a similar voyage in 1985. The first received Canada's reluctant permission; the second departed unannounced. In 1988 the U.S. government agreed to request surface ship passage through the Arctic islands, but it still does not formally recognize Canadian sovereignty in the waterways. This remains a source of irritation for Canadians.

More recently the longest international border in the world became a focus of some dispute. Concerns about illegal aliens passing from Canada to the United States, as well as older issues such as the smuggling of drugs and other illicit items, led American politicians to consider legislation in the late 1990s that would make crossing the border a more rigorous process. A collective cry of protest from Canadians forced the Americans to reconsider the changes. The failure to exclude Canadians from the Helms-Burton law of 1996 provided another irritant. The law permitted the prosecution of individuals who supposedly benefited from the "confiscated property" of people who fled Castro's Cuba. When a few Canadians were prevented from entering the United States because of this law, it inflamed popular passions. Nonetheless, these disputes between the two countries paled when compared with the explosive events of the past. Despite the fact that the image has its sharp critics, millions of

Canadians and Americans alike believed that their countries shared a special relationship on the eve of the twenty-first century.

Canada's Complex Face

The contest for power transpired on many fronts outside the realm of political party divisions and the historic struggle between francophones and anglophones. Late in the twentieth century, interest groups based on class, gender, and ethnicity sought to bring about changes and improve the lives of their members through political and social action. In 1867 the new dominion's leaders were overwhelmingly male anglophones of British heritage and elite francophones. After repeated struggles the country's power base had dramatically shifted to include women, Native peoples, and immigrants. As the Charlottetown Accord illustrated, these groups now needed to be included in all important national and provincial dialogues.

Women's Issues

After World War II, Canadian women accomplished considerable achievements. A rising tide of feminism, which was part of an international phenomenon, provided cohesion for women seeking to expand their rights and improve their positions in the workplace, home, and political arena. Many women were forced to leave their jobs in the postwar era. Those who remained earned lower wages than their male counterparts, who performed virtually the same task. The National Action Committee on the Status of Women (NAC), formed in 1972, lobbied extensively to enhance women's rights. Over 600 organizations under the NAC umbrella, representing over five million women, existed in the late 1990s. Central issues for these groups were equality in the workplace, political equity, domestic and public violence against women, day care, maternity leaves, family law, and educational rights. As the result of the efforts of some of these organizations, abortion was legalized in a 1987 Supreme Court decision. While the Charter of Rights and Freedoms suggested unambiguous gender equity, many women believed that the Constitution would not adequately protect them against discrimination if provinces elected to invoke the notwithstanding clause.

The growth of the number of women in politics was frustratingly slow during the twentieth century. From the first female in a provincial legislature in 1917, Alberta's Louise McKinney, to Kim Campbell, who became the country's first female prime minister for a brief period in 1993, women undeniably made significant gains in politics. Still, given the fact that women outnumbered men in Canada, their numbers remain disproportionately small in elected and appointed positions. In 2000's Parliament, for example, sixty women (twenty percent) sat in the House of Commons and thirty-two (thirty percent) served as Senators. As more than one feminist politician bitterly observed, at the contemporary pace it would take quite some time for women to gain parity with men in Canada's political sphere. As they entered the twenty-first century, Canadian women pointed with pride to their impressive gains in politics, society, and the workplace, but great imbalances and injustices remained to be addressed.

Native Peoples

Canada's Native peoples also made great strides in the late twentieth century. A revised Indian Act in 1951 extended more power to Native women and band councils; it also implied that assimilation would be a positive solution for bringing an end to centuries of injustices. A government study in 1969, reflecting Trudeau's "just society" principles, proposed that Native peoples should enjoy equal rights with other Canadians. This effectively meant that over time, they would lose their special rights. Reserves would be phased out, for example. The reaction among Native peoples was negative and swift, forcing Minister of Indian Affairs Jean Chrétien to shelve the recommendations.

Native peoples in the modern era became more politically and socially active then at any other point in the twentieth century. The Assembly of First Nations, formed in 1982, became one of the major political and lobbying groups for Native rights. Led by Ovide Mercredi, First Nations participated in the discussions leading to the Charlottetown Accord. While Canada's Native peoples were tremendously varied and articulated different perspectives, three issues illustrated their concerns in the closing years of the twentieth century: land claims, social issues, and self-rule (see "First Nations Charter" in the Documents section).

Native land claims rest on the fact that approximately half of Canada's landmass has never been formally signed over to governments in treaties. Some of the most dramatic land claim cases of the 1990s unfolded in British Columbia. At stake were vast timber reserves, coastal rights, and traditional tribal cultures. A contentious 1975 compromise involved Quebec's James Bay region. In the James Bay Agreement, Cree and Inuit gave up their historic land titles in return for territorial, hunting, fishing, and trapping rights, as well as financial payments. The Quebec government's massive hydroelectricity project in James Bay and its plans for further developments in the area still spark heated confrontations among Native peoples, the Quebec government, and environmentalists. Environmentalists argue that the ecosystem of northern Quebec has been damaged by the construction of massive dams and altered waterways.

Although large-scale conflict between Native peoples and whites had not broken out since the North-West Rebellion of 1885, several confrontations in the late twentieth century produced some violence. A 1990 clash involving the Akwasasne reserve in Quebec, Ontario, and New York State over land claims and gambling led to a protracted standoff between armed Mohawk and Quebec's police. One police officer died in the incident. In another episode at Kahnewake, a community on the outskirts of Montreal, Mohawk blockaded a popular commuter bridge. After seventy-eight days of deadlock between federal troops and Mohawk, the resistance collapsed. A subsequent government study determined that granting Native peoples more rights to self-rule would ease the tensions. Yet no obvious resolution materialized for these emotional issues. Native peoples across Canada generally supported the Mohawk, but many whites deemed armed resistance an inappropriate way to solve problems.

In a more positive vein, on April 1, 1999, the new self-governing territory of Nunavut, meaning "our land," came into being. This vast domain, about one-fifth of Canada's landmass, was carved off of the Northwest Territories. The Inuit, about eighty-five percent of the territory's 25,000 inhabitants, gained self-rule over their ancestral homelands. The new territory was designed with the administrative machinery to exercise a great deal of control over its domestic matters, social programs, and economic development, but it would receive most of its operating budget from the federal government. Nunavut remains a unique model of self-government in Canada and is testimony that land claims between indigenous peoples and governments can be resolved peacefully and equitably.

The New Immigrants

Canada's immigration patterns in the wake of World War II changed substantially; they literally altered the country's ethnic and cultural complexion. A point system introduced in the late 1960s shifted immigration policy away from making decisions based on national origin and race to considering the applicant's education, occupation, age, and language abilities. By the 1980s substantial numbers of immigrants came from the Caribbean, India, Indochina, and the Philippines. British and Americans, reflecting traditional migration patterns, also arrived. As the 1990s progressed, political and social tensions in Sri Lanka, Taiwan, and Hong Kong, which reverted to Chinese control in 1997, became significant sources of immigrants to Canada. During that decade, the country averaged over 200,000 immigrants a year. By the turn of the century almost five million residents, sixteen percent of the country's population, were born abroad.

Canada's vibrant medley of ethnic and cultural groups both strengthened the country and exposed unsavory attitudes. Immigrants flocked to urban areas. By 1991 Toronto's population was almost forty percent foreign born; Vancouver's was thirty percent. The cities and large towns of southern Ontario also became magnets for the new migrants. On the other hand, the Atlantic region and Saskatchewan received few immigrants. The introduction of distinct ethnic and cultural groups unsettled some Canadians who were accustomed to thinking of their society as an especially tolerant one. Harsh sentiments were aired in public, and occasional violence flared involving immigrants from Hong Kong, India, Haiti, and Southeast Asia. The Charter of Rights and Freedoms played a critical role as various ethnic groups defended their culture and language. In a highly publicized case, for example, a Sikh Mountie won the right to wear his turban on the job. Native-born Canadians expressed alarm that growing numbers of residents spoke neither official language. Roughly seventeen percent of the country's population in 1991 fell into this allophone category. Canadians faced an essential contradiction in 2000. The mosaic or multicultural ideal, so carefully constructed since the 1960s, had become a target of criticism by Canadians who feared the erosion of a unifying Canadian culture in the twenty-first century. (see "A Voice of New Canadians" in the Documents section).

Chrétien and the Return of the Liberals

After the Charlottetown Accord failed to be approved in the 1992 referendum, the fate of Mulroney's Conservatives seemed to be sealed. Westerners believed that the federal government was spending too much time and energy trying to appease Quebec. *Québécois* complained that it had not done enough. Free trade and NAFTA received severe criticism from Canadians who were concerned about the health of the country's economy and culture as a recession hit in 1990. The following year an immensely unpopular Goods and Services Tax of seven percent, to be levied on virtually every commodity except food and rent, pushed the prime minister's popularity ratings into the cellar. With Conservatives clambering for his removal because he was so obviously a political handicap, Mulroney retired in June 1993. He was replaced by an untested and largely unknown westerner named Kim Campbell, the country's first female prime minister. She inherited a $40 billion deficit and struggled to handle the baggage of Mulroney's administration, which was tainted by excessive patronage. Within months Campbell and the Conservatives were crushed by a resurgent Liberal party.

The election of 1993 brought Jean Chrétien into office as Liberal prime minister. Unkindly called "yesterday's man" by his opponents, he had indeed served in various capacities during Trudeau's administration. With promises to improve the economy and create jobs, Chrétien's Liberals took virtually every seat in Ontario and did well in the West and Atlantic region. The upstart Reform party captured many western votes. After the election, many Canadians no doubt had trouble identifying the greater of two shocks. Lucien

Bouchard's Bloc Québécois party (BQ) received enough seats to become the official opposition party in Parliament. Strikingly, the BQ's mandate was to work in conjunction with the Parti Québécois to seek Quebec's separation from Canada. Perhaps equally astounding was the almost total decimation of the Progressive Conservatives. Only two Tory members of Parliament survived the election. Voters had passed brutal judgment on Mulroney's policies, and the politics of regionalism had triumphed.

Despite a lack of enthusiastic popular support, the Liberals retained power for the remainder of the 1990s. While Chrétien had strongly criticized them during the election campaign, he did not dismantle the trade agreements with the United States and Mexico. Sweeping cuts in funding to provinces for welfare, health, and educational programs helped to bring the deficit under control. Thanks to an improved economy in the 1990s and a continued high tax burden, by 1998 the government was in the enviable position of declaring that it had a surplus. A spirited politician with working-class roots, Chrétien managed to navigate tricky party and regional divisions to remain firmly in control. In 1997 the Liberals won reelection. The most significant changes in that election were the modest recuperation of the Conservatives (humorists pointed out that they had nowhere to go but up) and the slippage of the Bloc Québécois into third-party status. The Reform party, still an overwhelmingly western organization, now assumed the role as the official opposition in Parliament. In the late 1990s, few Canadians displayed any evidence of liking or admiring their feisty prime minister. Yet with a roaring economy and surprising ease, Chrétien and his Liberals won a third majority government in the elections of November 2000.

Quebec and the Question of Sovereignty

The nagging issue of Quebec's reluctance to sign the Constitution continued to influence Canadian politics. Robert Bourassa's remarkable political comeback kept the Quebec Liberals in power from 1985 to 1994. The Liberals negotiated both the Meech Lake Accord and the Charlottetown Accord, passed Bill 178 in 1988 to protect the

French language, and agitated for more provincial control over programs. Bourassa stepped down in 1994. Later that year his successor, Daniel Johnson, lost the provincial election after taking a staunch federalist position. The return of the Parti Québécois in 1994 signaled a resurgence of separatist spirit. The new premier, Jacques Parizeau, a fluently bilingual and prickly academic, suggested another referendum in the near future. This time, he promised, the vote would be for a clear separation from Canada.

With Bouchard's Bloc Québécois as the official opposition party in Ottawa and the PQ now back in power in Quebec City, the atmosphere seemed favorable for the province's separation. The referendum question, scheduled for October 1995, asked for a sovereign Quebec with a "new economic and political partnership" with Canada. Canadians outside Quebec were profoundly discouraged. Most of Quebec's anglophones, Native peoples, and other ethnic groups deplored the repeat performance. The referendum campaign faltered badly in the summer. Premier Parizeau was roundly disliked and mistrusted, even by staunch separatists. Chrétien largely ignored the issue, confident in the thought that the PQ did not have enough support to approve the question. Then Bouchard and his supporters decided to take over the campaign directly. Almost overnight the immensely popular Bouchard, who had remarkably survived a bacterial flesh-eating disease that led to the amputation of one of his legs in 1994, reinvigorated the sovereignty cause. In the eleventh hour, frightened by the turn of events, federalists rallied. One massive and emotional gathering in Montreal a few days before the vote proclaimed that Quebec's position in Canada was critical for the country's survival. On October 30, 1995, Quebec voters cast ballots that left a victory in the hands of sovereignty opponents, but just barely. A shocking 49.6 percent supported the question. In the postreferendum haze, Canadians grasped the fact that the country had narrowly survived a dangerous moment.

Much like the aftermath of the 1980 referendum, the 1995 sovereignty vote led to conflicting feelings of utter exhaustion and renewed anger. Allegations of spoiled ballots, claims from PQ ministers that ethnic minorities had undermined sovereignty, and blame directed at the federalists for their lackluster efforts combined to leave Canadians in a sour mood. After 1995 the intensity of the separatism movement diminished. Bouchard, intent on restoring Quebec's financial health, replaced Parizeau as premier in early 1996. The PQ promised another referendum on sovereignty during its successful 1998 reelection campaign, but by 2000 Bouchard was maintaining that the party would not hold a vote until it had clear winning conditions. On another front, the Canadian Supreme Court unanimously determined in 1998 that provinces did not have the constitutional right to separate unilaterally. Yet the Court also indicated that if a substantial majority of *Québécois* ever supports a clear question about reformulating Quebec's relationship with Canada, the federal government would be obliged to negotiate in good faith. In 2000 Chrétien's government passed a Clarity Act that would require an unambiguous question in the event of another referendum. Additionally, the definition of an acceptable majority had yet to be resolved. Separatists argued that "50 percent plus one" positive votes would suffice. Opponents asserted that an issue of this magnitude should require an indisputable plurality, such as two-thirds. At the turn of the century the separatist movement seemed to be in a dormant phase, but, if recent history serves as a predictive gauge, it can easily be reinvigorated in the right political and social conditions.

Western Thunder: the Reform Movement

Offsetting the recent focus on Quebec was the growth of the Reform party after 1987. Rooted to a sense of western alienation, the party expanded rapidly under the leadership of Preston Manning. Several themes provided cohesion for Reform supporters. They wanted to protect the West from having its resources exploited by "central Canada." The Senate's regional composition, which heavily favors Ontario and Quebec and gives more senators to New Brunswick and Nova Scotia than to Alberta and British Columbia, was another common grievance among Reformers. The creation of a "Triple E" Senate became a popular rallying cry. Reformers tended to support cuts in social programs, more direct democracy, and less state intervention. Most also opposed bilingualism and the extension of special favors to Quebec. By the 1990s it had become the strongest right-wing party in Canada. In 1993 the Reform party fell just shy of becoming the official opposition in the House of Commons. Four years later it succeeded. Manning's leadership style generated a great deal of criticism among his own party members, however, and despite its efforts, Reform failed to make inroads with voters east of Manitoba. Considered by many westerners the only viable party that could save the country, Reform was often characterized as bigoted and reactionary by easterners and *Québécois*, in no small part because of the staunch moral conservatism of many of its supporters. In an attempt to broaden its appeal to incorporate Conservatives, the party changed its name to the Canadian Reform and Conservative Alliance (Canadian Alliance) in 2000. Perhaps as a sign of its new direction, an extremely right-wing and youthful Albertan named Stockwell Day defeated Manning to become the new party's leader. In the election of November 2000, the Canadian Alliance retained its status as the official opposition in Parliament.

Canada's Regions and Provinces at the Century's End

Some provincial governments also took a hard veer to the political right in the 1990s, while others moved to the left. Ontario experienced explosive growth after World War II. Vast swaths of farmland disappeared, the victim of developers' bulldozers for housing and shopping malls. In the midst of a recession, voters turned to a Conservative government in 1995 under Mike Harris, who promised a "common sense revolution." To the cheers of middle-class taxpayers and the chagrin of his many critics, Harris sliced deeply into social programs and attempted to balance the budget by reducing government spending. As a rich and populous province, Ontario continued to draw both the admiration and reproach of Canadians who were removed from the country's center of power.

The western provinces, quite distinct in their economies, politics, and populations, also expanded their influence in the modern era. Saskatchewan, still heavily dependent on its agricultural production, was one of Canada's few remaining bastions of the declining NDP. First elected in 1991, Premier Roy Romanow cultivated a program of modified socialism and attempted to balance the provincial budget. In neighboring Manitoba, a diverse province dominated by Winnipeg, political leadership vacillated between Conservatives and the NDP. Farther to the west, Alberta remained in the hands of Conservatives since 1971. Starting in 1992, Ralph Klein's government made national news with its draconian cuts in virtually all social services and programs. Few Albertans, or Canadians for that matter, expressed neutral viewpoints on Klein's conservative "revolutionaries." British Columbia remained a magnet for people across Canada and around the rest of the world who wanted to relocate to a bountiful and beautiful area. Vancouver absorbed thousands of Asian immigrants, for example, especially people fleeing Hong Kong before its reversion to Chinese control. For many years, the heartland of the Social Credit party, a legacy of the Depression era, British Columbia elected a series of NDP governments in the 1990s. Unfortunately, both parties achieved notoriety for their scandal-ridden administrations.

Although they exercised less influence in shaping the national agenda in the recent past, the Atlantic Provinces were also immensely diverse in economic, political, and cultural orientation. Swept by fickle trade winds and the impact of industrialization, the region's resource-based economy suffered mightily. The four eastern provinces experienced dramatic out-migration, especially in the postwar era to the 1970s, with thousands moving to Ontario and the developing West in search of employment. Newfoundland in the 1990s had the country's highest unemployment rate. Partially as a result of the 1992 federally mandated moratorium on Atlantic cod fishing, designed to give dwindling fish stocks a chance to regenerate, the province had the country's largest number of people per capita on government assistance. The brightest economic prospect for Newfoundlanders was the 1997 opening of the Hibernian offshore oil production project. Tiny Prince Edward Island also struggled to maintain its traditional way of life in an era of rapid change. Small farming, a vestige of the old tenant system, declined in the postwar era. Correspondingly, the tourist industry became more important for the province's economy. Thousands flocked annually to visit the Cavendish home of Prince Edward Island's most famous fictitious character, Anne of Green Gables, the creation of author Lucy Maud Montgomery. The most notable change for the Island was the construction of a fixed link to the mainland after a contentious plebiscite in 1988. Proponents of the bridge argued that it would improve tourism and facilitate the movement of agricultural and fishing products, whereas opponents maintained that it would ultimately destroy the quintessential lifestyle of the island and pose environmental risks. An engineering marvel that spans eight miles of the Northumberland Strait, the bridge opened for traffic in 1997.

New Brunswick also fought to remain competitive in the postindustrial world. The Liberal party under Frank McKenna led the country's only bilingual province for most of the 1990s. The expenses of providing all essential government services in two languages led to an unpleasant backlash when the Confederation of Regions party openly opposed bilingualism. The reliance on paper and pulp industries led to overcutting of timber stocks in the province's interior. Attempts to develop mineral industries, especially lead and zinc, met with mixed results. A growing telecommunications industry, on the other hand, proved more successful. Finally, the modern challenges faced by Nova Scotia mirrored those of its neighbors. As the most populous and diverse province in the Atlantic region, Nova Scotia adjusted to changing demands for its products. In particular, Cape Breton's coal and steel industry, once a powerful engine of the province's economy, was devastated by fluctuating markets, environmental concerns, and mining tragedies. As with Newfoundland, offshore energies provided a beacon of hope for Nova Scotians, especially the development of natural gas from Sable Island. Conservatives, Liberals, and New Democrats led various colorful and often scandal-plagued governments in the 1980s and 1990s. Ultimately, they failed to provide lasting resolutions to the province's numerous problems.

Canadians Look to a New Century

The closing two decades of the twentieth century bought momentous constitutional, political, and social changes to the country. With a host of progressive rights bestowed on each citizen and with shifting immigration patterns redefining the face of Canada, the political and social landscapes of a century earlier were barely recognizable. The

Cold War appeared to be relegated to the past, a subject that would hence be of greater interest to historians than to political scientists. In the 1990s few would have predicted the magnitude of virulent nationalism and anti-Western extremism in the Middle East that would capture global attention in the dawn of the twenty-first century. Dramatic and horrific events in New York, Baghdad, and Kabul would serve to recalibrate Canada's foreign policy. Issues that were gaining prominence in the late twentieth century, such as territorial sovereignty and environmental protectionism, would rapidly shift to center stage in the first decade of the new century. International markets and financial systems that had thrived in the 1990s because of an accelerated rate of trade would experience a sudden and devastating collapse a decade later. After 2008 Canadians would be forced to cope with a global recession that in many ways rivaled the catastrophic depression of the 1930s.

On the domestic front political parties seemed poised to tilt to the right, a direction that reflected contemporary patterns in much of Western Europe and the United States. The definition and location of the boundaries that separate federal and provincial responsibilities for a myriad of agendas and programs, from health care to resource extraction, continued to shape debate as Canadians sought to maintain the complicated balance that has essentially defined the country's nature since Confederation. Moreover, after almost two decades of life under the Charter of Rights and Freedoms, Canadians continued to seek a clearer definition to the nuances of their rights through the courts and in the halls of parliament and provincial legislative assemblies. Canadians greeted the new century with hope and anticipation. Some observers, no doubt mindful of the country's consistent place at the top of the United Nation's annual comparative ranking for quality of life during the 1990s, wryly wondered if Wilfrid Laurier's famous pronouncement that the twentieth century would belong to Canada would prove to be of greater veracity a hundred years later.

Chapter 11

Contemporary Canada (2001–2010)

Canadians Greet a New Century

It is axiomatic that contemporary events in any nation-state are profoundly shaped by the past. Canada's story in the first decade of the twenty-first century was undeniably defined to a great degree by long-standing patterns in its history; at the same time, new dynamics and challenges from inside and outside the country seemed to unfold at an accelerated pace that makes an assessment of what will have lasting import and what will be ephemeral virtually impossible. Nonetheless, in the recent past we can identify a striking political transition to conservative agendas, which in many ways mirrored European and American patterns as had been the case in the 1980s. Regionalism, always an essential ingredient for understanding Canadian history, remained an important factor in politics and the cultural landscape. The issue of sovereignty-association appeared to recede into the background in the early years of the new century, but the separatist agenda of the Bloc Québécois remained intact; polls regularly indicated that a significant proportion of Quebec voters supported a form of permanent separation from Canada.

Individuals and groups persisted in testing the boundaries of the Charter of Rights and Freedoms, now a quarter century old, in the

The icebreaker *Louis S. St-Laurent* makes its way through Baffin Bay in July 2008.

Source: Associated Press / Jonathan Hayward

courts and on the political front. The cycles of modern capitalism, with the strengths and weaknesses of the world's dominant economic system on full display, would have a great impact on the country. After enjoying several years of growth, Canada confronted the global recession that started in 2008 and for a time threatened to rival the Great Depression of the 1930s with its dismal unemployment figures, damage to numerous sectors of the economy, and disruption of trading patterns with the country's key partners. Canada's international role, which since Confederation has been shaped to a large extent by domestic policies, would be heavily stamped by swiftly moving events in the Middle East. In addition, the issue of sovereignty in the Arctic and along the border with the United States continued to be of great importance, especially because they were so thoroughly linked to environmental agendas and resource development. In 2010, according to practically any political, social, or economic criteria, Canada remains one of the world's strongest, most tolerant, and culturally attractive countries.

The Nuances of Modern Politics

The first decade of the new century brought a shift from Liberal to Conservative agendas in federal politics, yet the magnitude of that transition was tempered. A degree of ambivalence among voters has been apparent that since 2004 two minority governments have been returned. Moreover, voter turnout declined rather precipitously from a high of around seventy-five percent in 1993 to a record low of under sixty percent in the most recent federal election in 2008. Although it is premature to define with any measure of certainty the factors that accounted for this change, some political scientists think that a decline in voter attachment to parties has been a major element. The role and impact of smaller, issue oriented, and regional parties remained vital for understanding the complicated admixture of Canadian politics. Once again, we can see a clear example of contemporary themes that follow deeply etched patterns; in this case, it demonstrates the power of so-called "third party" behavior since Confederation.

The End of a Liberal Run

Prime Minister Jean Chrétien continued his rather improbable run into the early twenty-first century. Although he had been slighted since the outset of his leadership as a less than stellar machine politician, his detractors consistently underestimated his feisty appeal among voters and his sometimes uncanny ability to navigate tricky political waters. Chrétien's government focused a great deal of attention on a permanent solution that would undercut the impulse for separation in Quebec. In addition to the Clarity Act legislation of 2000 that stipulated an unambiguous question in the event of another referendum, the federal government exercised its largess by investing millions of dollars in programs and agencies in Quebec. The dynamic of using federal funds to temper regional discontent was a page from a well-worn playbook that had been used since the late nineteenth century to cajole provinces into Confederation and pacify regional critics. The complicated system of funneling federal dollars to the province led to a series of high profile scandals, which in turn triggered numerous official investigations into malfeasance. Federal agencies and the Royal Canadian Mounted Police explored the dubious nature of some of the programs that had been established. The most widely covered, the so-called "sponsorship scandal," exposed corruption and the deliberate misuse of taxpayers' funds, particularly for advertising programs, and cast a devastating pall over the Liberal government's ability to govern effectively throughout the country.

In a political maneuver designed in part to defuse the growing discontent with the Liberal agenda, Chrétien stepped down in December 2003 and turned the government over to his finance minister, Paul Martin, Jr. Martin's government, molded profoundly by a disappointing election in 2004 that left the Liberals with a minority status, never gained an effective distance from the corruption issues. Moreover, Martin struggled to find traction with a distinctive agenda that would give Canadians the sense that the Liberals would be capable of confronting the special challenges of the new century. In the twilight of Liberal rule, after over twelve years in power, Conservatives seized the opportunity to retool their platform to appeal to a broad spectrum of the electorate. In a federal election in February 2006, the resurgent Conservatives landed on the right message and capitalized on the fatigue from seemingly endless corruption scandals that had become a hallmark of the hapless Liberals.

The Conservative Resurgence

After a number of years in the political wilderness of the late 1990s, struggling to advance their ideals of smaller government, fiscal prudence, and social conservatism, Canada's Conservatives regrouped in the newly formed Canadian Reform and Conservative Alliance (Canadian Alliance) in 2000. The youth and relative inexperience of the party's leader, Stockwell Day, and the strong western regional stamp on crucial elements of the party's agenda, proved to be twin factors for tempering its success in the first few years of the new century. The tribulations of the Liberal Party provided Conservatives a hopeful beacon for recapturing control of the federal government, and in a well-orchestrated maneuver the Canadian Alliance merged in late 2003 with the old arm of the Progressive Conservative Party to form the new Conservative Party of Canada [CPC].

The CPC's platform was an amalgamation of the ideals of the older Reform Party, vintage agendas of Canadian Conservatives since the nineteenth century, and modern solutions for social and fiscal moderation. It included classic language about the compelling advantages of smaller and more decentralized government, proposals for substantial tax cuts, a scheme for reducing public debt, an argument for the election of Senators, and a plan to encourage individual ownership on First Nations' reserves. Assuming leadership of the reconfigured party was a former policy director of the Reform Party, Stephen Harper.

Harper and the CPC won a minority government in February 2006. The Liberals were led by Stéphane Dion, a young politician who made environmentalist policy initiatives, the so-called "Green Shift," a centerpiece of his campaign. Dion failed to kindle enthusiasm and gain the support of voters, and although Harper's demeanor was often stilted and aloof, the conservative appeal to strengthen the economy and plan to purge the country from years of corruption carried the day. In a subsequent election in October 2008 the

CPC was able to retain its leadership with another minority government. Still in power in 2010, Harper and his government will clearly have to await a future date for a judicious and dispassionate assessment of their successes and failures. Nonetheless, we can comfortably state that his agenda continues to reflect its right-wing base, primarily in the West. The party consciously appeals to the middle class for support, and its rhetoric is emblematic of conservative parties in Europe, the United States, and Australia. The focus, at least according the party's rhetoric, is on people who work diligently, pay their fair share of taxes, and adhere to traditional family values. On the delicate subject of the ongoing relationship between the federal government and the provinces, Harper's government has championed an "open federalism" that leans in the direction of more provincial autonomy in controlling social services and other programs. This fits squarely in a model of decentralized power, the ubiquitous conservative ideal of downsizing federal bureaucracies and putting more control in the hands of provincial governments, businesses, and citizens. As an illustration of this approach, Harper's government has passed a number of carefully worded— critics would say that they are purposefully ambiguous—resolutions that corroborate Quebec's stature as a nation within a nation. Whether or not these resolutions will have a positive impact remains to be seen; still, they are contemporary examples of the federal government's desire to gain Quebec's official support for the Canadian Constitution and abandon its periodic attempts to pursue sovereignty-association.

In the Balance: Other Political Parties in Contemporary Canada

As has been the case since Confederation, and particularly in the twentieth century, smaller parties continue to play a fundamental role in the country's political and social arenas. The Bloc Québécois, a legacy of the 1990s, remains a powerful force in Ottawa. In 2010 its forty-eight members of parliament make it the third largest party in the House of Commons. It is still committed—at least nominally—to Quebec's achievement of sovereignty-association. In practice, however, the party supports a government that actively stimulates the economy and equitably distributes tax dollars to the provinces. The BQ's ability to maintain its impressive stature in Ottawa no doubt rests in part on the support of a dedicated cohort of Quebec voters, approximately forty percent according to political scientists, who still envision a sovereign Quebec. Detractors maintain that the party has become anachronistic and that its provocative agenda undermines Canada's position in the international community.

Another important party that maintains its influence in determining public policy is the New Democratic Party (NDP), which has experienced fairly dramatic fluctuations in support and representation over the past few decades. Its platform still envisions social responsibility and a progressive role for government, yet it has somewhat tempered its rather provocative language about achieving an ideal socialist model for Canada. The NDP in 2010, with thirty-six members of parliament, is the fourth largest party in Ottawa. It enjoys its strongest federal support from voters in Ontario and British Columbia, and although it does have a few members of parliament from Quebec and the Atlantic Provinces, it continues to struggle with having its message resonate in the eastern region of the country. In the early twenty-first century the NDP has fared well in the provincial governments of Ontario, Manitoba, Saskatchewan, and British Columbia.

Numerous smaller parties also jostle for power at the provincial and federal levels, especially with the former. These include the Confederation of Regions Party, which was created in 1984 from a base of conservative populism and radical support for regional control; the Christian Heritage Party; the Progressive Canadian Party; and the Green Party of Canada. The Green Party was formed by academics and environmental activists in the early 1980s to promote environmental policies and progressive social planning. Strikingly, in each election since 2004 the party has run candidates in each of the country's 308 ridings; in the most recent federal election it garnered close to five percent of the total popular vote.

With a host of parties appealing for the support of voters in a classic environment of parliamentary give and take, and with a stubborn pattern of minority status for the larger parties at the federal level, even conservative governments such as that of Stephen Harper must remain receptive to "third-parties" if they want to remain in power and advance their agendas. For Harper, that means that his government needs to maintain its support for core Canadian programs and ideals, such as Medicare and sensitivity to the special concerns of provinces such as Quebec, and still placate its base by actively promoting conservative economic and social values.

The Cycles of Capitalism and Trade in a New Century

Canada's economy in the first decade of the twenty-first century has been, to a large extent, emblematic of modern capitalism. It has fluctuated rather significantly. The gains from a relative boom in the first half of the decade precipitously gave way to a severe global recession in 2008. Another quality that characterizes the country's dominant economic engine is its continuing reliance on international trade. The linkages between Canada and other countries, nurtured since the nineteenth century, mean that a commanding portion of the nation's economy is either dictated to or influenced by the economic health of its trading and commercial partners. In sum, the first decade of the century brought to the foreground an illustration of the exhilarating power and fundamental flaws of global capitalism. Unemployment figures, one important barometer of a country's economic health, demark the peaks and valleys of the country's economy. In 2010, with Canada still struggling to emerge from the decimation of the 2008 recession, the national unemployment rate hovers around eight percent. Newfoundland and Labrador, the province with the most alarming number of unemployed, remains around fourteen percent; Manitoba and Saskatchewan enjoy the best numbers at approximately five percent. The figures from the two Prairie provinces suggest, if nothing else, one of the sharp distinguishing features that separate the Dirty Thirties, a period when the country's heartland was shattered by record unemployment, and the recession of 2008.

Industrial production continues to be a centerpiece of the Canadian economy, despite the fact that key industries have suffered a decline in the early twenty-first century. The automobile industry, for example, was forced to contend with the twin forces of a growing popularity of foreign vehicles, especially from Japan, and with decline of the big three automobile manufacturers in the United States. General Motors closed plants in Quebec in 2002, and Ford followed suit by shutting factories in Ontario in 2006.

Resource production remains an important driver of the economy. Of particular note was the construction of offshore oil drilling platforms such as Newfoundland's Hibernia (1997) and Terra Nova (2002). These did not adequately counterbalance the deleterious effects of the decline in the cod fishing industry, but they did provide a much needed bright spot for economic growth in a beleaguered province. The massive hydroelectric projects that have become a fixture of modern Quebec's economy continue apace in the first decade of this century. In the West, resources remain a fixture of economic growth. An excellent example is found in the extraordinary attention that has been devoted to extracting oil and natural gas in Alberta. Noteworthy is the ongoing effort to perfect the technology and construct the infrastructure to refine petroleum products or produce crude oil from the province's massive deposits of tar sands. The question as to whether or not these expensive endeavors will ultimately be cost effective are as yet unanswered, but proponents of the project maintain that the finite nature of oil deposits in the world will mean that eventually the expensive and elaborate efforts will pay off. All of these resource projects raise alarming questions about the environmental costs and the impact on the lives of Canadians, especially indigenous people in the country's northern reaches, who are adversely affected and even dislocated by the insatiable pursuit of new and more resources (see "An Environmentalist's Perspective" in the Documents section).

Of special note in the modern era is the enduring strength of Canada's financial sector. The recession of 2008, which crippled banks and lending institutions throughout the world, also cast a spotlight on Canada's banks to find a success story in what was otherwise an overwhelmingly dismal set of statistics. Because of decades of strict oversight and relative fiscal prudence in lending practices, and the fact that the country has only six large banks that dominate and control about ninety percent of the country's total bank assets, Canada's financial institutions weathered the recession storm in relatively good shape. Canada's banks even expanded their role and influence in American markets in the early twenty-first century. One important contemporary example is TD Ameritrade, a broker business that is owned by the Toronto-Dominion Bank.

Trade continues to be the flywheel that determines so much of the country's economic might. In 2010 it comprises about three-quarters of the country's Gross Domestic Product (GDP); about forty percent of the country's total production is exported, and about thirty-five percent of the goods that Canadians consume are brought into the country from other countries. On a global level, the World Trade Organization (WTO) provides the single most important forum for shaping the country's trade policies. At the continental level, as has been the case since the twentieth century, the United States continues to be the country's most important trading partner. Although the percentage of import and export between Canada and the United States dropped somewhat after the 2008 recession, the current economic relationship between the two countries remains the largest and most comprehensive in the world. Contemporary figures indicate that about $1.6 billion in goods cross the Canadian-American border every day, and this in spite of the strengthened border security and a plethora of bureaucratic measures that have been implemented in the wake of the terrorist attacks on the United States in 2001. Although aggregate figures of trade fell off in the wake of the 2008 recession, trade in energy resources increased. In 2010 Canada is the largest single foreign supplier of energy to the United States; it accounts for seventeen percent of the oil and eighteen percent of the natural gas consumed by Americans.

Trade with its partners in NAFTA, especially the United States, remains problematic on other levels. Disputes among the trading partners, particularly in sectors such as grain and softwood, somewhat soured the relationship between the two countries in the first decade of the twenty-first century. For the most part, these disagreements concerned government subsidies for resource produ-cers, which inevitably are characterized as "unfair" by the trading partner. Two recent cases illustrate this tendency. In the important sector of softwood production, American producers repeatedly claimed that provinces such as British Columbia unfairly subsidized their timber production by exacting artificially low stumpage fees. The United States successfully challenged those practices under both NAFTA and the WTO. The contentious issue was resolved in 2006 in the Softwood Lumber Agreement: the United States agreed to return eighty percent of the $5 billion duties it had collected on Canadian softwood imports, and Canada agreed not to increase its current share of the American market, which at the time was about thirty-four percent.

A more recent issue illustrates the ways in which trade between the two countries can be governed by nationalistic sentiments. As will be discussed below in more detail, American patriotic rhetoric and assertion of its military might combined in the wake of 9/11 to fashion a difficult environment for its allies to navigate. Noteworthy were the growing efforts advanced by politicians and corporate leaders to protect American industry. In early 2009, much to the chagrin of Canadians and in an alarming affront to the terms and spirit of the Free Trade Agreement, a "Buy American" program for iron, steel, and manufactured products gained traction. The idea was couched in patriotic and politically positive terms. Moreover, in the same year legislative measures were designed to affix labels on a host of food products that clearly denote the country of origin; this was advanced with the clearly stated goal of having the consumer select a "homegrown" American product over an import. In another vein, current attempts on the part of President Barack Obama's administration to introduce a so-called "cap-and-trade" system to reduce carbon dioxide emissions, in environmental interest of improving air quality, might lead to the levying of tariffs on goods coming into the country that are produced with lower environmental standards. This could mean a tax on Canadian products, which would once again run afoul of NAFTA's terms.

On another note, and as yet another example of the impact of the global nature of contemporary capitalism, foreign investors continue to find Canada an attractive place to expend their capital. Mergers of Canadian companies with foreign companies, a process that has been underway since John A. Macdonald's National Policy inadvertently created an environment for foreign takeovers, continues in the modern era. Simultaneously ironic and disconcerting to a fair number of Canadians are several corporate mergers of the early twenty-first century. For example, Tim Horton's, the popular coffee and donut chain that is the stuff of contemporary Canadian lore, was bought out by the American hamburger company Wendy's. Of equal concern to dedicated Canadian nationalists, and also an affront to a virtual icon of Canadian identification, Molson merged with its North American brewery rival Coors. In sum, all indicators suggest that in spite of the vagaries of global recessions and spikes in nationalistic fervor on either side of the border, Canada will remain an important player in the global economy in the twenty-first century.

A Foreign Policy in the Post–Cold War Era

Canada's relationship with other countries, as well as its perception of how it should confront the challenges of the new century, adhered closely to past patterns and debates. A classic question, posed repeatedly by academics and journalists in the height of the Cold War, gained new life: Are Canadians peacemakers or warriors? This question succinctly captured the paradox of modern Canada in a global setting of intense regional conflicts and the aggressive behavior of the United States as it projected its interests abroad. It spawned a number of corresponding questions, such as how much should Canada support its primary ally in strengthening its defensive perimeters in North America? Should the country follow the lead of the United States in its military endeavor to attack Iraq in pursuit of elusive, and as it turned out nonexistent, weapons of mass destruction? And should it collaborate with its NATO partners in a protracted military exercise in Afghanistan to unseat the Taliban, indigenous tribal organizations that had abetted the terrorist organization al-Qaeda in its horrific attacks on 9/11? The challenges of the early twenty-first century raised yet again questions about the application and relevance of the now cherished middle power ideal. To a great degree, as it had been the case since the mid-twentieth century, the country's global response was carefully considered in the light of its relationship to the United States.

Jean Chrétien's administration pursued a classic balancing act of maintaining the country's middle power role of pursing an independent foreign policy in the context of a close relationship with the United States. Chrétien worked constructively on a number of fronts with President Bill Clinton's administration in the 1990s, and yet he continued to nurture ties to Cuba. These clearly chaffed with American policymakers and politicians. Canada's foreign policy continued its Cold War pattern, so clearly articulated under Trudeau's administration, of crafting many of its activities in the same spirit as its domestic policy. This captured the positive view that

Canadians held of themselves as a forward-looking nation that supported peaceful and progressive global agendas.

The infamous events of 11 September 2001 had a profound effect on Canadians; they also served to recalibrate the country's relationship with the United States and forced its citizens to revisit vintage questions of its broader role as a peacekeeper or warrior. They would bring to the foreground questions about national security, defense, and the country's commitment to helping its allies fight Islamic terrorism at its source: the Middle East.

Canada's response to the 9/11 attacks was swift, unambiguous, and genuine. The use of hijacked commercial aircraft to smash into the World Trade Center in New York City and the Pentagon in Washington led to an immediate rerouting of commercial flights from American airspace to Canadian airports. Approximately 150 planes landed at Canadian airfields, and in the immediate aftermath of the attacks almost 30,000 passengers were officially and unofficially assisted by Canadians in locations from Newfoundland to the West coast. Ordinary Canadians opened their homes and hearts to the stranded passengers. In a spontaneous and massive show of support, approximately 100,000 Canadians showed up on Parliament Hill in Ottawa to acknowledge a national day of mourning for the almost three thousand dead, which included at least twenty-four Canadians who died in the collapse of the World Trade Center. With poignant eloquence, Canada's prime minister sent a message to America: "You are not alone in this. We are with you."

The administration of Republican George W. Bush, which had been in power for eight months when the attacks occurred, was still in the process of articulating its foreign policy agendas. The 9/11 attacks would swiftly be incorporated by the Bush administration to invoke a generalized "war on terrorism" and pursue agendas that were designed to buttress the country's defensive perimeters in North America to preclude future terrorist attacks. In patriotic fervor, the United States rapidly moved to employ its overwhelmingly superior number of uniformed forces and military hardware to take the battle to enemies in the Middle East that sponsored or harbored, at least theoretically, terrorist organizations such as al-Qaeda. When President Bush overlooked Canada as he publicly listed the true friends of the United States a week after the attacks, Canadians were incensed and reminded yet again of their ambiguous relationship with their greatest trading partner and most important ally. As the Bush administration recast virtually its entire foreign policy through the lens of its war on terror, Canadian policymakers would struggle to determine their course of action.

A Question Reposed: Will Canadians Be Peacekeepers or Warriors?

The international response to the 9/11 terrorist attacks in many ways created a perfect metaphor for the ways in which Canadian politicians and policymakers had crafted a middle ground between showing support for the country's allies and yet maintaining an independent stance to protect Canadians. These themes unfolded as the country recrafted its relationship with Great Britain after Confederation and into the twentieth century; similar patterns emerged in its relationship with the United States during the Second World War and Cold War era. The country's cooperation with a multinational military coalition in attacking the Taliban in Afghanistan leans in the peacemaker or warrior direction, whereas the country's refusal to support the United States in its misguided war on Iraq demonstrates its more independent streak.

The most immediate response of many of the world's powers in the wake of the 9/11 attacks was to confront al-Qaeda in Afghanistan. Canada's military commitment with its NATO partners started in October 2001 by sending a naval task force and supporting aircraft to the region; this was followed by 2,000 light infantry soldiers who arrived in early 2002. Remarkably, the focal point for Canada's military mission in Afghanistan has not changed substantially since the beginning of the war. The Canadian forces have been fighting in the Kandahar region battling al-Qaeda and then their supporters, the Taliban. Canadian popular support for the war at the outset was overwhelming; only ten NDP members of parliament expressed an official opposition to the conflict. Canada, Britain, Australia, Germany, Denmark, Norway, and of course the United States, comprised the original military coalition.

The war has lasted through the three administrations of Chrétien, Martin, and Harper. By 2006 over half of Canadians still supported the mission, although mounting casualties and the growing sense that the military effort lacked a clear sense of victory eroded popular enthusiasm for the conflict. This trend accelerated as it became apparent that the terrorist forces of al-Qaeda were swiftly relocating operations to neighboring Pakistan, thereby leaving the coalition to battle the local Taliban. Harper's government received pressure from a growing number of Canadians, particularly women and Quebecers, to refocus its energies on peacekeeping rather than fighting an elusive enemy without a clear sense of mission and a defined exit strategy from the region. In 2008 a panel chaired by John Manley, a former deputy prime minister and foreign minister, recommended that Canada should remain committed to the war as long as more support was forthcoming from other NATO allies. It also suggested shifting an emphasis from combat to training Afghan troops and buttressing nonmilitary aid for development in Afghanistan. The Manley Commission led to a parliamentary resolution in March 2008 that the country would start a redeployment in July of that year and target a complete rotation of troops out of Kandahar by late 2011. As casualties have mounted—by summer 2010 over 150 Canadian forces have been killed while serving in Afghanistan—and time has passed, Canadian opinion has declined. Canada still maintains a military presence of about 2,000 combatants in the Kandahar region. Development aid from Canada to Afghanistan has reached almost $2 billion since the war began, a significant figure when compared with aid provided by other countries. Whether the forces will adhere to the planned withdrawal deadline remains to be seen, but there is little doubt that the war in Afghanistan has forced Canadians to revisit questions about when they should commit their military personnel and tax dollars to fighting foreign wars (see "A Celebration of Canada's Role in Afghanistan" in the Documents section).

The same question, when applied to the Bush administration's essentially unilateral decision to attack Iraq in early 2003 and topple the government of Saddam Hussein, was answered quite differently. As the Bush administration swiftly moved through a process of countering the bureaucracy of the United Nations and ignoring the conclusions of international observers that Iraq was not harboring storehouses of weapons of mass destruction, it sought a "coalition of the willing" to defeat Hussein's armies and occupy the country. Prime Minister Chrétien, supported by a majority in parliament, proclaimed that Canada would not send troops to Iraq unless further evidence of the necessity for the war was presented and more defined conditions were set. An overwhelming majority of Canadians have opposed the United States and its dwindling number of allies in its Iraq adventure, which continues in 2010. Most draw sharp distinctions between the wars in Afghanistan and Iraq; these illustrate a Canadian ability to distinguish between conflicts that are necessary and ones that are misguided and perhaps illegal.

Canada continues to follow a path of providing aid and peaceful support to countries around the world, although its commitment to peacekeeping has fallen off in the first decade of the twenty-first century. In 2004 the Martin administration issued a comprehensive statement on Canadian security: "Securing an Open Society: Canada's National Security Policy." It elaborated a plan to protect Canadians at home and abroad; moreover, in a note that echoed the sentiments of Mackenzie King on the eve of the Second World War, it indicated that Canada would not be used as a base to threaten its allies. In an important International Policy Statement in 2005, Martin announced that Canada's foreign policy would adhere to a multi-lateral system that would be grounded in clearly defined rules; support for human rights in an international context, enunciated so clearly during Trudeau's administration, would remain an essential ingredient of Canadian foreign policy. In 2005 a Security and Prosperity Partnership of North America was established with Mexican President Vicente Fox, Martin, and Bush to improve the collaboration between the three countries on the order of security, goods, environment, and technology. Development aid to countries became a priority, and this agenda has been reinforced by Harper's government. Finally, Canada's role as a major country in peace-keeping efforts dropped rather precipitously in the new century. After reaching a threshold in 2001, by 2007 it ranked about halfway down an international list of contributors, with a little over one hundred personnel on active peacekeeping duty.

North American Defense and Issues with the United States

The relationship between Canada and the United States in the first decade of the twenty-first century has been cast almost exclusively through the twin lenses of trade and 9/11. The Liberal administrations of Chrétien and Martin struggled to navigate the unilateral agenda of President George W. Bush's administration and the bellicose language of American policymakers as they settled into their nebulously defined "war on terrorism." The attacks of 9/11 dramatically intensified a focus on the border between the two countries, and as the decade unfolded the Bush administration turned its attention to reinvigorating its missile defenses in North America. Starting in 2002, the new Department of Homeland Security intensified its efforts to monitor the border. The ideal of catching terrorists who would use Canada as a route to enter the United States was one component; another was a growing attempt, clearly driven by political and popular support, to stem the flow of illegal immigrants into the United States. Traffic across the border became increasingly difficult as the decade unfolded and border security personnel became more alert and at times officious. The intensified security along the border, including the requirement by the end of the decade that Americans carry passports so they can return to the country from Canada, has impeded the flow of goods and become a concern for businesses on both sides of the border. Moreover, most Canadians who travel regularly to the United States can share anecdotal evidence of how the border has become more difficult, and sometimes unpleasant, to cross. At the close of this century's first decade the familiar axiom of the world's largest undefended boundary seems less applicable; perhaps it will recede as an iconic illustration of the relationship between the two countries.

More contentious and problematic was the Bush administration's reinvigoration of a defensive missile network to protect North America from terrorist attack. Most Canadians opposed the idea of resurrecting the missile defenses; many considered it a needless resurrection of technological policies that may have been appropriate at the height of the Cold War, but seemed to be largely irrelevant in the modern age of terrorism. The Bush administration created the U.S. Northern Command (USNORTHCOM) to solidify the defense of North America in 2002. Although pressures continued to be applied by the Bush administration for cooperation by his Canadian counterparts, opposition to the idea mounted. Paul Martin's government, with strong popular support, officially rejected an American plan to reconstruct a missile defensive network in 2005.

Bush was widely unpopular in Canada; indeed, on a number of occasions Canadians publicly voiced their harsh assessments of the American president. For example, Bush was variously called a "moron" and "a failed statesman" by politicians and representatives of the federal government. NORAD, a legacy of the Cold War, was renewed in 2006 after strained discussions with American policy-makers. The agreement was largely symbolic; nonetheless it indicated a reluctance on the part of Canada to completely jettison its well-established defensive connections with the United States.

Other issues have tested the resiliency of the relationship between the two countries recently. Tensions over the United States policy of torture and relocation of suspected terrorists to other countries for incarceration and interrogation have revealed some of the most glaring differences between the two countries. One case involved Maher Arar, a Syrian-born software engineer who was captured in New York in 2002 because of his suspected terrorist links. Arar was forcibly transported to Syria, where he was subjected to torture and deprivation. After his release in 2003 Arar mounted a legal campaign to expose his treatment and seek compensation from the Americans. The case triggered a sensitive diplomatic dispute, with the United States emphatically rejecting Arar's case or even acknowledging its role in his rendition to Syria. Ultimately the Canadian government compensated Arar for $11.5 million, but the United States maintained its decree that Arar could not enter the country. Another contentious case involved Omar Khadr, a Canadian citizen, who was fifteen years old when he was captured in Afghanistan after killing an American soldier with a grenade. His father was a member of al-Qaeda; Khadr was taken to the American military base at Guantanamo, which was swiftly became a lightening rod for opposition to America's draconian policies in the age of terrorism. For many years, and without a formal charge, he was severely interrogated. In 2010 he is still being held by the American authorities, and his case is winding its way through the judicial system at a glacial pace.

Other issues are less contentious, yet nonetheless instructive in defining the ongoing relationship between the two countries. For many Americans, the issue of importing cheaper prescription drugs from Canada became an important agenda in the early twenty-first century. The Canadian government's adoption of a plan to permit the medical use of marijuana and decriminalize recreational use of the drug set off a predictable firestorm of debate in the United States; American opponents of following a similar policy inevitably cast their Canadian neighbors in the role of left-leaning progressives or worse. Interestingly, as the American debate on a comprehensive plan for medical care intensified during the decade, Canadian Medicare became a foil for Americans. Proponents touted Canada's comprehensive system as one of the leading models of health care in the world; opponents sought out Canadian critics and cited supposed evidence of its flaws, including the system's inequality across the country, its cost, and the waiting lists for certain medical treatments, as reasons for not following Canada's lead.

Finally, Canadians closely watched the remarkable election of Barack Obama, the first African-American president of the United States. Most Canadians made little secret of their displeasure with Bush and his policies, and many openly supported the Democratic candidate in his campaign against Republican John McCain. Remarkably, with evidence that disappointed Stephen Harper, pollsters pointed out that not since the election of John F. Kennedy had an American president been more popular than a sitting prime minister. Despite his obviously different policy agendas of conservative governance, Harper continues to signal his desire to work closely with the United States on a number of issues. Instructively, however, and in a typically Canadian fashion, he remains vigilant about protecting Canada's interests: "Stand up for Canada" was one of his signature campaign slogans in 2006. Among other matters, trade, the border, and Arctic sovereignty loomed large.

Themes for the Twenty-First Century: Territorial Control and Environmentalism

Although it is impossible to predict where Canada's foreign policy will head in the twenty-first century, in the recent past it is abundantly clear that a powerful linkage connects environmental themes and border concerns. Canada signed the Kyoto protocol in 1997, which was designed to have the countries that signed cut their greenhouse gas emissions by certain deadlines, despite the fact that numerous and vocal opponents from the business community and resource developers had significant reservations with its terms and possible impact on the Canadian economy in the new century. Stephen Harper's scaled back Canada's support for the Kyoto terms when he became prime minister, but he continued to signal his government's interest in protecting the environment. Three brief case studies will illustrate the bonds that exist between environmental themes and Canadian interests.

Harper's government has made a priority of promoting Canada's case for sovereignty in its territorial claims in the Arctic. According to the 1982 United Nations Convention on the Law of the Sea, of which Canada was a signatory, countries enjoy a twelve-mile limit for full sovereignty in oceans. However, in international straits that link two major seas, a country cannot prevent the international passage of ships. At the same time, nations that lay claim to such waterways have the right to oversee and legislate for environmental themes. The Northwest passage through the Canadian archipelago of islands that connects the Pacific and Atlantic oceans, according to most international legal opinion, falls into the category of international space. Canadian claims an historical right to those waterways, a point that has not been accepted by other countries with an interest in the Arctic, including the United States, Denmark, and Russia. Since the late 1960s the United States has challenged the Canadian case by sending ships and submarines through the Northwest passage, sometimes with forewarning and sometimes without. In 2005 the Danes occupied Hans Island, which is situated between its possession in Greenland and Canada's Ellesmere Island. This led to a brief but intense diplomatic contretemps. In addition to the question of passage, the Arctic space has abundant yet mostly untapped resources that could promise to be of great value in the twenty-first century. With the northern icecap of the planet warming at an alarming pace—twice the global rate of temperature increase—some climate change scientists predict that perhaps half of the ice cover could disappear by the turn of the next century. This means that by mid-century ships might be able to make voyages through the Northwest passage, unimpeded by ice, in the summer months. Few Canadians, including its current prime minister, would disagree on the point that their claim to sovereignty in the Arctic will remain of paramount national interest as the century unfolds (see "Canada's Position on Arctic Sovereignty" in the Documents section).

Analogous themes that highlight the border and environmental themes include the case of Devils Lake, North Dakota. In 2003 the state made plans to construct an emergency outlet to expedite runoff in the case of flooding. Residents in neighboring Manitoba, including provincial officials and First Nations' people, were alarmed because the runoff could potentially affect Canadian waterways. Devils Lake is in a closed ecosystem, but the construction of an emergency outlet could release waters from the lake that are high in contaminates and pollutants such as phosphorous, sulfate, and mercury. The International Joint Commission, an organization that celebrated its one-hundredth birthday in 2009, studied the case and supported the arguments presented by the Canadians. Nonetheless, plans went ahead for the construction of the outlet.

A third example of the linkages between environmental concerns and territorial space involves the shared waterways between New Brunswick and Maine. Plans to construct a terminal to unload shipments of Liquefied Natural Gas (LNG) in Eastport, Maine, triggered a sharp response in neighboring New Brunswick because the massive tankers that are designed to carry the dangerous cargo would have to pass through Canadian waters on their way to Eastport. LNG tankers present a potential problem that concerns environmentalists, including the possibility of spills or a catastrophic accident similar to the fate of the *Exxon Valdez*, a supertanker that ran aground and spilled oil in Prince William Sound, Alaska, in 1989. Despite the fact that New Brunswick and Maine worked assiduously to improve their business and tourist connections, the issue triggered a difficult series of diplomatic discussions. New Brunswick Premier Shawn Graham and Maine Governor John Baldacci enlisted the support of their respective federal governments to advance their interests. The issue remains at a stalemate in 2010; the terminals have not been constructed, and New Brunswickers have not yielded on their position.

The twenty-first century will almost certainly witness more concerns that are shaped by the themes of resource extraction, environmental protection, and territorial sovereignty. The protection and distribution of freshwater will no doubt become of paramount importance as the century unfolds. Canada has about seven percent of the world's renewable freshwater, fourth in the world behind

Brazil, China, and Russia. The question of bulk water exports from Canada to thirsty regions of the United States, especially in the Southwest, has already become a contentious proposition in the first decade of the century. NAFTA regulations on the subject of the export of fresh water have been challenged by California, and no doubt more cases will follow. There is also little question that Canadians will remain vigilant as they protect their storehouse of freshwater—the world's most important resource.

Canadian Citizens Exercise their Rights

Canadians in the early twenty-first century have been active in pursuing their rights, and debate has played out primarily in the courts, the provincial legislatures, and the federal parliament in Ottawa. Much of the discussion has been contextualized by the Charter of Rights and Freedoms, which reached the quarter-century mark in the first decade of the century. The struggle for the articulation of rights can indeed be considered a global theme, and it should be of no surprise that the articulation and protection of essential human rights have become important barometers for understanding contemporary Canadian society.

First Nations continue their struggle to articulate the special rights of status Indians, especially in the contentious subject of marriage outside of tribal groups. In 2006 the Indian Residential Schools Settlement Agreement stipulated that about 80,000 Native peoples would be eligible for reparations. This agreement stemmed from the fact that Native peoples were forced to be educated in schools from 1874 to 1996 that were administered by the Department of Indian Affairs. These schools, according to the case made against them by First Nations, actively promoted assimilation by teaching Christian and western values to the students. In the early twenty-first century Canada's Native peoples still cope with high rates of alcoholism, mental illness, suicide, family violence, diabetes, and tuberculosis. Numerous court cases involving sovereignty and land claims have defined the judicial struggle for rights for aboriginal peoples in the new century. In 2006 the Six Nations Confederacy engaged in a well-orchestrated protest in blocking roads near Hamilton, Ontario. Their concern was that under the terms of a treaty in 1784, their band is not bound to recognize the sovereignty of Canadian law. Finally, land claims are ongoing in British Columbia with the Nisga'a; the issues are not settled, but they are being closely watched by other members of the First Nations. The creation of Nunavut in 1999, a self-governing territory, was a triumph of using the courts to win the argument for protecting the rights of Native peoples. Native peoples across the country have been quite successful in using the language of treaties and the Charter of Rights and Freedoms to advance their interests. The further resolution of land claims will undoubtedly be a central story of the twenty-first century.

The Charter of Rights and Freedoms has become the single most import wellspring for advancing the interests of Canadian citizenry. It has changed the court system and politics; individuals and groups actively use the Charter to pursue their rights and seek redress for their grievances. The Supreme Court, a creation of the early Confederation era, has moved to a place of central importance in determining the final resolution of cases that range from consumers' rights to a controversial case in 2004 that confirmed the rights for Canadians to have a same-sex marriage. This case determined that parliament could constitutionally allow for same-sex marriages, which it did in the Civil Marriage Act the following year. The court case set off a firestorm of debate that mirrored the more general arguments that have been made by detractors and advocates of the growing power of the judicial system. Proponents argue that the courts have the right to interpret laws, especially in the light of the Canadian Constitution and its Charter of Rights and Freedoms; they also generally agree that individual rights should trump the rights of the state in the cases where the boundaries between the two are ambiguous. Critics of the modern court dynamic, who are often equally skeptical of the expansive rights issued in the Charter and typically describe themselves political and social conservatives, believe that the courts often overreach their mandate. Instead, the critics argue, the courts should defer to the federal and provincial legislatures. Canada's courts have struck down dozens of laws in the early twenty-first century; of particular note are gains made on behalf of the gay and lesbian community, women, and individuals suspected of crimes. Despite these vociferous and ongoing debates, the Charter of Rights and Freedoms enjoys solid support among Canadian citizens. Most see the Charter, like the Medicare program, as one of the essential, if not quintessential, ingredients that represents a distinguishing feature of modern Canada.

Contemporary Canadian Culture

The definition and protection of a distinct Canadian culture have been two of the most enduring themes in the country's history since Confederation. First, the proliferation of American newspapers and magazines, and then the development of radio, movies, and television, created an almost century-long discussion of the impact that American culture has on Canadian self-identification. Despite the warnings of the Massey Commission in the early 1950s and the efforts of government agencies to ensure enough "Canadian content" in radio and television programming, Canadians continue to demonstrate a voracious appetite for all things American. They also consume products from around the world. Thus, the issue perhaps is not so much American in scope, but instead a product of the increasing internationalization of cultural industries. Canada's publishers and music producers, for example, have extraordinary high rates of foreign ownership. Nonetheless, Canada annually celebrates the superior contributions of its writers and artists. These ceremonies include the Juno Awards for music, the Genie Awards for films, and the prestigious Governor General's Awards for literature.

The Canadian-U.S. boundary seemed to matter little in a consumer zone of shared tastes in popular culture. Canadian-made films have captured the attention of American viewers, such as those directed by David Cronenberg, Atom Egoyan, and Denis Arcand. Vancouver and Toronto have become favorite locations for Hollywood's movies. Canadian actors continued to seek warmer locations to practice their art. The complete tally of Canadians in movies, comedy, and newscasting in the United States would be long indeed. A partial list from the late twentieth century included Robert MacNeil, Peter Jennings, Jim Carrey, Michael J. Fox, Donald Sutherland, Dan Aykroyd, William Shatner, and Hume Cronyn. While the impressive number of their compatriots in the American television and movie industries is a source of pride among Canadians, it is simultaneously a reminder of an ongoing talent drain to more lucrative markets.

Canadian writers and musicians also enjoyed international exposure. Some of the most respected writers of the modern era are Margaret Laurence, Robertson Davies, Margaret Atwood, Alice Munro, Timothy Findley, Antonine Maillet, Gabrielle Roy, Mordecai Richler, Michael Ondaatje, W. O. Mitchell, Michel Tremblay, and Farley Mowat. While many of their works were distinctively Canadian in setting and composition, they clearly addressed issues that touched a wider audience. A similar point can be made about Canadian musicians. The deep traditions of country music and jazz, as well as the rock industry of the postwar era, became international in scope. Canadian musicians whose compositions became familiar to millions included piano virtuosos such as Glenn Gould, jazz greats such as Oscar Peterson, folk singers such as Anne Murray and Gordon Lightfoot, and country crooners such as Hank Snow. From its inception the rock industry was replete with Canadians. An unbroken line reached from early rock stars such as Joni Mitchell and Neil Young to late twentieth century pop attractions such as Céline Dion, Bryan Adams, Alanis Morissette, and Shania Twain. More recently, groups and artists such as Barenaked Ladies, Nickelback, Broken Social Scene, and Drake have garnered an international following. The ease in which these artists move across the border suggests an international culture that can be interpreted in one of two ways: either it indicates positive connections, a variation on the "global village" theme, or it threatens the survival of a distinctive Canadian culture (see "Canadian Insights Using Humor" in the Documents section).

Canadians found themselves confronting similar dilemmas with the sports industry. The fate of the National Hockey League aptly illustrates the issue. Started in 1917 with four Canadian teams, by the 1920s the NHL was dominated by American teams. In the early twenty-first century the NHL's players come from Canada, the United States, and a growing number of European countries. As humorists have long pointed out, hockey is the closest Canadians come to having a national religion. Canada's narrow victory in a 1972 hockey series with the Soviets triggered an unusual demonstration of national pride. By 2000 Canada also had two professional baseball teams, the Montreal Expos and the Toronto Blue Jays. The beleaguered Expos, which never drew large numbers of fans to its home games, played their final game in 2004 and the franchise moved to Washington, D.C. The Canadian Football League struggled to compete for fans who increasingly preferred the National Football or American Football leagues. Strikingly, the CFL developed expansion teams in American cities such as Shreveport and Las Vegas. Canada enthusiastically hosted the 1976 Summer Olympics in Montreal, the 1988 Winter Olympics in Calgary, and the 2010 Winter Olympics in Vancouver. Canadians eagerly play and watch sports as varied as curling, swimming, ice skating, hockey, soccer, softball, baseball, lacrosse, and wrestling. Whether their devotion to sports makes Canadians more "American" or "global" is a question that will no doubt continue to be the subject of lively debate for the foreseeable future.

Canada and the Twenty-First Century

Questions addressing the survival of Canadian culture make an appropriate transition to a few concluding thoughts on the country at the close of the first decade of the twenty-first century. It is well known that professional historians, while comfortable in assessing the past, are notoriously inept at mapping the future. Most are reluctant to make predictions. Nonetheless, history provides many clues to determining the paths that Canada's thirty-four million diverse inhabitants might take.

Well-established patterns continue to shape the country's political, economic, social, and cultural dynamics. A francophone-anglophone duality undeniably has been a key factor in determining the Canadian past, although it has increasingly become a deficient model for understanding the country's development. Regionalism, a powerful phenomenon since the colonial era, is still quite pronounced. Regional distinctions, coupled with the tendency for provinces and states to seek north-south connections, make it difficult for nationalists to provide a political glue strong enough to keep Canada intact and moving forward. An essential contest between the federal government and the provinces has also accounted for much of Canadian history. The most contentious struggle might have been the question of Quebec's separation, but as events since

Confederation illustrate, the arenas for power clashes have been located in all of the provinces and territories. Moreover, Canada truly does have a mosaic of peoples. The popular image of groups that are peacefully allowed to keep their cultural identity remains debatable. Yet certainly Canadians, both those with deep family roots and recent immigrants, have constructed a successful country that has withstood periodic clashes and persistent divisions.

The scenarios for Canada's future are as varied as the imagination can conjure. Only a few, however, are plausible. A brief discussion of these images on a scale from the bleakest to the most optimistic seems the most appropriate way to close this book. The most sensational possibility is political dismemberment created by Quebec's withdrawal from Confederation. This could prompt a number of events, none of them pleasant to envision except by confirmed separatists. Quebec separation could lead to a reformulation of the remaining provinces and territories, despite the obvious problem of having the Atlantic region physically removed from the rest of Canada. Another possible model, one that Canadians have long discussed, greatly feared, and rarely embraced, is continental reconfiguration. Existing transnational regions might build stronger trading connections and perhaps create political zones in the event that Quebec leaves Canada. More linkages could materialize between the Atlantic Provinces and New England, Ontario and the Midwest, the provinces and states of the prairies, and British Columbia and the Pacific Northwest. Political connections, if any, would no doubt be the subject of protracted discussions. Finally, the most dramatic possibility would be the formal coupling of Canada's remaining provinces and territories with the United States. While this prospect might bring a smile to closet American imperialists, it is not likely to happen.

The most compelling view of Canada's future is the one that most closely follows the patterns of its past. History is never linear, despite our best efforts to bring order to a jumble of events, so trying to keep our thoughts concerning the country's future firmly set on the rails of the past would be folly. Nonetheless, Canadians will most assuredly continue their relationship. Political, social, and cultural bonds have been strained, sometimes to the point of breaking, but they have proved exceptionally resilient. Canada in the twenty-first century should maintain its sovereignty in a complex and interconnected world. For Canadians, survival has been a way of life for centuries, so there are powerful reasons to believe that the country will continue to flourish. Given the sweeping majesty of the land and the determination of its peoples, it would be most appropriate to end with the observation that the current century should be promising for one of the world's most intriguing countries.

Notable People in the History of Canada

Borden, Sir Robert Laird (1854–1937). Prime minister. The Conservative leader Borden defeated Sir Wilfrid Laurier in 1911 on the reciprocity issue. Prime minister during World War I, his government passed the War Measures Act, controlled the country's economy, developed conscription, and met regularly with other British Empire countries. He created a Union government in 1917 by inviting Liberals to join his party's war efforts. Borden pursued a distinctively Canadian agenda during the peace negotiations in 1919. To his supporters, Borden was a strong leader who successfully led Canada through a difficult war; to his critics, he was the architect of conscription and the Union government.

Bouchard, Lucien (1938–). Premier of Quebec and Bloc Québécois leader. Trained in law, Bouchard held cabinet positions in Brian Mulroney's Conservative government. He became ambassador to France in 1988. Bouchard left the Conservatives to form the Bloc Québécois in 1990, a party designed to send members to Parliament to work in conjunction with the Parti Québécois to seek Quebec's separation. He successfully led the BQ opposition in Parliament in 1993. During the second Quebec referendum campaign in 1995, Bouchard took a leading role. He resigned his BQ position in 1996 and became PQ premier of Quebec. After becoming premier, Bouchard focused his energies on Quebec's troubled economy and postponed another referendum on separation. Bouchard was an immensely popular leader among *Québécois*, who saw him as the guiding force behind modern separatism. His detractors considered him a political opportunist. He resigned as premier in 2001, but he returned to prominence in 2010 when he controversially proclaimed that Quebec should no longer seek sovereignty and focus instead on the economy and education.

Bourassa, Henri (1868–1952). Journalist and politician. The grandson of Louis-Joseph Papineau, Bourassa was elected to Parliament as a Liberal in 1896. He entered Quebec politics in 1907 and three years later helped to found *Le Devoir*, Canada's most influential French-language newspaper. Bourassa was an articulate and persistent opponent to British imperialism, the Boer War, the development of the Canadian navy, World War I, and conscription. He returned to Parliament from 1925 to 1935. Bourassa was not a separatist, but his ideas were used as beacons by French-Canadian nationalists. He believed that Canada should protect the integrity of French and English and act independent of both Britain and the United States.

Brown, George (1818–1880). Publisher and politician. The Scots-born Brown founded Toronto's *Globe*. A political reformer, he supported the Clear Grits and advocated popular representation by population and opposed close linkages between church and state. Brown entered the "Great Coalition" with John A. Macdonald and George-Étienne Cartier in 1864 and helped to design the terms of Confederation. Distrustful of French-Canadian power in the new government, he championed western development. Brown became a major figure in the developing Liberal party. He was appointed senator in the 1870s and remained active in Ontario politics. As the most powerful newspaper editor of his era, Brown promoted broader political representation and Canada's expansion into the West.

Cartier, Sir George-Étienne (1814–1873). Politician and Father of Confederation. As a young man Cartier was a *patriote* and active in the Rebellions of 1837–1838. He retreated to the United States, but later returned to Canada and became a politician and railroad promoter. As a *Bleu* leader, he formed an important ministry with John A. Macdonald and George Brown. Cartier was one of the most active French-Canadian politicians in the Confederation debates and a strong advocate of linking Canada with the Grand Trunk Railway and later the Canadian Pacific Railway. He served in Macdonald's government as minister of militia. Cartier is widely considered Canada's most influential French-Canadian political figure of the Confederation era who worked with Macdonald to improve the design of cooperative leadership.

Cartier, Jacques (1491–1557). Explorer. A French mariner who engaged in three significant trips to the New World from 1534 to 1542, Cartier explored the coast of Newfoundland and the St. Lawrence River system. Taking possession of the region for France, he quickly fell into troubled relations with the Iroquoian peoples he encountered. He took a group of Iroquois to France, including the chief Donnacona; they never returned. He failed to establish a settlement at Quebec and returned to France with "riches" that turned out to be worthless quartz and iron pyrite—fool's gold. One of Canada's most important and controversial of early explorers, Cartier helped to establish a foothold and give French place names in the New World.

Casgrain, Thérèse (1896–1981). Politician, feminist, and reformer. One of the most important female politicians and activists of the twentieth century, Casgrain worked tirelessly to advance women's rights in Quebec. She was active in the League for Women's Rights from the late 1920s until the early 1940s, and played a central role in winning the battle to have women receive the Quebec provincial franchise in 1940. After switching from the Liberal Party, she rose to prominence in the Co-operative Commonwealth Federation (CCF) after the Second World War. When she became the leader of the CCF in Quebec, Casgrain achieved notoriety for being the first woman to lead a major political party in Canada. She was a dedicated advocate of civil rights organizations, including Voice of Women, a pacifist group that opposed nuclear proliferation and the Vietnam war. Appointed a Senator in 1970, she served less than a year because of the mandatory age retirement. The title of Casgrain's autobiography was well chosen: *A Woman in a Man's World*.

Champlain, Samuel de (1570–1635). Explorer and founder of New France. A skilled cartographer and energetic explorer, Champlain took many trips to the New World in the early seventeenth century. He attempted to found a colony in Acadia in 1604. Four years later, he established a French settlement at Quebec. On various occasions he explored the St. Lawrence River system, Lake Champlain, and parts of Lakes Huron and Ontario. Champlain helped to establish trade with various Native peoples but also fought regularly with Iroquoian groups. He left detailed accounts and descriptions of his travels, elaborate drawings, and perhaps most important accurate maps of the eastern part of North America. Earlier generations called Champlain the Father of New France, a heroic image that masked a complex man. Yet undeniably his devotion to settling and exploring territory in the New World was extraordinary and of critical importance to France.

Charest, Jean (1958–). Politician. Educated as a lawyer, the Quebec-born Charest became the youngest cabinet member in Canadian history when he served in Brian Mulroney's administration in a number of positions, the most important of which was the Minister of the Environment. Charest was one of only two Conservative members of Parliament who survived the crushing Liberal victory in 1993. Remarkably, the popular Charest later agreed to assume the leadership role in Quebec's Liberal Party in a gambit to counteract the Parti Québécois's sovereignty-association agenda. Charest has served as Premier of Quebec since 2003. He has been a vocal backer of environmental reforms, although the actions of his government often suggest otherwise. Charest supports Quebec's recognition as a distinct society in Canada, and his government has actively promoted Quebec's connections to the international community. His detractors view him as a political opportunist, while his supporters claim that his temperate leadership has enabled Quebec to improve its relationship with Canada.

Chrétien, Jean (1934–). Prime minister. Born in Quebec of working-class roots, Chrétien was trained in law at Laval University. First elected to Parliament in 1963, he served in Lester Pearson's and Pierre Trudeau's cabinets. He held many positions, such as the minister of Indian Affairs, led the federalist forces against Quebec's referendum in 1980, and promoted the new Constitution in 1982. He became prime minister in 1993, a position that he retained after winning a third majority government in 2000. Much criticized for his belated opposition to the second Quebec referendum in 1995, Chrétien nonetheless led a strong Liberal party in the 1990s. His government was scandal ridden, and few Canadians seemed to embrace his folksy yet cagey political style of leadership. Critics and supporters alike attributed his continued leadership to the general prosperity of the 1990s rather than to his initiatives.

Currie, Sir Arthur (1875–1933). Soldier. Currie began his career as a businessman and real estate speculator in British Columbia. He was active in the provincial militia, so when the First World War broke out he was positioned to move into a position of leadership. He took command of a division of the Canadian Corps when it was created in 1915, and as a result of several campaigns along the Western Front, Currie became the first Canadian to become a full general. Currie was given credit for molding a professional and efficient fighting force, and he was known for resisting the practice of offering promotions for political reasons. After his participation in the Canadian victory at Vimy Ridge in 1917, Currie was appointed commander of the Canadian Expeditionary Force. Following the war he became president of McGill University. Unfortunately, his reputation was somewhat tarnished in the 1920s when he was accused of endangering the lives of his men to advance the interests of his career and the nation during the war. Nonetheless, he successfully defended himself against libel in a 1927 trial. Considered by many contemporaries and historians to be one of the most talented commanders on the Western Front, Currie's biography is a classic example of the citizen-soldier in Canadian history.

Diefenbaker, John George (1895–1979). Prime minister. Ontario born, Diefenbaker moved to Saskatchewan and became a respected defense lawyer in the 1920s. After experience in provincial politics, he was elected to Parliament in 1940. He became leader of the Progressive Conservative party and was elected prime minister from 1957 to 1963. Diefenbaker promoted the ideal of "One Canada," passed the Canadian Bill of Rights, sought northern development, and supported the Commonwealth. Economic issues plagued his administration, and poor relations with the United States during critical moments of the Cold War such as the Cuban missile crisis helped to lead to his defeat. After losing to Lester Pearson, he remained in Parliament as an effective opponent to the Liberals. Diefenbaker's political style and insistence on creating a unified and mostly anglophone country, closer to the Commonwealth than to the

United States, divided Canadians who disagreed on the direction the country should take in the postwar era.

Douglas, Thomas C. (1904–1986). Premier of Saskatchewan and social reformer. The Scots-born Douglas became a Baptist minister and engaged in the social gospel movement of Christian activism to improve society. As a socialist politician he was an original member of the Co-operative Commonwealth Federation (CCF). A CCF member of Parliament from 1935 to 1944, he resigned to run for premier of Saskatchewan. An activist premier from 1944 to 1961, Douglas implemented social services and created a plan for socialized medicine that the federal government used as a model in the 1960s. The leader of the left-leaning New Democratic party after its creation in 1961 until 1971, Douglas championed pension plans for Canadians and improved rights for civil servants. Douglas pioneered programs for the modern welfare state. Not surprisingly, Canadians are deeply divided in their opinions of his political and social contributions.

Duplessis, Maurice (1890–1959). Politician. Trained as a lawyer, Duplessis gravitated to politics as a young man. He helped to form the Union Nationale party and served as Quebec's premier from 1936 to 1939 and from 1944 until his death in 1959. His leadership style and political programs made him one of the most controversial politicians of the twentieth century. Known as "*le chef*" because of his reliance on patronage, he fiercely opposed leftist organizations and the attempts of the federal government to conscript soldiers during the Second World War. Duplessis's agendas included creating a favorable business environment for the province, encouraging American investment, and developing a comprehensive rural electrification program. His detractors, including union organizers, complained of his autocratic behavior and pointed to his government's corrupt practices. His legacy remains the subject of some debate. Some highlight his passionate defense of Quebec's interests and modernization schemes; a greater number refer to his time in office as "*la grande noirceur*" (the great darkness). However, virtually everyone agrees that his death set the stage for Quebec's Quiet Revolution in the 1960s.

Groulx, Lionel-Adolphe (1878–1967). Roman Catholic priest and historian. Trained for the priesthood, Groulx became professor of Canadian history at the University of Montreal in 1915. Throughout a long and celebrated career, he maintained that French Canadians had survived repeated attempts by the British and anglophone Canadians to subordinate or assimilate them. He edited the journal *Action française* and a group of the same name. Groulx is justifiably considered one of the intellects behind modern Quebec nationalism. He was not a Quebec separatist, but he did mount a spirited defense of francophone ideals and implored his people to remember their struggles to survive since the era of New France.

Howe, Joseph (1804–1873). Journalist and premier of Nova Scotia. The editor of the influential *Novascotian*, Howe engaged in a long career as a political reformer. He helped to institute responsible government in Nova Scotia in the late 1840s and became premier from 1860 to 1863. Howe was one of Canada's most persistent opponents to Confederation, which he called a "Botheration Scheme." After failing to convince the British to let Nova Scotia immediately withdraw from Canada after 1867, he became a federal minister in John A. Macdonald's government. In his extensive writings and speeches, Howe effectively gave voice to the regional interests of Maritimers and raised questions about the wisdom of establishing a Canadian nation.

King, William Lyon Mackenzie (1874–1950). Prime minister. The grandson of rebel William Lyon Mackenzie was initially elected to Parliament in 1908. Interested in workers, he served as Wilfrid Laurier's labor minister and wrote *Industry and Humanity*. He became the prime minister in 1921, two years after becoming the leader of the Liberals. After briefly being out of office in 1926 and engaging in a constitutional struggle with Lord Byng, the governor general, he remained in power until 1930. Defeated by the Conservatives as the Great Depression deepened, he returned in 1935 and served as prime minister until his resignation in 1948. Canada's longest-serving prime minister at almost twenty-two years, King was known for his conciliatory behavior and attempts to prevent divisions between Quebec and the rest of Canada. His domestic programs included a pension plan, unemployment insurance, and the Family Allowance Act. During World War II, he reluctantly moved to conscription. A spiritual and withdrawn bachelor, he was poorly understood by contemporaries. Historians are fond of claiming that his greatest contribution was that he divided Canadians the least.

Laurier, Sir Wilfrid (1841–1919). Prime minister. Trained as a lawyer, Laurier emerged as the Liberal party leader in 1887. Canada's first French-Canadian prime minister (1896–1911), he developed a compromise for the Manitoba schools question, modified the National Policy, and vastly increased the number of immigrants. Laurier presided over Canada's voluntary commitment to the Boer War, created the Canadian navy in 1910, and fashioned a trade plan with the United States. The Liberals lost the election of 1911 on this issue, and thus reciprocity was not enacted. Laurier refused to join Robert Borden's Union forces or support conscription during World War I. A skilled compromiser who was devoted to national development, Laurier consistently angered conservative and Roman Catholic elements in his native Quebec.

Laval, François de (1623–1708). Bishop of New France. A French-born Jesuit priest, Laval became the first bishop of Quebec (1674–1685). An energetic leader who struggled in vain to stop the practice of using liquor in trade negotiations with Native peoples, he established the Quebec Seminary in 1663 to train Canadian-born clerics. Laval's legacy for New France was important. He "Canadian-ized" the clergy and strengthened connections between Quebec's Roman Catholic church and Rome. Laval also clashed repeatedly with governors in his attempts to maintain the church's influence in the New World.

Leacock, Stephen (1869–1944). Writer and educator. Born in England, Leacock grew up in Ontario. He studied economics and political science, and received a Ph.D. from the University of Chicago. Leacock taught at McGill University from 1908 to 1936. A regular contributor to magazines and author of books, he achieved fame for his humorous pieces. One of his most famous works, *Sunshine Sketches of a Little Town*, satirized life in small-town Canada and explored the impact of modernization on the lives of ordinary people. He also gained notoriety as a Conservative activist. In his time Leacock was perhaps Canada's most influential and widely read author, humorist, and critic.

Lévesque, René (1922–1987). Quebec premier and journalist. A correspondent during World War II, the bilingual Lévesque became a popular television commentator in the 1950s. As a Liberal politician, he worked under the Lesage government as the head of various ministries and was influential in creating Hydro-Quebec. After quitting the Liberals and helping to form an alliance of independence groups in the Parti Québécois, Lévesque became premier in 1976. His government passed Bill 101, the French-language charter, and led the sovereignty-association referendum in 1980. The PQ lost the referendum but was reelected in 1981. Lévesque bitterly opposed Pierre Trudeau's new constitution. After resigning as premier in 1985, he returned to journalism. The PQ's charismatic leader in its early phase of governance, Lévesque nonetheless failed to bring Quebec's sovereignty from Canada to fruition.

Macdonald, Sir John A. (1815–1891). Prime minister and chief architect of Confederation. Scots born, Macdonald moved to Canada and became a lawyer in Kingston. He fought against the rebels in the Upper Canadian Rebellions of 1837–1838. In 1864 he formed the "Great Coalition" with George-Étienne Cartier and George Brown as a Liberal-Conservative, the forerunner of the Conservative party. The chief designer of the British North America (BNA) Act, Macdonald is still called the Father of Confederation. Canada's first prime minister, Macdonald served from 1867 to 1873 and 1878 to 1891. He supported the development of the Canadian Pacific Railway and was defeated by Alexander Mackenzie in the Pacific Scandal of 1873. On his return in 1878, he promoted the National Policy. Macdonald was federal leader during the Red River and North-West rebellions. He died in office. An exceptionally skilled politician with numerous personal flaws, Macdonald stands as Canada's most important nation builder of the nineteenth century.

Mackenzie, Sir Alexander (1764–1820). Explorer and fur trader. The Scots-born Mackenzie was an energetic fur trader and partner in the North West Company who explored the continent's western and northern reaches in the late eighteenth century. The massive river system that carries his name disappointed him by reaching Arctic waters instead of the Pacific. Mackenzie is best known for his successful overland passage with a small group to the Pacific Ocean in 1793. His published journals and history of the fur trade reinforce the fact that he was one of the most important white explorers in Canadian history.

Mackenzie, William Lyon (1795–1861). Publisher, politician, and rebel. Born in Scotland, Mackenzie emigrated to Upper Canada and became a newspaper publisher and politician. He was elected Toronto's mayor in 1834. An admirer of American democracy, he regularly criticized the elitist Family Compact. He also published a series of grievances against the British control of Upper Canada. In December 1837 he helped to incite a rebellion against British and loyal Canadian forces. He immediately fled to an island in the Niagara River and was arrested in the United States for violating neutrality laws. After serving a jail sentence, he returned to Canada and was elected to the legislature of the Canadas in the 1850s. A controversial figure, Mackenzie was Canada's most influential anglophone rebel.

Macphail, Agnes (1890–1954). Politician, teacher, and reformer. An Ontario born school teacher, Macphail entered politics in the United Farmers of Ontario. In 1921, shortly after the passage of women's suffrage, she became the first female elected to Parliament. She remained in the House of Commons from 1921 to 1940, first as a member of the Progressive party, then later in the newly formed Co-operative Commonwealth Federation. She also served in the Ontario legislature and was the first woman appointed to Canada's League of Nations delegation. Macphail championed farmers' rights and prison reform, but she is best known for her work in pursuing women's issues. One of Canada's most influential feminists in the first half of the twentieth century, Macphail overcame substantial prejudice to become an effective politician in an arena that was overwhelmingly inhabited by males.

Massey, Vincent (1887–1967). Diplomat, Governor General. The son of a prosperous Methodist family, the Toronto-born Massey spent his early career in university administration and as president of the Massey-Harris farm implement company. He was appointed Canada's first Minister to Washington from 1926 to 1930, and then served as High Commissioner to London from 1935 to 1946. As a reflection of his stature, Massey was appointed Canada's first native-born Governor General in 1952. He is perhaps best known for chairing the Royal Commission on National Development in the Arts, Letters and Sciences, which is still referred to as the Massey Commission. A strong Canadian nationalist, Massey believed that his country would be strengthened by improving its education, protecting its culture, and nurturing its multilateral relationships. Massey, called *The Imperial Canadian* in the title of Claude Bissell's biography, was one of Canada's most able and humane statesmen of the twentieth century.

McClung, Nellie (1873–1951). Reformer, suffragist, and politician. Ontario-born, McClung moved to Manitoba as a child. She became an activist in the Women's Christian Temperance Union and the struggle for female suffrage rights. The author of numerous novels, opinion pieces, and an autobiography, McClung also lectured widely on women's and reform issues. Her actions helped in 1915 to bring women's suffrage to Manitoba, the first province to do so in Canada. She also pursued reforms for workers, especially in factories, and was elected to Alberta's legislature as a Liberal from 1921 to 1926. McClung was appointed a delegate to the League of Nations in 1938 and served on the board of governors for the CBC. She was one of Canada's most influential reformers and women's rights activists in the first half of the twentieth century.

McGee, Thomas D'Arcy (1825–1868). Journalist, politician, Father of Confederation. Born in Ireland, McGee worked as an editor in the United States before he returned to his birthplace to support the Young Ireland movement. He escaped to the United States after a failed rebellion in 1848, and moved to Montreal in the late 1850s. He formed the *New Era* newspaper and was elected to the Province of Canada's assembly. McGee became a strong opponent of both the ultra-Protestant Orange Order and the controversial Irish nationalist organization of Fenians. He became part of the coalition that supported Confederation, and his varied interests included separate schools for Catholics, opposition to American expansion, railway construction, and an intriguing vision to promote Canadian literature to define the new country's character. McGee was assassinated by a Fenian sympathizer in Ottawa in 1868, and to this day he is one of the very few Canadian politicians to suffer that fate.

Mercredi, Ovide (1946–). Assembly of First Nations leader. Born in Manitoba of Cree heritage, Mercredi received a law degree and became an expert on constitutional law. He rose to prominence as the national chief of the Assembly of First Nations from 1991-1997.

During his tenure he worked to advance the interests of Native peoples in both the Meech Lake Accord and the Charlottetown Accord. In particular, he sought to add more inclusive language to the new Constitution. He is one of Canada's leading proponents of non-violent activism. The co-author, with Mary Ellen Turpel, of *In the Rapids: Navigating the Future of First Nations*, Mercredi is currently chancellor of University College of the North and a leader of Manitoba's Misipawistik Cree Nation.

Moodie, Susanna (1803–1885). Author and pioneer settler. An English writer and antislavery activist, Moodie married a British officer and emigrated to Upper Canada in 1832. Settling in the backwoods, she was forced to adjust to pioneer life and the people she encountered. Over time she dropped her aristocratic outlook and grew to appreciate the ingenuity and culture of the hard-working backcountry farmers. She wrote novels, short stories, and verse. Her most famous work, *Roughing It in the Bush*, was published in 1852. The rigors of pioneer life and her own attempts to be successful at farming provided Moodie with material for her novels and magazine pieces. As with the works of her sister, Catherine Parr Traill, another well-published author, Moodie's literary contributions give readers important insights into nineteenth-century rural life in Canada.

Mulroney, Martin Brian (1939–). Prime minister and businessman. Quebec born of Irish heritage and fluently bilingual, he trained in law and became president of the Iron Ore Company of Canada in 1977. With little political experience, he became leader of the Conservatives in 1983. The next year he was elected prime minister. Mulroney presided over the Meech Lake and Charlottetown accords to gain Quebec's signature to the Constitution, both of which failed. His government arranged a free trade agreement with the United States and the North American Free Trade Agreement (NAFTA) with the United States and Mexico. Mulroney left office in 1993 with extremely low popular support. He returned to practicing law and sits on many corporate boards of international firms. Many Canadians still blame Mulroney for linking Canada too closely to the United States and for personally profiting during the 1980s boom. His supporters remember that he was dedicated to improving federal relations with Quebec.

Murphy, Emily (1868–1933). Women's rights activist and writer. The Ontario-born Murphy moved to Alberta and became involved in the movement for improving women's rights. She used the pen name "Janey Canuck" in her various writings. In 1916 Murphy became the first female magistrate in the British Empire, serving in Edmonton. She campaigned against narcotic drugs and championed other social issues. Murphy helped to win the "Persons Case" of 1928–1929. In this celebrated issue, the British Privy Council overturned a Canadian Supreme Court decision that women could not serve in the Senate. Murphy wrote extensively on a woman's experience abroad and in Canada; she was one of Canada's most important reform advocates of her times.

Papineau, Louis-Joseph (1786–1871). Lawyer, politician, and rebel. Born to a landholding family and trained in law, Papineau entered politics. He led the Parti Canadien and spearheaded an independence movement from British colonial rule in Lower Canada. He helped to compose the Ninety-Two Resolutions in 1834. After being instrumental in fomenting the rebellion in 1837, he escaped to the United States. After 1845 he returned to his seigneury and reentered politics. French Canada's most influential rebel, Papineau was an immensely controversial figure because of his flawed leadership during the rebellions and his complex personality.

Pearson, Lester (1897–1972). Statesman and prime minister. Pearson served in the army and Royal Flying Corps during World War I. After teaching history at the University of Toronto in the 1920s, he became involved in Canada's diplomatic corps. Pearson served in England from 1935 to 1941 and the United States from 1942 to 1946. As a Liberal politician, he worked in Mackenzie King's and Louis St. Laurent's administrations. Pearson achieved international fame as president of the UN General Assembly in 1952 and for his peacekeeping efforts during the Suez crisis of 1956. For the latter he received the Nobel Peace Prize in 1957. Elected Liberal prime minister from 1963 to 1968, his government instituted a variety of medical and social plans while it tried to achieve "co-operative federalism." Pearson was arguably Canada's most widely respected diplomat of the twentieth century and an architect of the modern welfare state.

Poundmaker (1842–1886). Cree leader. Poundmaker was a Plains Cree chief who was born in present-day Saskatchewan. He helped to negotiate Treaty 6 in 1876, which covered an extensive territory in the North-West, and led his band on a newly created reserve. Concerned about the growing hunger of his people and the Canadian government's inattention to promises made in the treaty, Poundmaker sought assistance at Fort Battleford. Government troops unsuccessfully attacked a Cree camp near Cut Knife Hill in May 1885; Poundmaker was not a participant in the fight, and he instructed his men to let the military forces retreat without further struggle. At the conclusion of the brief hostilities in the North-West Poundmaker voluntarily surrendered. Convicted of treason-felony with his fellow Cree leader, Big Bear, he served seven months in prison. Plagued by declining health, he died in 1886. Oral history and traditional sources suggest that Poundmaker worked to improve the lives of his people and that he consistently sought a peaceful solution to the North-West crisis.

Riel, Louis (1844–1885). Métis leader. Born in the Red River settlement, the Métis Riel was educated in Quebec. He led the Red River resistance against the encroachment of the Canadian government in 1869 and 1870 by forming a provisional government and presenting a "List of Rights" that became the foundation of the Manitoba Act. After struggles broke out, he fled to the United States. He subsequently returned and was elected to Parliament from Manitoba, but he was prevented from sitting in the House of Commons. Following brief stays in Quebec mental asylums, Riel moved to Montana and became an American citizen. Invited by Métis and Native peoples to join their struggle against Canadian expansion in the Saskatchewan region, Riel was captured during the North-West Rebellion of 1885. After a dubious trial, he was hanged for treason in Regina. Probably no other figure in Canadian history remains as controversial as Riel. Lauded by Métis, Native peoples, and Quebecers as a noble opponent to a variety of injustices, his detractors consider him a deranged and misguided traitor.

Smallwood, Joey (1900–1991). Politician, journalist. Born in a small Newfoundland community, Smallwood began his career as a journalist. As he worked on newspapers in New York, Boston, and Nova Scotia, he embraced the ideals of labor unions and leftist organizations. After returning to Newfoundland and trying his hand as a pig farmer, he became interested in politics. He ran a popular radio program starting in the late 1930s, and after the Second World War he was elected to the National Convention to decide Newfoundland's future. Smallwood visited Ottawa and became a staunch advocate of joining Canada. He helped to win the case for Confederation after two referendums in 1948, and became the province's first premier the following year. As premier, a position he held until 1972, Smallwood supported economic development and welfare programs. He was the driving force behind the massive *Encyclopedia of Newfoundland and Labrador*. His critics stressed his overbearing style, his failed schemes to industrialize the province, and his dramatic reversals on policies. Undeniably eccentric, Smallwood was a tireless promoter of Newfoundland's unique history and culture.

Stowe, Emily Howard (1831–1903). Physician and women's rights activist. Born in Upper Canada, Stowe decided to pursue a career in medicine. Prevented from being educated in Canada, she received her training at the New York Medical College for Women. She set up a practice in Toronto during the 1860s and helped to form the Woman's Medical College in Toronto in 1883. She also assisted in founding the Toronto Women's Literary Club in 1876, which was primarily a suffragist organization. Stowe tirelessly advocated the enfranchisement and improved property rights for women in Ontario. She was one of Canada's foremost advocates of women's rights and a pioneer in breaking into the male-dominated medical profession of the late nineteenth century.

Thomson, Tom (1877–1917). Painter. As a young man, the Ontario-born Thomson apprenticed in a machine shop. He gravitated towards the commercial arts in Seattle and Toronto and, without formal training, he developed a dramatic painting style using the medium of oil. He developed relationships with an impressive number of budding artists, the most celebrated of which formed the Group of Seven in the 1920s. Drawn to the rugged landscape of the Canadian Shield, he became a fishing ranger and guide in Algonquin Park, Ontario. His death as a result of a canoeing accident in 1917 sparked various theories that he may have been murdered, but those controversial claims have never been proved. There is no doubt, however, that Thomson's paintings influenced the Group of Seven and gave his fellow citizens some of the most enduring and iconic images of the country's forests and lakes. "The Jack Pine" and "Northern River," to cite just two works, are instantly recognizable to many Canadians.

Trudeau, Pierre Elliott (1919–2000). Prime minister and lawyer. The son of a wealthy Quebec family, Trudeau trained for the law. He opposed the political style of Maurice Duplessis and helped to found the newspaper *Cité Libre*. A law professor at the University of Montreal in the 1960s, he was elected to Parliament in 1965. Trudeau served on Lester Pearson's cabinet and became prime minister in 1968. During his leadership from 1968 to 1979, he coped with the October Crisis, implemented bilingualism, and faced economic difficulties. Defeated by the Conservatives in 1979, he returned within a year. From 1980 to 1984, he opposed Quebec's referendum and "patriated" the Constitution. He retired from politics in 1984 but continued to practice law in Montreal until his death. Trudeau was one of Canada's most controversial modern prime ministers, both admired and criticized for being a staunch federalist, a proponent of the welfare state, and a fierce opponent of Quebec separatists.

Woodsworth, James Shaver (1874–1942). Minister, politician, and reformer. An Ontario-born Methodist minister, Woodsworth became interested in the plight of immigrants to Canada. He wrote *The Strangers Within Our Gates* (1909) and labored to improve the lives of lower-class Canadians as part of the social gospel movement, an activist organization of Christian reformers. A pacifist during World War I, Woodsworth supported the workers during the Winnipeg General Strike of 1919. He was elected to Parliament in 1921 as a labor candidate and remained in that seat until his death in 1942. As one of the founders of the Co-operative Commonwealth Federation in 1933, he became that party's first leader. Woodsworth opposed Canada's declaration of war in 1939. Called "a prophet in politics" by his biographer, Woodsworth was clearly one of the country's greatest social reformers of the twentieth century.

Timeline of Historical Events

18,000–10,000 B.C.	Aboriginal peoples migrate to North America
700–1000 A.D.	Inuit migrate to North America
1000	Leif Eriksson's voyage
1497	John Cabot's voyage makes contact with Newfoundland and Cape Breton
1524–1528	Giovanni da Verrazano's voyages; New France named
1534–1542	Jacques Cartier's three voyages; St. Lawrence River explored
1604	Attempt to settle Acadia by Sieur de Monts and Samuel de Champlain
1608	Quebec founded by Champlain
1610	Henry Hudson's European discovery of Hudson Bay
1611	Port-Royal established
1621	Nova Scotia granted to Sir William Alexander
1627	Company of New France established
1628	Kirke brothers raid New France
1632	Quebec returned to the French
1640s	Huron decimated by Iroquois raids and disease

1642	Montreal established by Paul de Chomedey de Maisonneuve and Jeanne Mance
1663	New France put under royal control
1670	Hudson's Bay Company chartered
1689–1697	King William's War
1702–1713	Queen Anne's War
1713	Treaty of Utrecht cedes Newfoundland and Acadia to Britain; Louisbourg established
1744–1748	King George's War
1749	Halifax established
1755–1762	Acadian deportation
1756–1763	Seven Years' War leads to Conquest
1759	Quebec City falls to the British
1763	Treaty of Paris cedes most of North America to British; Royal Proclamation reformulates British North America
1774	Quebec Act extends Quebec's territory and grants limited rights to French
1770s–1780s	Loyalists arrive in British North America
1783	Treaty of Paris; United States victorious in Revolutionary War
1784	New Brunswick established by Loyalists
1791	Constitutional Act (Canada Act) creates Upper and Lower Canada
1793	Alexander Mackenzie reaches Pacific Ocean by overland route
1812	Selkirk grant in Red River (Assiniboia)
1812–1814	War of 1812
1817	Rush-Bagot Agreement
1818	Convention of 1818 creates boundary with the United States at forty-ninth parallel
1821	Hudson's Bay Company and North West Company merge
1829	Welland Canal opened
1832	Rideau Canal completed
1837–1838	Rebellions in Lower and Upper Canada
1839	Durham's Report; "Aroostook War"
1841	Act of Union creates Canada East and Canada West

1846	Oregon Boundary settlement
1848–1855	Responsible government established in British North American colonies
1849	Annexation Manifesto
1854–1866	Reciprocity Treaty with United States
1858	British Columbia Colony formed
1864	September: Charlottetown Conference; October: Quebec City Conference
1867	July 1: Dominion of Canada formed
1869–1870	Red River Resistance
1870	Manitoba Act
1871	British Columbia enters Confederation
1872	Dominion Lands Act
1873	Prince Edward Island enters Confederation; Supreme Court created
1878	National Policy introduced
1880	Canada acquires Arctic islands from Britain
1885	North-West Rebellion; Canadian Pacific Railway completed
1888	Jesuits' Estates Act
1890–1897	Manitoba schools controversy
1899–1902	South African War (Boer War)
1903	Alaska Boundary award
1905	Saskatchewan and Alberta join Confederation
1909	Boundary Waters Treaty establishes International Joint Commission
1910	Naval Service Act creates Canadian navy
1911	Reciprocity Agreement with United States rejected
1914–1918	World War I
1914	War Measures Act passed
1917	Battle of Vimy Ridge; Halifax explosion; conscription; Union government formed
1917–1920s	Canadian National Railway created
1918	Women's suffrage for federal elections
1919	Winnipeg General Strike
1921	Agnes Macphail elected, Canada's first female member of Parliament

1923	Halibut Treaty with United States
1925–1926	King-Byng controversy
1929	Stock market crash leads to Great Depression
1931	Statute of Westminster
1932	Unemployment Relief Camps organized; Canadian Broadcasting Corporation formed
1932–1933	Co-operative Commonwealth Federation established
1935	Richard Bedford Bennett's "New Deal"; On-to-Ottawa Trek
1939–1945	World War II (Canada enters war in September 1939)
1940	Rowell-Sirois Report on Dominion-Provincial Relations; Ogdensburg Agreement with United States
1941	Hyde Park Agreement with United States; Canada declares war on Japan
1942	Conscription pledge plebiscite; Dieppe raid
1942–1947	Japanese-Canadian relocation
1944	Normandy invasion; PC 1003 grants workers the right to collective bargaining
1945	Canada joins United Nations as charter member
1949	Newfoundland enters Confederation; North Atlantic Treaty Organization (NATO) formed
1950–1953	Korean War
1951	Massey Commission reports
1952	Vincent Massey becomes first Canadian-born governor general
1956	Suez Crisis and UN peacekeeping forces organized
1957	Hospital Insurance Plan; North American Air Defense Agreement (NORAD) formed
1959	St. Lawrence Seaway opens
1960s	"Quiet Revolution" in Quebec
1961	New Democratic Party (NDP) formed
1962	Cuban missile crisis strains Canadian-American relations

1965	Canada Assistance Act; Medicare; Canada Pension Plan
1967	Montreal Exposition '67
1969	*Manhattan* incident; Official Languages Act
1970	October Crisis
1971	National Action Committee on the Status of Women (NAC)
1973	Foreign Investment Review Agency (FIRA) created
1975	Petro-Can formed; James Bay Agreement between Quebec government, Cree, and Inuit
1976	Parti Québécois (PQ) elected in Quebec
1977	Bill 101, Charter of the French Language, passed in Quebec
1980	National Energy Program; Quebec Referendum on Sovereignty-Association; Canada joins Organization of American States (OAS)
1982	Constitution Act passed, including Charter of Rights and Freedoms; Assembly of First Nations formed; Canada agrees to UN Convention on the Law of the Sea
1987	Meech Lake Accord; Reform party formed
1988	Bill 178 passed in Quebec
1989	Free trade agreement with United States implemented
1990	Gulf War fought with Canada's participation; Mohawk tensions in Quebec
1992	Charlottetown Accord
1993	North American Free Trade Agreement (NAFTA) created with United States and Mexico; Bloc Québécois forms official opposition in Canadian Parliament
1995	Second Quebec Referendum
1997	Canada signs Kyoto Protocol
1999	Nunavut, a self-governing territory, established
2000	Canadian Alliance formed
2001	Canada sends military forces to Afghanistan
2003	Conservative Party of Canada (CPC) formed

2005	Civil Marriages Act legalizes same-sex marriage
2006	Indian Residential Schools Settlement Agreement
2008	Economic Recession
2010	Vancouver Winter Olympics

Primary Documents

The following book excerpts, articles, legal documents, and letters are designed to support various points in the previous chapters, and each includes a helpful introduction.

The Vancouver Winter Olympics and the Press

The Vancouver Winter Olympics in 2010 provided an opportunity for Canada to host a popular sporting event and showcase the country to the world. By all accounts the Olympics were a tremendous success, despite the anxiety over uncooperative weather patterns that threatened a lack of adequate snow cover for numerous events and the tragic death of a participant in the dangerous luge competition. The event was closely observed by Canadians from coast to coast. Predictably, observers came to strikingly different conclusions about the relative strengths and weaknesses of the Olympics for representing the entire country and the greater impact that the event would have on Canadian nationalism in the early twenty-first century. The following excerpts from two newspaper accounts provide a sampling of that wide-ranging opinion.

"Shades of Vimy," by Lorne Gunter, in *National Post*, 3 March 2010.

Will our success at the Winter Olympics cure us of our national inferiority complex? God, I hope so.

Military historians have argued that Canada became a nation on the slopes of Vimy Ridge in France, when, in 1917, all four divisions of the Canadian Expeditionary Force fought together for the first time and overwhelmed a massive German stronghold most thought unconquerable. Perhaps, then, in the not-too-distant future, our

Lorne Gunter, "Shades of Vimy," in *National Post*, 3 March 2010.

nation will be seen to have become fully grown up and cast off its adolescent obsession with cultural engineering on the slopes of Whistler and Cypress Mountain and the ice surfaces of Vancouver and Richmond.

Not only did our athletes do us—so proud—so did the Vancouver Organizing Committee, the thousands of volunteers, and the people of the Vancouver region. What a world-class celebration.

The Canadian Olympic Committee and the associations for each of the winter sports deserve credit, as well. Without their help to make our athletes as good as they could be—without their courage to demand excellence and not settle for personal bests—we would not have raked in all those golds and other medals.

And we Canadians ourselves deserve a pat on the back for not apologizing for coming first so often.

But when I refer to casting off our national inferiority complex, I don't mean the permission we suddenly seem to have given ourselves to be overjoyed by our nation's athletic accomplishments. Rather, I'm talking about the way most of our major national policies of the past half-century have really just been masks for our national angst. Multiculturalism, universal health care, soft power diplomacy, economic and cultural nationalism and others are all, in part, efforts to downplay our own fear that we are an insignificant nation. Through them, we reassure ourselves of our moral superiority, especially toward the Americans.

Maybe Vancouver finally made us willing to stop defining ourselves through our belief in giant government programs and our fear and resentment of the United States.

Now, perhaps, we can also give ourselves permission to stop trying to manufacture a distinctively Canadian culture and just let one evolve naturally.

We are not Americans. We are never going to be Americans. No amount of economic or cultural protectionism is going to keep the U.S. influences out. But also, American influences were never going to impoverish us or strip our identity away....

Perhaps instead of sneering at the Americans about their melting pot approach to immigration and insisting our multicultural approach is superior, we'll now come to see the two as different sides of the same coin.

I think we have already come to understand that while we were tremendous peacekeepers under the UN, what the world needs now is peacemakers. There was nothing wrong with our old role. We were very good at it. But now we have moved on. We have re-equipped ourselves and are getting on with the heavy lifting of fighting in hot spots and bring aid directly to stricken regions.

Those who still cling to the old notion of Canada as only ever a non-fighting nation, that works only through the UN and cares deeply what the rest of the world thinks of us, have been left behind by events.

Maybe it's a generational thing. The Canadians most excited by the Olympics seemed to be the 20-somethings.

They are not defined by the culture wars of the 1960s and 1970s. They don't know national unity battles (except through their textbooks). They take our cultural diversity largely for granted and are eager to be part of the global pop/youth culture.

Indeed they are already a part of the global Twitter/Facebook/You-Tube/texting/Avatar/iPod society.

They are more relaxed about being Canadian, less concerned about being sucked into the American vortex, positively deaf to arguments that we need to be sheltered if we are to compete.

It will be years before the political legacy of Vancouver is understood completely. But let's hope some day we look back and see how the games moved us away from our old collectivist goals.

"Vancouver Games Quickly Turn Sour for Quebec," by Kalli Anderson, in *Globe and Mail*, 16 February 2010.

The Olympic spirit may be alive and well in Vancouver, but it was an altogether different story in the Quebec press over the weekend. The francophone media kicked off their coverage of the Games with a collective uproar over the not-quite-French-enough opening ceremony in Vancouver on Friday.

Kalli Anderson, "Vancouver Games Quickly Turn Sour for Quebec," in *Globe and Mail*, 16 February 2010.

A headline in *La Presse* cheekily declared, "French is as rare as snow in Vancouver." The article quoted Canada's Commissioner of Official Languages, Graham Fraser, who described the opening ceremony as a "show conceived and performed in English with a French song tacked on at the end."

Quebec politicians were quick to criticize the Vancouver Organizing Committee for failing to include more French in the ceremony. Premier Jean Charest told reporters that he would have liked to have seen "a stronger presence of French during the ceremony...."

Insufficient French wasn't the only criticism of the opening ceremony in the Quebec press. In a report from Vancouver, *La Presse*'s Jean-Francois Bégin wrote that what was "equally, if not more shocking" was the organizers' decision to "snub Gaétan Boucher." Mr. Bégin deplored the fact that the former Olympic champion speed skater did not make an appearance during the ceremony....

In his *Journal de Quebec* column, Donald Charette lamented an overall lack of recognition of *la belle province* during the ceremony....He suggested that [the organizing committee] should have made a greater effort to "show the world that this country was founded by two great peoples, that Quebec represents a quarter of [Canada's] population...."

In what was surely the angriest (and most surreal) response to the opening ceremony published in the Quebec press, *La Presse* sports columnist Réjean Tremblay decided to write part of his column in English, in mock-deference to [the organizing committee]. In a sarcasm-drenched fury, Mr. Tremblay praised the opening ceremony for so accurately representing Canada through depictions of "the Rockies, the Prairies and the Maritimes, while jumping right over Quebec."

Joe Canadian Rant

Late in the winter of 2000 the Molson company sponsored one of the most successful advertisement moments in all of Canadian history. The "Joe Canadian Rant," as it was instantly dubbed, captured a sense of Canadian pride and nationalism at the dawn of a new century. The actor who delivered the lines, as a sort of everyman, began his pitch in modest cadence, only to complete the commercial in strident volume and an emotional flourish. The advertisement cleverly used classic stereotypes and skillfully drew out enduring distinctions that separate Canadians from their neighbors in the United States.

Hey. I'm not a lumberjack or a fur trader. And I don't live in an igloo, or eat blubber, or own a dogsled. And I don't know Jimmy, Sally, or Suzy from Canada, although I'm certain they're really, really nice. I have a Prime Minister, not a President.

I speak English and French, not American. And I pronounce it "about," not "aboot."

I can proudly sew my country's flag on my backpack. I believe in peacekeeping, not policing; diversity, not assimilation. And that the beaver is a truly proud and noble animal. A toque is a hat, a chesterfield is a couch, and it is pronounced "zed" not "zee."

Canada is the second largest land mass, the first nation of hockey, and the best part of North America!

My name is Joe, and I *am* Canadian! Thank you.

Patrick James and Mark Kasoff, eds., *Canadian Studies in the New Millennium* (Toronto: University of Toronto Press, 2008), 143.

Champlain's Assessment of Native Peoples

Samuel de Champlain, in addition to being a masterful cartographer, wrote extensively about his various trips to the new world and commented on the indigenous peoples that he and his contemporaries encountered. His narratives give us a powerful insight to the European viewpoint, but they are of course skewed entirely to the outlook and sensibilities of French explorers in the seventeenth century. The following passage comes from his published account: Des Sauvages, ou, voyage de Samuel Champlain, de Brouage, fait en la France nouvelle, l'an 1603 (Of Savages: or the Voyage of Samuel Champlain of Brouage to New France in the Year 1603).

The savages are cheerful and laugh a lot, but they aren't excitable. They speak deliberately, as if to make sure you understand them, and they often stop to think. This is especially true when they are speaking in council, which is attended only by the chiefs and elders and never by women or children.

Sometimes they are so short of food, on account of the cold and the snow, that they are sorely tempted to eat one another, for the game and fowl they live on migrate in winter to warmer countries. But I feel sure that if anyone showed them how to cultivate the soil they would learn quickly enough, for they are sensible and intelligent and ready to answer any questions you put to them.

Samuel de Champlain, *Voyages to New France*, trans. Michael Macklem (Ottawa: Oberon Press, 1971), 72–76.

One bad thing about them is that they are very given to revenge. They are also great liars. You shouldn't trust them unless you have good reason to do so and even then you have to be on your guard. They make great promises but seldom keep them.

They have no laws, so far as I could make out from what the grand Sagamo told me. He did tell me that they believe in a God who made all things. I asked him where he thought mankind had come from. He said that after God had made the world He took a number of arrows and stuck them in the ground and they turned into men and women. I told him that this was wrong, that there was but one God who made all things in heaven and earth....

I then asked him if he thought there was more than one God and he said they believed there were four—God, his mother, his son and the sun—but that God Himself was the chief of these. The son and the sun were good to his people, he explained, but the mother was wicked and ate them up when she could. The father, he added, wasn't much better....

All Christians, I explained, believe in God the Father, God the Son and God the Holy Ghost—three persons in one God, with no first and no second, no greater and no lesser. By virtue of prayers, I explained, we are given the strength we need to resist the devil. I added that if they believed in God they would have everything they needed and the devil wouldn't be able to do them any harm.

The Sagamo admitted that this made sense. I then asked him how they prayed to their gods, and he said they didn't have any ceremonies, that each man prayed in his own way. This of course is why they have no principles and know nothing of God and behave like animals. My own opinion is that if the country were settled they would readily enough become good Christians and would be the better for it.

The Old World Becomes the New World

The French imperial powers collaborated with members of the Roman Catholic church to carry out a plan for populating New France with emigrants from France. A typical argument in favor of such a design was articulated by Father Le Jeune. "How It Is a Benefit to Both Old and New France, To Send Colonies Here," *is taken from one of the richest documentary sources from the colonial period:* The Jesuit Relations. *This vast and heavily edited resource consists of correspondence and reports from Jesuit missionaries over the course of two centuries. Careful scholars treat the Jesuit Relations with healthy skepticism because the authors typically crafted their arguments to place their activities in a positive light, and the reports probably went through numerous approval stages before they were released.*

It is to be feared that in the multiplication of our French, in these countries, peace, happiness, and good feeling may not increase in the same ratio as do the Inhabitants of New France. It is much easier to control a few men than whole multitudes; yet it must be confessed that it would be an enterprise very honorable and very profitable to Old France, and very useful to the New, to establish settlements here, and to send over Colonies.

Reuben Gold Thwaites, ed., *The Jesuit Relations and Allied Documents: Travels and Explorations of the Jesuit Missionaries in New France, 1610–1791*, Vol. VIII (Cleveland: Burroughs Brothers, 1897), 9, 11, 13, 15.

Shall the French, alone of all the Nations of the earth, be deprived of the honor of expanding and spreading over this New World? Shall France, much more populous than all the other Kingdoms, have Inhabitants only for itself?

Geographers, Historians, and experience itself, show us that every year a great many people leave France who go to enroll themselves elsewhere....Would it not be better to empty Old France into New, by means of Colonies which could be sent there, than to people Foreign countries?

Add to this, if you please, that there is a multitude of workmen in France, who, for lack of employment or of owning a little land, pass their lives in poverty and wretched want. Many of them beg their bread from door to door; some of them resort to stealing and public brigandage, others to larceny and secret frauds, each one trying to obtain for himself what many cannot possess. Now as New France is so immense, so many inhabitants can be sent, here that those who remain in the Mother Country will have enough honest work left them to do, without launching into those vices which ruin Republics....

Now there is no doubt that there can be found here employment for all sorts of artisans. Why cannot the great forests of New France largely furnish the Ships for the Old? Who doubts that there are here mines of iron, copper, and other metals? Some have already been discovered, which will soon be worked; and hence all those who work in wood and iron will find employment here. Grain will not fail here, more than in France. I do not pretend to recite all the advantages of the country, nor to show what can give occupation here to the intelligence and strength of our French people; I will content myself by saying that it would be an honor and a great benefit to both old and new France to send over Emigrants and establish strong colonies in these lands, which have lain fallow since the birth of the world.

A Portrait of Life in New France

Many French made their way to New France in the seventeenth century to observe the colony or to remain for a portion of their lives. Accounts written by those visitors and colonists were undeniably subjective; nonetheless, they give us a sense of the promise of the New World and the challenges that European settlers faced. One such account was originally published in 1664 by Pierre Boucher, a French-born emigrant who arrived in Quebec as a young man and rose in prominence to become a Governor of Three Rivers. Particularly noteworthy in the following passage are Boucher's negative perceptions of Native peoples, especially the Iroquois, and his comparison of New France to the more established English colonies.

During my stay in France, various questions on the subject of New France were put to me by worthy people. I think I shall oblige the curious reader by mentioning them here and by making a chapter of them and of my answers to them....

Are there not prairies of which hay can be made? Do not oats grow there? Perfectly well, and there are beautiful prairies; but hay making is rather dangerous, particularly near the settlements at Three-Rivers and Montreal, and will continue to be dangerous so long as the Iroquois make war on us, for the mowers and hay makers are always in danger of being killed by them. For this reason we make but little

Pierre Boucher, *Canada in the 17th Century*, trans. Edward Louis Montizambert (Montreal: George E. Desbarats & Co., 1883), 69–79.

hay, although we have fine large prairies on which there grows very good grass for making it. . . .

Are there many settlers? To this question I cannot give any positive answer, except that I have been told that there are about eight hundred at Quebec; as for the other settlements there are not so many there. . . .

Have the settlers many children? Yes, and they grow up well formed, tall and robust, the girls as well as boys; they are, generally speaking, intelligent enough, but rather idle, that is to say it is difficult to attend to their studies. . . .

But how can we make money there? What can we get out of it all? This is a question that has often been put to me, and that gave me an inclination to laugh every time it was put to me; I seemed to see people who wanted to reap a harvest before they had sowed any thing. After having said that the country is a good one, capable of producing all sorts of things, like France, that it is healthy, that population only is wanting, that the country is very extensive, and that without doubt there are great riches in it which we have not been able to bring to light, because we have an enemy who keeps us pent up in a little corner and prevents us from going about and making discoveries; and so he will have to be destroyed, and many people will have to come into this country, and then we shall know the riches of it. . . .

Our neighbours, the English, laid out a great deal of money at the outset on the settlements; they threw great numbers of people into them; so that now there are computed to be in them fifty thousand men capable of bearing arms; it is a wonder to see their country now; one finds all sorts of things there, the same as in Europe, and for half the price. They build numbers of ships, of all sorts and sizes; they work iron mines; they have beautiful cities; they have stage coaches and mails from one end to the other; they have carriages like those in France; those who laid out money there, are now getting good returns from it; that country is not different from this; what has been done there could be done here. . . .

Here is another set of questions that have been put to me, namely: how we live in this country, whether justice is administered, if there is not great debauchery, seeing that numbers of worthless fellows and bad girls come here, it is said. . . .It is not true that those sort of girls come hither, and those who say so have made a great mistake. . .for before any can be taken on board ship to come here some of their relations or friends must certify that they have always been well-behaved; if by chance there are found among those who have, some who are in disrepute, or who are said to have misconducted themselves on the voyage out, they are sent back to France.

As for the scapegraces, if any come over it is only because they are not known for what they are, and when they are in the country they have to live like decent people, otherwise they would have a bad time of it: we know how to hang people in this country as well as they do elsewhere, and we have proved it to some who have not been well behaved. Justice is administered here, and those who are not satisfied with their decisions can appeal to the Governor and the Sovereign Council, appointed by the King, and sitting at Quebec.

Hitherto we have lived pleasantly enough, pleased God to give us Governors who have all been good men, and besides we have had the Jesuit Fathers who take great pains to teach the people what is right so that all goes on peaceably; we live much in the fear of God, and nothing scandalous takes place without its being put to rights immediately; there is great religious devotion throughout the country.

A Church Perspective on Women and Their Clothing

Although the Roman Catholic church undeniably had a powerful influence on the spiritual and cultural life of virtually all settlers in New France, ample evidence suggests that it was not able to control social behavior as much as the clerics might have wished. The following edict in 1682 offers an insight to the preferred attire of some women in Quebec. It comes from Mandements des Évêques (Mandates from the Bishops).

"Against Luxury and Vanity of Women and Girls in Church, Quebec, February 26, 1682"

If the Fathers and Doctors of the Church censure with force against the luxury and vanity of girls and women who, forgetting the promises of their baptism, appear dressed and ornamented with displays of Satan which they so solemnly renounced, it is to indicate to us the extreme horror that God has of such a disorder, which makes those who are guilty of it all the more guilty before Him, in that, wishing to please the eyes of men, they make themselves the captives and instruments of the Demon who uses this luxury to make them, and those who see them, commit an infinity of sins. . . . If these vain appearances displease God so strongly . . . of what crime are they not guilty, and what punishment might be expected by those who wear this ostentatious apparel . . . in our churches, appearing in these

Cameron Nish, *The French Regime* (Scarborough, Ont.: Prentice-Hall of Canada, 1965), 75–76.

consecrated places to pray and do penance in indecent apparel, showing a scandalous nudity of arms, shoulders, and throats, contenting themselves with covering them with a transparent fabric which only serves to give lustre to these shameful nudities; the head bared or but covered with a transparent net and the hair curled in a manner unworthy of a Christian person....

For these causes we expressly prohibit all women and girls of no matter what rank or consideration to approach the sacraments...in the indecent manners specified....

François

A Military Perspective During the Seven Years' War

For many decades historians have explored the inequities in population size and economic might in New France and the American colonies to the south. The complicated internal struggles between the governing representatives and military leaders in Quebec added another important dimension to the question of whether or not the conquest and collapse of New France was demographically and logistically inevitable. Contemporaries also grappled with that important question. The Marquis de Montcalm, who was in command of the French forces in the colony, offered his assessment of the colony's precarious position and his contempt for the civilian leadership. The following excerpts come from two letters that were written on the same day: 12 April 1759.

M. de Montcalm to M. de Cremile

The war has changed character in Canada. The vast force of the English, our example determines them on continuous operations in a country where the Canadians thought they were making war, and were making, so to speak, hunting excursions. Our principles of war, considering our inferiority, ought to be, to contract our defensive, in order to preserve at least, the body of the Colony, and retard its loss; to combine with the system of European tactics the use to be made of

E.B. O'Callaghan, ed., *Documents Relative to the Colonial History of the State of New York* (Albany, NY: Weed, Parsons, 1858), 958–962 [CIHM microfiche series; #53993].

the Indians. This is what I am always saying, but the prejudices or councils of quacks are followed. No matter, I serve the King and the State. I shall always express my opinion. I shall execute to the best of my ability....To retreat would be the ruin of the Colony....

M. de Montcalm to Marshal de Belle Isle

Canada will be taken this campaign, and assuredly during the next, if there be not some unforeseen good luck, a powerful diversion by sea against the English Colonies, or some gross blunders on the part of the enemy.

The English have 60,000 men, we at most from 10 to 11,000. Our government is good for nothing; money and provisions will fail. Through want of provisions, the English will begin first; the farms scarcely tilled, cattle lack; the Canadians are dispirited; no confidence in M. de Vaudreuil or in M. Bigot. M. de Vaudreuil is incapable of preparing a plan of operations.

Everybody appears to be in a hurry to make his fortune before the Colony is lost, which event many, perhaps, desire, as an impenetrable veil over their conduct. The craving after wealth has an influence on the war, and M. de Vaudreuil does not doubt it. Instead of reducing the expenses of Canada, people wish to retain all; how abandon positions which serve as a pretext to make private fortunes? Transportation is distributed to favorites. The agreement with the contractor is unknown to me as it is to the public....

The enemy can come to Quebec, if we have not a fleet; and Quebec, once taken, the Colony is lost. Yet there is no precaution....

The general census of Canada has at last been completed. Though it has not been communicated to me, I think I'm correct, that there are not more than 82,000 souls in the Colony; of these, twelve thousand, at most, are men capable of bearing arms; deducting from this number those employed in works, transports, bateaux, in the Upper countries, no more than seven thousand Canadians will ever be collected together, and then it must not be either seed time or harvest, otherwise, by calling all out, the ground would remain uncultivated; famine would follow. Our eight battalions will make three thousand two hundred men; the Colonials, at most, fifteen hundred men in the field. What is that against at least fifty thousand men which the English have?

The Acadian Experience

The British treatment of the Acadians in the eighteenth century stands as one of the most troublesome events in all of Canadian history. Numerous documents of the experience attest to the struggles that the Acadians had with the decision of whether or not to take the oath of fidelity; others provide accounts of the forced deportation and subsequent relocation (le grand dérangement) of Acadians to the American colonies and elsewhere. One such account from John Baptiste Galerm, an Acadian who was transported to Pennsylvania, is reprinted below.

"A Relation of the Misfortunes of the French Neutrals, as laid before the Assembly of the Province of Pennsylvania, by John Baptist Galerm, one of the said People"

[W]e were summoned to appear before the Governor and Council at Halifax, where we were required to take the Oath of Allegiance without any Exception, which we could not comply with because, as that Government is at present situate, we apprehend that we should have been obliged to take up Arms; but we are still willing to take the Oath of Fidelity, and to give the strongest Assurance of continuing peaceable and faithful to his Britannick Majesty, with that Exception, But this, in the present Situation of Affairs, not being satisfactory, we were made Prisoners, and our Estates, both real and personal, forfeited for the King's Use; and Vessels being provided, we were some time after sent off, with most of our Families, and

N.E.S. Griffiths, ed., *The Acadian Deportation: Deliberate Perfidy or Cruel Necessity?* (Toronto: Copp Clark, 1969), 150–152.

dispersed amongst the English Colonies. The Hurry and Confusion in which we were embarked was an aggravating Circumstance attending our Misfortunes; for thereby many, who had lived in Affluence, found themselves deprived of every Necessary, and many Families were separated, Parents from Children, and Children from Parents. Yet blessed be God that it was our Lot to be sent to Pennsylvania, where our Wants have been relieved, and we have in every Respect been received with Christian Benevolence and Charity. And let me add, that notwithstanding the Suspicions and Fears which many here are possessed of on our Account, as tho' we were a dangerous People, who make little Scruple of break-our Oaths. Time will manifest that we are not such a People: No, the unhappy situation which we are now in, is a plain Evidence that this is a false Claim, tending to aggravate the Misfortunes of an already too unhappy People; for had we entertained such pernicious Sentiments, we might easily have prevented our falling into the melancholy Circumstances we are now in, viz: Deprived of our Subsistance, banished from our native Country, and reduced to live by Charity in a strange Land; and this for refusing to take an Oath, which we are firmly persuaded Christianity absolutely forbids us to violate, had we once taken it, and yet an Oath which we could not comply with without being exposed to plunge our Swords in the Breasts of our Friends and Relations. We shall, however, as we have hitherto done, submit to what in the present Situation of Affairs may seem necessary, and with Patience and Resignation bear whatever God, in the course of his Providence, shall suffer to come upon us.

One Loyalist's Perspective

The Loyalists who arrived in British North America were extremely diverse; they came from all the American colonies, and they represented virtually every class and ethnic group in America. The reasons for loyalty to the Crown also varied dramatically, as did perspectives of a Loyalist ideal and the most suitable course of action to take in the interest of improving the lives of the thousands who migrated to the northern colonies of the British empire. Among many Loyalists who arrived in Nova Scotia, the argument was advanced to create a separate colony that would reflect the ideals of loyalism. Some, like Massachusetts-born and Harvard-educated Edward Winslow, who served in the British forces during the Revolutionary War, believed that a new loyalist colony of New Brunswick would become a model of enlightened governance in North America. An excerpt of his extensive correspondence follows.

I'll introduce another argument in favour of dividing this province [Nova Scotia], which (if not of equal weight with others) is of some consequence. You will I think enter into the spirit of it. A large proportion of the old inhabitants of this country are natives of New-England, or descendants from New Englanders, they, from their situation, never experienced any of the inconveniences which resulted from the violence of political animosity, they remained quiet during all the persecutions in the other provinces—they retained a natural (perhaps laudable) affection for their country. The rebel party were more industrious, and their doctrines and principles were more

Rev. W.O. Raymond, ed., *Winslow Papers, A.D. 1776–1826* (Saint John, NB: Sun Printing Co., 1901), 192–193.

greedily adopted, than those of the other side, by degrees the Nova-Scotians became firmly persuaded of the justice of their cause. Of this complexion are the public officers, generally. On our side the principal people are men who have served in a military line—irritable from a series of mortifications—scarcely cooled from the ardor of resentment—jealous to an extreme, some of 'em illiberally so. Either of these kinds of men may form useful societies among themselves—but they can't be mixed—separate them, and this very difference of opinion will increase the emulation and contribute to the general good; together—wrangles and contests would be unavoidable.

Lord Sydney's declaration quoted in your letter, "That he will make Nova-Scotia the envy of the American States," has excited a kind of general gratitude, I cannot describe it. Other ministers and Great men have by their patronage of new settlers, relieved individuals from distress, and rendered services to their country, but it is a Godlike task that Lord Sydney has undertaken. Such an event as the present, never happened before—perhaps never will happen again. There are assembled here an immense multitude (not of dissolute vagrants such as commonly make the first efforts to settle new countries,) but gentlemen of educations—Farmers, formerly independent—& reputable mechanics, who by the fortune of war have been deprived of their property. They are as firmly attached to the British constitution as if they never had made a sacrifice. Here they stand with their wives and their children looking up for protection, and requesting such regulations as are necessary to the weal of society. To save these from distress, to soothe and comfort them by extending indulgencies which at the same time are essentially beneficial to the country at large, is truly a noble duty. By Heaven we will be the envy of the American States.

Mackenzie's Call to Arms

As is the case with many rebellions in history, the rationale for violently opposing the existing form of government was presented by literate people with access to the press. William Lyon Mackenzie, Upper Canada's most energetic and articulate advocate of severing the colony's ties with Great Britain, used newspapers and printed handbills to encourage others to join in his cause. One such appeal, a broadside that was distributed in late November 1837, is presented below. Noteworthy in this document are Mackenzie's skillful use of rhetorical questions and his reliance on provocative language to make his points.

BRAVE CANADIANS! God has put into the bold and honest hearts of our brethren in Lower Canada to revolt—not against "lawful" but against "unlawful authority." The law says we shall not be taxed without our consent by the voices of the men of our choice, but a wicked and tyrannical government has trampled upon that law—robbed the exchequer—divided the plunder—and declared that, regardless of justice they will continue to roll their splendid carriages, and riot in their palaces, at our expense—that we are poor spiritless ignorant peasants, who were born to toil for our betters. But the peasants are beginning to open their eyes and to feel their strength....

CANADIANS! Do you love freedom? I know you do. Do you hate oppression? Who dare deny it? Do you wish perpetual peace, and a government founded upon the eternal heaven-born principle of the Lord Jesus Christ—a government bound to enforce the law to do to

Margaret Fairley, ed. *The Selected Writings of William Lyon Mackenzie* (Toronto: Oxford University Press, 1960), 222–225.

each other as you would be done by? Then buckle on your armour, and put down the villains who oppress and enslave our country—put them down in the name of that God who goes forth with the armies of his people, and whose bible shows us that it is by the same human means whereby you put to death thieves and murderers, and imprison and banish wicked individuals, that you must put down, in the strength of the Almighty, those governments which, like these bad individuals, trample on the law, and destroy its usefulness....We contend, that in all laws made, or to be made, every person shall be bound alike—neither should any tenure, estate, charter, degree, birth or place, confer any exemption from the ordinary course of legal proceedings and responsibilities whereunto others are subjected....

MARK MY WORDS, CANADIANS! The struggle is begun—it might end in freedom—but timidity, cowardice, or tampering on our part will only delay its close. We cannot be reconciled to Britain—we have humbled ourselves to the Pharaoh of England, to the Ministers, and great people, and they will neither rule us justly nor let us go—we are determined never to rest until independence is ours—the prize is a splendid one. A country larger than France or England; natural resources equal to our most boundless wishes—a government of equal laws—religion pure and undefiled—perpetual peace—education to all—millions of acres of lands for revenue—freedom from British tribute—free trade with all the world—but stop—I never could enumerate all the blessings attendant on independence!

UP THEN, BRAVE CANADIANS! Get ready your rifles, and make short work of it; a connection with England would involve us in all her wars, undertaken for her own advantage, never for ours; with governors from England, we will have bribery at elections, corruption, villainy and perpetual discord in every township, but Independence would give us the means of enjoying many blessings. Our enemies in Toronto are in terror and dismay—they know their wickedness and dread our vengeance....Aye, and now's the day and the hour! Woe be to those who oppose us, for "In God is our trust."

A Perspective of Life in the Backwoods

Many accounts remain that document the challenges that people faced when they emigrated to the interior of British North American, carved out farmland, and constructed homes. Two British-born sisters, Susanna Moodie and Catharine Parr Traill, experienced the rigors and joys of settling in Upper Canada; they were among the most prolific and widely published authors of the mid-nineteenth century on the subject of life in British North America. The following excerpts come from two letters written by Traill. The first, written in 1834, was addressed to her friends James and Emma Bird. The second was sent to Canon Richard Gwillym and written in 1845. In the latter Traill references her most popular work, The Backwoods of Canada, *which was published in London in 1836.*

To James and Emma Bird:

[Our son] James has his youthful faults and who has or had them not at his age but on the whole he is a good boy and I hope will prove himself worthy of parents of whom he is justly proud. He has his ups and downs in this country all classes have their trials and hardship, they may be called with truth, and James's situation does not exempt him from his share. They will I trust fit him the better for a settler's life when he becomes his own master, a period as yet distant. At present he is become intimately acquainted with the customary work of a

Carl Ballstadt, Elizabeth Hopkins, Michael A. Peterman, eds., *I Bless You in My Heart: Selected Correspondence of Catharine Parr Traill* (Toronto: University of Toronto Press, 1996), 40–41, 51–52.

Canadian farm. I could edify his Suffolk friends by telling them of chopping, under-brushing logging making brush heaps and log heaps, burning and branding a fallow, sowing and harrowing in wheat and rye, planting corn, ie Indian corn, for we do not here mean all sorts of grain by the term corn as at home, setting pumpkinseed and turnips, raising potato-hills etc. He could talk very learnedly of Raising-Bees, Logging Bees, Carpentering Bees and Husking Bees. Discuss the merits of Buck & Bright, the orthodox names for Canadian oxen, go through the logging exercise with stentorian lungs....

We are now comfortably settled in our new house....When writers in this country speak of the rapid manner in which houses are put up upon one day or two they mean the icy walls merely. If you do not mean to live in a habitation divested of all comfort, much longer time is required. The difficulty of measuring lumber sawn board is inconceivable especially if it so happens you are distant from a saw mill or a town. The badness of roads in this country, the slowness of conveyance, want of proper artificers etc. etc. are seldom taken into consideration by writers who write only to sell a book. When they talk of the advantages and comforts of a settlers life they pass over the intervening and necessary hardships and privations and talk of the future as if the present....

To Canon Richard Gwillym:

Your opinion of my Backwoods was very gratifying to me coming from a scholar, and a gentleman. I suppose it has merits in spite of many faults by the interest it has excited and the friends it has won for me. One thing bear in mind my dear brother that my work was not written with the design of inducing any one to leave their own fair homes in Britain to seek a wooden hut in Canada but rather to cheer and advise such as were by stern necessity compelled to emigrate to make the best of a bad bargain and if any one has been nerved to energy and to the encouraging of a contented spirit by my little book the end for which it was written has been gained. After twelve years residence in Canada my opinions remain much as they were. I love the country on many accounts and I have some valued friends in it but misfortunes have fallen heavily upon us and kept us back. [O]ur own state is less prosperous than when full of hope I wrote my Backwoods but this is merely the result of untoward circumstances. [W]hile we have made little advance others who started with less means have pressed on and are far ahead of us in all comforts but I blame not my adopted country for this, and I rejoice in the increasing prosperity of its inhabitants and hope yet to see my sons and daughters happy and honorable members of society beneath the shades of her mighty forests.

The Argument in Favor of Confederation

Strident arguments in favor of Confederation were advanced by a number of political luminaries in the 1860s, but two stand out for their clear and eloquent arguments of the many reasons for the union of the British North American colonies. The following excerpts come from the Confederation debates in the Province of Canada in 1865. The first is from a speech delivered by John A. Macdonald, who at the time was Attorney General West in the Province of Canada; the second passage comes from a speech by one of the most influential francophones in support of Confederation, Attorney General East George-Étienne Cartier. Of particular interest in Macdonald's text are the many references to the weaknesses in the American system of governance. Cartier echoed some of Macdonald's thoughts on the challenge presented by the United States and paid close attention to the idea that Confederation would provide a positive context for racial collaboration.

Hon. John A. Macdonald:

All the statesmen and public men who have written or spoken on the subject admit the advantages of a union, if it were practicable: and now when it is proved to be practicable, if we do not embrace this opportunity the present favorable time will pass away, and we may never have it again. . . .If we are not blind to our present position, we must see the hazardous situation in which all the great interests of

P.B. Waite, ed., *The Confederation Debates in the Province of Canada, 1865,* 2nd ed. (Montreal: McGill-Queen's University Press, 2006), 22–30.

Canada stand in respect to the United States. I am no alarmist. I do not believe in the prospect of immediate war. I believe that the common sense of the two nations will prevent a war; still we cannot trust to probabilities....

The Conference having come to the conclusion that a Legislative union, pure and simple, was impracticable, our next attempt was to form a government upon federal principles, which would give to the General Government the strength of a legislative and administrative union, while at the same time it preserved that liberty of action for the different sections which is allowed by a Federal union. And I am strong in the belief—that we have hit upon the happy medium in those resolutions, and that we have formed a scheme of government which unites the advantages of both, giving us the strength of a Legislative union and the sectional freedom of a Federal union, with protection to local interests. In doing so we had the advantage of the experience of the United States. It is the fashion now to enlarge on the defects of the Constitution of the United States, but I am not one of those who look upon it as a failure. I think and believe that it is one of the most skilful works which human intelligence ever created; is one of the most perfect organizations that ever governed a free people. To say that it has some defects is but to say that it is not the work of Omniscience, but of human intellects. We are happily situated in having had the opportunity of watching its operation, seeing its working from its infancy till now....[The Americans] commenced, in fact, at the wrong end. They declared by their Constitution that each state was a sovereignty in itself, and that all the powers incident to a sovereignty belonged to each state, except those powers which, by the Constitution, were conferred upon the General Government and Congress. Here we have adopted a different system. We have strengthened the General Government. We have given the General Legislature all the great subjects of legislation. We have conferred on them, not only specifically and in detail, all the powers which are incident to sovereignty, but we have expressly declared that all subjects of general interest not distinctly and exclusively conferred upon the local governments and local legislatures, shall be conferred upon the General Government and Legislature. We have thus avoided that great source of weakness which has been the cause of the disruption of the United States....

One of the great advantages of Confederation is, that we shall have a united, a concerted, and uniform system of defence....The criminal law too—the determination of what is a crime and what is not and how crime shall be punished—is left to the General Government. This is a matter almost of necessity. It is of great importance that we should have the same criminal law throughout these provinces—that what is a crime in one part of British America, should be a crime in every part—that there should be the same protection of life and property as in another. It is one of the defects in the United States system, that each separate state has or may have a criminal code of its own....

Hon. George-Étienne Cartier:

Confederation was, as it were, at this moment almost forced upon us....The matter resolved itself into this, either we must obtain British American Confederation or be absorbed in an American Confederation. The question for us to ask ourselves was this: Shall we be content to remain separate—shall we be content to maintain a mere provincial existence, when, by combining together, we could become a great nation?

Nations were now formed by the agglomeration of communities having kindred interests and sympathies. Such was our case at the present moment. Objection had been taken to the scheme now under consideration, because of the words "new nationality." Now, when we were united together, if union were attained, we would form a political nationality with which neither the national origin, nor the religion of any individual, would interfere. It was lamented by some that we had this diversity of races, and hopes were expressed that this distinctive feature would cease. The idea of unity of races was Utopian—it was impossible. Distinctions of this kind would always exist. Dissimilarity, in fact, appeared to be the order of the physical world and of the moral world, as well as of the political world. But with regard to the objection based on this fact, to the effect that a great nation could not be formed because Lower Canada was in great part French and Catholic, and Upper Canada was British and

Protestant, and the Lower Provinces were mixed, it was futile and worthless in the extreme. Look, for instance, at the United Kingdom, inhabited as it was by three great races. Had the diversity of race impeded the glory, the progress, the wealth of England? Had they not rather each contributed their share to the greatness of the Empire? Of the glories of the senate, the field, and the ocean, of the successes of trade and commerce, how much was contributed by the combined talents, energy and courage of the three races together? In our own Federation we should have Catholic and Protestant, English, French, Irish and Scotch, and each by his efforts and his success would increase the prosperity and glory of the new Confederacy. He viewed the diversity of races in British North America in this way: we were of different races, not for the purpose of warring against each other, but in order to compete and emulate for the general welfare. We could not do away with the distinctions of race. We could not legislate for the disappearance of the French Canadians from American soil, but British and French Canadians alike could appreciate and understand their position relative to each other. They were placed like great families beside each other, and their contact produced a healthy spirit of emulation. It was a benefit rather than otherwise that we had a diversity of races.

The Argument Against Confederation

Arguments against Confederation were eloquently and passionately made as well during the debates and political campaigns of the 1860s, and many lingered well into the early Confederation era of the late nineteenth century. Opponents of the Confederation plan ranged widely in their concerns, but many shared a core belief that groups and provinces would lose their distinctive qualities and control over their destinies in a larger union. Two of the most articulate and persistent critics of the union principle were Joseph Perrault, a francophone politician from Canada East, and Joseph Howe, an extremely influential newspaper editor and politician from Nova Scotia. Perrault's speech was delivered to the Legislative Assembly of Canada in 1865. Howe's long and detailed speech—an excerpt of which is provided below—was delivered at Dartmouth, Nova Scotia, in May 1867.

Joseph Perrault's Legislative Assembly Speech:

Formerly France possessed all this part of the continent. The settlers of that period, the farmers, fishermen, hunters, and trappers travelled over the whole extent of those immense possessions which were known by the name of New France. At the moment what remains to her of a territory that was equal in extent to Europe itself? A wretched little island at the entrance of the Gulf, a foothold for her fisheries, and a few acres of beach on the coast of Newfoundland. When we consider that fact, when we see French power completely destroyed

Janet Ajzenstat, et al., eds., *Canada's Founding Debates* (Toronto: Stoddart Publishing: 1999), 349–351.

on this continent, are we not justified in looking closely into the project of constitution now submitted to us, which has for its object, I repeat, simply to complete the destruction of the influence of the French race on this continent? Has not the past taught us to dread the future? Yes, Mr. Speaker, the policy of England has ever been aggressive, and its object has always been to annihilate us as a people. And this scheme of Confederation is but the continued application of that policy on this continent; its real object is nothing but the annihilation of French influence in Canada....

If we study the history of our struggles since the cession of Canada [the Conquest], we shall find that our public men were always attached to the crown of England up to the time when they were compelled by the arbitrary and unjust conduct of the imperial government to have recourse to arms to obtain respect for our political rights and our liberties; and it was thus in 1837 that we gained responsible government. But in order to hold up to view the spirit of aggression and encroachment which has always characterized the English population in America, I shall give a historical sketch of the struggles through which we had to pass, in the course of a century, to attain at last our present constitution, which it is my wish to preserve, but which our ministers wish to destroy in order to substitute for it the scheme of Confederation. This historical sketch will demonstrate to us that we owe no gratitude to England for those political reforms which were obtained for us only through the unyielding patriotism of our great men, who, with intelligence, energy, and perseverance, valiantly strove for the constant defence of our rights. We shall also see that, if they obtained the system of government and the political liberty for which they struggled, it was because we had for our neighbours the states of the American union, and that side by side with the evil was its remedy. We shall see that whenever England stood in need of us to defend her power, she made concessions to us; but that when the danger was once over, colonial fanaticism always attempted to withdraw those concessions and to destroy the influence and liberties of the French race....

Joseph Howe's Dartmouth Speech:

A year ago Nova Scotia presented the aspect of a self-governed community, loyal to a man, attached to their institutions, cheerful, prosperous and contented. You could look back upon the past with pride, on the present with confidence, and on the future with hope. Now all this has been changed. We have been entrapped into a revolution. . . . You are a self-governed and independent community no longer. The institutions founded by your fathers, and strengthened and consolidated by your own exertions, have been overthrown. Your revenues are to be swept beyond your control. You are henceforward to be governed by strangers, and your hearts are wrung by the reflection that this has not been done by the strong hand of open violence, but by the treachery and connivance of those whom you trusted, and by whom you have been betrayed. . . .

But it is said, why should we complain ? We are still to manage our local affairs. I have shown you that self-government, in all that gives dignity and security to a free state, is to be swept away. The Canadians are to appoint our governors, judges and senators. They are to "tax us by any and every mode" and spend the money. They are to regulate our trade, control our Post Offices, command the militia, fix the salaries, do what they like with our shipping and navigation, with our sea-coast and river fisheries, regulate the currency and the rate of interest, and seize upon our savings banks. . . .

Hitherto we have been a self-governed and independent community, our allegiance to the Queen, who rarely vetoed a law, being the only restraint upon our action. We appointed every officer but the Governor. How were the high powers exercised? Less than a century and a quarter ago, the moose and the bear roamed unmolested where we stand. Within that time the country has been cleared—society organized. . . . It is thus that our country grew and throve while we governed it ourselves, and the spirit of adventure and of self-reliance was admirable. But now, "with bated breath and whispering humbleness," we are told to acknowledge our masters, and, if we wish to ensure their favour, we must elect the very scamps by whom we have been betrayed and sold.

J. A. Chisholm, ed., *The Speeches and Public Letters of Joseph Howe* (Halifax: Chronicle Publishing Co., 1909), 509, 513, 515.

The British North America Act

The British North America Act was a detailed statute that essentially served as Canada's governing constitution from 1867 to 1982. Designed by the so-called "Fathers of Confederation" and lightly modified by the British, its pragmatic language reflected the overriding interests of its architects. Although each section of the BNA Act provided an important building block for creating the apparatus to govern the new dominion, three sections were considered particularly essential for capturing the essence of the Confederation design. Sections #91 and #92 articulated the powers of the federal and provincial governments respectively, and Section #133 addressed the central question of language. These three sections are reprinted below.

The Powers of the Dominion Government

91. It shall be lawful for the Queen, by and with the Advice and Consent of the Senate and House of Commons, to make Laws for the Peace, Order and Good Government of Canada in relation to all Matters not coming within the Classes of Subjects by this Act assigned exclusively to the Legislatures of the Provinces; and for greater certainty, but not so as to restrict the Generality of the foregoing Terms of this Section, it is hereby declared that (notwithstanding anything in this Act) the exclusive Legislative

J.T. Copp, Marcel Hamelin, eds., *Confederation: 1867* (Toronto: Copp Clark, 1966), Appendix: 89–92.

Authority of the Parliament of Canada extends to all Matters coming within the Classes of Subjects next hereinafter enumerated, that is to say:

1. The Public Debt and Property.
2. The Regulation of Trade and Commerce.
3. The Raising of Money by any Mode or System of Taxation.
4. The Borrowing of Money on the Public Credit.
5. Postal Service.
6. The Census and Statistics.
7. Militia, Military and Naval Service and Defence.
8. The fixing of and providing for the Salaries and Allowances of Civil and other Officers of the Government of Canada.
9. Beacons, Buoys, Lighthouses and Sable Island.
10. Navigation and Shipping.
11. Quarantine and the Establishment and Maintenance of Marine Hospitals.
12. Sea Coast and Inland Fisheries.
13. Ferries between a Province and any British or Foreign Country, or between Two Provinces.
14. Currency and Coinage.
15. Banking, Incorporation of Banks and the Issue of Paper Money.
16. Savings Banks.
17. Weights and Measures.
18. Bills of Exchange and Promissory Notes.
19. Interest.
20. Legal Tender.
21. Bankruptcy and Insolvency.
22. Patents of Invention and Discovery.
23. Copyrights.
24. Indians and Lands reserved for the Indians.
25. Naturalization and Aliens.
26. Marriage and Divorce.
27. The Criminal Law, except the Constitution of the Courts of Criminal Jurisdiction, but including the Procedure in Criminal Matters.
28. The Establishment, Maintenance and Management of Penitentiaries.

29. Such Classes of Subjects as are expressly excepted in the Enumeration of the Classes of Subjects by this Act assigned exclusively to the Legislatures of the Provinces.

And any Matter coming within any of the Classes of Subjects enumerated in this Section shall not be deemed to come within the Class of Matters of a local or Private Nature comprised in the Enumeration of the Classes of Subjects by this Act assigned exclusively to the Legislatures of the Provinces.

The Powers of the Provincial Governments

92. In each province the Legislature may exclusively make Laws in relation to Matters coming within the Classes of Subjects next hereinafter enumerated; that is to say:

1. The Amendment from Time to Time, notwithstanding anything in this Act, of the Constitution of the Province, except as regards the Office of Lieutenant-Governor.
2. Direct Taxation within the Province in order to the raising of a Revenue for Provincial Purposes.
3. The Borrowing of Money on the sole Credit of the Province.
4. The Establishment and Tenure of Provincial Offices, and the Appointment and Payment of Provincial Officers.
5. The Management and Sale of the Public Lands belonging to the Province, and of the Timber and Wood thereon.
6. The Establishment, Maintenance, and Management of Public and Reformatory Prisons in and for the Province.
7. The Establishment, Maintenance, and Management of Hospitals, Asylums, Charities and Eleemosynary Institutions in and for the Province, other than Marine Hospitals.
8. Municipal Institutions in the Province.
9. Shop, Saloon, Tavern, Auctioneer, and other Licenses, in order to the raising of a Revenue for Provincial, Local, or Municipal Purposes.

10. Local Works and Undertakings, other than such as are of the following Classes....
11. The Incorporation of Companies with Provincial Objects.
12. The Solemnization of Marriage in the Province.
13. Property and Civil Rights in the Province.
14. The Administration of Justice in the Province, including the Constitution, Maintenance, and Organization of Provincial Courts, both of Civil and of Criminal Jurisdiction, and including Procedure in Civil Matters in those Courts.
15. The Imposition of Punishment by Fine, Penalty, or Imprisonment for enforcing any Law of the Province made in relation to any Matter coming within any of the Classes of subjects enumerated in this Section.
16. Generally all matters of a merely local or private nature in the Province.

133. Either the English or the French Language may be used by any person in the Debates of the Houses of the Parliament of Canada and of the Houses of the Legislature of Quebec; and both those languages shall be used in the respective records and journals of those Houses; and either of those languages may be used by any person or in any pleading or process in or issuing from any Court of Canada established under this Act, and in or from all or any of the Courts of Quebec.

The Acts of the Parliament of Canada and of the Legislature of Quebec shall be printed and published in both those languages.

Louis Riel on Trial

The nature and impact of Louis Riel's role in Canadian history continues to spark debate among historians. Particularly contentious and open to interpretation is the sequence of events that led to Riel's execution. At the center of this ongoing discussion is the question of Riel's sanity throughout his adult life, but especially during the period when he sought to create a self-governing space in the North-West for Métis and Native peoples. The following excerpt comes from a speech given by Riel in his own defense during his trial in Regina in late July and early August 1885. Note especiallly Riel's studied and careful references to the question of his sanity and his explanations for pursuing an agenda of using force to ensure the survival of Native peoples in the Canadian West.

Your Honors, gentlemen of the jury: It would be easy for me to-day to play insanity, because the circumstances are such as to excite any man, and under the natural excitement of what is taking place to-day (I cannot speak English very well, but am trying to do so, because most of those here speak English), under the excitement which my trial causes me would justify me not to appear as usual, but with my mind out of its ordinary condition. I hope with the help of God I will maintain calmness and decorum as suits this honorable court, this honorable jury.

You have seen by the papers in the hands of the Crown that I am naturally inclined to think of God at the beginning of my actions. I wish if you—I do it you won't take it as a mark of insanity, that you

Desmond Morton, ed., *The Queen v. Louis Riel* (Toronto: University of Toronto Press, 1974), 311–319. Reprinted with permission of the publisher.

won't take it as part of a play of insanity....To-day, although a man I am as helpless before this court, in the Dominion of Canada and in this world, as I was helpless on the knees of my mother the day of my birth.

The North-West is also my mother, it is my mother country and although my mother country is sick and confined in a certain way, there are some from Lower Canada who came to help her to take care of me during her sickness and I am sure that my mother country will not kill me more than my mother did forty years ago when I came into the world, because a mother is always a mother, and even if I have my faults if she can see I am true she will be full of love for me.

When I came into the North-West in 1884, I found the Indians suffering. I found the half-breeds eating the rotten pork of the Hudson Bay Company and getting sick and weak every day. Although a half-breed, and having no pretension to help the whites, I also paid attention to them. I saw they were deprived of responsible government, I saw that they were deprived of their public liberties. I remembered that half-breed meant white and Indian, and while I paid attention to the suffering Indians and the half-breeds I remembered that the greatest part of my heart and blood was white and I have directed my attention to help the Indians, to help the half-breeds and to help the whites to the best of my ability. We have made petitions, I have made petitions with others to the Canadian Government asking to relieve the condition of this country. We have taken time; we have tried to unite all classes, even if I may speak, all parties....

It is true, gentlemen, I believed for years I had a mission, and when I speak of a mission you will understand me not as trying to play the roll [sic] of insane before the grand jury so as to have a verdict of acquittal upon that ground. I believe that I have a mission....

I say that I have been blessed by God, and I hope that you will not take that as a presumptuous assertion. It has been a great success for me to come through all the dangers I have in that fifteen years....When I see British people sitting in the court to try me, remembering that the English people are proud of that word "fair-play," I am confident that I will be blessed by God and by man also.

Even if I was going to be sentenced by you, gentlemen of the jury, I have this satisfaction if I die—that if I die I will not be reputed by all men as insane, as a lunatic....The agitation in the North-West

Territories would have been constitutional, and would certainly be constitutional to-day if, in my opinion, we had not been attacked....

I know that through the grace of God I am the founder of Manitoba. I know that though I have no open road for my influence, I have big influence, concentrated as a big amount of vapour in an engine. I believe by what I suffered for fifteen years, by what I have done for Manitoba and the people of the North-West, that my words are worth something. If I give offence, I do not speak to insult. Yes, you are the pioneers of civilization, the whites are the pioneers of civilization, but they bring among the Indians demoralization....

As to religion, what is my belief? What is my insanity about that? My insanity, your Honors, gentlemen of the jury, is that I wish to leave Rome aside, inasmuch as it is the cause of division between Catholics and Protestants. I did not wish to force my views, because in Batoche to the half-breeds that followed me I used the word, *carte blanche*. If I have any influence in the new world it is to help in that way and even if it takes 200 years to become practical, then after my death that will bring out practical results, and then my children's children will shake hands with the Protestants of the new world in a friendly manner. I do not wish these evils which exist in Europe to be continued, as much as I can influence it, among the half-breeds....

My condition is helpless, so helpless that my good lawyers, and they have done it by conviction...my condition seems to be so helpless that they have recourse to try and prove insanity to try and save me in that way. If I am insane, of course I don't know it, it is a property of insanity to be unable to know it. But what is the kind of mission that I have? Practical results.

Sifton's Rationale for Immigration

Historians typically give Wilfrid Laurier's interior minister, Clifford Sifton, a great deal of credit for putting together a comprehensive design for bringing immigrants to Canada. The full scope of the impact of the substantial immigration during Laurier's administration is still being explored, but in his many writings and speeches Sifton left doubt as to the kind of settlers he envisioned would make the most appropriate new Canadians and provide the muscle for making the West an agricultural heartland. The following excerpt comes from one of Sifton's most celebrated statements; it was published in Maclean's in 1922, long after Sifton had left his position as interior minister. Observe his recognition of the source of a substantial number of immigrants from the United States and Great Britain, his characterization of peasants, and his expectations that those peasants would become the docile and hardworking backbone of the Canadian West.

People who do not know anything at all about the policy which was followed by the Department of the Interior under my direction quite commonly make the statement that my policy for Immigration was quantity and not quality. As a matter of fact that statement is the direct opposite of the fact....

Howard Palmer, ed., *Immigration and the Rise of Multiculturalism* (Toronto: Copp Clark, 1975), 34–38.

When I speak of quality I have in mind, I think, something that is quite different from what is in the mind of the average writer or speaker upon the question of Immigration. I think a stalwart peasant is a sheep-skin coat, born on the soil, whose forefathers have been farmers for ten generations, with a stout wife and a half-dozen children, is good quality. A Trades Union artisan who will not work more than eight hours a day and will not work that long if he can help it, will not work on a farm at all and has to be fed by the public when his work is slack is, in my judgment, quantity and very bad quantity. I am indifferent as to whether or not he is British-born. It matters not what his nationality is; such men are not wanted in Canada, and the more of them we get the more trouble we shall have.

I am of the deliberate opinion that about 500,000 farmers could be actually put on land in the next ten years by a thorough, systematic and energetic organization, backed with all needful legal authority and money....

There is the practical question of ways and means. Where and how shall we put these settlers? So far as the United States is concerned I am quite clear in my views as to the methods that should be adopted....If I were working for the purpose of getting American settlers into our North West I should endeavor to work through [land and colonization companies]....

As to the other places from which settlers can be procured, I could turn loose the organization upon the North of England and Scotland. There are some young mechanics in the North of England and Scottish towns who have been born on the land and brought up by farmers. Very nearly all of them are willing to emigrate. I would search out individually every one of these men that can be got, as well as farm laborers and the sons of small farmers. I would make a most intensive search, because experience shows that these men are of the very best blood in the world and every one of them that can be procured is an asset to the country.

In Norway, Sweden, Denmark, Belgium, Bohemia, Hungary and Galicia there are hundreds of thousands of hardy peasants, men of the type above described, farmers for ten or fifteen generations, who are anxious to leave Europe and start life under better conditions in a new country. These men are workers. They have been bred for generations to work from daylight to dark. They have never done anything else and they never expect to do anything else. We have some hundreds of thousands of them in Canada now and they are among our most useful and productive people.

The Necessity for Victory

As the Great War deepened and the fighting between the Allied and Central powers settled into a virtual stalemate along the killing grounds of a ragged series of trenches that came to be known as the Western Front, the call to supply reinforcements became a thorny political issue. Prime Minister Borden, who had long been an advocate of his country's unflagging support in the war effort, traveled to Europe in 1917 to meet with Canada's allies and visit the troops. He returned more convinced than ever that the struggle was of paramount importance for Canada's future, and quickly steered the government's attention to a conscription plan to offset declining enlistments. The following excerpt from one of Borden's speeches in the House of Commons in May 1917 provides an excellent illustration of his thoughts on Canada's war effort.

Now, as to our efforts in this war—and here I approach a subject of great gravity and seriousness, and, I hope with a full sense of the responsibility that devolves upon myself and upon my colleagues, and not only upon us but upon members of the Parliament and the people of this country. We have four Canadian divisions at the front. For the immediate future there are sufficient reinforcements. But four divisions cannot be maintained without thorough provision for future requirements....I think that no true Canadian, realizing all that is at stake in this war, can bring himself to consider with toleration or seriousness any suggestion for the relaxation of our efforts. The months immediately before us may be decisive....I

Robert L. Borden, *Canada at War* (Ottawa: s.n., 1917) [CIHM microfiche series; #76128].

myself stated to Parliament that nothing but voluntary enlistment was proposed by the Government. But I return to Canada impressed at once with the extreme gravity of the situation, and with a sense of responsibility for our further effort at the most critical period of the war. It is apparent to me that the voluntary system will not yield further substantial results. I hoped that it would. The Government has made every effort within its power, so far as I can judge. If any effective effort to stimulate voluntary recruiting still remains to be made, I should like to know what it is. The people have cooperated with the Government in a most splendid manner along the lines of voluntary enlistment. Men and women alike have interested themselves in filling up the ranks of regiments that were organized. Everything possible has been done, it seems to me, in the way of voluntary enlistment.

All citizens are liable to military service for the defence of their country, and I conceive that the battle for Canadian liberty and autonomy is being fought today on the plains of France and of Belgium. There are other places besides the soil of a country itself where the battle for its liberties and its institutions can be fought; and I venture to think that, if this war should end in defeat, Canada, in all the years to come, would be under the shadow of German military domination....

Now, the question arises as to what is our duty....I believe the time has come when the authority of the state should be invoked to provide reinforcements necessary to sustain the gallant men at the front who have held the line for months, who have proved themselves more than a match for the best troops that the enemy could send against them, and who are fighting in France and Belgium that Canada may live in the future. No one who has not seen the positions which our men have taken, whether at Vimy Ridge, at Courcelette, or elsewhere, can realize the magnitude of the task that is before them, or the splendid courage and resourcefulness which its accomplishment demands. Nor can any one realize the conditions under which war is being carried on. I have been somewhat in the midst of things at the front. Yet I feel that I cannot realize what the life in the trenches means, though I know that I can realize it better than those who have not been as near to the front as I have been. I bring back to the people of Canada from these men a message that they need our help, that they need to be supported, that they need to be sustained, that reinforcements must be sent to them. Thousands of them have made the supreme sacrifice for our liberty and preservation. Common gratitude, apart from all other considerations, should bring the whole force of this nation behind them....

Therefore, it is my duty to announce to the House that early proposals will be made on the part of the Government to provide, by compulsory military enlistment on a selective basis, such reinforcements as may be necessary to maintain the Canadian army today in the field as one of the finest fighting units of the Empire.

An Argument Against Conscription

A diverse number of Canadians disagreed with Borden's government on a host of issues having to do with the war effort. Sparking some of the most contentious debates were the questions of loyalty and the need for conscription. Henri Bourassa, the politician and journalist who was considered by many contemporaries to be one the most indefatigable defenders of francophone interests, spoke and wrote extensively about those questions. The following piece, which was originally published in Le Devoir *on 12 July 1917, provides a fine illustration of a francophone interpretation of national identity and Canada's role in the Great War.*

We are opposed to further enlistments for the war in Europe, whether by conscription or otherwise, for the following reason: (1) Canada has already made a military display, in men and money, proportionately superior to that of any nation engaged in the war; (2) any further weakening of the man-power of the country would seriously handicap agricultural production and the other essential industries; (3) an increase in the war budget of Canada spells national bankruptcy; (4) it threatens the economic life of the nation and, eventually, its political independence; (5) conscription means national disunion and strife, and would thereby hurt the cause of the Allies to a much greater extent than the addition of a few thousand soldiers to their fighting forces could bring them help and comfort....

Henri Bourassa, *Win the War and Lose Canada* (Montreal: s.n., 1917) [CIHM microfiche series; #71868].

If Canada persists in her run towards extreme militarism, in order to supply the armies of Europe with a number of men wholly insufficient to influence the fate of arms, she will soon find herself utterly unable to give to the Allied nations the real help which ought to be, and could be, her most valuable contribution to the common cause: nourishment. . . .

We, Canadian Nationalists, hold that Canada has not the right to commit suicide for the sake of any European or humanitarian cause, excellent as it may be. It must live and do honour to its own obligations. It must also keep the *pax Americana*, and not sow the seeds of future strifes with its only neighbor. British politics brought it twice to war with the United States, in 1774 and 1812, and twice at least on the verge of conflict, during the Secession war and the Venezuela embroilment. We do not want Canada to raise a quarrel of its own; we do not want to see it reduced to such as state of financial despondency that the money lenders in the United States will have to recoup themselves at the expense of our national independence. A free Canada—free politically, free economically—and a peaceful America are more important to us than the establishment of democratic governments in Europe, or the settlement of the Balkan problem. . . . .

Conscription is sure to bring serious troubles in the labour circles. Indiscriminate enlistment has already disorganized labour conditions. Rightly or wrongly, labour leaders apprehend that conscription is sought for not so much for military purposes as with the object of controlling wages and work. The enforcement of conscription will certainly be resisted by the organized labour of Canada. . . .

Much has been said about the small number of French-Canadians who have enlisted for the war; but very little about the large numbers of European-born volunteers in the so-called "Canadian" force. The truth is, that the over proportion of British-born volunteers, as compared with the Canadian-born volunteers of English or Scottish extraction, is as great as between English-speaking and French-speaking *Canadians*. The fact is that the proportion of enlistments, among Canadians of various extractions, has been in *inverse ratio* to their enrootment in the soil.

The only trouble with the French Canadians is that they remain the only true "unhyphenated" Canadians. Under the sway of British imperialism, Canadians of British origin have become quite unsettled as to their allegiance: they have not yet made up their mind whether they are more British than Canadian, or more Canadian than British; whether they are the citizens of a world-scattered empire, of members of an American community. The French-Canadians have remained, and want to remain, exclusively Canadian and American. . . .

Opposition to conscription and war-madness in Canada is not anti-patriotic: it is essentially patriotic and clear-sighted.

A Case for Women's Suffrage

The movement for opening the franchise to women unfolded in the nineteenth century and gathered pace in the first two decades of the twentieth century. Proponents of women's suffrage presented a number of reasons to support their case. Strikingly, some of the most dedicated advocates of suffrage were quite moderate in their predictions of the impact that the female vote would have on politics. Two very different positions on the rationale for and potential benefits of women's suffrage are presented below. The first is a piece from Olivar Asselin in Montreal's Daily Herald *of 26 November 1913; the second is from Nellie McClung, one of Canada's leading suffragettes, in an article published in* Maclean's Magazine *in July 1916 and entitled "What Will They Do With It?"*

Olivar Asselin:

[I]f the family be looked upon as the basic unit of the state, the head of the family, man, is the natural spokesman of the family in the public councils. For myself, I am inclined to think that conception the wiser in principle. But then, the logical consequences would be the barring of unmarried men from suffrage. Since the family unit has, the world over, been given up for the man unit, and since woman has a far greater interest in government than unmarried men, there is no reason why women should not be allowed to share the right of government....

In modern communities, woman, through the press, has just as effective a means of apprising herself of the needs of the

Ramsay Cook and Wendy Mitchinson, eds., *The Proper Sphere: Women's Place in Canadian Society* Copyright © Oxford University Press Canada 1976, 312–313, 319–324. Reprinted by permission of the publisher.

commonwealth without injuring the home, as man without injuring his private business. So much for the practicality of woman suffrage....

Education, liquor selling, city and town planning, public health and police, child labor, public charities, and dozens of other pithy questions would be nearer a proper solution if women had the vote....

The fear has been expressed that the atmosphere of the polling booth might deny the character of our women. I would rather expect woman's presence to purify the atmosphere of the polling booth. There are of course bad women, and plenty of them, but woman has a native moral cleanliness which men lack, and the chances are that her entrance into the political field would be something like her sudden advent into a circle of "gentlemen" while the latter are engaged in telling nasty stories....

I favor woman suffrage not so much out of a belief in equal rights as because I am convinced that woman suffrage would help to lift politics out of the slush into which personal appetites and capital's corporate greed have caused them to sink.

Nellie L. McClung:

And now the question naturally arises, "What will they do with it?" There are still some who fear that the franchise, for all its innocent looks, is an insidious evil, which will undermine and warp a woman's nature, and cause her to lose all interest in husband, home and children. There are some who say it will make no difference. There are others who look now for the beginning of better things. Every one is more or less interested; some are a bit frightened....

Women have not tried to get into Parliament in the countries where they have the franchise and I venture the prediction that it will be many years before there are women legislators in Canada. And when they are elected it will be by sheer force of merit; for there will be a heavy weight of prejudice against women which only patient years can dispel!

The first work undertaken by women will be to give help to other women, particularly mothers of families....It seems a fitting thing that women should use their new political power to make motherhood easier, to rob colonization of its fears and dangers, to give the lonely woman on the outposts of civilization the assurance that she is part of a great sisterhood and is not left alone to struggle with conditions which may prove too hard for her!

More and more the idea is growing upon us that certain services are best rendered by the state, and not left to depend on the caprice, inclination, or inability of the individual....As it is now many a man, woman, and child, suffers agony, or perhaps becomes a menace to their family, because medical aid cannot be afforded. Why should a child suffer from adenoids, which makes him stupid and dull in school, and give him a tendency to tubercular trouble, just because his father cannot afford to pay the doctor's fee, or maybe does not know the danger?

One of the most hopeful signs of the advent of the woman voter is the quiet determination to stay out of party politics. Party lines are not so tightly drawn in the West. Great issues have been decided by people outside of politics. The temperance fight in Alberta and Manitoba obliterated the lines of party, and when that once happens they can never be quite so strong again. It is no uncommon thing to hear public men say: "I have voted both ways, and will change my politics any time I want to." The women have no intention of forming a woman's party. They see no future for such a movement. But they do see that a great body of intelligent women, who study public questions, fairly and honestly, uncontaminated by party hypothesis, not trying to fit their opinion to the platform of any political leader, may become a powerful influence in forming the party of a Government, or perhaps in making the platform of an opposition.

Letters from the Heartland

An extraordinarily large number of Canadians suffered hardship during the Depression. As the provincial relief programs rapidly became exhausted and the ranks of the unemployed grew, many citizens looked to support from the federal government. Prime Minister Bennett received an extraordinary number of letters from struggling Canadians during his term in office. Many made appeals for government action to get people back to work; others sought immediate financial assistance. The two selections below come from a remarkable edited collection of these letters to Bennett. They give us an insight to a difficult time from two regions of the country, as well as an illustration of gender differences in assessing the impact of the economic crisis. The first is from R.D. in Ottawa, and the second is from Mrs. R. Paddy from Burton, Alberta.

Ottawa, 4 March 1932

Dear Sir,

   I am just writing a few lines to you to see what can be done for us young men of Canada. We are the growing generation of Canada, but with no hopes of a future. Please tell me why is it a single man always gets a refusal when he looks for a job. A married man gets work, & if he does not get work, he gets relief. Yesterday I got a glimpse of a lot of the unemployed. It just made me feel downhearted. To think there is no work for them, or in the future, & also no work for myself. Last year I was out of work for three months. I received work with a local

L.M. Grayson and Michael Bliss, eds., *The Wretched of Canada* (Toronto: University of Toronto Press, 1971), 20–21, 117–118. Reprinted with permission of the publisher.

farm. I was told in the fall I could have a job for the winter; I was then a stable man. Now I am slacked off on account of no snow this winter. Now I am wandering the streets like a beggar, with no future ahead. There are lots of single men in Ottawa, who would rather walk the streets, & starve, than work on a farm. That is a true statement. Myself I work wherever I can get work, & get a good name wherever I go. There are plenty of young men like myself, who are in the same plight. I say again whats to be done for us single men? do we have to starve? or do we have to go round with our faces full of shame, to beg at the doors of the well to do citizen. I suppose you will say the married men must come first; I certainly agree with you there. But have you a word or two to cheer us single men up a bit? The married man got word he was going to get relief. That took the weight of worry off his mind quite a bit. Did the single man here [*sic*] anything, how he was going to pull through? Did you ever feel the pangs of hunger? My Idea is we shall all starve. I suppose you will say I cant help it, or I cant make things better. You have the power to make things better or worse. When you entered as Premier you promised a lot of things, you was going to do for the country. I am waiting patiently to see the results. Will look for my answer in the paper.

Yours Truly,
R.D., Ottawa

Dear Mr. Bennett:

I suppose I am silly to write this letter but I haven't any one else to write to so am going to hope and pray that you will read this yourself and help me or us, rather.

We are just one of the many on relief and trying to keep our place without being starved out. Have a good ½ section not bad buildings and trying to get a start without any money and 5 children all small. . . .Am so worried on account of the children as we never have any vegetables except potatoes and almost no fruit and baby hasn't any shoes have kept him in old socks instead. . . .Just had 70 acres in last year and the dry spell just caught it right along with the grasshoppers although we poisoned most of them there were hardly any left by fall. I cant hardly sleep for worrying about it.

My husband doesn't know I am writing this letter but I just don't know what to do for money the children come to me about everything it's the women & children who suffer in these terrible times, men don't notice things. I suppose you think I am maybe making things out worse than they are but I am not. Please help me by lending me some money and I will send you my engagement ring & wedding ring as security....If you would just lend me $50.00 even I would be the happiest woman in Alberta and you would be the best Premier of Canada because you would have been the means of saving a whole family guess I had better go to bed. My two rings cost over a $100.00 15 years ago but what good are they when the flour is nearly all done and there isn't much to eat in the house in the city I could pawn them but away out here. I haven't been off the farm this winter. Will expect to hear from you hope to anyway I am sure you will never be sorry any way if you do help us.

Yours sincerely,
Mrs. R. Paddy

The CCF Platform

The Depression gave rise to a number of new political parties that promised to tackle the economic crisis more effectively than the Liberals or Conservatives, and some offered controversial plans to alter Canada's reliance on capitalism. The most important of those upstart parties was the Co-operative Commonwealth Federation. The following document states the party's agenda in unambiguous language; it comes from the CCF's Programme that was adopted at the First National Convention, Regina, Saskatchewan, 1 July 1933.

The C.C.F. is a federation of organizations whose purpose is the establishment in Canada of a Co-operative Commonwealth in which the principle regulating production, distribution and exchange will be the supplying of human needs and not the making of profits.

We aim to replace the present capitalist system, with its inherent injustice and inhumanity, by a social order from which the domination and exploitation of one class by another will be eliminated, in which economic planning will supersede unregulated private enterprise and competition, and in which genuine democratic self-government, based upon economic equality will be possible. The present order is marked by glaring inequalities of wealth and opportunity, by chaotic waste and instability; and in an age of plenty it condemns the great mass of the people to poverty and insecurity. Power has more and more become concentrated into the hands of a small irresponsible minority of financiers and industrialists and to

Kenneth McNaught, *A Prophet in Politics: A Biography of J.S. Woodsworth* (Toronto: University of Toronto Press, 1959), 321–330. Reprinted with permission of the publisher.

their predatory interests the majority are habitually sacrificed. When private profit is the main stimulus to economic effort, our society oscillates between periods of feverish prosperity in which the main benefits go to speculators and profiteers, to catastrophic depression, in which the common man's normal state of insecurity and hardship is accentuated. We believe that these evils can be removed only in a planned and socialized economy in which our natural resources and the principle means of production and distribution are owned, controlled and operated by the people.

The new social order at which we aim is not one in which individuality will be crushed out by a system of regimentation. Nor shall we interfere with cultural rights of racial or religious minorities. What we seek is a proper collective organization of our economic resources such as will make possible a much greater degree of leisure and a much richer individual life for every citizen.

This social and economic transformation can be brought about by political action, through the election of a government inspired by the ideal of a Co-operative Commonwealth and supported by a majority of the people. We do not believe in change by violence. We consider that both the old parties in Canada are the instruments of capitalist interests and cannot serve as agents of social reconstruction, and that whatever the superficial differences between them, they are bound to carry on government in accordance with the dictates of the big business interests who finance them. The C.C.F. aims at political power in order to put an end to this capitalist domination of our political life. It is a democratic movement, a federation of farmer, labor and social organizations, financed by its own members and seeking to achieve its ends solely by constitutional methods. It appeals for support to all who believe that the time has come for a far-reaching reconstruction of our economic and political institutions and who are willing to work together. . . .

A Portrait of the Fighting Forces

The Second World War was the most documented conflict in history, and Canada's participation in the war provides an excellent illustration of that dynamic. The engagements of Canada's military forces were covered extensively by journalists and often captured on film. There was certainly a tendency to glorify the efforts of the men and women in uniform. Nonetheless, the accounts from journalists who reported from the front lines or were attached to units offer a valuable insight to the gritty commitment of Canadian forces during the war. The following excerpt comes from Canada's most popular news magazine, Maclean's. *Entitled "Tank Battle," by L.S.B. Shapiro, it describes in detail one component of the country's military engagement in northern France in September 1944.*

Some day—if the war lasts long enough—when tanks have developed armament capable of meeting fixed antitank weapons on even terms or better, we may see them sweeping like cavalry into enemy positions. Today they are being used in close support of the infantry...sometimes they are used in place of infantry for defensive flank protection. They are distributed in small packets among battalions and companies. But the men who command tanks long for the day when they can be employed as popular imagination would have—in open battles of magnificent scope and decisive result....

Michael Benedict, ed., *On the Battlefields: Two World Wars that Shaped a Nation*, Vol. II (Toronto: Penguin Canada, 2002), 355–364.

Their job is like an airman's, with something added. It requires nerves of steel, quick decision, technical skills of the most exacting kind. And something more—an ability to maintain the mind at trigger edge for many hours under the mental torture of imminent death. The airman's moment of battle climax is come and gone in a moment; the violence of a tank battle is slow and excruciating.

He lacks the soaring freedom of the fighter pilot, or the comforting sense of catlike mobility which comes to a rifleman when he is advancing over a battlefield. The tankman sits with four others in a Sherman, surrounded by high explosive shells, with every moment bringing new possibility that he will be holed and shattered. The tank commander shares the confined space with his driver and co-driver, who doubles as a loader, gunner, and wireless operator. He has a very keen sense of claustrophobia; occasionally he leaves his turret open though it would be safer to shut it.

He rolls into the shadow of a hedge, keeping his eyes on the skyline. Suddenly the silhouette of a tank rises over the distant ridge. Its dappled camouflage tells him it is German. His mind must be faster and sharper than he ever thought it could be. Is the enemy a Panther? Or a Tiger? Has it an 88 or a 7.5? Should he take a shot at it? Is it 1,200 or 1,800 yards off? Why has it suddenly and boldly silhouetted itself? Are there other enemy on the reverse slope, planning to ambush him? Has he been seen? Is the terrain right for a winning battle by a Sherman? Can he get around to the Panther's soft side or are their 88's within range?

The answers to these and a dozen other questions must fall into his mind immediately—before the plan of battle can be formulated. Sometimes he has less than five seconds to weigh the answers and put the conclusions into lethal operation.

Day in and day out the tankman undergoes this ordeal. He is the toughest warrior of them all.

A Japanese-Canadian Perspective

The treatment of Japanese Canadians during and immediately following the Second World War stands as one of the bleakest episodes in the entire scope of the history of the Canadian government's treatment of its citizens. Many Japanese Canadians documented their experiences, so historians have abundant resources to consult as they assess the role that fear and prejudice played in bringing about the relocation of thousands of Canada's citizens from British Columbia. One such individual, Muriel Kitagawa, contributed regularly to the New Canadian *in the 1940s. The following pieces come from her papers, manuscripts, and essays. These were collected by Roy Miki and published with an extensive collection of letters to her brother, Wes Fujiwara. They eloquently address the issues of citizenship and racism in the context of the Second World War.*

We'll Fight for Home! [January 1942]

The tide of panic, starting from irresponsible agitators, threatens to engulf the good sense of the people of British Columbia. The daily press is flooded with "letters to the editor" demanding the indiscriminate internment of all people of Japanese blood, alien or Canadian-born; demanding the immediate confiscation of our right

Muriel Kitagawa and Roy Miki, eds. *This Is My Own: Letters to Wes & Other Writings on Japanese Canadians, 1941–1948* (Vancouver: Talonbooks, 1985), 180–182.

to work as we like; our right to live like decent human beings. One and all, they add to the height of sardonic cynicism; if we are as loyal as we say we are, then we ought to understand why we ought to be treated like poison. . . . .

For the very reason that or Grade School teachers, our High School teachers, and our environment have bred in us a love of country, a loyalty to one's native land, faith in the concepts of traditional British fair play, it is difficult to understand the expression of a mean narrow-mindedness, an unreasoning condemnation of a long suffering people. We cannot understand why our loyalty should be questioned.

After all, this is our home, where by the sweat of our endeavours we have carved a bit of security for ourselves and our children. Would we sabotage our own home? Would we aid anyone who menaces our home, who would destroy the fruits of our labour and our love? People who talk glibly of moving us wholesale "East of the rockies," who maintain that it is an easy task, overlook with supreme indifference the complex human character.

They do not think what it would mean to be ruthlessly, needlessly uprooted from a familiar homeground, from friends, and sent to a labour camp where most likely the deficiencies will be of the scantiest in spite of what is promised. They do not think that we are not cattle to be herded wherever it pleases our ill-wishers. They forget, or else it does not occur to them, that we have the same pride and self-respect as other Canadians, who can be hurt beyond repair. In short, they do not consider us as people, but as a nuisance to be rid of at the first opportunity. What excuse they use is immaterial to them. It just happens to be very opportune that Japan is now an active enemy.

On Loyalty [February 1942]

The quality of loyalty is difficult to define in exact terms. There is a oneness with one's country, just as there is the blood tie with one's mother. There is the fighting urge to defend that country should it be threatened in any way. There is a passionate, unquestioning, unqualified affinity with the land that excludes the pettiness of a manmade—and therefore imperfect—government. All this and active service for the country is loyalty.

Who can glibly say I am a Japanese National of Japan just because I am of the same race with black hair and yellow skin? Who can rightfully tell me where my heart lies, if I know better myself? Who can assume with omniscience that I am disloyal to Canada because I have not golden hair and blue eyes? What are these surface marks that must determine the quality of my loyalty? Nothing, nothing at all!

Yet because I am Canadian, must hate be a requisite for my patriotism? Must I hate vengefully, spitefully, pettily? Will not hate cloud my good sense, muddy the clean surge of willing sacrifice, the impulse to rally strongly to the flag of this country? Hate never fought as fiercely as love in the fight for one's country. Hate impedes, while love strengthens.

Therefore it is not hate for a country one has never known, but love for this familiar Canadian soil that makes me want to use my bare fists to uphold its honour, its integrity.

Who is there, unless he does not know the quality of loyalty, who will question mine?

Smallwood's Argument for Confederation

Joey Smallwood was one of the most colorful and eccentric political figures of twentieth-century Canada. His rationale for supporting Newfoundland's confederation with Canada was repeatedly made during two grueling referendums on the future of the province in 1948. The following document comes from Smallwood's autobiography, which he fittingly titled I Chose Canada. *His self-assurance, never in short supply during his political career, comes through clearly in the pages of his autobiography. Note also his appeal to Newfoundlanders to see the benefits of becoming a part of Canada's growing number of social programs in the postwar era.*

I was going to bring Newfoundland and Canada together as one country. I was going to get the National Convention to ask Canada to state the terms and conditions of Newfoundland's entry in the Confederation....

Our people had no notion at all of what Confederation was or what it meant. They had no conception of a federal system of government. Their only experience of government was what they had had before the coming of the Commission system. In Newfoundland up to this time, one Government alone...had performed all the functions of government that in most other countries were performed by federal, provincial or state, municipal, county or other forms of local administration....

Joseph R. Smallwood, *I Chose Canada* (Toronto: Macmillan of Canada, 1973), 226–228.

It was to people whose knowledge and experience of government was so simply defined that I undertook to explain the complexities of Confederation; and not merely to explain, but to convince them of its rightness for them—a mammoth task!

[Our arguments] enabled them to understand how it could be that, under Confederation, a province would have its own elected Provincial Government, to handle purely local matters, while at the same time there would be a great Central Government at Ottawa that would coordinate national affairs for all the provinces. This Central or Federal Government would be answerable to the Parliament of Canada, just as the local Provincial Government would be answerable to the Provincial House of Assembly. Each Legislature and each Government would have its duties and rights clearly spelled out. And, I used to say triumphantly, Newfoundlanders, like the people in the other nine provinces, would have the right to elect that Parliament of all Canada and would be represented in it by their own Members of Parliament and their own Senators. In addition—a fact that appealed to so many people then—Newfoundlanders, besides paying Canadian federal taxes to the Federal Government of Canada, would share in the huge amounts that this Government paid out to individual provinces! I drove home, repeatedly and endlessly, the fact that there were "have" and "have-not" provinces, that Newfoundland would be one of the have-nots, and that therefore we would receive from Ottawa far, far more than we contributed.

Diefenbaker and Nuclear Weapons

Prime Minister Diefenbaker's attempts to define a Canadian role in the Cold War led to significant problems for his administration; they also illustrated the delicate balance the country faced as it tried to support its superpower ally and still maintain enough distance from the United States' more unpopular policies. The question of nuclear weapons on Canadian soil represented an especially thorny dilemma for Canadians in the early 1960s. The following passages, which come from the House of Commons Debates in late January 1963, clarify Diefenbaker's defense of his decision to alter Canada's original agreement with the United States to arm Bomarc anti-aircraft missiles with nuclear warheads.

During 1958 the Canadian government studied intensively the arms required by Canadian forces in modern circumstances, and we reached the decision we would provide aircraft for the purposes of NATO. At that time I made it perfectly clear...that those forces would have to be equipped, in order to be fully effective, with defensive nuclear weapons if and when the need arose. That was recognized in taking the decision that was announced in September, 1958, to install Bomarc anti-aircraft missiles in Canada....

Every now and then some new white hope of rocketry goes into the scrap pile. We established the Bomarc, the two units. They are effective over an area of only a few hundred miles. People talk about

J.L. Granatstein, ed., *Canadian Foreign Policy Since 1945: Middle Power or Satellite?* (Toronto: Copp Clark, 1970), 119, 120, 123, 125.

change. Who would have thought three years ago that today the fear would be an attack with intercontinental ballistic missiles? This program cost Canada some $14 million. The United States put up the major portion of the total cost. I do not want to repeat, but it is necessary to do so, that with the advent more and more into intercontinental ballistic missiles the bomber carrier is less and less the threat that it was.

So what should we do? Should we carry on with what we have done in the past, merely for the purpose of saying, "Well, we stated, and having started and having proceeded, we will continue"? Should we do this in an area where mistakes are made? ... More and more the nuclear deterrent is becoming of such a nature that more nuclear arms will add nothing materially to our defences. Greater and greater emphasis must be placed on conventional arms and conventional forces. We in Canada took the lead in that connection....

What course should we take at this time? I emphasize what I have already stated, that we shall at all times carry out whatever our responsibilities are. I have said that strategic changes are taking place in the thinking of the western world, and there is a general recognition that the nuclear deterrent will not be strengthened by the expansion of the nuclear family. With these improvements in the international situation, this is no time for hardened decisions that cannot be altered. We must be flexible and fluid, for no one can anticipate what Khrushchev will do....[W]e are living in a new and changing world of defence realism....

Canada has a proud record....All of us should be true Canadians when facing a problem that touches the heartstrings of each and every one of us. My prayer is that we will be directed in this matter. Some may ridicule that belief on my part. I believe that the western world has been directed by God in the last few years, or there would have been no survival. I believe that will continue. My prayer is that we shall so live as to maintain not only the integrity of Canada and its high reputation by carrying out our responsibilities, but at the same time that we will be right, that the Canadian people will be able to say that, whatever decision is made, it was made with every consideration being given to all those moral and psychological things that form one's make-up.

Recommendations of the Massey Report

In the late 1940s the federal government created a commission to explore the current state of Canadian culture and to make recommendations for its future development. Chaired by the well-known diplomat, Vincent Massey, the Royal Commission on National Development in the Arts, Letters, and Sciences issued a detailed report of its findings in 1951. The report was responsible for laying the groundwork either to improve or to create a wide range of government-sponsored agencies in the following decades. These included federal aid for students, the Canada Council for the encouragement of arts, letters, humanities, and social sciences, the National Gallery, the National Library, archives, the National Film Board, and numerous museums. Excerpts of that report, which attempted to define Canadian culture and suggested ways to ensure its survival in the modern world, are presented below.

Our task has been neither modest in scope nor simple in character. The subjects with which we have dealt cover the entire field of letters, the arts and sciences within the jurisdiction of the federal state. But although numerous and varied they are all parts of one whole. Our concern throughout was with the needs and desires of the citizen in relation to science, literature, art, music, the drama, films, broadcasting. In accordance with our instructions we examined also

R. Douglas Francis and Donald B. Smith, eds., *Readings in Canadian History: Post-Confederation* (Toronto: Holt, Rinehart, and Winston of Canada, 1982), 526, 533, 544, 545.

research as related to the national welfare, and considered what the Federal Government might do in the development of the individual through scholarships and bursaries. Such an inquiry as we have been asked to make is probably unique; it is certainly unprecedented in Canada. . . .

Canadians, with their customary optimism, may think that the fate of their civilization is in their own hands. So it is. But this young nation, struggling to be itself, must shape its course with an eye to three conditions so familiar that their significance can too easily be ignored. Canada has a small and scattered population in a vast area; this population is clustered along the rim of another country many times more populous and of far greater economic strength; a majority of Canadians share their mother tongue with that neighbour, which leads to peculiarly close and intimate relations. One or two of these conditions will be found in many modern countries. But Canada alone possesses all three. What is their effect, good or bad, on what we call Canadianism? . . . .

But the institutions, the movements, the activities we have examined share something more than a purpose; they suffer in common from lack of nourishment. No appraisal of our intellectual or cultural life can leave one complacent or even content. If modern nations were marshaled in the order of the importance which they assign to those things with which this inquiry is concerned, Canada would be found far from the vanguard; she would even be near the end of the procession. . . .

It seems to us that two things are essential to restore in Canada the balance between the attention we pay to material achievements and to the other less tangible but more enduring parts of our civilization. The first must be of course the will of our people to enrich and to quicken their cultural and intellectual life; our inquiry has made clear that this will is earnest and widespread among our fellow-citizens. The second essential is money. If we in Canada are to have a more plentiful and better cultural fare, we must pay for it. Good will alone can do little for a starving plant; if the cultural life of Canada is anaemic, it must be nourished, and this will cost money. This is a task for shared effort in all fields of government, federal, provincial and local.

A Voice of the New Quebec

The Quiet Revolution affected virtually every aspect of life in Quebec. In addition to the social, religious, and educational changes that became synonymous with its transformative impact, it reinvigorated the old question of the nature of the province's relationship with Canada. A number of politicians, including René Lévesque, put their efforts into building an argument for fundamentally changing Quebec's ties to Canada. The following selection, published in 1968, comes from Lévesque's exposition of a plan that would quickly evolve into the sovereignty-association movement.

Now, in the last few years we have indeed made some progress along this difficult road of "catching up," the road which leads to the greater promise of our age.

At least enough progress to know that what comes next depends only on ourselves and on the choices that only we can make....

On this road where there can be no more stopping are a number of necessary tasks which must be attended to without delay. Neglecting them would endanger the impetus we have acquired, perhaps it would slow it down irreparably.

And here we encounter a basic difficulty which has become more and more acute in recent years. It is created by the political regime under which we have lived for over a century.

We are a nation within a country where there are two nations. For all the things we mentioned earlier, using words like "individuality," "history," "society," and "people," are also the things one includes

René Lévesque, *An Option for Canada* (Toronto: McClelland and Stewart, 1968), 18, 20–21.

under the word "nation." It means nothing more than the collective will to live that belongs to any national entity likely to survive.

Two nations in a single country: this means, as well, that in fact there are *two majorities*, two "complete societies" quite distinct from each other trying to get along within a common framework. That this number puts us in a minority position makes no difference; just as a civilized society will never condemn a little man to feel inferior beside a bigger man, civilized relations among nations demand that they treat each other as equals in law and in fact.

Now we believe it to be evident that the hundred-year-old framework of Canada can hardly have any effect other than to create increasing difficulties between the two parties insofar as their mutual respect and understanding are concerned, as well as impeding the changes and progress so essential to both.

It is useless to go back over the balance sheet of the century just past, listing the advantages it undoubtedly has brought us and the obstacles and injustices it even more unquestionably has set in our way.

The important thing for today and for tomorrow is that both sides realize that this regime has had its day, and that it is a matter of urgency either to modify it profoundly or to build a new one.

As we are the ones who have put up with its main disadvantages, it is natural that we also should be in the greatest hurry to be rid of it; the more so because it is we who are menaced most dangerously by its current paralysis.

The Underside of Canadian Society

At the same time that Canadians were celebrating their stature as a leading industrialized nation with progressive ideals, critics were uncovering evidence that pointed to the country's profound social and economic inequities. One landmark scholarly study of the 1960s, John Porter's Vertical Mosaic, *tackled one of the most tenacious Canadian myths: that the country was classless and thus essentially egalitarian. Through the lens of sociological methodology, Porter discovered persistent inequities based on ethnic identification; he suggested that class might indeed exist in Canada. Porter's provocative work triggered a generation of debate among scholars. Excerpts from the introduction and conclusion to his work should suffice to give the reader a sense of the context of his work and of his major conclusions.*

One of the most persistent images that Canadians have of their society is that is has no classes. This image becomes translated into the assertion that Canadians are all relatively equal in their possessions, in the amount of money they earn, and in the opportunities which they and their children have to get on in the world. An important element in this image of classlessness is that, with the absence of formal aristocracy and aristocratic institutions, Canada is a society in which equalitarian values have asserted

John Porter, *The Vertical Mosaic: An Analysis of Social Class and Power in Canada* (Toronto: University of Toronto Press, 1965), 3, 4, 6, 557, 558. Reprinted with permission of the publisher.

themselves over authoritarian values. Canada, it is thought, shares not only a continent with the United States, but also a democratic ideology which rejects the historical class and power structures of Europe....

The historical source of the image of a classless Canada is the equality among pioneers in the frontier environment of the last century. In the early part of the present century there was a similar equality of status among those who were settlers in the west, although, as we shall see, these settlers were by no means treated equally....

Although the historical image of rural equality lingers it has gradually given way in the urban industrial setting to an image of a middle level classlessness in which there is a general uniformity of possessions....Modern advertising has done much to standardize the image of middle class consumption levels and middle class behavior. Consumers' magazines are devoted to the task of constructing the ideal way of life through articles on childrearing, homemaking, sexual behaviour, health, sports, and hobbies.

That there is neither very rich nor very poor in Canada is an important part of the image. There are no barriers to opportunity. Education is free. Therefore, making use of it is largely a question of personal ambition.

Images which conflict with the one of middle class equality rarely find expression, partly because the literate middle class is both the producer and the consumer of the image. Even at times in what purports to be serious social analysis, middle class intellectuals project the image of their own class onto the social classes above and below them. There is scarcely any critical analysis of Canadian social life upon which a conflicting image could be based. The idea of class differences has scarcely entered the stream of Canadian academic writing despite the fact that class differences stand in the way of implementing one of the most important values of western society, that is equality....

Canada, it may be concluded from the evidence...has a long way to go to become in any sense a thorough-going democracy....Even into the 1960's Canadian educational systems have yet to become democratized through to the university level. The possibilities for upward social mobility are reduced, and, at the same time, shortages of highly trained people for the new occupational structure continue.

In this respect Canada is behind twentieth-century democracy elsewhere.

Ethnic and religious affiliation in Canadian society have always had an effect on the life chances of the individual. If not its one distinctive value, that of the mosaic is Canada's most cherished. Legitimization for the mosaic is sought in the notion of collective or group rights which becomes confused with the legal foundation of individual rights. It seems inescapable that the strong emphasis on ethnic differentiation can result only in those continuing dual loyalties which prevent the emergence of any clear Canadian identity. From the point of view of our study of social class and power, it is likely that the historical patterns of class and ethnicity will be perpetuated as long as ethnic differentiation is so highly valued. Canada will always appear as an adaptation of its British and French charter groups, rather than as one of a new breed in a new nation....

Canada is a new society, and should have had great opportunities for institutional innovation, but so far it has been incapable of taking a lead in the changes and experimentation necessary for more democratic industrial societies. A fragmented political structure, a lack of upward mobility into its elite and higher occupational levels, and the absence of a clearly articulated system of values, stemming from a charter myth or based in an indigenous ideology, are some of the reasons for this retardation.

Keenleyside's Letter

As the Cold War deepened, a growing number of Canadians began to question the country's relationship with its superpower neighbor. In the late 1960s and early 1970s an impressive number of works were published by academics, policymakers, and journalists that had at their core a decidedly anti-American tone. The expansion of American military might, the most alarming example of which was the wrenching and protracted war in Vietnam, served as a key element for this growing skepticism of the historic relationship between Canada and the United States. Hugh Keenleyside, an experienced diplomat with a resume that included working with the United Nations, contributed the following piece to one of the most widely read collections of critical essays. Addressed to "Sam"—an obvious literary reference to the fictitious Uncle Sam—the letter explores some of the prevailing Canadian opinions of American political and cultural dominance in the Cold War era.

Dear Sam:

We have often talked about the attitude of Canadians towards the United States and, in particular, why it is so often, as you believe, unfairly critical. . . .

Let me say first, that the fact that you and so many other Americans are interested and even concerned about how you and your country appear to people from other lands illustrates one of the most attractive of your national characteristics—your willingness to invite frank and critical comment on your domestic and foreign policies and

---

John H. Redekop, ed., *The Star-Spangled Beaver* (Toronto: Paul Martin Associates, 1971), 6, 7, 12, 13, 14, 16, 20, 21, 22, 23.

behaviour. In this you are almost unique, especially among the so-called developed countries. We in Canada, for example, while indulging in almost perpetual self-criticism, are notoriously sensitive to criticism from others. . . .

As is the case with others, self-defence is the first preoccupation of the American Government. . . .In addition to developing a military power that has no close rival the United States has evolved a policy which, in spite of occasional variations and modifications, has had a certain coherence and consistence. It has used its economic power to organize and assist various programmes designed to promote economic and social progress in the under-developed countries and regions. . . .

The first thing to say about the Canadian reaction is that we realize that both our security and our economic welfare have been strengthened by the "good neighbour" policy that existed towards Canada long before President Roosevelt enunciated it in relation to Latin America. . . .This does not mean, however, that we are so comfortable in this warm relationship that we are satisfied or tempted to relax and enjoy the sunshine of your smile. American businessmen are just as sharp and aggressive in their dealings with Canada as they are elsewhere abroad, or, indeed, at home. Many of them don't hesitate to lie . . .or, when they can, to use the big stick of government intervention. . . .

We are concerned when we find that a large part of our industrial machine is owned or controlled by Americans and we object very strongly when we learn that parent companies in the United States have prohibited their Canadian subsidiaries from filling orders from countries, like China or Cuba, of whose governments the American State Department currently disapproves. We may or may not disapprove too, but we feel that Canadian companies and Canadian citizens, even if the companies are owned in the United States, should conform to Canadian not to United States rules. And we don't like to have Canadian citizens told that if they even visit such countries their associates in the United States will be greatly upset. . . .

It is when we come to problems of defence, of war and peace, of disarmament and proliferation of arms, of cold war debates and hot war threats and practices, that many foreign observers feel and express the most serious reservations about the leadership of the United States. . . .

You are, of course, aware that informed opinion throughout the world is generally critical of what they consider to be Washington's obsession with communism. The official American conviction that there exists a world-wide, monolithic, malevolent communist conspiracy guided from a single centre, employing unlimited funds, marked by diabolical cleverness, and using methods that are as unique as they are unscrupulous, is not generally accepted in other countries, including Canada. . . .

What worried Canadians and, I believe, many others as well, is not doubt of American power, but doubt of American wisdom. Above all we are frightened by the Pentagon's obvious preference for action rather than thought, and by the possibility that a weak or stupid President may at some crisis act on the advice of his Chiefs of Staff. . . .

There is, I believe, some significance in the fact that almost all Canadians think that the American people are better than their governments. . . .[I]n spite of doubts and even fears of some American policies, and in spite of our strong distrust of some American leaders, particularly in the Pentagon, we Canadians, who should know you better than anyone else in the world, would be the last people to ask for another neighbour. . . .

Sincerely,
Hugh Keenleyside

Perspectives of History and the Sovereignty-Association Question

The arguments in support of sovereignty-association and in opposition to the idea were important for setting the stage for the referendum of 1980. They were also instructive because the oppositional groups mustered their evidence in a fashion that was heavily colored by their respective views of history. The following excerpts come from the "New Deal" and "New Federalism" platforms that were designed to convince Quebec voters to support a direction for the province to take in reshaping its relationship with Canada. In these selections one can detect the pessimistic tones of the "New Deal" arguments for setting Quebec on a track towards sovereignty, as well as the more positive assessment of the historic relationship between Quebec and the rest of Canada in the "New Federalism" approach.

"Québec-Canada: A New Deal"

A study of our past will show that the path taken by Quebecers, no matter how original it is, follows the same laws that have prevailed through the ages as various peoples have assumed national sovereignty.

Québec-Canada: A New Deal (Quebec: Éditeur official, 1979), 3, 7, 8, 9, 10, 12.

Our ancestors put down their roots in American soil at the beginning of the 17th century, at the time the first British settlers were landing on the east coast of what would become the United States....By 1760, our community was already an established society along the shores of the St. Lawrence. North American by geography, French by culture, language and politics, this society had a soul, a lifestyle, a way of behaving, traditions, institutions that were its very own. Its struggles, its successes and the ordeals it endured had made it aware of its common destiny, and it was already impatient under the colonial ties.

Sooner or later, that society would have rid itself of the colonial yoke and acquired its independence, as was the case in 1776 for the United States of America. But in 1763 the hazards of war placed it under British control....

[In Confederation] Quebecers did gain responsible and autonomous government, but with its autonomy limited to jurisdictions seen then as being primarily of local interest....It is obvious that this new regime was a Confederation in name only....Under the terms of the British North America Act, Québec is not the homeland of a nation, but merely a province among others, first four, then five, then ten; a province like the others, with no more rights or powers than the smallest of them. Nowhere in the British North America Act is there talk of an alliance between two founding peoples, or of a pact between two nations; on the contrary, there is talk of political and territorial unity, and of a national government which essentially dictates the direction the regional governments are to take....

The federal regime thus sanctioned, and favoured as well, the supremacy of English Canada. It was natural that in such a regime the interests and aspirations of Quebecers and Francophones in other provinces should take second place....

Though some federal laws belatedly attempted to encourage bilingualism in central institutions...Francophones were never regarded in Canada as a society with a history, a culture and aspirations of its own. They were seen at best as an important linguistic minority with no collective rights or particular powers, one that must sooner or later melt into the Canadian whole, as English Canada long believed....

"A New Canadian Federalism"

At the moment when Quebecers are preparing to make an historic decision on their collective future, they have every right to ask that the major options competing for their loyalty be presented to them honestly and clearly.

The government of Quebec, led by the Parti Québécois, has already made public the broad outline of its option, sovereignty-association, in the white paper entitled "Quebec-Canada: A New Deal."

One objective emerges clearly from the white paper. The Parti Québécois and the present government, propose to make Quebec a fully sovereign country....

The Péquiste [supporters of the Parti Québécois] view of our collective future is new in terms of the radical solution it proposes. However, their resolutely pessimistic view of our past history and our present situation is all too familiar.

In this frame of mind, they perpetuate an attitude which was held by the opponents of Confederation in the last century.

During the years which preceded the proclamation of the BNA Act, the enemies of this new constitution pronounced it to be a suicidal adventure for the people of Quebec. They predicted freely that Quebec and its traditions would be devoured by the Canadian federation, that it would mark the end of our culture and our own institutions.

It is this same theme, with a few variations, which forms the basis of the Péquiste refrain.

But alongside this negative attitude, there has always existed in Quebec another viewpoint, resolutely open to a more optimistic perspective of confidence and co-operation.

R. Douglas Francis and Donald B. Smith, eds., *Readings in Canadian History: Post-Confederation* (Toronto: Holt, Rinehart and Winston of Canada, 1982), 606, 607.

Those who hold this vision have always defended the existence in Quebec of a distinct and unique society, with all the attributes of a national community. Far from denigrating the Quebec government's key role in the development of this community, they are its very architects, the ones who have built and strengthened it....

The Quebec Fathers of Confederation did not fear the assimilation of Quebec in 1867. They believed that the federal challenge presented a unique occasion for the disparate colonies of that day to form a great country, one in which Quebec would be called upon to play a major role.

Those who defend the federal tie today are the true inheritors of that vision.

It is certainly necessary to review in depth the constitutional arrangements bequeathed to us in 1867. The venture has become urgent in the light of current tensions which have been generated not only in Quebec but elsewhere, and particularly in Western Canada.

But a realistic and honest evaluation of the Canadian federation can lead to only one conclusion—the assets far outweigh the liabilities.

Charter of Rights and Freedoms

Clearly the most important addition to the Constitution Act when it was patriated in 1982 was the inclusion of one of the world's most progressive statements of individual rights. In unambiguous terms, the Charter deemed that all Canadian citizens would be able to enjoy the rights enumerated in the new Constitution. Although the meaning of some of the language in the document is open to interpretation, and the courts—especially the Supreme Court—have been busy in hearing cases brought forth by individuals and groups that use the Charter as an essential underpinning, it is useful to consider some of the key components of the original document. The Charter is detailed and comprehensive; excerpted below are some of its key provisions.

Fundamental Freedoms

2. Everyone has the following fundamental freedoms:
   (a) freedom of conscience and religion;
   (b) freedom of thought, belief, opinion, and expression, including freedom of the press and other media of communication;
   (c) freedom of peaceable assembly; and
   (d) freedom of association.

Equality Rights

15. (1) Every individual is equal before and under the law and has the right to the equal protection and equal benefit of the law without discrimination and, in particular, without

---

The Charter of Rights and Freedoms: A Guide for Canadians (Ottawa: Minister of Supply Services Canada, 1982), 3, 15, 27, 29.

discrimination based on race, national or ethnic origin, colour, religion, sex, age or mental or physical disability.

(2) Subsection (1) does not preclude any law, program or activity that has as its object the amelioration of conditions of disadvantaged individuals or groups including those that are disadvantaged because of race, national or ethnic origin, colour, religion, sex, age or mental or physical disability.

General

25. The guarantee in the Charter of certain rights and freedoms shall not be construed so as to abrogate or derogate from any aboriginal, treaty or other rights or freedoms that pertain to the aboriginal peoples of Canada including

(a) any rights or freedoms that have been recognized by the Royal Proclamation of October 7, 1763; and

(b) any rights or freedoms that may be acquired by the aboriginal peoples of Canada by way of land claims settlement.

27. This Charter shall be interpreted in a manner consistent with the preservation and enhancement of the multicultural heritage of Canadians.

28. Notwithstanding anything in this Charter, the rights and freedoms referred to in it are guaranteed equally to male and female persons.

An Argument Against Free Trade

The plans to create a Free Trade Agreement between Canada and the United States kindled an intense debate about the immediate and long-term effects of the arrangement. Although the Mulroney administration had the support of businesses and resource producers that were eager to sell their products in the United States without added tariffs, opponents of the FTA came from a broad spectrum of Canadian society. Many, like professor and economist James Laxer, argued that closer economic integration would imperil Canada's sovereignty. The excerpt below comes from Laxer's forceful book on the subject of free trade, Leap of Faith.

The proposed free trade agreement can best be understood as a formalized bargain between Canada and the United States. As everyone knows, there are two sides to every bargain. What the Canadian free traders want is complete and assured access to the American market for Canadian producers. In return for that access they will limit Canadian economic sovereignty, to lock Canada into the larger pattern of the American economy, to discard Canadian ways of doing things in favour of American ways of doing things. Limiting sovereignty, whether advertently or inadvertently, means, quite simply, limiting future choices; that is why it is so important to take such steps only with very great care. Once made, the free trade bargain will not be unmade. It will be more important to Canadians

James Laxer, *Leap of Faith: Free Trade and the Future of Canada* (Edmonton: Hurtig Publishers, 1986), 13, 15, 91, 92, 137.

than their own national constitution in determining what they can do and not do as a society....

Free traders want Canadians to emulate the American economic model. Their conclusion that free trade with the United States is the best option for the country rests on the assumption that the American market system is the highest expression of what is possible in an economy. They hope that by linking Canada with the vibrant U.S. economy, fresh air will course through the musty corridors of Canadian enterprise, calling people in this country to meet the challenge of competition by rising to new heights of entrepreneurial energy....

Canadians have often been told that the stakes in the debate about free trade with the United States are purely economic, that the issue is whether a sound business deal can be had. There is evidence, however, that what will be on the table in the trade negotiations is no less than a series of key decisions about our way of life, the values of our society, the character of our communities. What is involved is "culture," not in the narrow sense of specific institutions and their products, but in the broad sense of the world view of our society....

I believe there are such differences between Canada and the United States, and that they are tangible, important to the way Canadians live, and that they are at stake in the trade talks. Four areas come to mind:

- Violence in the two countries
- The tone and design of Canadian and American cities
- Attitudes to social programs
- The importance of the military in the two countries

It is clear ... that entering a free trade arrangement with the United States means moving over to a more "market-driven economy." This means an economy in which strategic long-range planning is less, not more, possible. It means moving over to the American system at exactly the moment in history when that system is revealing its fundamental weakness. There could be no greater economic folly for Canada, no greater misreading of the history of our time.

First Nations Charter

Many groups in the late twentieth century made concerted efforts to articulate their objectives and advance their agendas in Canadian society. One such organization was the Assembly of First Nations, the country's largest coalition of peoples of aboriginal descent. The following excerpts come from the Charter of the Assembly of First Nations that was adopted in July 1985 at Vancouver, British Columbia. This important statement should be considered in the light of the new Constitution and the Charter of Rights and Freedoms. Of particular interest is the language that links the First Nations to the international community, as an expression of expanding aboriginal interests beyond Canada, and the appeal to treaties and the rule of law.

WE THE CHIEFS OF THE INDIAN FIRST NATIONS IN CANADA HAVING DECLARED:

THAT our peoples are the original peoples of this land having been put here by the Creator;

THAT the Creator gave us laws that govern all our relationships for us to live in harmony with nature and mankind;

THAT the laws of the Creator defined our rights and responsibilities;

THAT the Creator gave us our spiritual beliefs, our languages, our cultures, and a place on Mother Earth which provided us with all our needs;

Jeffrey Keshen and Suzanne Morton, eds., *Material Memory: Documents in Post-Confederation History* (Don Mills, Ontario: Addison-Wesley, 1998), 326–327.

THAT we have maintained our freedom, our languages, and our traditions from time immemorial;

THAT we continue to exercise the rights and fulfill the responsibilities and obligations given to us by the Creator for the land upon which we were placed;

THAT the Creator has given us the right to govern ourselves and the right to self-determination;

THAT the rights and responsibilities given to us by the Creator cannot be altered or taken away by any other nation;

THAT our aboriginal title, aboriginal rights and international treaty rights exist and are recognized by international law;

THAT the Royal Proclamation of 7 October 1763 is binding on both the Crowns of the United Kingdom and of Canada;

THAT the Constitution of Canada protects our aboriginal title, aboriginal rights (both collective and individual) and international treaty rights;

THAT our governmental powers and responsibilities exist; and

THAT our nations are part of the international community

ARE DETERMINED:

To protect our succeeding generations from colonialism;

To reaffirm our faith in fundamental human rights, in the dignity and worth of the human person, in the equal rights of men and women of our First Nations large and small;

To establish conditions under which justice and respect for the obligations arising from our international treaties and from international law can be maintained; and

To promote social progress and better standards of life among our peoples;

AND FOR THESE ENDS,

To respect our diversity,

To practice tolerance and work together as good neighbours,

To unite our strength to maintain our security, and

To employ national and international machinery for the promotion of the political, economic and social advancement of our peoples. . . .

A Voice of New Canadians

Canada's immigration patterns have shifted dramatically since the nineteenth century, but what has not changed are themes having to do with the ways in which immigrants struggle to maintain their cultural identity as they adapt to Canadian society. A particular challenge for immigrants and their children is to assess the positive and negative aspects of acculturation. Another is to determine the relationship between identifying with the nation and with one's ethnic roots. The documents below come from interviews with two Chinese-Canadian women. Although they were recorded in the late twentieth century, they speak to human matters that are timeless: pride, acceptance, dislocation, acculturation, and survival. The first selection is from an interview with Winnie Ng, a Hong Kong-born woman who came to Canada in 1968; the second is the testimony of Lily Welsh, a Chinese-born woman who arrived in Canada as an infant in 1951.

Winnie Ng

When my daughter, Claire, was about three years old, she came with a picture of herself with blond hair. I remember I got kind of upset, questioning her—"what colour is your hair?" I figured no matter how much you want to assimilate, there are people who say, "As long as you treat people well, you'll be reciprocated." But I don't think I believe that anymore. As a non-white Canadian, as a Chinese Canadian, you need to assert yourself.

Jin Guo, *Voices of Chinese Canadian Women* (Toronto: Women's Book Committee, Chinese Canadian National Council, 1992), 167–168, 169–171.

For me, the whole identification of myself as "Canadian" has been a very gradual process. I came here in 1968. When I was a student, I saw myself as a "student." I didn't see myself as part of the Chinese Canadian community. But once you get involved in working in the community, eventually there's a process of moving from identifying yourself as an immigrant to identifying yourself as a Canadian of Chinese origin. Having two children here sort of prompted that process—and the fact that those labels, at a certain point, are arbitrary.

Lily Welsh

I don't think my daughter is conscious of being Chinese. When she was a lot younger, she used to say, "I'm part Chinese and part white." I mean, I taught her that she's part Chinese and part white. So she would go to school and she'd tell other people. The other day she came home and told me she was walking home with a Chinese girl. Our daughter told this other girl that she was part Chinese and part white. The other girl, who is completely Chinese, told my daughter that *she* herself is also part Chinese and part white. . . .

I usually use the word, "Chinese Canadian." When I say "Canadian," I guess I think only about the white people—although I am actually a Canadian myself. I also use the term "Chinese," because, after all, I am a Chinese person. But because I grew up in Canada, I most often call myself a "Chinese Canadian." I don't really think about Chinese culture much because my parents didn't follow the customs that thoroughly. . . .

I don't think I'm a typical Chinese Canadian woman. I feel like I'm in between. To me, a typical Chinese Canadian woman is one who is so westernized that she follows everything the white person's way. And I don't feel that I'm like that because I know a lot of Chinese customs and I do mingle with a lot of Chinese people. . . .

I have not always felt proud to be Chinese. Sometimes I too have wished I was white, so I could be in the majority instead of being in the minority. I suppose I feel that way when I get depressed. I don't resent white people. I realize that even among the white people there are all different kinds. . . .

When I came out to the city, I got along very well with the Chinese people I met. If I made mistakes in speaking Chinese, I never felt bad. I could be excused because I grew up in Canada. But if I made a mistake speaking English, I felt really bad, I really put myself down.

Sometimes I feel very inadequate in my English. Maybe it's because I went through so many years of being very quiet. I find that's the case with a lot of Chinese. When you're in a minority, you feel different. And when you feel different, you feel kind of inadequate. It's only when you get older that you realize how silly that thinking is. But then, the thing is that when you go through life being so quiet, that quietness becomes a part of you.

An Environmentalist's Perspective

A host of environmental themes reached the public's consciousness in the late twentieth century. These included concerns about the quality of air and water, the finite nature of the earth's resources, and the long-term consequences of greenhouse gases and global warming. Canada, as a modern industrial power and major producer of resources, had become one of the world's leading polluters. Scientists and environmental activists called for Canada to be aggressive in protecting its environment, as well as to consider the context of a global ecosystem. Activist organizations such as Greenpeace, which had roots in Vancouver in the early 1970s, dramatized the environmental threats to animals and the earth. Without a doubt, the most public and prolific Canadian environmentalist in the modern era is David Suzuki. Now a retired professor, Suzuki sponsored the long-running CBC program, The Nature of Things. *The following text comes from one of his collections of essays on environmental themes; it concentrates on the impact of Quebec's massive hydroelectric project on the James Bay region.*

In our concern with serving the immediate needs of our own species, politicians make decisions based on economic, social, or political imperatives that have vast repercussions for other species, whole ecosystems and, eventually, other human beings.

Some of the planet's priceless and irreplaceable ecosystems in exotic places like Sarawak, the Amazon, and Zaire are now being invaded

David Suzuki, *Time to Change: Essays* (Toronto: Stoddart, 1994), 95–96, 97.

by human activity. But if poverty and ignorance in poor countries blind people to the consequences of their actions, what is *our* excuse?

At this moment, Hydro-Québec is pressing on to fulfill Premier Robert Bourassa's grand vision of harnessing for hydroelectric power all of the major rivers draining into James and southern Hudson bays from Québec. The James Bay Project (JBP) is the largest development ever undertaken in the history of North America and is a technological *experiment* with ecological repercussions that extend far beyond the confines of Québec. The land area affected is a large as France, while the enormous inland sea formed by James and Hudson bays will be seriously affected.

Every spring in these waters, ice formed with salt water melts in the bays and the freshwater runoff into estuaries stimulates a bloom of ice algae, the basis of a food chain extending to cod, seals, and whales. Each year, hundreds of beluga whales of the eastern herd return to the estuaries. In the fall, millions of migratory birds—ducks, geese, shorebirds—stop at biological oases on the bay edges to fatten up for flights as far as the tip of South America! . . . .

In the Arctic, *timing* is everything. Plants and animals in the north have evolved an impeccable synchrony with seasonal productivity in specific regions. Through narrow temporal and geographic windows, life has flourished, but unlike human beings, wild organisms can't change their growth cycle, feeding, nesting areas, or time of arrival. They are locked into a genetic destiny that has been honed over aeons of time. . . .

The fate of many ecosystems in Canada now seems to hinge on the application of an environmental assessment (EA) of proposed developments like dams. It's ironic that so much rests on an EA. Scientists are still trying to describe the elementary units of matter and how they interact, while our knowledge about how gene activity is controlled or cells function is primitive. When it comes to communities of organisms in complex ecosystems, most of the component species are not yet identified, so we have very little insight into their interaction and interdependence.

Given the state of our ignorance, the notion that in only a few months enough information can be collected to assess the con-sequences of massive projects like dams, aluminum plants, or pulp mills is absurd. The so-called "data" assembled in an EA are so limited in scale, scope, and duration as to be virtually worthless scientifically. At the very least, an EA should be initiated from a profound sense of humility at the inadequacy of our knowledge. At best, the EA can highlight questions, reveal areas of ignorance, and warn of potentially sensitive effects. Anyone who claims to know enough to predict with confidence the consequences of new developments simply doesn't understand the limited nature of scientific knowledge.

In our form of government, only *people* vote; owls, trees, or rivers don't. A minister designated to protect the environment must therefore act according to the demands of a human electorate. So a watershed, old-growth forest, ocean bottom, or newly discovered oil deposit can be assessed only in terms of potential human utility. If trees could vote, we would have radically different priorities. Since they can't, society must incorporate an ecological perspective in our value system. . . .

A Celebration of Canada's Role in Afghanistan

Canada's recent military commitment in Afghanistan has invoked many of the questions that have been asked since Confederation about the advisability of the country's participation in global conflicts. In addition, it has sparked an interesting conversation from the perspective of the forces that have been serving and fighting in the NATO-sponsored conflict since 2002. Some of these individuals, although they receive official backing from the government and some popular support as well, have made a concerted effort to publicize their reasons for serving in the all-volunteer Canadian Forces and to defend their efforts in the Afghanistan war. The passage below comes from a book written by one such member of the Canadian Forces, Lieutenant-Colonel John Conrad, who is a native Newfoundlander and now retired career officer.

The Canadian Forces achieved a great deal in 2006—not the least of which was denying control of Kandahar City to the Taliban. Our country and our tiny army are growing up around us in Kandahar. However, the considerable logistics derives from the leaders of the army remains shockingly and inappropriately slim....We succeeded in 2006 because the young men and women who fill the logistic ranks in the Canadian Forces are among the best in the world at what they do. They are mentally tough and technically superb. More important, I found them to be both discerning and compassionate while treading

Lieutenant-Colonel John Conrad, *What the Thunder Said: Reflections of a Canadian Officer in Kandahar* (Toronto: The Dundurn Group, 2009), 218–220.

on Afghan soil. The men and women with whom I served refused to lose. Kandahar represents Canada's most dangerous military mission since Korea. Even though our soldiers had not been involved in a sustained fight for generations, they met the challenge of Afghanistan, making sure that convoys would run, mail and supplies would flow, vehicles would get fixed in the centre of an infantry battle, and hamburgers would get flipped underneath barrages of mortar fire and rocket-propelled grenades, not because of any genius on my part or the part of the army staff or the headquarters in Ottawa but only because *they* willed it to be so. The projection of national power, the currency used to purchase the government's aims, has to be delivered by combat soldiers and underwritten by robust logistics troops. As proud as I am of the accomplishments of 1 PPCLI and the fine Canadian infantry battle groups that have followed, my heroes in Kandahar will always be those noble troops that lumbered north in 16-ton logistic trucks, Bison repair vehicles, aftermarket wreckers, and the like—no regimental bluster, no glitter, just sheer guts.

Your Canadian forces are made up of soldiers, sailors, and airmen and women from across this great country. They are your own sons, daughters, friends, and neighbours. They have different roles and functions inside the force from infantry through to personnel selection. The ones that deliver logistics have a specific, time-revered role. The value of their contribution has diminished in the eyes of some across the breadth of Canadian military history, but I tell you now the esteem they have earned and deserved could not be higher. The combat logistics troops I knew are among the finest Canadians I have had the privilege of meeting. As an officer, a father, and as a taxpayer I am so very proud of them. These soldiers have been measured by Canada's enemies on the contemporary battlefield around Kandahar and have been found not wanting. They know all about the hell where youth and laughter go. In point of fact they have been there many times.

Canada's Position on Arctic Sovereignty

In the recent past both of the country's main political parties have adopted an aggressive stance in laying claim to Arctic space and asserting Canada's control over the movement of international vessels through northern waters. In a point that serves as a wonderful illustration of symmetry in history, the Northwest passage that attracted the attention of numerous European explorers and thereby helped to shape such a great deal of history in the colonial era, has reasserted itself as a major focus for the now mature nation-state of Canada. Prime Minister Stephen Harper, like his predecessors, has repeatedly taken on the responsibility of defining the country's position on sovereignty in the Arctic. The following document comes from a speech delivered by Harper in Tuktoyaktuk, Northwest Territories, on 27 August 2008.

Thank you very much, Minister Baird. Greetings ladies and gentlemen. Greetings also to Mayor Gruben, to our Aboriginal elders and of course to all residents of Tuktoyaktuk who are hosting us here today. Special greetings, of course, to members of the Canadian Coast Guard who play a vital role in keeping the True North strong and free by patrolling and protecting Canada's Atlantic, Pacific and Arctic coasts, which are in total the longest shoreline in the world....

Prime Minister of Canada, "Prime Minister Harper Announces Measures to Strengthen Canada's Arctic Sovereignty and Protection of the Northern Environment," http://pm.gc.ca/eng/media.asp?id=2259 (accessed 19 September 2008).

Exactly 100 years ago this summer the federal government dispatched Captain [Joseph-Elzéar] Bernier on a mission to claim the Arctic Archipelago for Canada.....Bernier's mission was a crucial event in Canadian history, as important as our national destiny in the North as the building of the Canadian Pacific Railway was in the West. But not even Captain Bernier could have imagined how important the Arctic would become to Canada and the world.

Its economic and strategic value has risen exponentially over the years. The rising global demand for energy and mineral resources has sparked a so-called "cold rush" of countries to the Arctic region, and with the retreat of the ice pack, record numbers of ships are plying our Northern waters. Canada must therefore move quickly to affirm and protect its sovereignty over the archipelago, including the navigable waterways within it, and the undersea extensions of our continental shelf.

Now sovereignty, as you know, is not an abstract notion. It conveys a source of authority and protection. The people of Tuktoyaktuk know from history how important it is for Canada to exercise control and provide order in the Arctic. Between 1890 and 1910, unregulated foreign whalers brought influenza to the Mackenzie Delta that decimated the community.

Today the threats are different, but no less dangerous. The proliferation of international shipping in the North raises the potential for shipwrecks, smuggling, illegal immigration, and even threats to national security. But more specifically it raises the potential of environmental threats like oil spills, poaching and contamination. These are particularly acute in the sensitive Arctic ecosystem. Protecting and understanding the Arctic environment is one of the four pillars of our Government's Northern Agenda, and it is one that we have been acting on....

Today our government is further strengthening Canada's control over our Arctic environment with two important announcements. First, our government will introduce legislation to expand the reach of our Arctic Waters Pollution Prevention Act. The act currently limits Canada's ability to regulate Arctic shipping to within just 100 nautical miles from our coastline. We intend to double our jurisdiction to 200 nautical miles....Second, the Government will amend the Canada Shipping Act to require vessels entering Canadian

Arctic waters to report to the Coast Guard's NORDREG reporting system. . . .

These measures will send a clear message to the world: Canada takes responsibility for environmental protection and enforcement in our Arctic waters. This magnificent and unspoiled ecological region is one for which we will demonstrate stewardship on behalf of our country, and indeed, all of humanity.

Canadian Insights Using Humor

Canadians share a deep tradition of enjoying satire that pokes fun at their idiosyncrasies and at the same time makes serious points about society, politics, and Canada's relationship with other countries. The inimitable Stephen Leacock, for example, skewered his contemporaries as he offered insightful observations about life in Canada in the early twentieth century. More recently an impressive number of comedians and satirists have plied their trade in live performances and programs such as Second City Television, *a popular Toronto-based series that ran during the 1970s and 1980s. One of the premier comedians of contemporary Canada comes from the Atlantic region. Rick Mercer, through the vehicle of television programs such as* This Hour Has 22 Minutes *and* Talking to Americans, *has used humor to offer pointed critiques of political figures, Canadian culture, and the ignorance that many Americans have of their northern neighbor. The following excerpts come from one of Mercer's collections of essays.*

"Back to School Days," 10 January 2006

Usually when there's an election, there's a script that both sides follow, and the rest of us read along. We all know our parts. In a federal election, the leaders fly around the country and make all sorts of promises that we take with a grain of salt. But based on those promises, we decide who we're going to vote for.

But the promises, whether they're kept or not, are generally within the realm of sanity. This time is completely different. The leaders are acting like this isn't a real federal election, or a provincial election, or even a municipal election for that matter. And for the longest time, I couldn't figure out what it was that it reminded me of. And then it dawned on me: high school student council.

In high school elections, 90 per cent of the candidates are very serious, but some guy always gets up there, high as a kite, and makes all sorts of insane announcements, and everyone loves him. When I was in grade ten, some dude with a mullet promised free beer in the fountains and a smoking room inside the school. My, how we cheered. And that's what Martin and Harper are like. Or they're like divorced parents trying to buy their children's love. We're the kids, they're our two dads. Except this time they're not trying to buy our love with just an Xbox or a few Easy-Bake-Ovens.

No, they've gone completely off their heads. Martin is spending like Belinda Stronach in a shoe store. We're talking billions of dollars every time he turns around. And Harper is outspending him. There's a rumour going around that Harper's about to promise everyone in Ontario a Ferris wheel and a pony.

This is not good, Canada. I hate to be old-fashioned here, but Stephen, Paul—where in God's name is all the money coming from? It's a bad sign when the worst-case scenario is that whoever wins this election actually keeps his promise. Because at the end of the day, free beer in the fountains is a great idea—I just don't want to pay for it.

"Go Invade Yourself," 6 February, 2004

Just looking at George Bush you can tell he's as mad as hell. He can't believe that after all this time there are still no weapons of mass destruction. And I think he's actually surprised. Things were looking good there a couple of weeks ago when they found a can of Raid and a Bic lighter, but since then, nothing.

Which is why Bush has announced the formation of a special investigation into weapons of mass destruction. Basically he wants to know just what the hell he's been up to for the past year and a half. He's saying, I don't trust me, I'm going to get to the bottom of this, I'm either with me or against me. So he's going to spend a fortune figuring out just how intelligent U.S. intelligence is.

Boy, it's a shame to see someone waste their money isn't it? I could just go knock on the door of the embassy and tell them what the rest of us already know. But no. He wants to know why it is that when he said there were weapons of mass destruction everyone knew he was lying except for him.

And you know why he didn't know, don't you? Dick Cheney forgot to tell him. I just hope he doesn't take the news too hard; otherwise he might have no choice but to go invade himself. And no getting around it, that's going to hurt.

Bibliographic Essay

The most comprehensive and approachable survey on Canadian history is the two-volume text by R. Douglas Francis, Richard Jones, and Donald B. Smith: *Origins: Canadian History to Confederation* and *Destinies: Canadian History Since Confederation*, both 6th ed. (Toronto: Harcourt Canada, 2008). A readable and opinionated work by Desmond Morton requires some background on Canada's past before it is consulted: *A Short History of Canada*, 6th rev. ed. (Toronto: McClelland & Stewart, 2006). For a book with plenty of interesting visual material, see Robert Craig Brown, ed., *The Illustrated History of Canada*, 5th ed. (Toronto: Key Porter Books, 2007). For a broad selection of article-length studies on aspects of the country's political, social, and cultural history, see R. Douglas Francis and Donald B. Smith, eds., *Readings in Canadian History: Pre-Confederation* and *Readings in Canadian History: Post-Confederation*, both 7th ed. (Toronto: Thomson Nelson, 2006). Readers who are interested in collections of sources should consult two fine volumes edited by Thomas Thorner and Thor Frohn-Nielsen: *A Few Acres of Snow: Documents in Pre-Confederation Canadian History*, 3rd ed. (Toronto: University of Toronto Press, 2009), and *"A Country Nourished On Self-Doubt": Documents in Post-Confederation Canadian History*, 3rd ed. (Toronto: University of Toronto Press, 2010).

The best bibliography of historical works on Canada is the two-volume *Canadian History: A Reader's Guide*. Volume 1, *Beginnings to Confederation* (Toronto: University of Toronto Press, 1994), which is edited by M. Brook Taylor. Doug Owram edited volume 2, *Confederation to the Present* (Toronto: University of Toronto Press, 1994). The most thorough bibliography of articles, reviews, and dissertations published since 1964 can be found in *America: History and Life*. This source is not easy to navigate; nonetheless, it is the best resource for serious students of the histories of Canada and the United States. A valuable general bibliography on Canadian themes is edited by J. A. Senécal, *Canada: A Reader's Guide* (Ottawa: International Council for Canadian Studies, 1993).

Readers interested in the lives of important Canadian figures should use the impressive and ongoing *Dictionary of Canadian Biography* (Toronto: University of Toronto Press, 1966–). Currently at fifteen volumes, it is arranged chronologically by the individual's date of death. The massive three-volume *Historical Atlas of Canada* (Toronto: University of Toronto Press, 1987, 1990, 1993) is a stunning production. A much more concise work is D. G. G. Kerr, *Historical Atlas of Canada*, 3rd rev. ed. (Don Mills, ON: Thomas Nelson & Sons, 1975). No updated general history of Canada's international relations exists. Still serviceable are C. P. Stacey's two-volume *Canada and the Age of Conflict: A History of Canadian External Policies* (Toronto: University of Toronto Press, 1977, 1984) and G. P. de T. Glazebrook's two-volume *A History of Canadian External Relations* (Toronto: McClelland & Stewart, 1966). A useful addition to the scholarship is a collection of essays edited by Phillip Buckner, *Canada and the British Empire* (Oxford: Oxford University Press, 2008). A thorough history of the country's foreign relations during the Cold War era is Robert Bothwell's *Alliance and Illusion: Canada and the World, 1945–1984* (Vancouver: University of British Columbia Press, 2007). American readers will no doubt be interested in the entertaining, yet scholarly work, by John Herd Thompson and Stephen J. Randall, *Canada and the United States: Ambivalent Allies*, 4th ed. (Athens, GA: University of Georgia Press, 2008).

Many works cover Canada's provinces and regions. Understandably, much of Quebec's history is written in French. For solid works in English, see John A. Dickinson and Brian Young, *A Short History of Quebec*, 4th ed. (Montreal: McGill-Queen's University Press, 2008), and Susan Mann Trofimenkoff, *The Dream of Nation: A Social and Intellectual History of Quebec*, 2nd ed. (Montreal: McGill-Queen's University Press, 2002). Two fine companion pieces effectively cover the full scope of Atlantic Canada's history: Phillip A. Buckner and John G. Reid, eds., *The Atlantic Region to Confederation: A History* (Toronto: University of Toronto Press, 1994), and E. R. Forbes and D. A. Muise, eds., *The Atlantic Provinces in Confederation* (Toronto: University of Toronto Press, 1993). Readers interested in Ontario might start with Robert Bothwell, *A Short History of Ontario* (Edmonton: Hurtig, 1986). The history of the prairies is adeptly interwoven in

Gerald Friesen, *The Canadian Prairies: A History* (Toronto: University of Toronto Press, 1984). Howard and Tamara Palmer produced a useful survey: *Alberta: A New History* (Edmonton: Hurtig, 1990). Canada's far West receives attention in Jean Barman's, *The West beyond the West: A History of British Columbia* (Toronto: University of Toronto Press, 1991). An excellent place to begin a study of the North is Morris Zaslow, *The Northward Expansion of Canada, 1914– 1967* (Toronto: McClelland & Stewart, 1988).

For the history of Native peoples, see Olive P. Dickason and David T. McNab, *Canada's First Nations: A History of Founding Peoples from Earliest Times*, 4th ed. (Don Mills, ON: Oxford University Press, 2009). Readers should also consider J. R. Miller, *Skyscrapers Hide the Heavens: A History of Indian-White Relations in Canada*, 3rd ed. (Toronto: University of Toronto Press, 2000). Virtually all of Canada's major ethnic groups have been the subject of historical study. Notable is Robin Winks's work, *The Blacks in Canada*, 2nd ed. (Montreal: McGill-Queen's University Press, 1997).

Several works can be recommended to readers who are interested in women's history. The best overview is Alison Prentice et al., *Canadian Women: A History*, 2nd ed. (Toronto: Harcourt Brace, 1996). Excellent collections of specific studies should also be noted: Adele Perry, Mona Gleason, eds., *Rethinking Canada: The Promise of Women's History*, 5th ed. (Don Mills, ON: Oxford University Press, 2006), and the two volumes by Alison Prentice and Susan Mann Trofimenkoff, eds., *The Neglected Majority: Essays in Canadian Women's History* (Toronto: McClelland & Stewart, 1977, 1985).

For studies of workers in Canada, see Craig Heron, *The Canadian Labour Movement: A Short History* (Toronto: James Lorimer, 1996), and Bryan D. Palmer, *Working-Class Experience: Rethinking the History of Canadian Labour, 1800–1991*, 2nd ed. (Toronto: McClelland & Stewart, 1992).

While they change more frequently than most of us would wish, Web sites on Canadian themes abound. The following are quite useful:

www.canadahistory.com – general Canadian history
www.collectionscanada.gc.ca – Library and Archives Canada
www.statcan.gc.ca – Statistics Canada

www.cs.cmu.edu/afs/cs.cmu.edu/Web/Unofficial/Canadiana/ –
    a Canadian resource page

www.civilization.ca/cmc/explore/online-resources-for-canadian-
    heritage – resources for Canadian Heritage

atlas.nrcan.gc.ca/site/english/index.html – Atlas of Canada

www.biographi.ca/ – *Dictionary of Canadian Biography* online

Index

About the Author

Scott W. See is Libra Professor of History at the University of Maine. He is the author of *Riots in New Brunswick: Orange Nativism and Social Violence in the 1840s* (1993), as well as numerous articles and book chapters on aspects of Canadian history.